MEASURING THE MUSIC:

ANOTHER LOOK AT THE CONTEMPORARY CHRISTIAN MUSIC DEBATE

SECOND EDITION

JOHN MAKUJINA

Old Paths Publications

Old Paths Publications
1 BITTERSWEET PATH
WILLOW STREET, PA 17584 USA
...ask for the old paths... Jer. 6:16

ISBN   1-889058-14-9

Cover Design: Debra Tremper
Cover Photos: Clint Anderson

Contents

Foreword

AS I WRITE THIS foreword we are halfway through the last year of the last century of the second millennium A.D. Far from being a warmed-over cyclical version of previous epochs, this century of centuries birthed much that was genuinely new: unparalleled advances in science, technology, computer systems, and powerful media cartels for both the dissemination of information and the molding of public opinion.

Yet the most invasive innovation, the broadest and deepest revision, was the transformation of society into a new type of culture with a concomitant change in societal values which goes to the very heart of life and living. This phenomenon, which I loosely term "pop culture," like the developments in science and technology, is genuinely new. As critic Ken Myers has noted, twentieth-century popular culture is "a complete novelty in human history." The result of mechanistic invention, philosophical disarray, and numerous alternative social, ethical, moral and aesthetic codes, its most conspicuous manifestation may be seen in the popular musical forms of the day. Actually, a case could be made for the popular musical arts not only reflecting changing societal values, but in fact creating them. Here I speak not about pop's words but about its music, because it is in the music that we hear pop's real message. There is little doubt that we are reaping today the results of the music sown yesterday. Not that popular music is the only protagonist in this move to a culture driven by pop values. But it does have more responsibility for the overall shaping of our national life than we are generally willing to admit.

So powerful has pop culture become that now it is society's dominant mode of apprehending reality. Because it is believed to be the epitome of normality and is so pervasive, it is difficult for the average person to set aside its norms and look critically at the worldview values which drive such a system. Nowhere is this more true than in the Christian church. Somehow the body of Christ has embraced the accoutrements of a society in desperate need of the gospel, absorbing the nation's popular cultural values in its own life, both intentionally and unintentionally. Not surprisingly then, the issue of religious pop music in the chancel is about as dead as yesterday's news. Evaluation of the church's adoption of pop culture is believed to be irrelevant, unnecessary, and a waste of valuable time and energy.

Yet a new assessment of church pop is just what author John Makujina asks us to do in this book. Though the acceptance of popular culture (and in the case of music, pop music) within the Christian church is now an established fact, its very normality across the face of virtually every variety of Christian theological persuasion is telling. In a climate of extreme multi-culturalism, pluralism, and relativism satiated with the notion that music is value-neutral and worldview-free, church music has been cut off from history, tradition, theology, aesthetic norms, and ultimately the Word. The result has been a breakdown of church music standards along with a collateral weakening in other areas of life as well.

The problem with Christian pop music is that pop changes the gospel! The musical medium remakes the message into a reflection of pop's own muse. Indeed, a gospel proclaimed by popular musical forms becomes transformed into a different gospel. It is this essential point which is at the heart of this book. The author, not content with the "biblical witness" fomented by popular musical forms such as "Contemporary Christian Music," gives the reader a biblically based, philosophically sound rationale for questioning its use, not as a matter of taste but as a matter of biblical principle. Taking on the musical fruit of the entire twentieth century as presently practiced in almost all Christian churches is a gargantuan task, staggering in scope and complexity and immense in its implications. Nevertheless, with courage and conviction, John Makujina takes the reader step by step through a series of well-thought-through insights which go to the heart of the church's adoption of popular musical culture. It is a meaty, detailed, thought-provoking treatise which should be read by every pastor, musician, church official, and parishioner. If there was ever a need for such a cleansing and prophetic work, it is now.

—Calvin M. Johansson
Evangel University

Preface

SINCE I FIRST ENCOUNTERED CCM in the early eighties and formally debated the issue in college several years later, to the time of this writing on the eve of the third millennium I have watched CCM progress from an underdog to a contender to an overwhelming favorite. Throughout those years my own views on Christian music have developed and changed as my interest in this amazingly complex issue have grown. Although speaking on the subject to youth and adults, I never imagined myself expending the time and energy necessary to write a book on something so controversial and explosive. I would have preferred to have been burdened with an issue that all Christians could agree on. But it was not to be. What may seem like a dead or petty issue to many, from my perspective has serious ramifications for both Christian orthodoxy and orthopraxy, and so deserves 'another look.'

There are many individuals who need to be thanked for their unselfish contribution to this project: John Blanchard and Calvin Johansson, who have given of their time to read two versions of this manuscript and have offered much counsel and encouragement; Frank Garlock, who has been a true friend, advisor, and encouragement throughout the length of this eight year project; ex-rock musicians Ron Barrie and Albert Svenddal for their expertise, input, and guidance; all those within the CCM industry who kindly answered my letters and e-mails; Mrs. Beatrice Jillson and Mrs. Debra Bauder who generously gave of their time to proofread the manuscript; David A. Noebel, Daniel Moxley, and Lenny Seidel for reviewing the manuscript; the University of Pennsylvania libraries and librarians for their assistance in obtaining obscure and difficult-to-locate sources; and finally Schmul Publishing Company for the strength of their conviction and their willingness to bear with me the reproach that this type of position and book is likely to generate. To all of them I extend my gratitude.

By way of disclaimers, I should stress that the opinions expressed in this book are mine alone and not (necessarily) those of the students or faculty of Westminster Theological Seminary (Philadelphia), the institution that I currently attend. Likewise, I take full responsibility for any infelicities in the published version of this book. Lastly, it needs to be mentioned that—although I have no intention of equivocating on my position—much of the thinking in this book is seminal and in need of fine-tuning and development, something that I hope to do at a later time and in which I invite responsible Christian scholars, theologians, musicians, and musicologists to accompany me.

—John Makujina
November 30, 1999
Philadelphia

Preface to the Second Edition

A SECOND EDITION OF *Measuring the Music* was necessary only because of a change of publishers, now Old Paths Publications. Therefore this is not an expanded edition. I have also taken this opportunity to make minor revisions, chiefly typographical errors. Further, this edition incorporates larger fonts for more comfortable reading, hence the expansion in page numbers from 303 to over 360. I should note here that the first edition actually consisted of two strains: the original printing in February of 2000 and a later reprint in October of 2000. The February edition can be identified by the copyright, which belongs to Schmul Publishing Co., whereas the October edition has it assigned to the author. Moreover, the October edition contains a slight change in pagination and minor corrections.

I cannot fail here to express my gratitude to several individuals for their support, interaction, and guidance, especially Kevin Bauder, Doug Bachorik, Greg Stiekes, Cory Rintala, and Doug Roman. I am also deeply indebted to Miss Linda Russell whose careful proofreading has rescued me from much embarrassment.

The publisher and I hope that the second edition will reach many more individuals who are concerned about the direction of church music in the new millennium.

—John Makujina
January 15, 2002
Central Baptist Seminary

Introduction

FEW TOPICS HAVE AROUSED as much hostility among Christians as contemporary Christian music (CCM).[1] Just the mention of it in the wrong context has brought ordinarily peaceful members of the same church or fellowship nearly to blows. The controversy of course is not as divisive as it used to be, with the opposition to CCM lessening considerably since its freshman days when Paul Baker and company (Ralph Carmichael, Billy Ray Hearn, and Kurt Kaiser) had to campaign with their backs to the wall for the propriety of the movement.[2] With the passage of time and increase of tolerance, the prospect arose that by the conclusion of the second millennium this inflammatory issue may be settled. Indeed, today CCM has experienced times of unprecedented prosperity and acceptance and is setting its sights on final victory.[3]

The evidence is all around us: most Christian bookstores and catalog retailers carry CCM labels. In 1996 alone CCM record sales neared $550 million—with concert tickets and merchandise included, $750 to $900 million.[4] The incredible revenue potential has inspired corporate giants to share in the profits, to the point where most CCM record labels are now owned by secular companies. CCM also has its own video programs, an annual award show (the Dove Awards, a spin-off of the Grammys), and every major city in the U.S. has at least one radio station that carries CCM (500 nationwide in 1996).[5] Further, CCM stars have actually received Grammys, been guests of celebrities like Johnny Carson and Jay Leno, and have opened for popular secular groups and artists like Sting and Garth Brooks. Andraé Crouch sang backup vocals for Madonna, while Peter King of Dakoda Motor Company has hosted MTV's *Sandblast*![6] Even more impressive is the induction of Petra into London's famous Hard Rock Cafe.[7]

In the print media CCM boasts a wide selection of popular periodical literature, past and present, including *Contemporary Christian Music, MusicLine, Release, HM* (formerly *Heaven's Metal*), *Rizzen*

Roxx, Take a Stand, 7Ball, Counter Culture, and *Buzz* (U.K.). Moreover, major evangelical publishers like Zondervan, Bethany House, Tyndale House, InterVarsity, Broadman & Holman, and Baker have supported the cause of CCM by publishing works that defend it. Likewise, CCM has received authorization from most denominations, church leaders, para-church ministries, and Christian schools and colleges—with some even offering degrees in CCM (e.g., Prairie Bible College and Greenville College). Finally, we should not overlook the success of CCM music festivals like Fishnet, Creation, Cornerstone, Ichthus, and Greenbelt (U.K.), which can attract as many as 50,000 individuals in any given summer.[8] By all accounts it appears that CCM is here to stay.

Yet pockets of resistance still exist. These dissenters are usually far from the mainstream and often forced to self-publish or use underground presses. 1992 gave birth to at least three conservative works on Christian music. Frank Garlock and Kurt Woetzel, Calvin M. Johansson, and Tim Fisher have attempted to halt the tidal wave of CCM within their respective spheres of influence.[9] A little earlier (1989) the team from England—John Blanchard, Peter Anderson and Derek Cleave—revised *Pop Goes the Gospel* (first edition 1983), displaying no intention of surrendering to an overwhelming opponent. And of course there is always Bill Gothard, that indefatigable adversary of CCM, who since the 1970s has taken the issue to the seminar floor. In 1993 he supplemented his offensive with a short book on conquering the addiction of rock music.[10] Four years later Kimberly and Lee Smith issued the brief and user-friendly *Oh, Be Careful Little Ears*, which approaches the controversy with a more pastoral and irenic spirit. At the same time the very confrontational *Confronting Contemporary Christian Music: A Plain Account of Its History, Philosophy, and Future* by H. T. Spence also made its appearance. Finally, in the spring of 1999 David W. Cloud submitted the most voluminous single treatment of the subject. His *Contemporary Christian Music Under the Spotlight* consists of 450 pages of aggressive critique, focusing on the personal lives, philosophies, theology, and affections of CCM personalities and the secular rock artists who have influenced them.[11]

In recent years, however, these conservative enclaves have been the target of mop-up activity. Still fearing the specter of fundamentalism, two major works in defense of CCM rolled off the presses in 1993. Both Steve Miller (*The Contemporary Christian Music Debate*) and Harold M. Best (*Music Through the Eyes of Faith*) have mounted spirited and sometimes sophisticated arguments in defense of CCM.[12] 1993 also produced a little-known but passionate defense of Christian rock by Angelo De Simone, *Christian Rock: Friend or Foe?*, and Robert H. Mitchell's much shorter, *I Don't Like This Music*—which essentially points in the same direction as the others, but focuses on music for Christian worship. During the same year a secular apology for heavy metal music also entered the arena. Although Robert Walser's *Running with the Devil* does not deal directly with Christian rock, many of the issues it raises and appeals it makes interface well with the CCM debate. In 1996 Al Menconi with Dave Hart released *Staying in Tune: A Sane Response to Your Child's Music*, a revised edition of Menconi's 1990 *Today's Music: A Window to Your Child's Soul*. The book is primarily a biblical critique of secular rock music and advice to parents on how to counsel children who listen to it. It does, however, contain important chapters justifying and promoting CCM, and so has been added to the critique.

In 1997 theologian John Frame stirred up much controversy through his *Contemporary Worship Music: A Biblical Defense*. Common ground between contemporary worship music and CCM would include pragmatism, contextualization, and similar perspectives on music and evangelism, but on the whole most right-wingers will probably not find Frame's proposal as troubling as Miller's or Best's. Frame's chief concern seems to be to convince traditional (Reformed) churches to adopt newer, more contemporary styles of music in worship (e.g., "Father, I Adore You").

An even more recent work to come upon the scene is *The Sound of Harvest: Music's Mission in Church and Culture* by J. Nathan Corbitt (1998). In his attempt to provide a "comprehensive, educational, and entertaining look at the holistic ministry of music in global Christianity," Corbitt spends a good deal of time exonerating CCM and cultural diversity in musical practice while criticizing the ethnocentricity of traditional approaches.[13] His position is very similar to Best's and Mitchell's, with whom he shares a similar pilgrimage from a puristic to a relativistic view of music, as well as a considerable dependence on ethnomusicology.

The final year of the second millennium saw to publication Charlie Peacock's controversial *At the Crossroads: An Insider's Look at the Past, Present, and Future of Contemporary Christian Music*. This is clearly not a defense of the musical styles that comprise CCM, which Peacock accepts without question, but a rebuke to members of his own guild and a plea to chart a more biblical course for the future. Its significance to the debate, however, is that it offers a theology of music that indirectly, though unmistakably, reflects Peacock's convictions on musical style as amoral and integrative rather than moral and prohibitive. It is also important because Peacock's candid exposure of the movement's dirty laundry all but hands CCM opponents a fresh club with which to beat it. *The Music of Angels: A Listener's Guide to Sacred Music From Chant to Christian Rock* by Patrick Kavanaugh was also published in 1999. In that it dedicates a chapter to CCM and treats it rather sympathetically, it is eligible for critique.

Much more impactive, however, than Kavanaugh's book is Jay R. Howard and John M. Streck's *Apostles of Rock: The Splintered World of Contemporary Christian Music* (1999). In what bills itself as an outsider's critique of CCM—the authors are noticeably clandestine about their own religious allegiance—Howard and Streck attempt to understand the divisions that have "splintered" CCM throughout its brief history through the grid of H. Richard Neibuhr's *Christ and Culture*. Although the book predominately wrestles with tensions within CCM, as does Peacock's, its occasional comments—neither entirely sympathetic nor critical—on the suitability of rock music as a medium for Christian lyrics are stimulating and worthy of discussion.[14]

A final book that deserves mention is *The Rock and Roll Rebellion: Why People of Faith Abandoned Rock Music—And Why They're Coming Back* by Mark Joseph. Like Peacock, Joseph's burden is to move CCM out of the bunker of evangelical subculture and into the mainstream. The importance of his book, along with Peacock's and Howard and Streck's, is that it forecasts a shift in concerns, the death of an old nemesis and the birth of a new one. Whereas in the early nineties CCM and its opponents were still rattling their sabers over the admissibility of the rock style, by 1999 the conflict has become internal, revolving around the issue of lyrics, crossover artists, and secular performing venues. This is evident in all three books, which combined dedicate but a millimeter of real-estate to the controversy concerning style, and even that in historical retrospect.

Despite this realignment of priorities, today CCM opponents aspire to keep the debate over musical style alive—well, at least once more. This is one way of officially breaking the silence (as if it were not already obvious) and confessing that the present book sides unashamedly with the dissenters and attempts to form a response to CCM's latest defense. By "latest defense" I am referring to major publications defending CCM during the last decade or so. This will include the books mentioned above, select articles in popular periodicals and on the internet, as well as what I have gained from personal encounters and interaction with CCM supporters. When relevant I will also refer to older material.

The justification for yet another book opposing CCM lies in the fact that the newer apologetic endeavors of authors such as Best and Miller have not been challenged, and some earlier arguments have not been adequately addressed. It is not my intention to repeat the work of my predecessors, but to look at the issue afresh and bring to the debate new and overlooked insights from biblical scholarship, systematic theology, musicology, history, and the social sciences.

Moreover, my experience with Campus Crusade for Christ in the early-to-mid eighties puts me in a unique position: it allows me to be intimately familiar with the subculture of CCM, their concept of Christian liberty, moral purity, culture, entertainment, music, and pragmatism, as well as their rationalizations for each. As one who shared their presuppositions and walked in their moccasins, I consider myself to be in a better position than many to criticize the movement and its theology. But familiarity also involves a measure of equity. Although I sternly disapprove of the entire concept of Christian rock music and name specific individuals and incidences, I do not wish to accuse anyone of *intentionally* dishonoring the Lord through their music, mannerisms, or dress. Most of the individuals involved with CCM genuinely desire to please God and live the Christian life to the best of their understanding.

As far as biblical passages are concerned, for the most part I have decided to furnish my own translations. Where I have employed a Bible version, it is clearly cited within the body of the text. Further, information that was based on eyewitness encounters and experience (mine or someone else's) was not documented in the endnotes. Over the years I have had many opportunities for interaction with CCM advocates and have found some of my experiences, and those of others, to be beneficial to the debate.

Moreover, the reader should be advised that due to the sometimes erotic nature of this topic, certain portions will be suitable for mature readers only. I have, however, removed offensive language (common in popular music journalism) from direct quotes and replaced it with euphemisms enclosed in brackets. Therefore, in such circumstances the word or phrase in the brackets should not be construed as an explanatory gloss, in the custom of professional writing, but the exchange of a vulgarism for a euphemism.

I would recommend reading the entire book, although I realize that some portions may be tough sledding for those not acquainted with the issues or terminology of this debate. I have tried to satisfy all levels of readership, but inevitably I project that this book will be more manageable for the studious type. That is simply the (inexcusable) price for writing a book while also finishing up a dissertation—for which I beg forgiveness beforehand. Further, the nature of this book, a critique, requires that arguments be dismantled, sifted, and tested, which is often an involved and complicated process. Nevertheless, there is much material that is practical and digestible at every educational level. Therefore, I encourage the reader to press on until the barbed wire of details gives way to horizons of clarity, understanding, and simplicity; with time they shall come. More complex discussions are reserved for the appendices for those who choose to examine the issues in greater detail. Additionally, a full bibliography of works cited and consulted has been included to facilitate follow-up and future research.

Since both sides of the debate accept the authority of Scripture as final, I have chosen to begin the discussion by ironing out differences in the interpretation and application of important biblical passages relating to the CCM controversy. From there peripheral, but important, issues of dancing, body image, celebrity worship, and dress styles are pursued (chapters two and three). Chapters four and five deal with the nucleus of the debate, the neutrality or non-neutrality of music and aesthetics. Chapter six will interest those who have followed the joustings over the physiological effects of rock music, while chapter seven grapples with some important junctures in the long history of church music. Finally, chapter eight contains the conclusion of the book. Another kind of conclusion then awaits—the reader's of course.

Endnotes

[1] CCM is really a generic label that refers to any modern style of music whose lyrical content reflects the Christian values or worldview of its composers and performers. Consequently CCM can include within its domain country and jazz. Nevertheless, my use of the term will be limited to pop and rock based genres such as rock, hard rock, disco, heavy metal, thrash, rap, grunge, alternative, punk, new wave, industrial, techno, ska, pop, middle-of-the-road, and their permutations.

[2] Charlie Peacock, *At the Crossroads: An Insider's Look at the Past, Present, and Future of Contemporary Christian Music* (Nashville: Broadman & Holman, 1999), 62, 63; Carol Flake, *Redemptorama: Culture, Politics, and the New Evangelicalism* (New York: Penguin Books, 1984), 173.

[3] Peacock, *At the Crossroads*, 11, 62, 78. According to Jay R. Howard and John M. Streck, "it is perhaps not surprising that there are only a few, however vocal, who still argue that rock and roll is the devil's music." CCM still faces major hurdles but they are internal and lyrically related. Jay R. Howard and John M. Streck, *Apostles of Rock: The Splintered World of Contemporary Christian Music* (Lexington, KY: The University Press of Kentucky, 1999), 45.

[4] Peacock, *At the Crossroads*, 11; Steve Rabey, "Age to Age," *Contemporary Christian Music*, July 1998, 21; Howard and Streck, *Apostles of Rock*, 44.

[5] Christopher John Farley, "Reborn to Be Wild," *Time*, 22 January 1996, 62.

[6] Rabey, "Age to Age," 40; Michael Ciani, "All Aboard," *Contemporary Christian Music*, July 1996, 37; Howard and Streck, *Apostles of Rock*, 79.

[7]Patrick Kavanaugh, *The Music of Angels: A Listener's Guide to Sacred Music from Chant to Christian Rock* (Chicago: Loyola Press, 1999), 254.

[8]Howard and Streck, *Apostles of Rock*, 59.

[9]Frank Garlock and Kurt Woetzel, *Music in the Balance* (Greenville, SC: Majesty Music, 1992); Calvin M. Johansson, *Discipling Music Ministry: Twenty-First Century Directions* (Peabody, MA: Hendrickson, 1992); Tim Fisher, *The Battle for Christian Music* (Greenville, SC: Sacred Music Services, 1992).

[10]*How to Conquer the Addiction of Rock Music* (Oak Brook, IL: Institute in Basic Life Principles, 1993).

[11]Earlier polemical books include Frank Garlock, *The Big Beat: A Rock Blast* (Greenville, SC: Bob Jones University Press, 1971); Bob Larson, *Rock and the Church* (Carol Stream, IL: Creation House, 1971); *The Day the Music Died* (Carol Stream, IL: Creation House, 1972); David A. Noebel, *The Marxist Minstrels* (Tulsa: American Christian College Press, 1974); *Christian Rock: A Stratagem of Mephistopheles* (Manitou Springs, CO: Summit Ministries, n.d.); Lowell Hart, *Satan's Music Exposed* (Huntingdon Valley, PA: Salem Kirban, 1981); David Wilkerson, *Set the Trumpet to Thy Mouth* (Springdale, PA: Whitaker, 1985); Richard Peck, *Rock: Making Musical Choices* (Greenville, SC: Bob Jones University Press, 1985); Jimmy Swaggart and Robert Paul Lamb, *Religious Rock 'n' Roll: A Wolf in Sheep's Clothing* (Baton Rouge, LA: Jimmy Swaggart Ministries, 1987); Ken Lynch, *Gospel Music: Blessing or Blight* (Chester, PA: n.p., 1987); Leonard J. Seidel, *Face the Music: Contemporary Church Music on Trial* (Springfield, VA: Grace Unlimited Publications, 1988); Jeff Godwin, *The Devil's Disciples: The Truth About Rock Music* (Chino, CA: Chick Publications, 1985); *Dancing with Demons: The Music's Real Master* (Chino, CA: Chick Publications, 1988); *What's Wrong with Christian Rock?* (Chino, CA: Chick Publications, 1990).

[12]Miller's book was reprinted in 1997 by O. M. Literature.

[13]J. Nathan Corbitt, *The Sound of Harvest: Music's Mission in Church and Culture* (Grand Rapids: Baker Books, 1998), 9.

[14]Earlier defenses of CCM include Harold Myra and Dean Merrill, *Rock, Bach and Superschlock* (New York: Holman, 1972); Paul Baker, *Why Should the Devil Have All the Good Music?* (Waco, TX: Word Books, 1979); Tom Allen, *Rock 'n' Roll, the Bible and the Mind* (Beaverlodge, AB, Canada: Horizon House Publishers, 1982); J. Brent Bill, *Rock and Roll* (Old Tappan, NJ: Revell, 1983); Dan Peters, Steve Peters, and Cher Merrill, *What About Christian Rock?* (Minneapolis: Bethany House, 1986); Steve Lawhead, *Rock of This Age: Real and Imagined Dangers of Rock Music* (Downers Grove, IL: Inter-Varsity, 1987); Dana Key with Steve Rabey, *Don't Stop the Music* (Grand Rapids: Zondervan, 1989).

1

Worldliness According to the New Testament

Introduction

ANY DEFENSE OF CCM must first lay to rest charges of worldliness brought against it by its opponents. Because rock and roll was forged in the crucible of popular culture and has been implicated with counter-culture values from its inception, it has been unable to escape the stigma of worldliness and condemnation from conservative Christians. The response from CCM advocates has been one that demands clarification of terms and a scriptural definition of worldliness, rather than an all-inclusive one that fails to make distinctions between that which simply originates from the world and that which originates from the world but stands in clear antipathy to biblical standards.

Perhaps no one has taken these charges more seriously or better represents the CCM position on this issue than Steve Miller. Miller attempts to answer these allegations by properly defining "world" and by showing the inconsistencies of those who make such accusations. The primary texts with which he deals are Romans 12:2, "And do not be conformed to this age, but be transformed by the renewing of your mind..." and 1 John 2:15-17, "Do not love the world, nor the things in the world...." When Miller complains that "world" in these contexts does not mean "everything that finds its origin or use in the sinful world," he is correct.[1] He rightly explains that the Greek language originated in a pagan society and was used for unrighteous as well as righteous purposes, such as the writing of the New Testament. He therefore concludes that items such as language could not have been what Paul and John meant.[2] His understanding of worldliness elsewhere is also respectable: "In other words, worldliness involves participation in those attitudes or those activities of the world that God has labeled 'sin,' either by direct teaching or by principle."[3]

Romans 12:2 and 1 John 2:15-17

Since Romans 12:2 and 1 John 2:15-17 are the most definitive passages in the New Testament on this subject, a few observations are in order. Paul's use of the term "this age" is roughly equivalent to John's "world" and refers to the old corrupted order of things, dominated by sin and death.[4] In Romans 12:2 Paul contrasts two antithetical modes of thinking: one that stems from the newness of the regenerated mind and the other from the darkness of this fallen and sin-contaminated age, "the world turned away from God, rebellious and hostile toward him (cf. Rom. 3:16, 19; 2 Cor. 5:19), depraved mankind that is headed for judgment (Rom. 3:6; 1 Cor. 11:32)."[5] Elsewhere he acknowledges that the citizens of this age have a wisdom of their own, alien to the wisdom of God (1 Corinthians 2:6f). Rather than specifics, then, Paul is concerned with patterns, grids, systems, principles, myths, and mind-sets. Further, the idea of conformity implies that the evil of this age can sometimes be subtle and unwittingly absorbed into Christian doctrine or lifestyle.

John's focus, however, is on sins of attraction ("do not love") that are embraced by the world (the human system opposed to God's order). He has in mind things that appeal to the sinful nature—pleasures that God has not ordained for man's fulfillment and happiness, but are institutionalized within human culture and elevated for easy admiration.[6] He further describes these lusts as transitory ("shall pass away") along with the world system itself, "all that is in the world, the lust of the flesh [the sinful cravings of man] and the lust of the eyes [sinful cravings that result from what is appealing to the eyes] and the pride of life [the glory that results from position or possessions], is not from the Father but is from the world" (1 John 2:16). Like the dualism in Romans 12:2, the last statement—"is not from the Father but is from the world"—indicates the irreconcilability of the two orders.

When taken together, Romans 12:2 and 1 John 2:15-17 forbid the adoption of patterns of thinking, modes of behavior, attitudes, philosophies, outlooks, grids of evaluation, affections, gratifications, priorities, and value systems that are sinful and a manifestation of the world's perverted understanding of what is true, good, and brings lasting happiness. Even so this is not to be taken as a categorical condemnation of culture, only unbiblical elements within it.

In conclusion, then, I find myself largely in agreement with CCM's interpretation of these passages.[7] We both concur that worldliness can only be applied to those things of the world that are clearly sinful. The key area of disagreement lies in the application of these passages, which must wait to be resolved after the neutrality of music and the moral ethos of rock music have been thoroughly discussed. For now it can only be said that there is a great deal of evidence to demonstrate that music should be included within the morally conditioned activities of culture. Music by way of symbol and referent is capable of transmitting human feelings and ideologies, some of which have deep ethical implications.

Paul on Mars' Hill: Acts 17:22-31

One of CCM's responses to accusations of worldliness has been to capitalize on examples of biblical personalities imitating pagan concepts. Of these Paul's citation of Greek poets in his famous address on Mars' Hill (Acts 17:22-31) may be the most popular.[8] In this passage Paul quotes the Greek poet Epimenides when he says, "'for in him we live and move and exist,' even as some of your own poets have said" (17:28), and the Cilician poet Aratus (as well as Cleanthes), "'For we also are his offspring'" (17:28). For many in CCM, Paul's deployment of Greek poets is an indication that even the most pagan elements of society can be used for the furtherance of the gospel.

Nevertheless, I will argue that the points of contact between today's concept of witness music and Paul's example in Athens are not of the kind that warrant these conclusions. Paul quoted Greek poets because they demonstrated his theology of general revelation. In doing so, Paul was not intimating that popular culture could be exploited freely for the sake of the gospel. Neither was he attempting to flatter the Athenians with their celebrities nor basing his teaching on the assertions of these men. Rather, he was proving the genuineness of the revelatory principle in Romans 1:19-20 through the theology of individuals who were familiar to his audience:[9] "Because that which is known of God is evident in them. For God has revealed it to them. For his invisible attributes, both his eternal power and divinity, have been clearly seen since the creation of the world, being understood by what is made, so that they may be without excuse."

Before proceeding to the next point in his message (a denunciation of idolatry, v. 29), Paul had to establish God's sovereignty as the creator and sustainer of life. Therefore, by quoting their philosophers, he was confirming that the divine attributes he was explaining were not as new to them as they might have first believed since God's sovereignty, divinity, and providence are part of the natural revelation that was available to all men and was already apprehended, in some way, by their own. John F. MacArthur, Jr. further clarifies Paul's intentions:

> Oddly enough, when Epimenides said, "In him we live and move and have our being," he was talking about Zeus. Why would Paul quote this paean for an idol and apply it to God? Because he was making a defense of the faith. His point may be paraphrased like this: "Your own poets, with no knowledge of the true God whatsoever, nevertheless gave testimony to the inescapable fact that there had to be a sovereign, life-giving, all powerful creator. Zeus does not fit that description. But the God I declare to you, whom you don't know yet, is that Almighty One."[10]

Put another way, Paul was implying that "in him [that is God, not Zeus] we live and move and exist" (Acts 17:28). The Greek poet demonstrated some recognition of divine providence but attributed it to the wrong divinity. It is significant that following this citation Paul remarks, "as even some of your own poets have said." The phrase "as even," though subtle, indicates that this nugget of theology did not originate with their poets, but was simply recognized by them (albeit imperfectly).

Paul's message on Mars' Hill demonstrates that he was well informed and able to comment intelligently on Greek religion, philosophy, and culture.[11] More so, his corrective language, evident elsewhere in the message, assures us that he was not trying to flatter his audience by recognizing their favorites.[12] He simply took advantage of the fact that an example of biblical doctrine was unknowingly espoused by their prophets in order to lay the foundation for the rest of his message. He was essentially appealing, "Don't just listen to me, listen to your own prophets." (Calling attention to divine principles operating through common grace within sinful men can be a powerful demonstration of the veracity of God's Word.) Also by interacting with their societal paragons, Paul demonstrated that his appeal to them was based on a firm knowledge of their philosophies and creeds. Paul's familiarity with their cult would thwart any accusation that he was inconsiderate of their religious circumstances when he reproved their system as false and demanded repentance.

So then, what we can learn from Paul's speech is the importance of understanding the religious and philosophical outlook of the culture in which we live and minister. It also teaches us that it is acceptable to support an argument by using an opponent's own words and ideas against him. But to glean from this example a precedent to plunder almost any artifact of popular culture, such as music, and harness it for the gospel is clearly invalid.

Becoming "All Things to All Men": 1 Corinthians 9:19-23

Along with Acts 17, the CCM faithful have traditionally favored 1 Corinthians 9:19-23 for demonstrating that, far from "worldliness," Scripture actually endorses the use of popular forms of discourse in evangelism. In fact 1 Corinthians 9:19-23 has developed into one of the most effective passages for justifying the use of contemporary music styles and other entertainment forms in evangelism and worship.[13]

> For though I am free from all men, I have enslaved myself to all in order that I might gain the majority. And I have become to the Jews as a Jew that I might gain the Jews; to those who are under the Law, as under the Law (though not myself being under the Law) that I might gain those who are under the Law; to those who are without law as without law (though not being without the law of God, but being subject to the law of Christ) that I might gain those who are without law. To the weak I became weak that I might gain the weak. I have become all things to all men that I might altogether save some. And I do all things for the sake of the gospel that I might be a partaker of it (1 Corinthians 9:19-23).

From a cursory reading, Paul's words seem to be the perfect charter for CCM and other types of witness music. After all, how can we possibly insist that rock music cannot be used to win the lost when Paul himself became "all things to all men"? A closer look at the passage and its context, however, unmasks something altogether different.

The context of 1 Corinthians 9:19-23 reveals that it is concerned with the issue of individual freedom and spreading the gospel. The entire chapter is a personal demonstration of Paul's teaching in 1 Corinthians 8, which commands the forfeiture of individual rights in order not to offend a weaker brother.[14] Paul in 9:19-23, as elsewhere in the chapter, stresses his abandonment of personal, social, and religious liberties for the sake of evangelism. In 9:4-12 he explains to the Corinthians that even though he is in a position to expect material support from them, he would rather deprive himself of the right than hinder the gospel through its use. From this specific example Paul moves on in 9:19-23 to outline his overall policy regarding societal adaptation for evangelism. Contextually, then, what Paul meant by becoming "all things to all men" was doing all things possible to avoid certain prohibitions, strictures, and offenses peculiar to a culture.[15] Paul had in mind such things as social and religious customs (1 Corinthians 10:31-33), the violation of which could insult its adherents and make it difficult to preach the gospel.[16]

All Things to the Jews

When Paul preached, "to the Jews I became as a Jew" (1 Corinthians 9:20), he was referring to things such as observing Jewish feast days, circumcision, and dietary laws. This is aptly demonstrated in Acts 16:3 where Paul has Timothy circumcised, not for his salvation, but because of the Jews, who knowing that Timothy's father was a Greek would not have accepted either of them.[17] Since circumcision is not in itself sinful, Paul had Timothy circumcised in order to become all things to the Jews and not offend them. Paul would also observe Jewish dietary customs in the presence of Jews to be accepted among them in order that he might preach the gospel.[18] He was relinquishing his freedom in Christ to eat all kinds of meats in order to win the Jews. An important factor in all of this, as Paul is sure to explain, is that although he followed Jewish customs, he was never under the Law (9:20). His knowledge and attitude toward the Law insulated him from the legalism often associated with it.[19]

All Things to the Gentiles

Paul's strategy toward the Gentiles involved being "without law" as they were. To be without law referred to the ceremonial Jewish law that was no longer in effect, not the moral law of God. Paul is quick to insert this qualifier when explaining that he is without law, "though not being without the law of God, but being subject to the law of Christ" (9:21). The law of God refers to God's moral law, binding at all times, not the ceremonial law, which was instituted only for a limited time and purpose. Paul makes it clear that he will become as the Gentiles in so far as it does not violate any biblical principles. He had in mind eating meats offered to idols (10:32-33)—for an idol is nothing—and not observing Jewish dietary and ceremonial codes while in the company of Gentiles. As with the Jews, this was done to avoid needlessly offending them.

Paul's Intentions

It is evident, then, that Paul's evangelistic approach in 9:19-23 of becoming "all things to all men" was *preventative* and *defensive*— dealing with life-style, behavior, Christian liberty, and personal preference. It was intended to avoid social taboos and needless offenses that would immediately short-circuit the preaching of the gospel, as is apparent from the context of the chapter and the letter as a whole.

So then, Paul's evangelistic doctrine here is *defensive* (or passive). It is not *offensive* (or active), which it must be if it is to support CCM's interpretation of the passage. Nowhere in this chapter or in the New Testament does Paul advocate communicating the gospel by means that appeal to the masses. Becoming "all things to all men" does not refer to an *offensive* strategy of inventiveness, creativity, persuasiveness, or accommodation to new modes of evangelism that key in on the latest public novelty. Paul's references here are purely *preventative*. He simply wished to eliminate any nonessential barriers that would hinder his proclamation of the gospel.

"The Foolishness of the Message Preached"

We encounter Paul's *offensive* strategy in 1 Corinthians 1-2 as the preaching of the cross, "not in persuasive words of wisdom, but in demonstration of the Spirit and of power" (1 Corinthians 2:4, NASB). Furthermore, he explains in 1:21 that "God was pleased through the foolishness of the message preached to save those who believe."[20] This refers to method as well as message, as the context recommends.[21] Such phrases as "cleverness of speech" (1:17), "persuasive words of wisdom" (2:4), "eloquence of speech or wisdom" (2:1), and "debater of this age" (1:20) refer to the persuasive techniques of skilled Hellenistic orators and debaters, who used such tactics to convince their audiences of their position.[22] Raymond C. Ortlund explains what was involved in these strategies:

> The words translated "lofty words or wisdom" (ὑπεροχὴν λόγου ἢ σοφίας) by the RSV are technical terms in the rhetorical theory of the day for the ideals which every public speaker sought to exemplify in order to win a hearing. These were the standards by which a powerful and attractive speaker was judged. If a speaker failed to take advantage of these secrets to success, he was dismissed as a loser. To impress, to entertain, to please, so to adapt oneself to the audience that one wins their allegiance and moves them deeply—this tested the skill of the orator. And the pay-off for the successful virtuoso was nothing less than public adoration. If it seemed expedient to indulge in self-display, to distort the truth, to pander to the vulgar appetites of the mob, to trivialize an issue to score a cheap point, well, one had to do whatever it takes to achieve results.[23]

More importantly, Paul disclosed that the use of such forms—which he was certainly capable of employing—would "empty the cross of its power" (1:17), i.e., create "an inappropriate response in the audience."[24] Burton L. Mack comments on style in proclamation:

> Early Christians were alert to the problem of style. Mark's reference to Jesus' authority and Paul's disavowal of eloquence were stylistic observations pertinent to the issue of how an audience might respond to their

messages. In general, early Christian rhetoric was marked by unusual claims to authority, claims intended to enhance the privileged status and seriousness of the message even while creating imposing obstacles to its entertainment.[25]

Likewise, Jeffrey S. Lamp discusses why rhetoric was depreciated by Paul:

> The σοφία λόγου [cleverness of speech] valued in Greco-Roman rhetoric, in contrast, relies upon human oratorical strategies to secure a predetermined response from the audience.... The persuasive techniques of rhetoric, in Paul's thinking, implicitly asserted that more than the proclamation of the cross was necessary to produce saving faith in the hearers.[26]

At this point it is important to realize that in Acts 17:22-31 Paul remained consistent with his theology of proclamation. It is often overlooked that Paul "proclaimed" his message to the inquisitive philosophers at Areopagus: "Therefore, that which you worship in ignorance, this I proclaim to you" (Acts 17:23). The pivotal word here is *kataggelein*, "to proclaim," used elsewhere of the authoritative proclamation of God's Word and the gospel (Acts 13:5; 15:36; 1 Corinthians 9:14). This is exactly the kind of verb that we would *not* expect if Paul intended to use the argumentative strategies popular at the time, since such verbs of declaration "describe a form of speaking which is at its core the antithesis of rhetorical behavior."[27]

So then, I propose that both the method and message of the gospel were in Paul's mind in 1 Corinthians 1:21. To Paul, the only appropriate method of communicating the seemingly absurd message of a crucified redeemer was preaching—a means that was as unappealing to the unconverted (in the context of Greco-Roman rhetoric) as its message.[28] Therefore, not only does 1 Corinthians 9:19-23 fail to support the modern concept of witness music (which is not limited to pop styles), but chapters 1 and 2 emphasize the very opposite—dependence on preaching with all its "foolishness."[29]

Conclusion

We may compare Paul's defensive strategy in 1 Corinthians 9:19-23 with CCM's offensive one by using a scale of integers with negative and positive numbers. In Paul's model he becomes "all things to all men" in order to move from a negative number, which represents a stumbling block or barrier to hearing the gospel, to zero, neutral ground from which he may preach Christ crucified.

Paul's Model:

CCM's strategy, however, has Paul beginning on neutral ground (zero) or lower, and then moving to higher positive numbers, which represent a persuasive advantage with his hearers when the gospel is presented. This is clearly not what Paul intended since such methods do away with the offense of the cross as well as its power (1 Corinthians 1:17).

CCM's Model:

In conclusion then, CCM's appropriation of 1 Corinthians 9:19-23 turns out to be patently un-Pauline because (1) it represents an offensive evangelistic approach (whereas Paul espouses only a defensive one); (2) it employs man-pleasing methods in spreading the gospel, which, like rhetoric, invalidate the power of the cross (1:17); and (3) unlike many other methods that appeal to the populace, rock music is gravid with counter-Christian values—as will be demonstrated—and so is also 'without the law of God and [not] subject to the law of Christ' (9:21).[30]

1 Corinthians 14:22-25

Yet another passage in 1 Corinthians has been mustered to support the use of indigenous musical styles for evangelism, 1 Corinthians 14:22-25. Miller feels that Paul's awareness of unbelievers in the church service at Corinth and his concern that adjustments be made for their benefit gives some basis for our accommodating the music service to the tastes of unbelievers.[31] Although this appears to be a reasonable application, an examination of the context leads to a different conclusion.

Some of the issues that Paul was addressing in 1 Corinthians 14 were church order and the priority, purpose, and use of spiritual gifts. Among other things, he was commanding that three adjustments be made in the Corinthians' exercise of tongues in the worship service: he insisted that no more than two or three should speak during a service, that only one should speak at a time, and that an interpreter be present (14:27). Thus, the true intention of tongues in worship, which was for the edification of the body, would be facilitated.

With regard to unbelievers (14:22-25), Paul was complaining that the congregation's overemphasis and improper use of tongues would have an adverse effect on visitors, who would be repulsed by the resulting chaos. Instead of tongues being a sign for them, it would be a stumbling block and hinder evangelism. It would undermine evangelism because the message would be unintelligible and the service would have the appearance of madness and confusion (14:23). Paul's concern was that unbelievers comprehend the message and come away with a positive impression of church decorum. Therefore, he preferred prophecy because it eliminated both these barriers to the unbeliever and edified the church.

Consistent with 1 Corinthians 9:19-23, Paul is again espousing defensive evangelistic measures. Paul's only accommodations to the unbeliever are those of public image (in the conservative sense) and language—perfectly legitimate ones. There is not a hint of using man-pleasing techniques or adjusting the service to the preferences of the unchurched. In fact, Miller overlooks one crucial point: the same corrections in the Corinthian service would have had to have been made in any case, unbelievers or not! Paul's line of thought in this section is *body*-centered, and his admonitions were ultimately designed to dissolve the notion among some that speaking in tongues was the most important spiritual gift. He also wished to establish proper procedures and conduct in the worship service because "God is not a God of confusion but of peace" (14:33). His digression to unbelievers in vv. 22-25 merely reveals an *additional* consequence of their misuse of tongues. It was not the main issue, but a supporting reason for how else these corrections would benefit the Corinthians. Therefore, this text gives no basis for the idea that the unbeliever's tastes should influence the style of Christian music.

Colossians 3:16

Miller also feels that Paul's command in Colossians 3:16 to teach and admonish with "psalms and hymns and spiritual songs" could be stretched to include evangelism in that the nature of evangelism is really *teaching* about the gospel.[32] Much like the previous example, however, this is more a case of special pleading than sound hermeneutics, since it is plain that Paul expects this commandment to be exercised within the community of believers, i.e., "one another." To apply it to an evangelistic sphere is clearly outside the context of this passage and unsupported elsewhere. (There is a considerable difference between using songs to instruct regenerate individuals, who already accept the authority of Scripture, and using music as an element of attraction or persuasion in reaching unbelievers.) This text is even less appropriate since by psalms, hymns, and spiritual songs Paul is probably referring to the Jewish music of the synagogue and temple.[33]

Although an argument from silence is inconclusive, I still feel that it is worth asking why Holy Scripture does not sanction, by direct command or implicit example, the use of music in evangelism if it is indeed God's desire that we employ it to reach the lost. Is it simply a coincidence that we find multifarious functions for music in the Bible and yet not one clear reference to its evangelistic use?[34]

This alone, however, does not lead to the conclusion that witness music is unbiblical. Yet, 1 Corinthians 1:17ff decidedly supports the Bible's silence on this point in that, like Greco-Roman rhetoric, evangelistic music would constitute an offensive, manipulative strategy that would undermine the power of the cross. On the contrary, Paul insists that it is through the gospel preached that God is pleased to save those who believe (1 Corinthians 1:21) in that it does not empty the cross of its power (1 Corinthians 1:17), appears foolish like its message (1 Corinthians 1:17-18), and demonstrates the Spirit's power in salvation rather than man's ingenuity (1 Corinthians 2:4).[35]

Although I do feel there may be some place for reverent music in an evangelistic setting, as an act of worship by believers, any dedication of a service or meeting to musical evangelism (whatever the style) falls under Paul's condemnation of persuasive methods that drain the cross of its power (1 Corinthians 1-2).

Further, since music can be a powerful emotional catalyst, it has the tendency to underemphasize or neglect the cognitive involvement that is vital in making a decision for Christ. Music has powers of its own, powers of persuasion and sentimentality that often counterfeit the work of the Holy Spirit. Even some CCM promoters like J. Nathan Corbitt have acknowledged this:

> Because of its power to motivate, music has a tremendous appeal. For this reason, music is often used as an attractive part of proclamation events. Crusades, evangelistic rallies, and revivals often feature a soloist or music group who will appeal to the musical tastes of an audience. At the same time, music can also be manipulative. The power of music to affect the emotions can create an atmosphere in which people respond solely out of emotion without cognitive understanding. Like people who may be motivated by advertising to change brands because the tune is catchy, people may also be motivated to change religions because they like the music—and they never understand the meaning of their decision.[36]

Likewise, CCM custodian Al Menconi warns, "If the music, the environment, and the attitude all say 'Rock out,' how can that encourage a deeper commitment to Jesus or a rational decision to repent?"[37]

As Menconi has recognized, this condition is most graphically realized at Christian rock concerts where the sheer volume, penetrating rhythms, pyrotechnics, frenzied gymnastics of the performers, and carnival atmosphere block out intellectual and rational faculties as the individual is swept away in a torrent of blistering sound to a decision that is contaminated with secondary influences. Quentin J. Schultze et al. briefly describe the power of a rock concert: "The high-tech rock show aims for a total sensory envelopment that embodies and enhances the absorptive power of the music itself. In a concert, sound, light, image, and performance carry as much power and meaning as any purely musical or lyrical 'message.'"[38] Indeed, some groups do pause to explain the message of the gospel, and often in a very serious manner; yet, as with anything else, their actions speak louder than their words when they suddenly relapse into their crowd-pleasing exhibitions, rebaptizing the gospel in the muddy waters of entertainment and assuring the listener that its demands are not as serious as they just appeared.[39]

With so many external factors such as the music, volume, lighting, costumes, showmanship, dancing, and mob psychology influencing the "conversion" process, how can the words of the apostle in 1 Corinthians 2:4-5 ring true? "And my message and my preaching were not with persuasive words of wisdom but with the demonstration of the Spirit and of power [i.e., the demonstration of the Spirit's power][40] so that your faith might not be in the wisdom of man but in the power of God." Consequently, I feel that Miller has failed again to find scriptural support for musical evangelism.

On Adopting Pagan Worship Forms

Baptism

As CCM defenders have become more sophisticated, they have looked to the expanding field of comparative studies in biblical scholarship to expose the futility of making sharp distinctions between what is sacred and secular in society. The apparent borrowing and redefinition of pagan symbols by God's people in both testaments is considered an important example of the potential for even the most offensive practices of pop culture and religion to be rehabilitated for sacred use.[41] With dependence on G. R. Beasley-Murray's *Baptism in the New Testament*, Miller finds just such an example in the ordinance of baptism. Beasley-Murray feels that New Testament baptism and Old Testament ceremonial washings were predated by and patterned after "animistic views of the supernatural nature of water."[42] It should be pointed out, however, that Beasley-Murray offers no evidence beyond the similarity of the washings in form and purpose, which leads me to believe that his conclusions are based on too simplistic a view of cultural exchange. In other words, simply because one event follows another and is similar to the other does not necessarily mean that the second is the product of the first.

Washing the body in water is a common religious metaphor for spiritual cleansing or renewal, where dirt serves as a tangible symbol for sin. To assume that this symbol of spiritual cleansing is limited to one group and alien to all others, except by imitation, is extremely difficult to prove. For example, certain Greek mystery religions included ablutions (religious washings) in their ceremonies. One of the initiations into the mysteries of Osiris consisted of washing the body to prepare the candidate for further religious rites.[43] The Eleusinian mysteries also included an ablution in sea water, as J. Gresham Machen elaborates: "The candidates went to the sea-coast, where they made sacrifice of a pig and purified themselves by washing in the sea water."[44] Also telling is the testimony of Tertullian, a third century church father, who describes the ablutions of the mystery cults:

> In some sacred rites a bath is the means by which they become initiates of some Isis or other or of Mithras. Even their gods themselves are carried in procession for ceremonial washings. Water is carried round and sprinkled as a ritual purification of their country villas,…even whole cities. Mass baptisms take place at the Apollinarian and Pelusian games, which are performed in the confidence that they will lead to rebirth and release from their broken oaths.[45]

Perhaps even more convincing are examples of ablutions from eastern religions, which were geographically and theologically removed from both Judaism and Christianity. For example, religious washings are important to worshipers in the Shinto religion, where serious devotees rinse their hands and mouth before entering a shrine.[46] Similarly, in the southern Buddhist tradition a monk is expected to wash in a pool before engaging in meditations.[47] Finally, there is the example of the famous River Ganges in India, which is a mythical source of life-giving water and ablutions for myriads of Hindus.[48] For these reasons I submit that the example of water baptism should be disqualified from the discussion of cultural dependence.

Canaanite Music

Another example of exploiting comparative studies to support CCM's position comes from David B. Pass, who assumes that the music of the Israelites was probably no different from that of surrounding cultures. Yet citing Sigmund Mowinckel—"beyond all doubt the temple singing in Israel can be traced back to Canaanite patterns"—only hurts his case.[49] Mowinckel was a radical form critic who tried to place the book of Psalms within the context of a supposed New Year's enthronement festival for Yahweh, based on superficial analogies with the enthronement festival of the Mesopotamian god Marduk. His views of the enthronement festival are almost unanimously rejected today and correctly seen as unsupported—making him a superb example of early twentieth-century parallelomania (see below).[50] Though it is probably true that Israel shared in the musical milieu of its neighbors, it is not true that Israel "used the music available to it from its own populace and neighbors without qualm (as far as we can tell)."[51] Alfred Sendrey points out that "whatever did not meet with their artistic approval, they either repudiated—as for instance the noisy and orgiastic music of the Ishtar cult—or transformed to a greater or lesser degree."[52]

More Borrowing?

In much the same way, many Old Testament religious practices are credited to pagan religions by liberal and conservative scholars alike. Archaeological digs in Canaanite shrines have uncovered bones of the right foreleg of sacrificed animals, resembling the statute in Leviticus

7:32, "And the right leg you shall give to the priest as a contribution from the sacrifices of your peace offerings."[53] Moreover, several ancient Near Eastern societies besides Israel offered first fruits and tributary offerings to their gods.[54]

Far more formidable are the apparent connections between New Testament events, doctrines, and ordinances and Greek mystery religions and Zoroastrianism, which if true, would render Christianity as a mere duplication of already established pagan cults. Disturbing parallels of deities suffering, dying, and being resurrected are said to have existed in Egypt, Syria, Phoenicia, and Asia and are thought by some critics to be the source of the Christian doctrine of the death and resurrection of Christ.[55] Moreover, could the Gospels' record of Christ's resurrection have been influenced by the cult of Osiris, who died on the 17th and was raised from the dead on the 19th (3 days)?[56] Could the apostle Paul's "negative" view of angels (1 Corinthians 4:9; 6:3; 11:10; 2 Corinthians 12:7; Colossians 1:20) have come from a similar negative outlook on angels by Gnostics?[57] Without attempting to refute these examples (since others have admirably done so already),[58] I will offer some general principles that, individually or corporately, can explain most parallels.

Fluctuations in Comparative Studies

First, it is necessary to understand that in ancient Near Eastern scholarship comparative studies have experienced considerable mood swings during this century. They began with the extreme of seeing Israel as entirely dependent on the surrounding cultures for its traditions, literature, and religion; later shifted to the opposite extreme where Israel was thought to be completely autonomous in these areas; and finally arrived at the current position, which rests somewhere in the middle.[59] The issues are certainly more complex than simply discovering similarities between cultures, determining which culture is older, and then drawing the conclusion that the younger must have borrowed from the older. This type of flat hermeneutic often results in the types of false parallels that CCM crusaders sometimes appeal to. According to Tremper Longman III, in any situation where there is a marked similarity between two cultures, one of four courses is possible: "(1) Culture A borrowed from Culture B, (2) Culture B borrowed from Culture A, (3) Both Culture A and B are dependent on Culture C, or (4) Culture A and B developed the similar trait independently of one another."[60] I have argued that in the case of Christian baptism, the fourth option is to be preferred.

Some Reasons for Similarity

Second, some similarities between civilizations of the ancient Near East, apart from borrowing, can be traced to limited resources and technology, common environment, circumstances, purposes, and universal archetypes.[61] For example, similar purposes and circumstances may result in similar types of praise in cultures separated by continents and eras. Claus Westermann explains the universality of praise conventions among various people groups:

> Narrative praise, as a response to God's deed by a person who has been liberated, heard, healed, and delivered is something which has occurred everywhere where people live their lives in the presence of a personal god. Even in the prayers of primitive peoples we find this.... A prayer of the Khonds (Africa) is, "You have rescued me, O God!" Some form of narrative praise is found in most religions.[62]

There is no causal relationship between the praise of the Khonds and similar Hebrew praises in Psalms 44:7; 56:13; 86:13, and 116:8, except similar purpose and circumstance.

Reinstituting the Rites of Primitive Yahwism

A third factor should be kept in mind, especially when it comes to *religious* similarities between Israel and her neighbors. We are told in Genesis 8:20 that after the flood Noah offered sacrifices to the Lord and exercised priestly functions. More so, even at this point there were distinctions between clean and unclean animals (Genesis 7:2, 8; 8:20) and offerings described specifically as "burnt offerings" (Genesis 8:20). Further, eating blood was also prohibited (Genesis 9:4) as in Leviticus 17:10-14. It is probable then that the cultic situation at that time was far more sophisticated than ordinarily imagined and that God instructed

Noah's covenant community—perhaps in great detail—in the proper procedures of worship.[63] These procedures, then, would have been passed on to Noah's sons Shem, Ham, and Japhet, whose children populated the earth. Further, God may have given (prior to the confrontation at Babel, Genesis 11) additional religious instructions to the children of Shem, Japhet, and Ham. Of course many of those rituals would have been abrogated, replaced, or perverted by human design as the religion of Noah's sons was propagated. But we would expect that some of them, especially those of the line of Shem, would have been preserved in a relatively unaltered form. We may assume then that the cultic regulations instituted in the Pentateuch as part of the Sinaitic covenant would have contained some of the same procedures used by Noah's altar community or his children's.[64] This would explain how God could be consistent in desiring to distance Israel from associations with pagan worship and at the same time seemingly institute rites that were similar or identical to them. Admittedly, there is a degree of speculation here, but it is not unreasonable, improbable, or without warrant (Genesis 7:2, 8; 8:20; 9:4).

The Crucible of Ancient Near Eastern Culture

Fourth, we should recognize that when God selected the line of Shem, and thereby Abraham, he enlisted the raw materials of the culture that developed from Shem as the basic orientation for his new nation in accordance with his will and purpose. It is evident that he did not wish to develop the nation of Israel in a cultural vacuum, choosing rather to retain several elements of Shem's culture while adapting or jettisoning others that were aberrant. Moreover, his choice of this societal sphere reflects his *general* approval of it. He could have chosen the Hamite or Japhetite culture as the womb for his new nation. Yet it seems that Shem's society was closer to his divine pattern and would require the least pruning (after all Shem and Japhet covered Noah's nakedness and received a blessing, Genesis 9:23-27). But just as every custom in the line of Shem was not admissible, so also there were elements within the line of Ham (Genesis 10:6) that were beneficial and could be incorporated within Israelite culture.

Consequently, it is not to be denied that there are genuine elements of culture, literature, and religion that the nation of Israel had in common with its neighbors. The Israelites were after all citizens of the ancient Near East and shared with other nations similar customs, language, literary conventions, figures of speech, metaphors, poetic imagery, military and civil practices, just to name a few. It should be realized, though, that such a network of conventions remained fairly resilient since during much of Israel's existence its culture was relatively sedentary, except for times when it underwent natural, military, or political upheaval.[65] Consequently, these similarities were not the result of faddish imitations as would be the case in today's fast changing society.

Conclusion

Therefore, the unique circumstances pertaining to the similarities between Israel and her neighbors must be taken seriously when attempting to use Israel as a paradigm for present-day cultural integration. In a positive light it does teach us that some elements of non-Christian culture can be useful to Christians. To go beyond this, however, and uncritically annex any discourse medium of society for the sake of the gospel not only violates the clear teaching of the New Testament (1 Corinthians 1:17ff), but does not accord in principle with the example of Israel in the Old Testament.

Finally, before resorting to a comparative approach, we must consider the possibility of the biblical examples being copied by neighboring religions, as well as simple coincidence.[66] We should also keep in mind the general disposition of the early church in such matters. Machen insists, "In the Christian Church, on the other hand, there was a strong objection to such procedure [syncretism]; Christianity from the beginning was like Judaism in being exclusive. It regarded with the utmost abhorrence anything that was tainted by pagan origin...."[67]

This chapter has been occupied with CCM's most recent attempts to secure its theory of music in ministry and evangelism on the bedrock of Holy Scripture in order that it might satisfy the complaints of its critics who insist that CCM is a violation of scriptural admonitions against worldliness. As has been demonstrated, however, the interpretation and application of the passages examined leaves much to be desired. In each case an alternative interpretation has been offered, which proves to be more consistent with the spirit of the passage, its book, and the Bible as a whole.

Endnotes

[1] Steve Miller, *The Contemporary Christian Music Debate: Worldly Compromise or Agent of Renewal?* (Wheaton, IL: Tyndale House, 1993), 43.

[2] Ibid., 43, 44.

[3] Ibid., 46.

[4] Geerhardus Vos, *The Pauline Eschatology*, 1930, reprint (Phillipsburg, NJ: Presbyterian & Reformed, 1994), 12-13.

[5] Herman Ridderbos, *Paul: An Outline of His Theology*, trans. John Richard De Witt (Grand Rapids: Eerdmans, 1992), 92.

[6] There is a certain sense of organization, order, collective agreement, and community within John's use of *kosmos*, "world," that bespeaks the inculturation of these sinful desires.

[7] Cf. Charlie Peacock, *At the Crossroads: An Insider's Look at the Past, Present, and Future of Contemporary Christian Music* (Nashville: Broadman & Holman, 1999), 148, 156.

[8] Warren Anderson, "Josh McDowell: Bridging the Gap," *Contemporary Christian Music*, June 1990, 36; Miller, *Christian Music Debate*, 44.

[9] Since Paul establishes the creator-creature distinction (contra Stoicism) early in his message (v. 24), "The God who made the world and everything that is in it," he is able to utilize what was correct in the Stoic conception of the divine, without endorsing its pantheistic underpinnings. Cf. Donald A. Carson, *The Gagging of God: Christianity Confronts Pluralism* (Grand Rapids: Zondervan, 1996), 499.

[10] John F. MacArthur, Jr., *Ashamed of the Gospel: When the Church Becomes Like the World* (Wheaton, IL: Crossway Books, 1993), 147. I would like to recommend chapter 7 (pp. 137-151) in MacArthur's book, which fully supplements my brief treatment of this passage and discusses areas that I have not pursued.

[11] We should note, however, that by Paul's time Aratus' poem was so familiar that it alone can hardly be an index of Paul's academic stature. Everett Ferguson, *Backgrounds of Early Christianity*, 2d ed. (Grand Rapids: Eerdmans, 1993), 335.

[12] For examples see MacArthur, *Ashamed of the Gospel*, 146-49.

[13] Cf. Bob Larson, *Rock and the Church* (Carol Stream, IL: Creation House, 1971), 48; Miller, *Christian Music Debate*, 38, 49, 86, 91-92, 97, 190, 206;

Angelo De Simone, *Christian Rock: Friend or Foe* (New Haven: Selah Production Agency, 1993), 65, 201; John M. Frame, *Contemporary Worship Music: A Biblical Defense* (Phillipsburg, NJ: Reformed & Presbyterian, 1997), 56, 96.

[14]Cf. MacArthur, *Ashamed of the Gospel*, 92.

[15]Gordon D. Fee, *The First Epistle to the Corinthians*, The New International Commentary on the New Testament (Grand Rapids: Eerdmans, 1987), 432.

[16]Cf. MacArthur, *Ashamed of the Gospel*, 92-93.

[17]Cf. MacArthur, *Ashamed of the Gospel*, 98-99.

[18]Cf. MacArthur, *Ashamed of the Gospel*, 96.

[19]It is worth noting that Paul's accommodations to Jewish religious customs could not be duplicated with pagan religions. Paul would never have adhered to Greco-Roman cultic practices in order to achieve the same effect with Gentiles. Judaism is unique in the sense that, although its ceremonial statutes were no longer necessary, because they were instituted by God, they were wholesome when properly understood.

[20]Cf. NASB.

[21]Cf. Raymond F. Collins, *First Corinthians*, Sacra Pagina Series, ed. Daniel J. Harrington, vol. 7 (Collegeville, MN: The Liturgical Press, 1999), 105. For a detailed treatment of why *kērugma*, "message preached," in 1 Corinthians 1:21 refers to both method and message see Appendix A.

[22]Burton L. Mack, *Rhetoric and the New Testament* (Minneapolis: Fortress Press, 1990), 9.

[23]Raymond C. Ortlund, "The Power of the Gospel in the Church Today," *Trinity Journal* 18 (1997): 4.

[24]Duane Litfin, *St. Paul's Theology of Proclamation: 1 Corinthians 1-4 and Greco-Roman Rhetoric* (Cambridge, England: Cambridge University Press, 1994), 190, 192.

[25]Mack, *Rhetoric*, 33.

[26]Jeff Lamp, "Gospel and Rhetoric in 1 Corinthians 1-4: Ruminations Over Implications for Christian Apologetics," paper presented at the 47th Annual Meeting of the Evangelical Theological Society, November, Philadelphia, PA, 1995, 4.

[27]Litfin, *Paul's Theology of Proclamation*, 195-96. Contra Jason Q. vonEhrenkrook, who fails entirely to deal with 1 Corinthians 1-2. "A Rhetorical Analysis of the Areopagus and Its Missiological Implications," *Calvary Baptist Theological Journal* 14 (Fall 1998): 1-15.

[28]Cf. Lamp, "Gospel and Rhetoric," 4; Litfin, *Paul's Theology of Proclamation*, 197, 200.

[29]We should note here that Paul is not advocating that evangelistic preaching should be boring or simply a shouting match. Neither is Paul disavowing argumentation since it is obvious that both he and other New Testament writers used it. He is probably referring to rhetoric that was mischievously

eloquent, manipulative, irresistible, and appealing, rather than to more intuitive, direct, and less sophisticated forms of argumentation. Cf. Litfin, *Paul's Theology of Proclamation*, 191-92, 201, esp. 132-34, 256-57.

Lamp, however, suggests that Paul's prohibitions against rhetoric were limited to evangelistic settings so that the work of salvation could be attributed to nothing other than the power of God. Consequently he feels that Paul would have had no objection to its use (based on the rhetorical devices appearing in his epistles) in discipleship contexts. Lamp, "Gospel and Rhetoric," 16. Although either view is possible, I prefer the first since Paul did use some argumentation with the unconverted at Areopagus (vv. 28-29) and since much of Lamp's evidence is circumstantial as he himself admits (p. 14). In either case it becomes quite clear that persuasive or manipulative practices in evangelism subvert the power of God, which he has purposely invested in the method of preaching.

[30]It should be noted here that witness music is not the only method that violates Paul's theology of the cross. Other methods that replace biblical preaching with entertainment are just as guilty: comedy, drama, movies, magic, dance, etc.

[31]Miller, *Christian Music Debate*, 86.

[32]Ibid. Unlike Miller, J. Nathan Corbitt and Al Menconi do not try to biblically justify the use of music in evangelism; they just assume it—with Corbitt offering guidelines for its use. J. Nathan Corbitt, *The Sound of Harvest: Music's Mission in Church and Culture* (Grand Rapids: Baker Books, 1998), 111-39; Al Menconi and Dave Hart, *Staying in Tune: A Sane Response to Your Child's Music* (Cincinnati, OH: The Standard Publishing Co., 1996), 151.

Donald P. Ellsworth, who also believes in the propriety of musical evangelism, is, nevertheless, forced to admit: "The Bible does not, however, have anything specific to say concerning music being used in evangelism. But the evangelical's practice of using music for his witness does seem to be founded on historical practice." And, "the evangelical musician looking for some biblical authority to support the use of music in evangelism will not find anything very specific." Donald Paul Ellsworth, *Christian Music in Contemporary Witness: Historical Antecedents and Contemporary Practices* (Grand Rapids: Baker Book House, 1979), 16, 165.

[33]Alfred Sendrey, *Music in Ancient Israel* (New York: Philosophical Library, 1969), 64, 190.

[34]Cf. John Calvin, *Institutes of the Christian Religion*, book 1, chapter 14, section 3.

[35]Cf. MacArthur, *Ashamed of the Gospel*, 113-14.

[36]Corbitt, *Sound of Harvest*, 119. See also pp. 118, 156.

37Al Menconi, "What's Wrong with Christian Music? An Open Letter to Contemporary Christian Musicians," *Contemporary Christian Music*, June 1987, 20.

38Quentin J. Schultze et al., *Dancing in the Dark: Youth, Popular Culture, and the Electronic Media* (Grand Rapids: Eerdmans Publishing Co., 1991), 147-48.

39For example Toby McKeehan of dc Talk interrupts a concert to read 2 Peter 1:5-7, which, among other things, exhorts believers to add self-control to their other virtues. This, however, is followed by McKeehan and another band member throwing themselves into a mosh pit and body surfing over the frantic crowd. Self-control? Jay R. Howard and John M. Streck, *Apostles of Rock: The Splintered World of Contemporary Christian Music* (Lexington, KY: The University Press of Kentucky, 1999), 74.

40Cf. Lamp, "Gospel and Rhetoric," 11n.

41See David B. Pass, *Music and the Church* (Nashville: Broadman Press, 1989), 33.

42G. R. Beasley-Murray, *Baptism in the New Testament* (Grand Rapids: Eerdmans, 1962), 2.

43J. Gresham Machen, *The Origin of Paul's Religion* (New York: The Macmillan Co., 1936), 233.

44Ibid., 218.

45Tertullian, *On Baptism* 1-9 *CCL* I, 277-84, in Maurice Wiles and Mark Santer, eds., *Documents in Early Christian Thought* (New York: Cambridge University Press, 1993), 176-77. With rites that have post-Christian dates such as this, Machen reserves the possibility that Christian practices were adopted by the pagan cults, considering their syncretistic nature. *Paul's Religion*, 255-90.

46Winfried Corduan, *Neighboring Faiths: A Christian Introduction to World Religions* (Downers Grove, IL: InterVarsity Press, 1998), 318.

47*The New Encyclopedia Britannica*, 1973 ed., s.v. "Ablutions."

48R. Pierce Beaver et al., *Eerdmans' Handbook to the World's Religions* (Grand Rapids: Eerdmans, 1982), 171.

49Pass, *Music and the Church*, 33.

50See Tremper Longman III, *Fictional Akkadian Autobiography: A Generic and Comparative Study* (Winona Lake, IN: Eisenbrauns, 1991), 26. Gerhard von Rad, whom Pass also cites, is scarcely more disciplined in this area.

51Pass, *Music and the Church*, 33.

52Sendrey, *Music in Ancient Israel*, 423.

53R. K. Harrison, *Introduction to the Old Testament* (Grand Rapids: W. B. Eerdmans Publishing Co., 1969), 600.

54Ibid., 601.

55Wilhelm Bousset, *Kyrios Christos*, trans. John E. Steely (New York: Abingdon Press, 1970), 57.

[56]Ibid., 58.

[57]Ibid., 257.

[58]For the New Testament I suggest Craig L. Blomberg, *The Historical Reliability of the Gospels* (Downers Grove, IL: Inter-Varsity Press, 1987); Machen, *Paul's Religion.*

[59]Longman, *Akkadian Autobiography*, 24-30.

[60]Ibid., 33.

[61]Cf. John H. Walton, *Ancient Israelite Literature in Its Cultural Context: A Survey of Parallels Between Biblical and Ancient Near Eastern Texts* (Grand Rapids: Zondervan Publishing House, 1989), 142, 144, 161, 164, 235, 236.

[62]Claus Westermann, *The Psalms: Structure, Content, and Message*, trans. Ralph D. Gehrke (Minneapolis: Augsburg Publishing House, 1980), 76.

[63]Even if one were to argue that these were the anachronisms of a later author, the point remains that the rites of Noah's covenant community were still quite involved.

[64]Gordon J. Wenham considers it "characteristic of Gen 1-11 to trace back the fundamental religious institutions to primeval times." Gordon J. Wenham, *Genesis 1-15*, Word Biblical Commentary, vol. 1 (Waco, TX: Word Books, 1987), 177.

[65]For example, most scholars recognize the beginning of a cultural renaissance during the reign of Solomon when times of peace and prosperity encouraged the arts and cultural interchange.

[66]Cf. Machen, *Paul's Religion*, 255-90. Interesting examples of coincidence occur when comparing biblical teachings with far removed cultures such as our own Native Americans. For example, like Samson in the Bible, shamans of the Tlingit tribe (Alaska) are not permitted to cut their hair. If they do, they lose their spiritual power. The same tribe also has marital codes similar to the levirate law in the Old Testament (Deuteronomy 25:5-10). In Tlingit society the brother-in-law or sister-in-law of a widow or widower must marry the surviving spouse. Corduan, *Neighboring Faiths*, 170, 178.

[67]Machen, *Paul's Religion*, 238.

2

Rock Music and Body Image

Introduction

NOW THAT WE HAVE dealt with important biblical passages relevant to the CCM controversy, it is time to explore several practices associated with rock music, apart from the music itself, that will plainly demonstrate that rock music as a social activity is indeed consistent with the biblical understanding of worldliness presented in the foregoing chapter. It is necessary to take this approach because rock music is not simply a one-dimensional listening activity, but a multidimensional mode of entertainment that also involves visual and physical participation. This chapter and the following, then, will provide a description and critique of rock-related dancing, stage antics, celebrity worship, and dress styles. The actual message of the musical style will be tackled later.

Dancing

Dancing is the physical activity that most naturally accompanies rock music and visually articulates its meaning. According to Robert Levin, "Rock began as visceral music, a body music, and, for sure, it must always be music that calls the body to dance."[1] Rock's danceability is due predominately to its emphasized syncopated rhythms, which invite the listener to supply the missing first and third beat, either mentally or through a series of physical gestures such as dancing.[2] Thus dancing becomes a vicarious anatomical reflex to the beat of the music. Although there are several variations, rock-based dance styles include everything from a spasmodic bucking and heaving of the anatomy and pelvic grind, to jolting upper-body flexions, flailing limbs, self-assured and assertive head movements, and power gestures—a spectacle of bodily excess and ritualistic extreme. As Judith Lynne

Hanna explains, "Youth dances often exhibit a contrary stance toward the mainstream establishment and their parent's generation. Alienated and rebellious, some youth who find themselves in a world they did not make or in any way approve of invest their psychic energies in dance."[3] According to Robert P. Snow, "dance styles ranging from the Twist and Frug of the 1960s to the 'nameless' style of the 1980s consist of repetitive body movements instead of choreography. It all came together as a rhythm and tempo achieved and sustained for its own sake and, as such, it was pure play."[4] Schultze et al. detail elements within the composition of the music that contribute to this objectionable style of dancing:

> At rock concerts and dance clubs, distinctions of melody, harmony, and rhythm are blurred to achieve anarchic, contourless, all-engulfing noise; in plunging into the music, teens largely put aside rational and conventional social limits and distinctions to join a community that celebrates, paradoxically, a number of distinct themes that characterize rock as a whole.[5]

Tom Manoff adds, "Obviously, here is a rhythmic style that purposefully seeks 'abandonment' and 'loss of control.' Rock music thrives on highly emphasized, unleashed dance impulse."[6] He also explains the communicable power of modern dance with an example from *Soul Train*: "In a real sense, the dance becomes a drama as the performers express and enhance the meaning of the words through movements and gestures."[7]

Aphrodisiac Dancing

Of greater concern for Christians is the fact that throughout history dancing has proven to be an effective medium for sexual desire and expression.[8] Hanna argues that

> sexuality and dance share the same instrument—the human body. Using the signature key of sexuality, essential for human survival and desirable for pleasure, dance resonates universal behavioral needs...and particular concerns. With the medium as part of the message, dance evokes, reinforces, and clarifies desires and fantasies, some of which would otherwise be incoherent.[9]

She adds that "dance often displays a person's sexual appeal, provides stimulating fantasy or foreplay, and communicates information as a prelude to encounters that lead to mating;"[10] and,

> In sum the body language of dance may carry a more immediate wallop than verbal communication on sexuality and in modeling gender because of its motion-attracting attention, language-like qualities, replete multilayered meanings, multisensory assault, composite of variables that change attitudes and opinions, and accessibility and humanity.[11]

It is even more unsettling to learn that from their very inauguration rock-related dance styles were considered erotic, as Susan McClary elaborates:

> The explosion of rock 'n' roll in the mid-1950s brought a vocabulary of physical gestures to white middle-class kids that parents and authorities quite rightly perceived as subversive of hegemonic bourgeois values. Sheltered Northern adolescents picked up on the dance rhythms of the Southern honky-tonk and black R & B, and their notions of sexuality....[12]

In fact sociologists trace most forms of social dance in the United States during this century to the African-American community, which over time blended Anglo-Saxon motions with those from their native cultures.[13] According to Hanna, "Afro-Americans meshed the African style of loose, flexible torso, extending and flexing knees with an easy breathing quality, shuffling steps, and pelvic swings and thrusts."[14] The erotic nature of these symbols, especially the pelvic thrust, is well documented in the fertility dances of African tribal cultures like the Ubakala of Nigeria: "They symbolize fertility with the stylization of female movement: undulations and hip shifts and rotations. The counterclockwise circle predominates as women move with flexed knees, the upper torso inclined forward at a forty-five-degree angle, and the pelvis tilted backward (the buttocks upward)."[15] Curt Sachs, likewise, reports of the "wild and erotic pelvic motions" of Bantu dancers in Africa.[16]

An aside: This disclosure is not in any way intended to be racist or to promote stereotypes of African-Americans. Many African-American

Christians themselves reject this form of dancing and recognize its sexual punctuation. "Racism" has often been used by CCM advocates as a silver bullet to win arguments against their opponents. (Not all of their accusations are groundless!) But in doing so, they tend to overlook a legitimate form of racism, one that encompasses the entire human race and condemns it as sinful, regardless of skin color, ethnic origin, or nationality (Romans 3:9-18, 23). We need to be aware that just because mannerisms become socialized and characteristic of a culture, they are not, therefore, immune to biblical critique. Culture should never serve as an excuse for carnality.

That this type of body language is not localized but cross-cultural and universally apprehensible is plainly evident when compared to the aphrodisiac dancing of the Cook Islanders—a Polynesian people racially, ethnically, and geographically unrelated to African tribal cultures. Hanna describes the erotic elements in the dance of the Islanders:

> Males and females, trained from puberty in sexual techniques, take pride in their sexual prowess. The ideal male lover has stamina for pelvic thrusting motions, the woman for hip rotations and swings. Stylized lovemaking movements are aesthetically pleasing. Their meanings, symbolic of mythic, romantic, and mundane male virility and female seductiveness, characterize the dance which varies in style and sexual explicitness among the Islands.[17]

The following account of an actual Cook Islander dance reveals remarkable points of contact with that of the Ubakala, again suggesting that these movements form the kernels of a universal language of sexuality:

> Women move their hips from side to side, lifting them with each step, while men, in a semicrouched position on the balls of their feet, move their thighs in and out to the music. The man, smiling, looks at his partner's hips; she, aware of his attention, gazes coyly into space.
>
> In the Cook Island *tuki* dance, or challenge, "the woman turns sideways to the man and accentuates her hip movements. The man crouches lower, keeping his thighs moving rhythmically, and moves as close as he can to the woman with arms extended on either side of her. The woman allures and entices; the man thrusts and tries to 'capture' the woman. But the woman also crushes with her hips, bumping his genitals if he gets

close enough. The man teases by dancing around just out of reach, or below her dangerous hips.[18]

Returning to a more familiar sector of the globe, Nik Cohn remembers the "Twist," the western counterpart of Polynesian and African aphrodisiac dances:

> Its [the Twist's] cuteness was simply that it allowed kids to do something that would have gotten their faces slapped for them in an earlier generation; namely to stand up in public and promote their [buttock]. And all right, so it looked foolish, but it felt illicit.[19]

Simon Frith adds, "The most obvious feature of dancing as an activity is its sexuality—institutionalized dancing, a peculiarly constrained form of physical interaction, is redolent with sexual tensions and possibilities, as private desires get public display."[20] Deena Weinstein agrees, "dance is understood in the modern West as an erotic activity."[21] Angela McRobbie finds that the BBC dance program *Top of the Pops* "confirms and illustrates the convention of dance as sexual invitation."[22] Other sociologists concur: "Rock and roll seemed to acknowledge publicly that teens possessed genitals and that it was *all right* to have them. Dancing became a vertical expression of horizontal desire."[23] Finally, Stan Hawkins, in reference to the rock group the Pet Shop Boys, remarks, "Erotic qualities of the musical ideas are expressed through the somatic [bodily] property of dance, and can be charged for sexing the groove."[24]

It is important to acknowledge that social dancing (pop or rock) from a female perspective is also a leisure activity, involving more than just sexual expression. Women often dance simply for the pleasure of it.[25] The problem is, however, that although there are other dimensions to social dancing (for men and women), sexuality can never be subtracted from the equation. "For women and girls, dance has always offered a channel, albeit a limited one, for bodily self-expression and control," says McRobbie. "It has also been a source of pleasure and sensuality."[26] More importantly she observes that social dancing articulates adolescence and girlhood with femininity and female sexuality and it does this by and through the body. This is especially important because it is the one pleasurable arena where women have some control and know what is going on in relation to physical sensuality and to their own bodies.... dance offers an escape, a positive and vibrant sexual expressiveness and a point of connection with the other pleasures of femininity like getting dressed up or putting on make-up.[27]

We should not assume at this point that dance styles at Christian concerts offer much improvement; they are almost identical as anyone who has attended them or viewed videos can testify.[28] Furthermore, denials of sensual and irreverent intentions by Christians who dance—though no doubt sincere—are hardly satisfactory.[29] As Hanna explains,

sometimes the dancers are unaware of their kinetic statements and their messages. And sometimes their messages may only be unconsciously absorbed by the viewer. In most social dance settings, participants will say they are dancing to have a good time. Some will admit they seek social or sexual partners. The health conscious often aver, "It's good exercise." Yet dance may simultaneously convey a spectrum of messages.[30]

More so, very little seems to be off-limits at these performances, even in the interest of impressionable youth who are in attendance. Joe Battaglia, reporting in *Contemporary Christian Music* magazine, writes (approvingly) of one such incident involving CCM artist Bryan Duncan:

Bryan Duncan lets his energy get to him sometimes even during his concerts. Recently while playing a gig at Nyack College (a Christian college in New York), Bryan decided to jump out into the audience and begin dancing with a certain promotion director from a certain Christian radio station. And he did this while still playing his guitar and singing. What a talented guy![31]

Duncan is not alone. As Michael McCall documents, Michael W. Smith "will sometimes jump from the stage to dance with the young women who have rushed the stage."[32] If such exhibitions are not reprehensible in themselves, the reader should realize that both Duncan and Smith were married and parents when they engaged with members of the opposite sex (in Smith's case, teenagers) in this lewd form of bodily discourse.

Moshing

Lastly, we need to take a close look at moshing, a rock-based dance style that is so menacing that it even has some CCM advocates concerned. Although moshing has adapted itself to a variety of rock formats, it has its roots in the hardcore genres of punk rock and thrash metal, a hybrid of punk and heavy metal.[33] Robert Walser describes thrash or speed metal as one of the "underground styles of metal [that] tended to be more deliberately transgressive, violent, and noisy."[34] Concerned with themes of death, violence, and madness, it is not difficult to understand why Walser would note that the "thrash guitar is even more distorted than in other kinds of heavy metal"[35] and is accompanied by "a vocal style that is rough, percussive, and nonvirtuosic [, which] make thrash metal darker than other metal—angrier, more critical and apocalyptic."[36] Others describe it as a "deliberately cacophonous, turbocharged merger of feedback-laden electric-guitar riffs and the speed freak drumbeat of classic Sex Pistol punk."[37]

Thrash metal is represented in the secular market by such bands as Metallica, Megadeth, Iron Maiden, and Slayer and in Christian circles by groups like Vengeance, Deliverance, and Tourniquet. Both musically and vocally Vengeance is in keeping with the brutality of thrash metal, "play[ing] an extreme form of thrash metal, with demonic-sounding vocals."[38] The same band cryptically presents themes of Christ's atonement, crucifixion, and the slaying of the beast (Revelation 13) under such gruesome song titles as "Human Sacrifice," "Fill This Place with Blood," and "Beheaded."[39] Although Vengeance would claim that these titles refer to biblical themes, non-Christian headbangers will in most cases identify them with other slaughterhouse titles such as Ozzy Osbourne's "Bloodbath in Paradise" and Slayer's "Kill Again." The point of such slight-of-hand evangelism is, of course, to draw metalheads by first appealing to their fascination with death and carnage and then reorienting their desires toward the message of the gospel. Yet, like other pragmatic measures, approaches that excite carnal desires and disguise true intentions in the interest of evangelism find no basis in Scripture.[40]

The actual practice of moshing is no less pernicious than its musical accompaniment. Eyewitness Jeffrey J. Arnett provides the first report:

> In it [the mosh pit] there are bodies crashing into one another, and the more you watch the more it becomes apparent that they are doing this deliberately, in a violent dance. This is what metalheads call "moshing" or "slamdancing." They often slam against one another so hard that one or both of them end up on the floor. After one especially forceful collision you see a boy put his hand to his head as he pulls himself up from the floor. He appears to be bleeding but he is smiling in a pained way.[41]

More useful are insights gained from his interviews with actual participants:

> "It looks like one huge brawl," as one subject described it. Most spoke of it as a release of aggression, barely contained and channeled into a social ritual: "It's violent fun," said one; "any aggressions you have, you let them out," said another; and one subject said half seriously, "I don't feel fulfilled if I don't come away with a scratch or a bloody nose."[42]

Another slamdancer comments, "Nothing you could possibly do [while slamdancing] could be socially unacceptable. You could walk up and pound someone in the face, and it's all in good fun."[43] Yet another confides: "One of the reasons I like to slam dance is that I am a teenager. What I mean is that I am angry at my parents, angry at school, angry at my peers, and angry with the world."[44] Likewise, a metalhead named Nick, "It beats going home and kicking your stereo over, or beating your best friend up."[45]

Next, Jon Savage describes moshing at a Nirvana concert:

> The dance floor is a war zone: a simulated war zone to be sure, but still not for the faint-hearted. Hundreds of young men ricochet off each other at high speed in the 'moshpit', creating flows and eddies that take on a life of their own. And then, by a combination of individual effort and group will, one of them will crest on the surf of this human tide, splaying his body out in pure abandonment before disappearing again. It's a communal, physical release.[46]

Even a comparatively mild illustration of moshing as found in *Contemporary Christian Music* magazine can be enough to condemn it:

Sometimes known as "slam-dancing" or "thrashing," moshing involves enthusiastic, energetic people running or gyrating wildly in a circle (called the "mosh pit") to the sound and speed of the music. "It's 'ring-around-the rosey' heavy metal style," says [Bob] Beeman [of L.A.'s Sanctuary, a heavy metal church]. "It's basically skipping with your arms up." "Moshing is like a man-powered merry-go-round," explains [Roger] Martinez [of Vengeance], "with the emphasis on 'merry.'"

"It's like playing football without the ball," says Julio Rey, guitarist for the Lead. "I think it's just a new way of dancing."

This "new dance" is a spectacle to observe. Like thrash music itself, which upon casual listening appears to be merely noise, a "mosh pit" appears as a crowd out of control. It conjures visions of a shark feeding frenzy.[47]

Gina Arnold recalls the mayhem on the floor of a punk rock concert (secular) in 1995:

The arena floor looked like it had been hit with a fifty-thousand-watt jolt of electricity. Every single person standing on it shot straight into the air, arms flailing, legs pumping, torsos jutting forward, a veritable Hieronymus Bosch painting come frighteningly to life. Huge new [mosh] pits were forming right and left, while kids in the balcony practically fell down the stairwells, the better to throw themselves on top of the crowd, releasing high-pitched shrieks of idiot glee.[48]

The last activity that Arnold described is known as "stagediving," a daring and dangerous maneuver where a member of the audience runs on stage and dives into the crowd expecting to be caught by onlookers below. The reason? A quick thrill, an exhibition of "courage," and sometimes a rite of passage. The following interview by Arnett provides a window into the experiences of one stagediver and the injuries he suffered:

I stagedive a lot. The security guards are brutal [if they catch you]. They just beat the c... out of you. [When I stagedived at a recent concert] one of them grabbed me by the foot and kind of kicked me in the face. Threatened my life. [At another concert] I jumped off the balcony [into the crowd]. [How far down?] About eleven feet. [Were people waiting to catch you?] Well, I was jumping into the crowd, but the crowd was moshing, so they were moving around. [They moved apart at the wrong time and] I kind of hit at the wrong angle. My knees swelled up like balloons.[49] (Italics and brackets original.)

Somewhat less risky is body surfing, the practice of passing an individual over the crowd, hand by hand. Surfing requires that the person (usually male) be momentarily held by any available body part—legs, arms, back, even buttock. This in turn introduces the possibility of *eros* when members of the opposite sex are doing the handling, as is often the case.

Moshing for Jesus?

Sadly, moshing, stagediving, and body surfing also take place at Christian rock concerts (alternative, punk, metal, thrash, etc.) and more regularly than one could wish to imagine. Body surfing, for example, is a familiar sight at such performances; at times even the band members (e.g., dc Talk) surf the crowd.[50] Furthermore, the erogenous hazards of body surfing are as real on the Christian dance floor as anywhere else. A picture of body surfing at a Rez Band concert reveals a young man in shorts kept aloft by generous hands (not all male), clutching everything from his elbows to his hindquarters.[51] The problem is magnified when young ladies dare to surf—not unheard of at Christian concerts[52]— somehow imagining that their brothers below, already overdosed on hormones, will resist the opportunity for a cheap thrill.

Likewise, moshing and stagediving have become fixtures within the hardcore genres of CCM. Live performances of the Christian punk rock group One Bad Pig promise "stage diving, pogoing, moshing and freaking out."[53] A review of the Christian rock group Narnia boasts, "Narnia hit the stage and woah!... now things started to happened! [*sic*] The audience was really moving, hair was flying, people were stage diving and we had a great time!"[54] When Extol took the stage, a similar response: "They were headbanging and doing the helicopter all the time...all of them!... Lots of hair was flying during their set."[55] Many others could be mentioned.

Moshing even occurs at concerts held in churches: "'We've played shows where there's a lot of moshing in the church,' said Mark Stuart, lead vocalist for Audio Adrenaline. 'If the churches book us, they usually know what to expect. We're not timid about what we do. It's a rock concert.'"[56] Stuart goes on to describe some of these church-occupied moshpits: "People leave sweating. Sometimes they pass out. People are skanking in the church aisles just like any rock 'n' roll show."[57] Absolutely! There is barely a sliver of difference between Christian and secular moshpits, as Dean Smallwood elaborates, "Yes, it looks like a rock concert, it sounds like a rock concert, and in every aspect except for the lyrics, it's just like any standard rock concert by today's teen-oriented bands: plenty of flash and lots of thrash on stage; heads bobbing and bodies moshing in the crowd."[58]

Moreover, the risk of injury is as much of an issue at Christian concerts as it is at secular ones. Pillars on dance floors of Christian concerts are often cushioned with layers of carpet or other impact absorbers in anticipation of crashing bodies and flailing limbs. Further, some bands set age limits, load up on liability insurance, or require injury waivers before individuals are permitted on the moshing floor.[59] Jay R. Howard and John M. Streck describe a moshpit at Ichthus 93, a Christian rock festival:

> The music continues, and the energy increases. A few of the younger moshers weave their way out of the crowd as the dancing gets rougher. Still the majority seem to effectively use their hands to bounce off each other and avoid the most painful collisions. Nonetheless, one mosher staggers out with a bloody nose and stands near me pinching his nostrils shut. With a nod of his head, he accepts the tissues I pull from my pocket and offer to him.[60]

A Newsboys-Audio Adrenaline concert (1995) saw two youngsters hospitalized, after which the town fire marshall ordered the moshing to stop.[61]

Eric Boehlert of *Rolling Stone* magazine recalls a moshing incident that went out of control at Jesus Northwest, another Christian rock festival:

> When Seattle's Grammatrain unleashed their three-man mayhem from the Jesus Northwest stage, all hell breaks loose in the mosh pit. Festival organizers, stunned by the careening bodies, airborne shirts and water

bottles spewing into the air like fountains, stop the show midsong, lecture the fans about their behavior and threaten to cancel the show unless things settle down.[62]

Perhaps the organizers should consider what role the musical "mayhem" and hyper-kinetics of the band may have played in the incident before placing the blame entirely on the fans. This is precisely the principle behind Dave Canfield's (of Cornerstone Festival) complaint: "If you bring in a band like MxPx or Black Cherry Soda [punk bands] and don't want to have any movement, why are you having the band? Because every kid's going to be bummed at all the people repeatedly asking them not to do what is utterly natural for them to do."[63] Lastly, just as Grammatrain contributed to the lunacy at Jesus Northwest, so Audio Adrenaline is certainly responsible for the neck injury (though not serious) to an eleven-year-old boy who butted heads with another at the insane exhortation of the band, "If you're happy and you know it, bang your head."[64]

After this series of disclosures, I would imagine that not only Christians but anyone with common sense and decency would outlaw such undisguised displays of savagery and anarchy. Unfortunately this is not the case. Although some within CCM have reservations about moshing—for fear of injury and other practical concerns—there is almost no recognition of the obvious antisocial and anti-religious significance of this loathsome ritual.[65]

Stage Antics

Another degrading form of body language encountered at rock concerts involves the stage histrionics of the performers. First, we must establish that stage antics were never intended to simply add excitement, as some CCM activists contend,[66] but constitute genuine forms of visual communication, saturated with cultural values. Charles Brown remarks, "The body language of a performer, the way he or she dresses, and the stage presentation are forms of nonverbal communication...."[67]

From its infancy rock boasted a stage choreography that, like its dance forms, brimmed with sexual innuendoes, thanks in no small part to the pelvic experiments of the legendary Elvis Presley. Brown explains Elvis' ability to communicate with his body: "He was called 'Elvis the Pelvis' because of the way he worked his hips. This movement, which was most certainly natural, conveyed an obvious sexuality (whether or not he meant it to), but it was also very rhythmic and accented the beat of the song."[68] Steve Simels agrees, but feels that his movements were certainly deliberate:

> Mostly, though, there was the famous gyrating pelvis. The young Presley, who cribbed his pelvic action from various black performers..., knew exactly how it was going to affect his female admirers.... "A male strip teaser," was the verdict of Jack O'Brien of the *New York Daily Mirror*, and to be fair, the man had a point. That was, in fact, exactly what Elvis was: the first white male performer to flaunt himself unmistakably as a sex object.[69]

Phallic Rock

Even though no serious rock genre is divorced from sexual posturing to one degree or another, the most formalized and transparent exhibitions of sexual iconography in rock music can be observed in the stage performances of heavy metal musicians, as Frith illustrates:

> In male music, [phallic]-rock performance means explicit, crude, "master-ful" expression of sexuality.... [Phallic]-rock performers are aggressive, boastful, constantly drawing audience attention to their prowess and control. Their bodies are on display (plunging shirts and tight trousers, chest hair and genitals), mikes and guitars are phallic symbols (or else caressed like female bodies), the music is loud, rhythmically insistent, built around techniques of arousal and release.[70]

Walser, reaching the same conclusion, reports,

> Visually, metal musicians typically appear as swaggering males, leaping and strutting about the stage, clad in spandex, scarves, leather, and other visually noisy clothing, punctuating their performances with phallic thrusts of guitars and microphone stands.[71]

He adds, "Heavy metal is as much as anything else, an arena of gender, where spectacular gladiators compete to register and affect ideas of masculinity, sexuality, and gender relations."[72] A description of the heavy metal group KISS is no less disturbing: "Meanwhile, the

band's members are stalking around in their foot-high platforms...,
sucking on their fingers, humping their instruments, and rotating their
pelvises."[73] As for its effect on women, rock journalist Cheryl Cline
considers "a sharp-dressed man with a low-slung guitar" to be sexual
stimuli.[74] Duran Duran adds, "You've got to be pretty sexless to hold a
guitar, dance with it on stage and not put over some kind of sexuality."[75]

Furthermore, Dave Laing reveals that the erotic symbolism of the
electric guitar and its handling are not confined to the heavier styles:

> It was not necessary for the guitarists to adopt the extravagances of a
> Jimi Hendrix or standard heavy metal soloist. The macho connotations
> of electric guitar playing in rock were also to do with the height at which
> the instrument was held and how it was held. The 'natural', 'right',
> 'powerful' way was at waist level with the neck pointing upwards at an
> angle of about 30 degrees. Machine gun or [genital] substitute, the im-
> pact was powerfully phallic, whether or not the players knew it, whether
> or not their songs were sexist.[76]

Finally, Mavis Bayton adds these careful and developed observations of the electric guitar's role as a phallic symbol in rock music:

> For a man, a good performance on the electric guitar is simultaneously a
> good 'performance' of 'masculinity'. The 'heavier' the rock the more
> true that is....The electric guitar, as situated within the masculinist dis-
> course of rock, is virtually seen as an extension of the male body. This is
> always implicit and sometimes explicit, as when men mime masturbat-
> ing their 'axes'. Heavy metal guitarists unashamedly hold their guitars
> like a [phallus]. Prince even has substance [coming out] from his guitar!
> (Male) musical skills become synonymous with (male) sexual skills.
> With legs firmly planted akimbo, the guitarist is able to lean back in a
> parody of sexual ecstasy. Metal fans may argue that this whole bodily
> stance is knowing, ironic, and fun. That may be so. The fact remains that
> it is an exclusively *masculine* idiom.
>
> It is not only the shape [of the guitar] which is symbolic, but also the
> sheer volume and attack of the instrument which connotes phallic
> power....
>
> ...Rock guitarists (unlike classical and jazz players) typically hold their
> instrument low down in front of their genitals, radically adapting the
> fingering style to suit. Yet most players actually find it easier to hold
> their guitar on their chest or at their waist. The main reason given, by

men and women, for playing the guitar at pelvic level (or lower) is that it 'just looks right'. I would argue that the only reason for this is the silent encoded phallocentric message. If you play it higher up it is seen as less 'masculine'.[77]

Unfortunately, with modification of only the most extreme behavior, the above-mentioned body language and wardrobe have been faithfully reproduced by Christian rock and metal bands at every professional level. Further, it is important to recognize the remarkable resilience of these sexual codes, which have endured for over three decades. The chronology of the preceding citations (1978, Frith; 1983, Duran Duran; 1985, Laing; 1992, Cline; 1993, Walser; and 1997, Arnold and Bayton) demonstrates that CCM has experienced no success in reinterpreting or reversing the sexual codification of phallic rock or rock in general—due, no doubt, to the strong coefficient between the visible signs and their phallic or sexual referents. (After all, in what Christian sense can impassioned thrusts with an electric guitar situated over the male reproductive organs be interpreted?) Rather, rock's sexual iconography has gained momentum since its beginning with Elvis and has become ossified through over thirty years of relentless reinforcement.

The situation is not to be taken lightly. Christian heavy metal, where this type of behavior is most apparent, still has a substantial following.[78] Further, grunge and alternative rock—which emerged from the ashes of heavy metal—as well as many other hard rock styles feature similar antics and body language. They can be witnessed in just about every current Christian rock group, whether the Newsboys, dc Talk, All Star United, Jars of Clay, or Audio Adrenaline.

Even more distressful is the fact that CCM sympathizers like Harold M. Best have been snookered into believing that this is the very kind of behavior that Christian bands avoid:

> The real break away from the secular—and it is truly significant—lies in CCM's consistent avoidance of anything overtly sexual, anything verbally or gesturally off-color, or anything smacking of violence and aberration…. And the very avoidance of sexual, abusive, and violent content in CCM,…is a strong testimony to those who continually find fault with it.[79]

What incredible charity! Nevertheless, sufficient documentation has already been provided to demonstrate that visual eroticism is not limited to the extremes of Jimi Hendrix or Prince, but is abundantly manifest in the standard discourse of rock music (including CCM) and has been since its beginning.

Violence in CCM

Moreover, CCM stage antics can express violence as well as eroticism, contrary to the denials of Best and Angelo De Simone.[80] At the 30th Annual Dove Awards, dc Talk unleashed their customary pitbull performance. The menacing looks of Michael Tait brandishing his muscular arms were only matched by bass player Otto Price, who entered the stage wearing a hideous gas mask. The already unruly performance concluded with what appeared to be an act of rehearsed violence. I watched in horror as Kevin Smith traveled across the stage and senselessly (but intentionally) barreled into his guitarist, flattening him to the ground before a nation of onlookers.

Likewise, Zoa, which describes itself as a Christian "alternative to classic rock" band and considers rage to be one of the "three strongholds of humans," ironically exhibits this very kind of behavior in its concerts.[81] The following is an account of one such occasion by a fan:

> Like Black Flag or Unbroken in their seminal heydays, Zoa are frightening to behold—knocking over cymbal stands, hurling guitars into the air and screaming aloud during moments that are otherwise silent. [Jesse] Smith [the drummer] has been known to shout into a drum mic once in a while during a song. On one occasion, [Daniel] Weyandt's raw emotion bubbled over so distinctly that he vomited all over the stage.[82]

Consistent with the antisocial ideals of punk rock, Carey "Kosher" Womack of One Bad Pig sometimes appears in concert with a grinding chainsaw, providing melody for his own bellicose screams.[83] (No comment necessary.) At Cornerstone 86 the same band beat an electric guitar "senseless against the hollow wooden stage,"[84] a practice repeated in subsequent concerts. Their artwork includes a cartoon of their mascot pig (complete with punk attire and mohawk) smashing a guitar with pugilistic vigor; they have even released a single entitled, "Smash the Guitar."[85]

In fact there seems to be quite a fixation with guitar smashing among Christian punkers, although it is seldom actually witnessed in live performances. This is not because it is considered out of line or inappropriate, but because most punk bands cannot muster the capital to replace damaged or destroyed instruments. Consequently, it usually remains in the realm of fantasy. For example the Christian punk rock group Unpopular features a short video, in simple stickman artistry, in which a lone punk guitarist turns from his maniacal dancing, runs over to the speaker, and smashes it to bits with his guitar. In the process the body of the guitar breaks off, strikes him in the face, and knocks him to the ground.[86]

Furthermore, violence sometimes erupts in the audience, inspired, in part at least, by the acrobatics of the performers and the reckless moshing. "People were stage-diving and having a good time," says the Underdog Conspiracy. "About halfway through our fourth song, somebody grabbed our giant stuffed dog and took it into the pit. It got ripped to shreds and it was like christmas [sic] man!"[87] Another Christian punk rock group, Upside Down Room, issues a similar report, "Upside Down Room has encountered many the insane show with fans going crazy to counter their parents' middle class structuralism. On their recent multi-state tour. [sic] Upside Down Room's bassist was nearly crushed when a kid slammed into his bass stack and knocked it over."[88]

Another method of expressing violence in punk is through criminal-concealment attire, like the Cambridge rapist mask.[89] Similarly, the members of Lust Control, a Christian punk band, sometimes wear ski-masks, typically identified with burglars, bank robbers, rapists, and hitmen. The intimidating image is enhanced by their predacious scowls and psychotic stares.[90] Almost as threatening is a logo for Prototype (also Christian punk), which consists of a clenched fist covered with spiked knuckles.[91]

Bernice Martin traces the beginnings of stage violence in rock to the early sixties and considers it to be one of the signifiers of anti-structure: "The symbols of anti-structure resided in the antics and body movements which culminated in such extravaganzas as physical fights on stage or aggressive competition between members to 'play each other off the stage' (Cream) or in smashing instruments (the Who)."[92] Violence is also one of the pillars of punk philosophy, as Savage underscores:

> The violence, real or represented, was the crucial link in punk rock's going public for real.... What the punks were doing was *representing* violence: because it meant that they got noticed, because it reflected apocalyptic politics and, frankly, because it was a bit of a thrill, a bit of a giggle.[93]

But more. The Christian hard rock/metal group Disciple staged a 'pro' wrestling match, the quasi-sport/drama of rabid, knuckle-dragging paleoliths who relish in choreographed violence. It was realistically performed in a ring with all the props and "everything from body slams to leg drops!" Following the match the band took the stage (rather ring) and "pounded the audience with some of the most incredible, bold Christian rock ever."[94] Indeed!

Violence and intimidation in the musical text are also not unheard of in CCM. The punk group Nobody Special has a single entitled "Finger Pointer," which considers love to be a solution to what it perceives to be self-righteousness. And yet the lyrics express anger, threaten injury, and then offer a slushy concept of love to cover it all up: "Point your finger at me and I'll bite it off/ I don't need you to tell me how to live/ Ease up, pal, where do you get off?/ Let's love one another; live and let live."

It needs to be emphasized that violence itself is not the issue, since otherwise we would have to condemn the Bible as well. The problem is not with reporting violence and treating it as a tragic consequence of life in a fallen universe, as we find in the Bible, but with glamorizing violence and turning it into a source of entertainment and pleasure, as is the practice of Hollywood, rock music, and in some cases CCM.

Conclusion

In this section ample evidence has been presented to demonstrate that the body language of rock music is not some neutral accessory of culture that is detached from the morally depraved world order. Rather, as we have seen, it is the idiom of illicit sexuality and, in the case of moshing, the discourse of barbarism. In either case rock-related dancing stands in clear antipathy to biblical ideals of truth, humility, reverence, chastity, submission, self-control, holiness, and love. Therefore, it would be more than mandated to expel this brand of bodily expression from any participation in Christian culture.

Celebrity Worship

Like secular rock concerts, many CCM concerts are visited with unabashed adulation, idolization, and celebrity worship. Young Christian fans often react with the same servile hysterics to CCM stars as secular rock fans do to theirs. Menconi disapprovingly writes, "I've been to Christian concerts where the audience was carried away in a near frenzy calling out the band's name or artist's name in unison."[95] Amy Grant, for example, has performed concerts to the demanding overtures of fans rhythmically chanting, "Amy! Amy! Amy!" I have witnessed the mere announcement of a Morgan Cryer concert mutate respectable daughters of Zion into "twisted sisters" ready to throw themselves at Cryer's feet. Likewise, Carmen concerts are often accessorized with the ear-splitting din of female groupies frantically screaming for their enchanting Romeo, bristling with sex appeal.

Corbitt, prior to conceding to the spiritual double-talk of CCM groups, had to confess,

> The sprawling church complex would soon be transformed into the stage of a Christian "rock" concert with hundreds of screaming young people dancing about the chancel to the music of their Christian "idols." The foyer of the church resembled a shopping mall. Brand T-shirts, performer pictures, cassettes, and CDs covered the walls and tables. Inside the auditorium electronic speakers, amplifiers, and theater lighting overflowed from the pulpit area. At that point, the usual complaints of CCM critics, "It's all commercial, they are in it for the money," were validated.[96]

In an interview, dc Talk remembers a time when they had to instruct the audience to stop screaming during an acoustical number because it (the number) was "so worshipful"—the interviewer perceptively suggesting that the very image they bore was responsible for the reaction.[97] At other times (not as worshipful I assume), no correction was necessary as the famous trio rocked their way into the heads of delirious fans, lunging from below, hoping just to touch the performers situated 'high and lifted up' on the platform.[98]

In the exercise of such behavior, devotees go far beyond simply giving "honor to whom honor is due;" neither can I accept the naive explanation that they are simply applauding the "Jesus who is in them." If that were the case, why do they not have similar reactions to Christians who live far more godly and sacrificial lives?

Recently, CCM has become painfully reacquainted with the relationship between celebrity status and idolatry.[99] During a 1996 symposium several CCM performers and industry leaders virtually admitted that they may have created a golden calf. Dan Harrell—artist manager of Amy Grant, Michael W. Smith, and others—agonizes:

> I believe that there's no difference, in a lot of respects, for what a new artist has to do in Christian music today to be successful, than what a new artist has to do on the secular label. And that really troubles me.... I don't have the answers. I'm not sure we should stop doing what we're doing, but I think we've got to be very careful as an industry as the stakes go up, and the pressure gets harder.[100]

CCM producer Reed Arvin is even more candid: "But that doesn't stop me from having a basic understanding that what drives this industry [CCM] is money. Period... When I say [this industry] doesn't represent Christ, I'm not talking about its intentions; I'm talking about its reality. That when I look at the Christian music industry, I don't see Jesus much."[101] During the same symposium, Toby McKeehan of dc Talk recounts, "a gentleman came up to me and said, 'Can I have your signature for my son? He totally idolizes you, Toby.' That's scary. I don't mind telling you, that makes me want to run from this industry."[102]

In an interview in *Contemporary Christian Music* magazine, Jason Carson, drummer for the Supertones, testified:

> This business really contradicts the heart of Christianity.... The whole New Testament is calling us to humble ourselves so we can lean on His power. But you get into this Christian music industry, and there's no persecution, no suffering. The trials we face are nothing compared to what we read about in the [Bible]—about people getting flogged and put in prison. We don't get any of that at all. We're constantly getting lifted up: 'You guys are the best, you guys are the greatest.'[103]

Other CCM celebrities like Kirk Franklin and Steven Curtis Chapman have expressed similar concerns.[104] And yet nothing seems to change. For example, Toby McKeehan has not run from the industry as he melodramatically suggested; dc Talk's latest promotions and performances are just as narcissistic as they were three years ago. Due to their unwavering conviction in the separation of form and content, behavior and meaning, CCM artists feel that a personal attitude adjustment is all that is needed. Some even try to deflect praise from themselves to God by pointing their fingers toward heaven. But this should in no wise be construed as reform, only damage control. Such measures make about as much sense as drilling a gaping hole in the bottom of a schooner and then reaching for the bailing pump. This is because the essential attributes of today's popular music—leavening everything from the performance to advertising, promotions, and body image—are self-attracting, self-aggrandizing, and at best man-centered. Therefore, we should not expect the situation in CCM to be any different when the methods of the secular music industry are replicated with such precision, as even Charlie Peacock affirms, "From music to marketing, CCM takes its cues from the world."[105]

To assume, then, that the accompanying idolatry is an unfortunate but correctable consequence of the music industry is entirely unrealistic. It may be unwanted, but it is neither accidental, avoidable, nor unsolicited. The wound is self-inflicted and cannot be healed until the true source is identified. In the meantime the personality cults continue, fan clubs grow, and fanzines roll off the presses. False worship, however, is taken much more seriously in the Bible than it is within the

CCM fraternity, and measures to stop it are much more drastic. I close with the following passages from Scripture that touch on the topic:

> Acts 14:11-15: And when the crowds saw what Paul had done, they lifted up their voice in the Lycaonian language saying, "The gods have become like men and have come down to us." And they were calling Barnabas, Zeus, and Paul, Hermes, since he was the main speaker. And the priest of Zeus, whose temple was before the city, brought oxen and garlands to the gate and, along with the crowds, wished to offer a sacrifice. But when the apostles, Barnabas and Paul, heard of this, they tore their garments and rushed into the crowd crying out and saying, "Men, why are you doing these things? We are men of like nature to you, preaching the gospel to you in order that you might turn from these vain things to the living God, who made the heaven and the earth and the sea and everything that is in them."[106]

> Revelation 19:10: And I fell before his feet to worship him. And he said to me, "See that you do not do it. I am a fellow servant of yours and of your brothers who hold the testimony of Jesus. Worship God."

> Revelation 22:8-9: And when I heard and saw, I fell down to worship before the feet of the angel who showed me these things. And he said to me, "See that you do not do it. I am a fellow servant of yours and of your brothers the prophets and of those who are keeping the words of this book. Worship God."[107]

Endnotes

[1]Robert Levin, "Rock and Regression: The Responsibility of the Artist," in *Twenty-Minute Fandangos and Forever Changes: A Rock Bazaar*, ed. Jonathan Eisen (New York: Random House, 1971), 270. See also Stephen Davies, *Musical Meaning and Expression* (Ithaca, NY: Cornell University Press, 1994), 292.

[2]Dave Laing, *One Chord Wonders: Power and Meaning in Punk Rock* (Philadelphia: Open University Press, 1985), 61.

[3]Judith Lynne Hanna, "Moving Messages: Identity and Desire in Popular Music and Social Dance," in *Popular Music and Communication*, ed. James Lull, 2nd ed. (London: Sage Publications, 1992), 180.

[4]Robert P. Snow, "Youth, Rock 'n' Roll, and Electronic Media," *Youth & Society*, 18, no. 4 (June 1987): 335.

[5]Quentin J. Schultze et al., *Dancing in the Dark: Youth, Popular Culture, and the Electronic Media* (Grand Rapids: Eerdmans Publishing Co., 1991), 164.

[6]Tom Manoff, *Music: A Living Language* (New York: W. W. Norton & Company, 1982), 459.

[7]Ibid., 99.

[8]Hanna, "Moving Messages," 180.

[9]Judith Lynne Hanna, *Dance, Sex, and Gender: Signs of Identity, Dominance, Defiance, and Desire* (Chicago: University of Chicago Press, 1988), xiii.

[10]Ibid., 4.

[11]Ibid., 22.

[12]Susan McClary, *Feminine Endings: Music, Gender, and Sexuality* (Minneapolis: University of Minnesota Press, 1991), 25.

[13]Hanna, "Moving Messages," 182, 185, 187; *Dance, Sex, and Gender*, 245.

[14]Hanna, "Moving Messages," 185.

[15]Hanna, *Dance, Sex, and Gender*, 79. See also pp. 55-56, 69, 78.

[16]Curt Sachs, *World History of the Dance* (New York: W. W. Norton & Company, 1937), 20.

[17]Hanna, *Dance, Sex, and Gender*, 55.

[18]Ibid., 55-56. On the cross-cultural distribution of pelvic dancing see Sachs, *World History of Dance*, 23-24.

[19]Nik Cohn, *Rock from the Beginning* (New York: Stein and Day Publishers, 1969), 108.

[20]Simon Frith, *Sound Effects: Youth, Leisure, and the Politics of Rock 'n' Roll* (New York: Pantheon Books, 1978), 19. See also Simon Frith and Angela McRobbie, "Rock and Sexuality," in *On Record: Rock, Pop, and the Written Word*, ed. Simon Frith and Andrew Goodwin (New York: Pantheon Books, 1990), 388; William Graebner, "The Erotic and Destructive in 1980s Rock: A Theoretical and Historical Analysis," *Tracking: Popular Music Studies* 1, no. 2 (1988): 12; Iain Chambers, "Popular Culture, Popular Knowledge," *OneTwoThreeFour* 2 (Summer 1985): 17.

[21]Deena Weinstein, *Heavy Metal: A Cultural Sociology* (New York: Lexington Books, 1991), 130.

[22]Angela McRobbie, "Dance and Social Fantasy," in *Gender and Generation*, ed. Angela McRobbie and Mica Nava (London: Macmillan, 1984), 139.

[23]Schultze et al., *Dancing in the Dark*, 150.

[24]Stan Hawkins, "The Pet Shop Boys: Musicology, Masculinity and Banality," in *Sexing the Groove: Popular Music and Gender*, ed. Sheila Whiteley (New York: Routledge, 1997), 118.

[25]McRobbie, "Dance and Social Fantasy," 144.

[26]Ibid., 132-33.

[27]Ibid., 144-45.

[28]There are some forms of reggae dancing that are so explicitly sexual that I assume even the most liberated Christian would not engage in them. See Chambers, "Popular Culture," 150.

[29]See Melanie Friebel, "Dancin' in the Church: Spreading the Good News Through Sanctified Dance," *Contemporary Christian Music*, November 1994, 51-53. Although refusing to apply the principle to CCM, Corbitt testifies of how various Christian groups around the world have recognized sensual elements within indigenous dance forms and avoided them. J. Nathan Corbitt, *The Sound of Harvest: Music's Mission in Church and Culture* (Grand Rapids: Baker Books, 1998), 330.

[30]Hanna, "Moving Messages," 177. See also p. 192.

[31]Joe Battaglia, *Contemporary Christian Music*, December 1986, 14.

[32]Michael McCall, "Michael's Forever Friends," *Contemporary Christian Magazine*, June 1986, 19.

[33]Robert Walser, *Running with the Devil: Power, Gender, and Madness in Heavy Metal Music* (Hanover, NH: Wesleyan University Press, 1993), 14.

[34]Ibid.

[35]Ibid., 157.

[36]Ibid., 158.

[37]John Podhoretz, "Metallic Rock That's Designed to Shock," *U.S. News & World Report*, 7 September 1987, 50.

[38]Weinstein, *Heavy Metal*, 55. Cf. Al Menconi, "A Serious Look at Christian Heavy Metal: 'Vengeance Is Mine,' Saith the Lord—Or Is It?" *Media Update*, January-February 1989, 13.

[39]Weinstein, *Heavy Metal*, 54. A similar double meaning strategy is evident in the names of Christian groups like Corpse, Torn Flesh, and Mortification.

[40]Phil Joel of the Newsboys seems to resonate with my complaint, at least in principle:

> I think there is a little bit of dishonesty in the old Christian concert model. In that sort of situation, kids definitely need to let kids know what's going to happen. In those old-fashioned sort of tactics, and I think that's what they are, they don't understand you're going to have power in integrity, power in honesty. That's where God hangs out. He hangs out in truth, he doesn't hang out in tricks. (Charlie Peacock, *At the Crossroads: An Insider's Look at the Past, Present, and Future of Contemporary Christian Music* [Nashville: Broadman & Holman, 1999], 188.)

[41]Jeffrey Jensen Arnett, *Metalheads: Heavy Metal Music and Adolescent Alienation* (Boulder, CO: WestviewPress, 1996), 10. Cf. Podhoretz, "Metallic Rock," 51.

[42]Jeffrey Jensen Arnett, "Adolescents and Heavy Metal Music: From the Mouths of Metalheads," *Youth & Society* 23, no. 1 (September 1991): 84.

[43]Arnett, *Metalheads*, 74.

[44]Linda Andes, "Growing up Punk: Meaning and Commitment Careers in a Contemporary Youth Subculture," in *Youth Culture: Identity in a Postmod-*

ern World, ed. Jonathan S. Epstein (Malden, MA: Blackwell Publishers, 1998), 223.

[45]Arnett, *Metalheads*, 83.

[46]Jon Savage, *Time Travel: Pop, Media and Sexuality 1976-96* (London: Chatto & Windus, 1996), 329-30.

[47]Doug Van Pelt, "Mosh for the Master?" *Contemporary Christian Music*, February 1989, 20.

[48]Gina Arnold, *Kiss This: Punk in the Present Tense* (New York: St. Martin's Griffin, 1997), 120.

[49]Arnett, *Metalheads*, 92.

[50]Jay R. Howard and John M. Streck, *Apostles of Rock: The Splintered World of Contemporary Christian Music* (Lexington, KY: The University Press of Kentucky, 1999), 74.

[51]Ibid., front piece.

[52]Amy Dixon, "To Mosh or not to Mosh? Christian Rock Concerts Incite Controversy," *Contemporary Christian Music*, February 1996, 22.

[53]On the World Wide Web at http://www.algonet.se/~kosher/obp.

[54]Johannes C. Jonsson, "BOBFEST '99-Stockholm, Sweden," *HM Electronic Magazine*, no. 78 (July/August 1999). Document available on the World Wide Web at http://www.christianmusic.org/cmp/hmmag/issue78/78Concert Reviews.htm.

[55]Ibid. The "helicopter" is the whirling effect created by the long hair of metalheads thrashing their heads back and forth. It is quite popular in fast metal.

[56]Troy Moon, "Christian Rock Embraces Diverse Styles and Attitudes," *Pensacola News Journal*, 1 March 1998, Life: 6E.

[57]Troy Moon, "Audio Adrenaline Vocalist: Christian Rock Differs Little from Secular Rock Music," *Pensacola News Journal*, 1 March 1998, Life: 6E.

[58]Dean Smallwood, "Christian Rockers All Set to Jam in Jesus' Name," *Huntsville Times*, 20 September 1998, G5. The differences would involve civilities like picking up someone who has fallen down. But as Steve Baker (manager of PFR) rightly discerns, if the dance itself is responsible for the fall, the offer is somewhat self-defeating. Dixon, "To Mosh or not to Mosh?" 24; Moon, "Christian Rock," 6E.

[59]Howard and Streck, *Apostles of Rock*, 73; Dixon, "To Mosh or not to Mosh?" 22, 24.

[60]Howard and Streck, *Apostles of Rock*, 2.

[61]Dixon, "To Mosh or not to Mosh?" 22.

[62]Eric Boehlert, "Holy Rock and Rollers," *Rolling Stone*, 3 October 1996, 24.

[63]Dixon, "To Mosh or not to Mosh?" 24. For further examples see below under the heading *Violence in CCM*.

[64]Ibid., 22.

[65]Van Pelt, "Mosh for the Master?" 20. Even if it is only for medical reasons, we should still be thankful that some, like Steve Baker and Tim Landis (Creation Festival), do oppose moshing. Dixon, "To Mosh or not to Mosh?" 24.

[66]Steve Miller, *The Contemporary Christian Music Debate: Worldly Compromise or Agent of Renewal?* (Wheaton, IL: Tyndale House, 1993), 97. Miller, for example, states, "For many serious concert-goers, a performance with static lighting and immobile band members sends a message that the band is not excited about their message." This is just one example of Miller's tendency to minimize powerful agents of human communication into their benign components (reductionism) in order to make them acceptable to critics. But if mere mobility was the desired entity, then a marching band would suffice. After all, are they not mobile? Such a concept is obviously senseless because it is not just mobility, as Miller claims, but a certain type of mobility that rock audiences desire.

[67]Charles Brown, *The Art of Rock and Roll* (Englewood Cliffs, NJ: Prentice-Hall, 1983), 6.

[68]Ibid., 67.

[69]Steven Simels, *Gender Chameleons: Androgyny in Rock 'n' Roll* (New York: Timbre Books, 1985), 16. See also Jonathan S. Epstein, David J. Pratto, and James K. Skipper, Jr., "Teenagers, Behavioral Problems, and Preferences for Heavy Metal and Rap Music: A Case Study of a Southern Middle School," *Deviant Behavior* 11 (1990): 394; Philip Gordon, "Review of Tipper Gore's *Raising PG Kids in an X-Rated Society* and *Dee Snider's Teenage Survival Guide*," *Popular Music* 8, no. 1 (January 1989): 120; Snow, "Rock 'n' Roll," 334; Bernice Martin, "The Sacralization of Disorder: Symbolism in Rock Music," *Sociological Analysis* 40, no. 2 (1979): 109.

[70]Frith, *Sound Effects*, 227.

[71]Walser, *Running with the Devil*, 108-09.

[72]Ibid., 111.

[73]Arnold, *Kiss This*, 140. Cf. Susan Hiwatt, "[Phallic] Rock," in *Twenty-Minute Fandangos and Forever Changes: A Rock Bazaar*, ed. Jonathan Eisen (New York: Random House, 1971), 145.

[74]Cheryl Cline, "*Essays from* Bitch: The Women's Rock Newsletter with Bite," in *The Adoring Audience: Fan Culture and Popular Media*, ed. Lisa A. Lewis (London: Routledge, 1992), 71.

[75]*Daily Express*, December 19, 1983; quoted in John Blanchard, Peter Anderson, and Derek Cleave, *Pop Goes the Gospel: Rock in the Church*, enlarged and revised (Darlington, England: Evangelical Press, 1989), 40.

[76]Laing, *One Chord Wonders*, 87. Cf. Schultze et al., *Dancing in the Dark*, 168.

[77]Mavis Bayton, "Women and the Electric Guitar," in *Sexing the Groove: Popular Music and Gender*, ed. Sheila Whiteley (New York: Routledge

1997), 43. See also Sara Cohen, "Men Making a Scene: Rock Music and the Production of Gender," in *Sexing the Groove: Popular Music and Gender*, ed. Sheila Whiteley (New York: Routledge, 1997), 28, 31; McClary, *Feminine Endings*, 113. Nevertheless, I have observed that some rock guitarists prefer to hold their instruments above the waist for better coordination and control.

[78]Christian or white metal bands no longer range in the hundreds as they did in the late eighties; nevertheless, they still have their patrons, and interest in their music is still high, as can be discerned by record sales, fanzines, and web sites. Cf. "Metal For Jesus Page," on the World Wide Web at http://surf.to/theMFJpage; *HM*; *The Narrow Path*; *Turn or Burn* (Germany); *Noizegate* (Sweden); Devlin Donaldson, "Barnabas: Forging Musical Horizons," *Contemporary Christian Music*, October 1998, 69; et al.

[79]Harold M. Best, *Music Through the Eyes of Faith* (San Francisco: Harper, 1993), 178-79.

[80]Ibid. Angelo De Simone, *Christian Rock: Friend or Foe* (New Haven: Selah Production Agency, 1993), 164-66. John E. Reid and Joseph R. Dominick's study found that "MTV and Christian videos did not differ in the amount of violence portrayed"—twenty-seven percent for MTV and sixteen percent for Christian videos. "A Comparative Analysis of Christian and Mainstream Rock Music Videos," *Popular Music and Society* 17, no. 3 (Fall 1993): 90.

[81]On the World Wide Web at http://www.geocities.com/SunsetStrip/Club/9541/index. html.

[82]On the World Wide Web at http://placetobe.org/cmp/artists/index.html; quoted in David W. Cloud, *Contemporary Christian Music Under the Spotlight* (Oak Harbor, WA: Way of Life Literature, 1999), 408.

[83]On the World Wide Web at http://www.algonet.se/~kosher/obp/carey.htm.

[84]"Music Interview—One Bad Pig," *Cornerstone*, 15:79, p. 46.

[85]On the World Wide Web at http://www.algonet.se/~kosher/obp.

[86]On the World Wide Web at http://www.members.linkopp.com/unpopular/home.html. Video on file.

[87]On the World Wide Web at http://www.sunflower.org/~dabeyes/un/unnews.htm.

[88]On the World Wide Web at http://memebers.xoom.com/_XOOM/udr/the band/reviews.html.

[89]Cf. Savage, *Time Travel*, 128; Dick Hebdige, *Subculture: The Meaning of Style* (London: Routledge, 1979), 108.

[90]Photo on file. The masks have nothing to do with the weather; the group is from Austin, Texas.

[91]On the World Wide Web at http://members.aol.com/craghater/prototype.html.

[92]Martin, "The Sacralization of Disorder," 107.

[93]Savage, *Time Travel*, 128.

[94]Scott Herrin, "Disciple Wrestling Match," *HM Electronic Magazine*, no. 78 (July/August 1999). Document available on the World Wide Web at http://www.christianmusic.org/cmp/hmmag/issue78/78ConcertReviews.htm.

[95]Al Menconi, "What's Wrong with Christian Music? An Open Letter to Contemporary Christian Musicians," *Contemporary Christian Music*, June 1987, 19.

[96]Corbitt, *Sound of Harvest*, 31-32.

[97]Kathy Bubel, "DC Talks At Last," *Release*, 4 May/June 1994, 18.

[98]Ibid., 17.

[99]I chose the term "reacquainted" because there have always been those within CCM who have criticized its commercialism, market-driven mentality, and artist deification. The more notable include Phil Driscoll, Keith Green, Dallas Holm, Steve Camp, and Mark Hollingsworth (Benson Records).

[100]"In the News: Artists, Pastors and Industry Leaders Discuss Issue of 'Fame and Ministry,'" *Contemporary Christian Music*, July 1996, 22.

[101]Ibid., 24.

[102]Ibid.

[103]Lou Carlozo, "Super Tone Deaf," *Contemporary Christian Music*, February 1999, 19, 22.

[104]Caryn D. Rivadeneira, "The Secrets of His Success," *Marriage Partnership*, Spring 1999, 44-45; James Long, "Mirror Christianity," *Contemporary Christian Music*, May 1995, 71-72.

[105]Peacock, *At the Crossroads*, 71. Cf. Lisa Miller, "Singing Songs of Love, Not God: It's Getting Harder to Find the Religion in Religious Bands," *The Wall Street Journal*, 23 April 1999, B4. For example, fans can acquire all kinds of paraphernalia including t-shirts laminated with full-color portraits of their favorite Christian artists. Further, for many years now promoters have made available realistic life-sized cardboard icons of CCM celebrities to be displayed in the music section of Christian book stores.

[106]Consider also Proverbs 29:5: "A man who flatters his friend spreads a net for his feet" and Psalm 115:1: "Not to us, O Lord, not to us, but to your name give glory."

[107]Although in Acts 14:11-15; Revelation 19:10, and 22:9 some sort of divinity is wrongly attributed to the objects of worship by worshipers—unlike our CCM scenario—anyone who is so fanatically esteemed should react like Paul and Barnabas or the angel in Revelation 22:9, "See that you do not do it. I am a fellow servant of yours and of your brothers the prophets and of those who are keeping the words of this book. Worship God."

3

The Language of Clothing

Introduction

AT LAST WE ARRIVE at what may be the most controversial appendage
to rock music, the dress styles of the performers. The apparel of CCM,
despite its variety, has succeeded in offending conservatives almost as
much as the style of the music. In response, CCM defenders have taken
various approaches to rationalize the dress styles of their performers,
which like other para-musical phenomena are often a mirror image of
their secular exemplars.

The earliest Christian rockers defended their counter-culture clothing simply by insisting that it lacked any inherent meaning. In other
words, clothing was thought to be entirely value-neutral, like music.
"The clear implication," say Howard and Streck, "was that the clothes
meant nothing and that any inference about the musicians based on
what they wore was an erroneous one.... As the industry moved into
the 1980s, more and more artists began to accept that argument, and
clear distinctions between the Christian and the secular became more
difficult to find."[1]

Contrast to Extremes

Around this core set of beliefs has developed a growing network of
supporting arguments, which through circulation and duplication have
achieved near credal status. One such tactic has been to contrast CCM
performers with the worst and most profane examples of immodesty in
secular music. For example, Miller mentions that "Cher dresses to kill"
in hopes that readers will notice the startling difference between Cher,
who has performed almost nude from the waist down, and female CCM
artists, who at least manage to keep their clothes on.[2] Yet, using extreme examples of sin as justification for other behavior—which in

comparison seems quite harmless—is hardly a legitimate response. This is because it displaces God's Word as the guideline by which conduct is to be judged and makes the worst of culture the (negative) standard. (In Cher's case, even some of her own children feel that she has gone too far.) Nowhere have the clothing choices of CCM performers been compared with biblical standards of modesty, which are considerably more stringent than what is acceptable in pop culture. If CCM would first compare its attire with biblical instead of cultural guidelines of modesty and nakedness, I am convinced that they would have to condemn the dress styles of both Cher and many CCM performers.

Worldly Critics?

Another strategy attempts to turn the tables on critics by demonstrating that they cannot live with their own definition of worldly dressing. The quintessential example of this is Josh McDowell speaking to a group of pastors during a Petra tour and addressing their complaints about the worldly adornment of the group:

> (He [Josh McDowell] scans the room and finds a gentleman in typical reverend rig—gray pinstripe suit, Oxford shirt, power tie, wing tips) [He says] Sir, are you a pastor? (A nod to the affirmative) You know, I can't begin to tell you apart from the world. In America, every single pastor who gets up on Sunday morning looks like the world—IBM from the word *go*. And when I visit your churches, I have to dress like I'm heading for Wall Street or most of you wouldn't let me speak to your congregations."[3]

McDowell essentially suggests that conservatives denounce CCM fashions because they resemble the world's. Therefore, all he has to do to mute the critics is to find one example in which their own clothing approximates that of the world. It is disappointing to see a man of McDowell's reputation resorting to blatant straw-man tactics in order to make his point. This argument is persuasive only because it misrepresents why conservatives are offended by CCM dress styles and then proceeds to tear down the premises of that illusory argument. Opponents of CCM apparel do not object to rock's regalia simply because it originates from the world, but because the styles are often revealing, immodest, or convey messages that are contrary to Scripture. McDowell has imputed a definition of worldliness to his critics that most of them do not hold.

Menconi, who uses the identical argument, secures it with 1 Samuel 16:7, a favorite among CCM advocates: "We must be careful about judging others based on appearance and never forget that, 'The LORD does not look at the things man looks at. Man looks at the outward appearance, but the LORD looks at the heart.'"[4] The exegesis and application of this text, however, are entirely amiss. In the context of the passage, what is meant is that future success is not based on a person's natural endowments—such as physical stature, outward beauty, or talent—but on one's inward desire to serve God. It is really a literary foil that hearkens back to 1 Samuel 9:2 and contrasts David's inward virtues with the outward promise of Saul. It is also in harmony with Paul's theology of the cross, discussed earlier, and intimates that God is not impressed with our version of "the most likely to succeed," but delights in demonstrating his power through the weak and neglected. It has nothing to do with God not being concerned with how a person dresses or what they may signify through their clothing. If anything, this passage defeats the celebrity complex, glitz factor, and pragmatism that are so much a part of CCM.

Therefore, just because a pastor, or any Christian, dresses like a Wall Street executive does not mean that they are worldly, as McDowell would surely agree. Men wear business suits—Christians and non-Christians—because in western society suits and ties signify propriety, professionalism, seriousness, respectability, and formality. Because this type of suit represents such qualities, it is certainly appropriate, even commendable, for Christians to wear. McDowell succeeds in his contention by having the reader believe that his opponents are against a style of clothing simply because non-Christians wear the same style when this is actually not the quarrel.

Just as a suit and tie represent formality, propriety, and respectability in our society, other dress styles represent different values. Dick

Hebdige expands on how subculture is able to communicate through clothing and other paraphernalia:

> The conventional outfits worn by the average man or woman in the street are chosen within the constraints of finance, 'taste', preference, etc.... Ultimately, if nothing else, they are expressive of 'normality' as opposed to 'deviance' (i.e. they are distinguished by their relative invisibility, their appropriateness, their 'naturalness'). However, the intentional communication [of subculture] is of a different order. It stands apart—a visible construction, a loaded choice. It directs attention to itself; it gives itself to be read.[5]

Likewise, Frith discloses that "fashion and style—both social constructions—remain keys to the ways in which we, as individuals, present ourselves to the world: we use the public meanings of clothes to say 'this is how I want to be perceived.'"[6] According to Orrin E. Klapp, style-rebellion is "more than a mere expression of taste in new and creative ways. It is protest which opposes a style with a different style that attacks, rebukes, shocks—puts down—prevailing standards. It is aggressive; it makes people angry; it has a flaunting, flouting, defiant quality."[7]

Indeed, the fashions endeared by many subcultures associated with rock music communicate deeply-felt ideologies and attitudes of rebellion. For example, Lorraine E. Prinsky and Jill L. Rosenbaum find that Cindi Lauper's "psychedelic hair and wild outfits are indications of her rebellion and anti-establishment ideal."[8] When one rocker was asked what his dress style communicated to others he answered, "That I'm a threat; to their way of life, to them physically."[9] In the same vein Iain Chambers observes, "Clothes become 'weapons,' 'visible insults' in a cultural war, and make-up becomes 'face-painting.'... It [dress style] may involve a confusion in sexual as well as consumer codes, in moral as well as sartorial tastes."[10]

Culture and Meaning

A third rejoinder wielded by CCM zealots involves removing an offensive article of clothing from its cultural context and placing it in another where it is welcomed. For example, Miller contends, "John

Wesley wore long hair, which was appropriate for his culture. First-century Roman soldiers wore skirts, and no one would dare call them feminine!"[11] Rick Cua insists, "What is wrong with leather? What is wrong with a leather jacket? I don't care who wears it! I don't care if the devil wears it! I mean its cowhide!... We forget about the hundreds of thousands of people who for years and years have worn leather!"[12] Both appeals refuse to acknowledge what the Bible, sociologists, rock musicians, and fans have realized all along, namely that even if an item of clothing is not intrinsically immodest, it can still function as a durable symbol of vice when invested with negative meaning by culture.

'The Shame of Their Nakedness'

Despite appeals to extreme examples, straw-men, and history, clear cases of immodesty by CCM performers are not difficult to come across and document. For example, the female artist for the Christian metal group Arsenal poses with the rest of the members, profiling her accentuated buttock enameled with leopard skin tights.[13] Likewise, a female vocalist for Gordon Gano's The Mercy Seat—a Donna Summer look-alike—wears a tight, black, and scandalously short miniskirt as she stands between other members of the group, gripping their shoulders with her long cat-like nails. Her noticeably extended hip, curvaceous figure, and inviting smile all suggest a rating somewhere between R and X.[14] The attractive Nancy Jo Mann of Barnabas, in similar upholstery—black slip (extremely short), black hose, and black heels—takes on the appearance of an eighties nihilist chic in search of deviant sex.[15] Others like Leslie Phillips and Melissa Brewer (Dakoda Motor Company) have also performed in miniskirts, silencing De Simone's protest that "I have yet to see a female singer who wears mini-skirts on the stage. Why are these people deliberately spreading lies?"[16]

Male CCM artists can be just as immodest, such as when they imitate the industry custom of performing without a shirt.[17] Drummers are especially fond of this type of exposure: Greg Jacques of Crashdog, Marcus Dahlström of Blindside, Ryan Shields of Never the Less, Robert Sweet of Stryper, and Efran Galicia of Paradox (all Christian groups).[18] Similarly, some of the members of the metal bands Barren

Cross and Paradox find no scruple in being photographed shirtless for a group picture.[19]

Less provocative, yet still immodest, pictures are more common. One promotion photograph shows a relaxing Kenny Marks casually flexing his biceps and tattooed forearm, in an unmistakable attempt to intensify his heartthrob image.[20] Likewise, Stormie Omartian with tight jeans and carefully turned hip strikes a sexy pose with her husband Michael in *Contemporary Christian Music* magazine.[21] Consider also the negligée look of Heather Miller on her album *Once Upon a Time* or Melissa Brewer with her slinky hip-protruding carriage and sassy "I'm in control here" stare.[22]

Amy Grant

No discussion of immodesty in CCM can afford to neglect the first lady of CCM, Amy Grant. Early in her career Grant confirmed complaints about her provocative postures and attire in this well-known citation from *Rolling Stone* magazine:

> Grant's also pragmatic about her career. Regarding her album covers and publicity photos, which portray her as a sexy, attractive young woman, the Christian pop star says, "I'm trying to look sexy to sell a record. But what is sexy? To me it's never been taking my shirt off or sticking my tongue out. I feel that a Christian young woman in the '80s is *very* sexual."[23] (Emphasis original.)

Other non-Christian reporters give similar testimonies. James Chute, for example, is convinced that "lyrics aside, Grant uses all the commercial weapons available, including sex, to promote her music."[24]

Recently Grant nailed her colors to the mast with some highly suggestive and arousing photographs, verifying earlier reports of her immodesty. The September/October, 1994 feature story in *Release* magazine reveals a striking cover-shot of Grant lying on silky white sheets in a black sleeveless evening gown, fully equipped with plunging neckline. The combination of her bare arms, highly visible upper chest, inviting eyes, and body emblazoned in black, positioned horizontally on crumpled bed sheets is so obviously stoked with sexuality that even the most sympathetic or naive onlooker would find it difficult to deny. The other bedroom pictures in the article reflect a similar soft-porn/*Cosmopolitan*-like layout.[25]

This style of restrained eroticism, however, is pushed to the limits in one of the most daring and seductive poses ever attempted by a CCM performer. On page 24-25 of the article, Grant teeters on the threshold of pornography. Her bare arms sprawling above her head, lips slightly parted, eyes closed, and expression identical to the look of sexual ecstasy so popular in centerfold layouts conjure images of a bathing Bathsheba, rather than a righteous Ruth. Further, her hair is so situated that it appears to be the only thing that shields her breasts from exposure. The overall impact of the picture is arresting. The viewer sees nothing but a mural of pink flesh, ornamented with a canopy of brunette locks and sexually-freighted countenance, all of which give the initial impression that Grant posed for this one in the nude.[26]

Those who have used pornography recognize the similarity in posture, photography, and facial expression (see below). Of course, by today's standards these pictures would not qualify as pornography proper, since there is no actual nudity. Yet, it is not necessary to uncover everything to produce arousal. Strategic body positioning, skin exposure and concealment, lighting, and photography have proven eye-teasing effects and are designed to generate a sinful curiosity about what the package will look like when it is fully unwrapped.

Assured of the fact that Grant fans would cry "foul," I decided to enlist the opinions of non-Christian men of various ages who knew nothing of Grant or my personal opinions concerning the last picture. One twenty-five-year-old man considered the woman in the picture to be "undressed or dressed very lightly in a quiet environment." When asked what type of message the picture communicated, he replied, "I think it would say, 'Hi, guys, look at me!'" I also asked men what one word would best describe the picture in question, providing them with a list of seventeen adjectives ranging in meaning from erotic to saintly. As expected none chose modifiers that would associate Grant with her professed faith such as "innocent," "conservative," "modest," "chaste," "pure," or "wholesome." Although some played it safe by choosing "beautiful," others echoed my opinion (unknown to them) and decided that words like "erotic," "sexy," "suggestive," and "tempting" best described the photograph.[27]

Lastly, I divulged the identity of the woman in the picture as a Christian and Top 40 recording artist and asked them to comment on the picture again. One viewer simply said, "She is trying to sell records." Another responded, "This is a very seductive photograph." Finally, when I exposed Grant's identity to a young painter, he developed a mischievous smile, rolled his eyes, and replied sarcastically, "She's a Christian? She should find a line of work in porno, man." I should mention here that most of the men surveyed, including all three just cited, were admitted users of pornography and so were well qualified to assess the moral (or immoral) content of the picture.

Those who still feel that this is baseless character assassination should be advised that Grant's past indiscretions provide sufficient warrant for this verdict. *Rolling Stone* columnist Michael Goldberg tells of one such occasion, "Following a listening session at A & M Records,…Grant casually told one company honcho about a recent vacation, during which she was discovered sunbathing naked with a girlfriend on an African beach."[28]

More Examples

CCM performers range in degree of immodesty, of course, and not all go to the same extent as Grant.[29] But it must be remembered that the above-mentioned performers and their outfits are readily accepted and stubbornly defended by the power-brokers of CCM. This is sometimes apparent in the kinds of pictures that CCM magazines allow to grace their pages. *Contemporary Christian Music* magazine, without apology, has printed lurid pictures of pop singer and professing Christian Mariah Carey; in one, Carey barely manages to cover her breasts and in another she deliberately arches her back to outline her voluptuous nymph-like figure, wrapped in a tight red Santa suit.[30] Likewise, country singer and Christian (?) Kathy Mattea appears uncensored and practically uncovered in a salacious cleavage-exposing frontal shot, which exposes more somatic real-estate than sartorial[31]—similarly disco queen Donna Summer.[32]

It should be no secret that the clothing choices of secular female rock performers do not arise out of a concern to please God or to appear chaste before their male audiences. Rocker Wendy Walman, when asked, "Do you feel you have to be sexy on stage?" replies, "I wear low-cut things, a lot of silver and a lot of jewelry, a lot of make-up and my hair down.... I've had some guys come on to me in a very rank way. It's OK because it's an idea that they're responding to. If they saw me sitting here in my orderly shoes with my hair in braids, they would probably not want to come on to me. It's the idea."[33] If this kind of motivation underlies fashion decisions in pop music, why do female Christian artists go to such lengths to replicate their secular counterparts?

Punk and Heavy Metal Styles

A more convincing case for rejecting the wardrobe of rock music can be made by examining rock genres that are especially reactionary and hostile to traditional culture, such as punk and heavy metal. Lamentably, even these excessively perverse styles are considered permissible and receive support from CCM fans, as we have already sampled. Yet in the following section, secular authorities will handily demonstrate the extraordinary capacity of clothing to communicate ideological meaning and the inability of a Christian context alone to dissolve the contract between a society, its symbols, and their morally-laden referents. We begin with one of the most deliberate attempts to convey moral corruption through clothing, punk rock.

Punk Styles

History credits Malcolm McLaren and Vivienne Westwood—whose fashion shop went under names like "Let it Rock" and "Sex"—as the architects of the subversive punk wardrobe, first worn by the Sex Pistols. Westwood once remarked, "I think fashion is the strongest form of communication there is."[34] And again, "It's [fashion] only interesting to me if it's subversive: that's the only reason I'm in fashion, to destroy the world 'conformity.'"[35] The elements of McLaren and Westwood that endured in the punk wardrobe included such articles as studded belts, chains, bondage pants, and dog collars. The outrageous "electrocuted" hair was first worn by Johnny Rotten of the Sex Pistols, but the practice of dyeing it in sundry colors was a later adaptation of the fans.[36]

Hebdige, who studied the punk subculture in England, describes the communicable power of punk clothing: "There was a homological relation between the trashy cut-up clothes and spiky hair,...the insurrectionary poses and the 'souless,' frantically driven music. The punks wore clothes which were the sartorial equivalent of swear words...."[37] Rock musician Brett Anderson of Suede relates something similar, "I started very early to play around with my image, cutting and dying my own hair, and making myself look absolutely dreadful. I had a punk phase, cut my hair like something that had survived a laboratory experiment. It's such a temptation to... [expletive] stir everyone up a bit."[38] Stir up indeed! A punker named Kathy remembers the punk style and the attitude that came with it: "My mom used to complain that my hair was too short and she hated the flaming red color. She'd say, 'You're going to turn off so many people.' I'd say, 'Well... [expletive] them!'"[39]

Finally, the reader should consider this lengthy but striking excerpt from Hebdige on punk attire and its signification:

> Objects borrowed from the most sordid of contexts found a place in the punks' ensembles: lavatory chains were draped in graceful arcs across chests encased in plastic bin-liners. Safety pins were taken out of their domestic 'utility' context and worn as gruesome ornaments through cheek, ear or lip. 'Cheap' trashy fabrics (PVC, plastic, lurex, etc.) in vulgar designs (e.g. mock leopard skin) and 'nasty' colors, long discarded by the quality end of the fashion industry as obsolete kitsch, were salvaged by the punks and turned into garments (fly boy drainpipes, 'common' miniskirts) which offered self-conscious commentaries on the notions of modernity and taste.... Hair was obviously dyed (hay yellow, jet black, or bright orange with tufts of green or bleached in question marks), and T-shirts and trousers told the story of their own construction with multiple zips and outside seams clearly displayed.... The perverse and abnormal were valued intrinsically. In particular, illicit iconography of sexual fetishism was used to predictable effect. Rapist masks and rubber wear, leather bodices and fishnet stockings, implausibly pointed stiletto heeled shoes, the whole *paraphernalia of bondage—the belts,*

straps and chains—were exhumed from the boudoir, closet and the pornographic film and placed on the street where they retained their forbidden connotations. Some young punks even donned the dirty raincoat—that most prosaic symbol of sexual 'kinkiness'—and hence expressed their deviance in suitably proletarian terms.[40] (Emphasis added.)

Summing up the impact of such apparel on society, Nathan Rubin states: "The willingness to wear purple-dyed hair and a safety-pin stuck through one's cheek gave freedom of thought and action a whole new dimension. After the Sex Pistols, anything was possible."[41] It is tragic, then, to learn of Christian punk rock groups spangled with many of the same emblems, presuming that Christian lyrics will somehow reverse the meanings of these long-standing tokens of violence, perversion, and anarchy.[42]

Heavy Metal Styles

Heavy metal musicians also developed a variety of clothing and accessories, which included freshly minted forms of counter-culture symbolism, as well as imitations of those already in vogue. Like the punkers, they were partial to black leather, studded collars and bracelets, and chains—all representing violence, bondage, and sadomasochism. Allison Lurie points out that "the wearing of black leather garments is an accepted signal that you are 'into' sadomasochism and interested in playing the part of master or slave either in harmless fantasy or dangerous reality."[43] Weinstein explains that "S&M regalia definitely influenced the heavy metal look. As metal costume designer Laurie Greenan declares, 'S&M was heavy metal long before heavy metal was.'"[44] (So much for Rick Cua's earlier ranting about the harmlessness of leather.) In Christian circles the S&M look was slavishly imitated by metal groups such as Saint and Philadelphia.

The S&M style was actually a permutation of an earlier outlaw image synonymous with motorcycle gangs and introduced into heavy metal in the 1970s by Judas Priest. What Weinstein calls the "biker-from-hell" look "meshed with a well-known symbol system of rebellion, masculinity, and outsider status that fit in with the other elements of the heavy metal culture."[45] Paul E. Willis describes the biker image as "aggressively masculine. The motorcycle gear both looked tough, with its leather, studs and denim, and by association with the motorbike, took over some of the intimidating quality of the machine."[46] Elianne Halbersberg profiles Judas Priest as "the embodiment of aggression and force; equipped with whips, chains, black leather, instruments and microphones, they transform into the authentic voice of heavy metal."[47] With this degree of counter-culture and anti-Christian iconography, I shudder at how Christian metal bands like the Rez Band, King James, the Daniel Band, Holy Soldier, and Sacred Warrior could have adopted some or all of the elements of the biker style—black leather, fingerless gloves, chains, studded bracelets and belts.

This brutish metal style achieved such popularity among fans that metal magazines like *Hit Parader* actually advertised, "Barbaric Jewelry! Authentic barbed wire look!"[48] Fans imitate other metal attire as well, which also expounds their counter-culture agenda. As Arnett explains, "the long hair, tattoos, earrings, and other trappings of the performers are ways of declaring, and of signifying to their metalhead followers, that they care little for the societal convention of how men should look, and little for the society that this convention represents."[49] Further, Jonathan S. Epstein reports that fans who dress in this manner are perceived by those *outside* their subculture as delinquent (and rightly so):

> Those who reported higher commitment to heavy metal dressed not unlike the stereotypical juvenile delinquent: They wore jeans, black t-shirts bearing the name of one of many popular heavy metal bands...black leather jackets, long hair, and one earring worn in the left ear.... It is possible that these students were singled out more often as behavior problems because they looked like the type of student who would be a behavior problem.[50]

Glam Metal

Yet, heavy metal boasted another sartorial approach that is even more inimical to a Christian worldview. Bands like Mötely Crüe, Ratt, Quiet Riot, Dokken, and Poison participated in a subversive brand of rock known as "glam metal," a unique subgenre of heavy metal that evolved in the mid-1980s and was distinguishable by its commitment to cross-dressing and androgyny.[51] As Walser explains,

> androgyny in heavy metal is the adoption by male performers of the elements of appearance that have been associated with women's functions as objects of male gaze—the visual styles that connote, as Laura Mulvey put it, "to-be-looked-at-ness." The members of bands like Poison or Mötley Crüe wear garish makeup, jewelry, and stereotypically sexy clothes, including fishnet stockings and scarves, and sport long, elaborate, "feminine" hairstyles. Though they are normally included within the genre of heavy metal, such "glam" bands are considered by most fans to be less "heavy" than the mainstream. This is due less to musical differences than to their visual style, which is more flamboyant and androgynous than that of heavier metal.[52]

Walser goes on to underscore the significance of this dress style, "Colorful makeup; elaborate, ostentatious clothes; hair that is unhandily long and laboriously styled—these are the excessive signs of one gender's role as spectacle. But onstage in a metal show, these signs are invested with the power and glory normally reserved to patriarchy."[53]

Far from simple attention-getting hype and one-upmanship, glam metal and other forms of androgyny in rock music represent a worldview that plants itself squarely in opposition to the biblical blueprint of creation and divinely instituted gender distinctions. Rubin reminds us that

> the wearing of glitter makeup and girls' clothing by male rock stars (and the glitter/glam movement it produced) told the world it could discard gender roles that had been in place through the whole of civilization. It told people they could be any sex. It reiterated what San Francisco beat poet Allen Ginsberg (by demanding social acceptance of homosexuality) had already announced.[54]

Walser echoes, "Glam metal has prompted a great deal of thought and discussion about gender by demonstrating, even celebrating, the mutability of gender, by revealing the potential instability of the semiotic or symbolic realms that support current gender configurations."[55] More to the point he states, "But heavy metal also participates in rock's tradition of rebellion, and some metal achieves much of its transgressiveness through androgynous spectacle."[56] Phil Gordon relates that

Dee Snider (of Twisted Sister), the most outrageous of the metal an-
drogynes, "grew his hair and wore women's clothes and make-up, not
merely to assert a difference between himself and his parents...but as a
carefully constructed style signifying attractiveness, energy and opposition to authoritative restrictions on particular pleasures."[57] Lastly,
Susan B. Kaiser points out that "androgyny aims to blur distinctions,
traditional or otherwise, between the sexes.... A male face adorned
with makeup, coupled with an elaborate hairstyle and earrings, for
example, calls into question traditional notions of masculinity versus
femininity."[58]

As the reader may have guessed, even glam metal, with its unquestionably seditious dress code, was not considered beyond the pale of
contemporary witness music. The early eighties saw a revolutionary
development in the history of CCM as Christian glam metal bands
began to materialize and gain popularity throughout North America.
They included groups like Stryken, Sacred Red, Electric, Eternal Ryte,
Neon Cross, and of course Stryper—which bears a remarkable resemblance in hair style, makeup, and other feminine features to Poison.[59]
For example, when in uniform, Robert Sweet of Stryper makes a convincing androgyne: his long platinum blond plumage and face battered
with makeup and finished with eyeliner keep him within striking distance of such androgynous renegades as Boy George, Freddie Mercury
(Queen), and David Bowie. The only element that reveals Sweet's true
male gender is his fully open shirt, shamelessly baring his chest and
body-hair![60] The other members of the band exhibit a similar case of
chromosome confusion.

When glam metal first infiltrated Christian rock, David Hazard detected the obvious contradiction and made these sobering comments:

> Some New-Wave Christian rock groups, comprised of young men,
> [s]how [sic] up on stage wearing eye make-up and with shirts split open
> to their navels and with pelvises grinding to a "heavy-metal" sound; and
> they tell teenaged boys who may be struggling with gender confusion
> how God can fulfill their masculinity, or try to convince teenaged girls
> that they must cap their sexual urges until they are married.[61]

Whether or not Christians should participate in this undeniable perversion of the created order scarcely needs scouting. As Christians we are to affirm gender distinctions, not confuse them. Stryper's popularity and acceptance is a sad commentary on the lack of cultural discernment within mainstream evangelicalism. Even though glam metal is no longer popular, long hair—an important signifier of androgyny—is still extremely common among CCM groups. Although parting with the heavy makeup, Michael Sweet, formerly of Stryper, has by and large maintained the half-man-half-woman look of days past, as is evident from recent pictures.[62] Further, there are many examples of the more subdued neo-androgyne look in CCM today (long hair, occasional facial hair, but no makeup), with perhaps Phil Joel (the Newsboys) standing out as the most successful of the recent CCM gender benders.[63]

Hair Length

As was just discussed, one of the most potent signifiers of androgyny in glam metal and rock music in general is long hair. Many arguments have been tendered in defense of Christian musicians wearing long hair, including wigs worn by Christian men in previous centuries.[64] The problem, however, is that whatever long hair on men may have signified in days past or in other cultures, in today's western society it functions as an insignia for various kinds of deviance and has done so since its introduction in the 1960s. This deviance can take the form of androgyny, rebellion against convention and society, identification with the heavy metal subculture, or any combination of the three.

The capability of long hair to signify gender confusion is due of course to the fact that men normally have short hair in western society (and in most societies) and women have comparatively longer hair.[65] In the United States these important signifiers of masculinity and femininity remained intact during the first half of the twentieth century until the 1960s when the Beatles, Rolling Stones, and Kinks began to popularize long hair[66]—which by today's standards is hardly considered long. Paul McCartney remembers the Beatles' contribution to the change: "There they were in America, all getting house-trained for adulthood with their indisputable principle of life: short hair equals men; long hair equals women. Well, we got rid of that small convention for them. And a few others, too."[67]

Savage elaborates:

The Beatles' trump card was their packaging, which took the concealed sexual divergence of the previous pop sensibility and made it explicit.... the Beatles became explicitly linked with femininity through their crucial visual hook: long hair. Their fresh masculinity was, meanwhile, reflected in their overall image.... This androgynous trend—a deliberate blurring of male/female qualities—was given further impetus by a new English subculture that the Beatles simultaneously heralded and exploited.[68]

He adds:

Just as England had packaged the external signifiers of American rock 'n' roll stars in the fifties, the Beatles' salespoint was their visual androgyny, the Beatles wigs that went on sale being the market leaders in a range of products that included lunchboxes, wallpaper, and stockings. The Beatles were like living dolls, lovable mop-tops packaged for a "passive" female consumer, yet their long hair contained messages that would be liberating to both men and women.[69]

Simels resonates: "No, the central theme of the Sixties, put simply, was hair. As in length of. Yes, the decade of the Sixties was when boys and girls, in large numbers and probably for the first time since the early nineteenth century, began to resemble each other (primarily) from the neck up."[70] He also credits the Beatles for initiating the new standard, "No, the major impulse behind the rock androgyny of the Sixties was, in fact, of foreign origin...: the Beatles."[71] Further, he affirms that the ideological referent of the long hair was androgyny: "No, what got everybody's... [expletive] in an uproar was that long hair was viewed as effeminate.... the haircuts were so revolutionary by Sixties standards that they were viewed as signs of incipient transvestism."[72] The long term result of this new look, as it was eagerly imitated by society's youth, was "a mass fudging of secondary sex characteristics."[73]

The argument, will of course, be advanced that "that was yesterday, but surely today the androgynous meaning has disappeared." As documented above, glam metal not only succeeded in keeping the feminine signification of long hair afloat, but catapulted it to new dimensions of depravity that have survived to the present day. As recently as 1996 Arnett confirmed the androgynous connotations of long hair in the subculture of heavy metal, "The long hair is intended to partly convey a daring androgyny, [and] partly to display a contempt for convention...."[74]

Aside from androgyny, extremely long hair on males can also be an indication of their dedication to metal music and its subculture. Weinstein explains:

> The body of the member of the metal subculture is also bound over to the subculture by hairstyle, which can be considered as a voluntary stigma. From the beginning the metal hairstyle of males has consisted of one simple feature: it is very long. Long hair is the most crucial distinguishing feature of metal fashion....
> Long hair is significant because it cannot be concealed. It is the one feature that excludes "weekend warriors," those with a part-time commitment to heavy metal. Long hair—especially as the other traces of counterculture fashion faded away—became a real sign of heavy metal dedication, a willingly embraced cross to bear. It functions to define the boundary of the subculture.[75]

Others, like John Podhoretz, observe the same thing, "Like punk rockers of the 1970s, committed metal fans...are immediately distinguishable from their contemporaries by their manner of dress and hairstyle."[76] David Lee Roth, former lead singer of Van Halen, comments on the meaning of his long hair: "It's a flag. It's Tarzan. I'll always be anti-establishment." He also describes its significance in history, "In ancient Rome the kids grew their hair and refused to comb it because they wanted to look like the barbarians."[77] Finally, David W. Cloud, a former hippie from the Vietnam era, testifies: "The long hair on males which was commonly associated with rock music's infancy was called a 'freak flag,' meaning the long hair identified the wearer as a 'freak,' a term describing a rebellious drug user."[78]

These are precisely the kinds of negative signals that led the apostle Paul to object to the Corinthian women praying and prophesying without a covering, inasmuch as the uncovered head signified some form of shameful behavior within the culture (1 Corinthians 11:1-16). But beyond this Paul appeals to nature, *phusis*, as a last resort to demonstrate the impropriety of their current practices: "Does not even nature itself teach you that if a man wears long hair, it is a dishonor to him?" (1 Corinthians 11:14). By "nature" Paul is referring to the natural order of things in terms of gender distinctions between men and women.[79] C. K. Barrett comments:

> Nature (i.e., God) has made men and women different from each other, and has provided a visible indication of the difference between them in the quantity of hair he has assigned to each; that is, in point of fact men have short, women have long hair, and though art can reverse this difference, the reversed distinction is, and is felt to be, artificial.[80]

There are several difficulties with Gordon Fee's understanding that *phusis* (nature) is used in a quasi-cultural sense so that it actually refers to social custom or "the 'natural feeling' that they shared together as part of their contemporary culture."[81] Actually, *phusis* carries the same sense here as it does in Romans 1:26, where it clearly means the natural created order, "for their women exchanged the natural use for that which is contrary to nature [*phusis*]."[82] Paul nowhere uses *phusis* in the sense that Fee suggests, nor do the other New Testament writers.[83] In fact I am not aware of such a sense for *phusis* anywhere in ancient Greek literature.[84] Rather, Paul uses *phusis* in a sense similar to that of the Stoic philosophers of his age—yet without submitting to their pantheistic aberrations. Often cited in connection with this text is the Stoic philosopher Epictetus (1.16.9-14):

> Come, let us leave the works of nature [*phusis*] and consider her secondary works. Is anything more useless than hairs on a chin? What then? Did she [nature] not use these in the most appropriate way that she could? Did she not distinguish male and female through them? Has not the nature of each one of us immediately cried out from afar saying, "I am a man...." Again, in regard to women, just as she [nature] has mingled in their voice something more tender, so also she has taken away the hair [from her chin].... On account of this, the signs that God has given ought to be preserved; they ought not to be abandoned, [and] as much as is within ourselves, the sexes, which have been divided, ought not to be confused.[85]

Henry Alford comments: "This is the argument. φύσις [*phusis*] is not *sense of natural propriety*, but NATURE,—the *law of creation....* The Apostle...makes no allusion to the *customs of the nations* in the matter, nor is even the mention of them relevant: he is speaking of the dictates of nature herself."[86] (Emphasis original.) Therefore, it is better to consider "nature," in this passage, as the natural order of creation than the norms of society. The *Dictionary of Biblical Imagery* cogently sums up the evidence, "By the time we reach the NT, Paul considers long hair to be the norm for women but degrading for men (1 Cor 11:14-15)."[87]

Since hair length is divinely ordained, and not the only indicator of gender, it can be superseded by divine decree to express consecration, as is the case with the Nazirite vow (Numbers 6:5, 9, 18, 19). In this specific instance the indication of gender that hair length ordinarily provides was to be overlooked so that the free flowing hair might serve as symbol of the Nazirite's consecration, much like a crown (*nēzer*). In this case long hair was "symbolic of being set apart to holiness—a sign of ascetic renunciation, not of physical attractiveness."[88]

The case of the Nazirite is of course exceptional and would not have resulted in confusion due to its place in Scripture and prominent Nazirites like Samson and Samuel. More so it attests that the normal hair length for men was short—with long hair ordinarily signifying barbarism.[89] The main point, however, is that long hair does not carry the meaning of special consecration in either Christianity or western culture today. Therefore, whether one agrees with the position that 1 Corinthians 11:14 refers to a universal gender distinction or whether one simply believes it was cultural, the end result for Christian males wearing long hair in modern western society should be the same: because of its debased connotations, it should be immediately discontinued.

'From the Mouths of Babes'

Yet, are such conclusions about clothing, symbolism, and moral meaning within a social setting merely the evaluations of academicians, moralists, and others who are out of touch with the youth subculture that embraces these symbols? Not according to a group of teenagers who responded to a contest in which the winners were given an opportunity to meet the members of Mötley Crüe. The contestants were asked to answer the question, "What would you do to meet the Crüe?"[90] Their answers offer invaluable insights into how the heavy metal subculture perceived the attire and paraphernalia of its own musicians.

As we begin, a thirteen-year-old girl writes, "They're [Mötley Crüe] good-looking, good and mean. They just look like guys who are out to party and have a good time."[91] Another thirteen-year-old writes, "I really like the way their faces look," while a seventeen-year-old describes the group as "wild and mean and evil."[92] Another female contestant offers the group sadomasochistic pleasures because to her "they look like the type that would like that. They look like women lovers."[93] More revealing is an entry from a fifteen-year-old girl who admits: "I really like Vince Neil's body. When he's on stage he wears a bunch of spikes and leather pants. I'd do whatever I had to do to meet him. I told my mother's boyfriend about it and he said, 'Whatever turns you on.'"[94]

Finally, this nineteen-year-old candidate furnishes the most compelling verification of the communicable power of heavy metal attire from the grassroots of its subculture. The young lady promises to wear leather straps, chains, and nails in an effort to please the rock group. In her own words, "I think they're all gorgeous. When I see them, I just naturally think of leather and whips and chains. I think that means that they're aggressive. I happen to love that image; it's a neat image. I think it's the kind of aggressiveness that a woman is always looking for."[95] What would these girls have thought of Christian heavy metal bands (Saint, Philadelphia, Stryken) who dressed in identical attire?

Biblical Support

The testimony of Scripture chimes with recent studies that document man's ability to communicate both negatively and positively through clothing. In Genesis 38 we read of how Tamar, by exchanging her widow's raiment for that of a prostitute, was able to communicate volumes to Judah without saying a word: "So she removed the garments of her widowhood from her and she covered herself with a veil and wrapped herself.... When Judah saw her, he thought she was a harlot because she had covered her face" (Genesis 38:14-15). This important example shows how localized and acute the symbolism of a veil was. The veil in other regions and times was not a sign of prostitution, but of modesty (Genesis 24:65). Yet the local culture determined this intrinsically modest item to be the banner of a harlot, which is how it was used by Tamar and perceived by Judah.

Another example comes from Proverbs 7:10 where Solomon describes the adulteress as decked out in the trappings of a harlot: "And, behold, a woman comes to meet him, wearing the apparel of a harlot and cunning in mind." Whatever constituted such apparel, it is obvious to Solomon that her clothing communicated her social and moral status. More important is the fact that he expects his readers to understand the moral culpability of the woman by describing her in terms of her clothing.

Finally, we return to the New Testament (1 Corinthians 11:4-16) and Paul's injunction to the women of the church in Corinth to have their heads covered in worship (a reference to either an external covering or hair length and style). Although no one can be certain as to why the uncovered head was shameful, according to Fee "the problem lay ultimately with a breakdown in sexual distinctions."[96] For our purposes what is important is that the wrong kind of communication was taking place, and that through appearance. Whether deliberately or unknowingly, the signification of the uncovered head associated the Christian women of Corinth with values, beliefs, or customs that were unbecoming for Christians, indeed 'disgraceful,' as Paul phrased it. Paul's concern, then, that the women cover their heads indicates that he recognized the power of the sartorial symbol and its ability to telegraph values, whether the wearer realized it or not.

Culture and Clothing

Nevertheless, because symbols are dynamic rather than static, they can take on new meaning. It may be that after a period of time certain less obvious counter-culture items will become so commonplace that they will no longer signify rebellion or moral deviance, but will be acceptable at every level of society. Until, and *if*, this happens, those symbols on Christians would still carry their original negative overtones, whatever they may be. Therefore, with items of clothing that do not carry intrinsic messages of indecency (such as black leather), the social and moral meaning of the article should be carefully considered within the context of culture and avoided if it diverges from Christian values.[97]

Miller's attempt to justify long hair and skirts on men reveals that he has overlooked the degree to which culture determines the meaning of clothing. Therefore, to intimate that skirts on Christian men in America are appropriate because Roman soldiers in the first century wore them is to miss the point. To several culture groups in India long skirts (*dhothi*) are normal and respectable apparel for men because the culture has determined so. This, however, is not the case in western society where skirts on men signify transvestism or some other form of sexual perversion, as they did on Kurt Cobain of Nirvana.[98] A Christian rock artist who is not intending to communicate counterproductive values by his or her dress will nevertheless do so because the culture that has generated the symbol—based on its worldview—will interpret its meaning according to what it has already determined (and is determining) that meaning to be. This is the poorest of missionary strategies and has unnecessarily sullied the reputation of the church.

Intrinsic Immodesty

So then we can isolate two types of immodesty that plague CCM performers. The most objectionable, of course, is the exposure of the body through either inadequate apparel or tight-fitting clothes. This type of immodesty was more prominent in Christian hard rock and heavy metal groups, who in order to become "all things to all men" remained loyal to the erogenous wardrobe of their musical genre, which required the display of an exorbitant amount of skin, especially in the shoulders, chest, and abdomen—areas obviously attractive to women.[99] Tight leather or spandex pants on men were also a fixture of the heavy metal industry, revealing as they did the forbidden contours of the lower body—another source of female arousal.[100] Cline forthrightly admits that "women are attracted to men who wear clothes that show off chest, biceps and [buttock] to good advantage, who do a credible bump & grind...."[101] She adds that "female rock fans do tend to notice when a Rock star is male, especially when the guy's wearing only enough to emphasize what he's covering up."[102] Sadly, this could describe many male Christian rock performers. Steve Rabey, writing in *Contemporary Christian Music* magazine, admits of Stryper that their "onstage look... [was] complete with chains, leather, studs and crotch bulges...."[103]

Symbolic Immodesty

The other kind of immodesty involves symbolism. Throughout the years CCM stars have adopted the dress code of the target culture or particular rock genre along with its counter-culture vocabulary. The most objectionable involve the hardware of sadistic sex, and of androgyny, which were discussed at length earlier. Although harmless in themselves, when these items are assigned meaning by the rock culture, they represent attitudes, lifestyles, and cultural myths that are contrary to Christian principles. Here the closing remarks of Albert LeBlanc are telling: "Others [rock stars] have used costume to defy convention and create outrage, saying that they are only doing what the public wants to but doesn't dare."[104]

Biblical Solution

So then, in determining the appropriateness of a dress style, we should first test it by biblical standards of modesty. This means that clothing should never be revealing or form fitting. God designed the male and female body to be mutually attractive, desirable, and arousing within the sacred confines of marriage. When this attractiveness is exported from that context and made available to the public, it turns into licentiousness and comes under the condemnation of the Almighty, whether or not it meets with the approval of popular culture. Second, if the clothing does qualify by biblical standards, but according to the culture communicates deviance through special accessories, color combinations, patterns, or cut, it must still be rejected. If, however, it is both biblically modest and has neutral or wholesome social connotations, then it is appropriate for Christian use.

The following description by J. A. Thompson summarizes the biblical understanding of modesty in a way that will give the reader some idea of the difference between biblical modesty and what is presently acceptable:

> It should be remembered that it is mostly in the modern times that clothes have been designed to reveal and emphasize a person's features. In Israel modesty was not only a virtue but a cultural characteristic; the skin-tight, see-through or skimpy garments of the twentieth century are themselves a reflection of a general attitude to the body and to sexuality. It is perhaps worth noting, however, that women of other cultures, contemporary with the Israelites, knew little of such modesty, to judge from such evidence as Egyptian tomb paintings.[105]

Conclusion

The last two chapters have helped us to realize that most of the activities and accessories associated with secular rock music and CCM are pregnant with immoral meaning and are in no sense suitable for Christian integration. Therefore, they would properly qualify as worldly, as the Bible itself defines the term, in that they represent a world system that is in direct opposition to God and his prescription for pleasure, happiness, and contentment. In the following chapters we shall see that the musical style itself suffers from the same malady.

Endnotes

[1]Jay R. Howard and John M. Streck, *Apostles of Rock: The Splintered World of Contemporary Christian Music* (Lexington, KY: The University Press of Kentucky, 1999), 52.

[2]Steve Miller, *The Contemporary Christian Music Debate: Worldly Compromise or Agent of Renewal?* (Wheaton, IL: Tyndale House, 1993), 25, 62.

[3]Warren Anderson, "Josh McDowell: Bridging the Gap," *Contemporary Christian Music*, June 1990, 36. Similarly John W. Styll, "Editor's Comment: How to Tell the Sheep from the Wolves," *Contemporary Christian Music*, June 1986, 4.

[4]Al Menconi and Dave Hart, *Staying in Tune: A Sane Response to Your Child's Music* (Cincinnati, OH: The Standard Publishing Co., 1996), 168.

[5]Dick Hebdige, *Subculture: The Meaning of Style* (London: Routledge, 1979), 101.

[6]Simon Frith, "Towards an Aesthetic of Popular Music," in *Music and Society: The Politics of Composition, Performance, and Reception*, ed. Richard Leppert and Susan McClary (Cambridge: Cambridge University Press, 1987), 139.

[7]Orrin E. Klapp, "Style Rebellion and Identity Crisis," in *Human Nature and Collective Behavior: Papers in Honor of Herbert Blumer*, ed. Tamotsu Shibutani (New Brunswick, NJ: Transaction Books, 1970), 71.

[8]Lorraine E. Prinsky and Jill Leslie Rosenbaum, "'Leer-Ics' or Lyrics: Teenage Impression of Rock 'n' Roll," *Youth & Society* 18, no. 4 (June 1987): 391.

[9]David A. Locher, "The Industrial Identity Crisis: The Failure of a Newly Forming Subculture to Identify Itself," in *Youth Culture: Identity in a Postmodern World*, ed. Jonathan S. Epstein (Malden, MA: Blackwell Publishers, 1998), 108.

[10]Iain Chambers, "Popular Culture, Popular Knowledge," *OneTwoThreeFour* 2 (Summer 1985): 15.

[11]Miller, *Christian Music Debate*, 93.

[12]Dan Peters, Steve Peters, and Cher Merrill, *What About Christian Rock?* (Minneapolis: Bethany House, 1986), 156.

[13]Picture on file.

[14]Picture on file. Gano's other group is the Violent Femmes.

[15]On the World Wide Web at http://www.leconte.com/barnabas/vintpics.htm. For the S&M coding of this type of apparel see E. Ann Kaplan, *Rocking Around the Clock: Music Television, Postmodernism, and Consumer Culture* (New York: Methuen, 1987), 103; Allison Lurie, *The Language of Clothing* (New York: Random House, 1981), 258; Hebdige, *Subculture*, 107-08.

[16]Mark Joseph, *The Rock and Roll Rebellion: Why People of Faith Abandoned Rock Music—And Why They're Coming Back* (Nashville: Broadman & Holman, 1999), 204; Howard and Streck, *Apostles of Rock*, 79; Angelo De Simone, *Christian Rock: Friend or Foe* (New Haven: Selah Production Agency, 1993), 194.

[17]Cf. Deena Weinstein, *Heavy Metal: A Cultural Sociology* (New York: Lexington Books, 1991), 221.

[18]Pictures on file.

[19]Picture on file.

[20]Picture on file.

[21]Steve Rabey, "Age to Age," *Contemporary Christian Music*, July 1998, 21.

[22]Michael Ciani, "All Aboard," *Contemporary Christian Music*, July 1996, 37.

[23]Michael Goldberg, "Amy Grant Wants to Put God on the Charts," *Rolling Stone*, 6 June 1985, 10. Like Miller earlier, Grant uses extreme examples from secular rock to gauge what is proper for Christians.

[24]James Chute, "What Hath Pop Wrought in Jesus' Name?" *The Milwaukee Journal*, 17 August 1986, 8E. Cf. David Hazard, "Holy Hype: Marketing the Gospel in the '80s," *Eternity*, December 1985, 39.

[25]See Roberta Croteau, "House of Amy," *Release*, September/October 1994, 22-26. For copies, one should contact Release Magazine, 2525-C Lebanon Pike Box 6, Nashville, TN 37214.

[26]Beneath the photographer's airbrushing, however, a swimsuit is barely noticeable.

[27]The choice of words was erotic, sexy, sensual, tempting, suggestive, exciting, beautiful, interesting, normal, uninteresting, innocent, conservative, modest, chaste, pure, wholesome, saintly, and other.

[28]Goldberg, "Amy Grant," 10.

[29]Precious few do strive for high standards, such as Point of Grace, whose members (all female) have a policy *not* to wear short skirts in concert or on album covers. Christopher John Farley, "Reborn to Be Wild," *Time*, 22 January 1996, 64.

[30]Gregory Rumburg, "Yahweh Rocks," *Contemporary Christian Music*, January 1999, 10; Deborah Evans Price, "'Tis the Season for Sounds of Joy,'" *Contemporary Christian Music*, December 1994, 24.

[31]Price, "'Tis the Season for Sounds of Joy," 23.

[32]Rabey, "Age to Age," 26.

[33]Katherine Orloff, *Rock 'n' Roll Woman* (Los Angeles: Nash Publishing, 1974), 19.

[34]Jon Savage, *Time Travel: Pop, Media and Sexuality 1976-96* (London: Chatto & Windus, 1996), 119.

[35]Ibid.

[36]Dave Laing, *One Chord Wonders: Power and Meaning in Punk Rock* (Philadelphia: Open University Press, 1985), 91-92.

[37]Hebdige, *Subculture*, 114.

[38]Savage, *Time Travel*, 344.

[39]Linda Andes, "Growing up Punk: Meaning and Commitment Careers in a Contemporary Youth Subculture," in *Youth Culture: Identity in a Postmodern World*, ed. Jonathan S. Epstein (Malden, MA: Blackwell Publishers, 1998), 223.

[40]Hebdige, *Subculture*, 107-08. See also Savage, *Time Travel*, 401; Laing, *One Chord Wonders*, 91-92, 94-95.

[41]Nathan Rubin, *Rock and Roll: Art and Anti-Art* (Dubuque, IA: Kendall/Hunt Publishing Co., 1993), 180.

[42]For example, see older punk groups like Undercover and Lightforce, and (early) One Bad Pig.

[43]Lurie, *Clothing*, 258.

[44]Weinstein, *Heavy Metal*, 30. See also Kaplan, *Rocking Around the Clock*, 103; Angela McRobbie, "Dance and Social Fantasy," in *Gender and Generation*, ed. Angela McRobbie and Mica Nava (London: Macmillan, 1984), 140.

[45]Weinstein, *Heavy Metal*, 30, 217.

[46]Paul E. Willis, *Profane Culture* (London: Routledge and Kegan Paul, 1978), 20; quoted in Weinstein, *Heavy Metal*, 104.

[47]Elianne Halbersberg, *Heavy Metal* (Cresskill, NJ: Sharon Publications, 1985), 30. See also Guy Garcia, "Heavy Metal Goes Platinum," *Time*, 14 October 1991, 85.

[48]Anne Fadiman, "Heavy Metal Mania," *Life*, December 1984, 112.

[49]Jeffrey Jensen Arnett, *Metalheads: Heavy Metal Music and Adolescent Alienation* (Boulder, CO: WestviewPress, 1996), 69.

[50]Jonathan S. Epstein, David J. Pratto, and James K. Skipper, Jr., "Teenagers, Behavioral Problems, and Preferences for Heavy Metal and Rap Music: A Case Study of a Southern Middle School," *Deviant Behavior* 11 (1990): 390.

[51]Robert Walser, *Running with the Devil: Power, Gender, and Madness in Heavy Metal Music* (Hanover, NH: Wesleyan University Press, 1993), 12. See also Menconi and Hart, *Staying in Tune*, 68-69.

[52]Walser, *Running with the Devil*, 124.

[53]Ibid., 131.

[54]Rubin, *Rock and Roll*, 167.

[55]Walser, *Running with the Devil*, 131. See also Savage, *Time Travel*, 160; Patrick Gray, "Rock as a Chaos Model Ritual," *Popular Music and Society* 7, no. 2 (1980): 78.

[56]Walser, *Running with the Devil*, 110-11.

[57]Philip Gordon, "Review of Tipper Gore's *Raising PG Kids in an X-Rated Society* and *Dee Snider's Teenage Survival Guide*," *Popular Music* 8, no. 1 (January 1989): 122.

[58]Susan B. Kaiser, *The Social Psychology of Clothing* (New York: Macmillan, 1990), 460.

[59]See the cover of Poison's album, *Look What the Cat Dragged In*.

[60]Picture on file.

[61]Hazard, "Holy Hype," 40.

[62]See *Release* May/June, 1994, 20-21. Stryper, which began in 1984, disbanded in 1992 when Michael Sweet left because of artistic differences.

[63]For Phil Joel see Deborah Barnes, "Green Cathedrals," *Contemporary Christian Music*, August 1998, 26. Menconi, who defends most varieties of CCM attire, at least acknowledges that "it is sinful for a man to dress in a way that would make him appear as if he wanted to be a woman, or for a woman to try to look like a man." He certainly recognizes the perversion of glam metal and may be hinting that the Christian version is also unacceptable—although he never charges Christian groups with the violation. Any-

way, I suspect this is what he means when he later voices his disapproval of his daughter's intrigue with a Christian rock group (Stryper?) whose appearance resembled Bon Jovi and was "unbecoming for Christians." Likewise, De Simone draws the line with makeup and opines, "A male musician doesn't need to look like a girl so he can reach someone." Menconi and Hart, *Staying in Tune*, 69, 168, 197-98; De Simone, *Christian Rock*, 202.

[64]The custom of long and elaborately managed hair on men in European society began in the early seventeenth century with King Louis XIII and gained momentum with his son Louis XIV, who considered himself the monarch, not only of France, but also of European fashion. It was popularized in England by Charles II, but was scathingly denounced by many Puritans as effeminate, vain, and lascivious. By the time of John Wesley long haired wigs on men were considered normal in England. Wesley himself, who grew his hair long, though not nearly as long as many, when commenting on 1 Corinthians 11:14 seems to indicate that the effeminacy of long hair was due not so much to its length, but to it being "carefully adjusted," i.e., coiffured. Bill Severn, *The Long and Short of It: Five Thousand Years of Fun and Fury Over Hair* (New York: David McKay Co., 1971), 38-63; James Laver, *Costume* (New York: Hawthorn Books, 1963), 69-70; Wendy Cooper, *Hair: Sex, Society, Symbolism* (New York: Stein and Day, 1971), 123-27; John Wesley, *Explanatory Notes Upon the New Testament*, 1754; repr. (Alec. R. Allenson Inc., 1966), 619.

[65]Cf. Klapp, "Style Rebellion," 71.

[66]Jon Savage, "The Enemy Within: Sex, Rock, and Identity," in *Facing the Music*, ed. Simon Frith (New York: Pantheon Books, 1988), 154.

[67]Barbara Ehrenreich, Elizabeth Hess, and Gloria Jacobs, "Beatlemania: Girls Just Want to Have Fun," in *The Adoring Audience: Fan Culture and Popular Media*, ed. Lisa A. Lewis (London: Routledge, 1992), 102.

[68]Savage, "The Enemy Within," 154. See also Savage, *Time Travel*, 159.

[69]Savage, "The Enemy Within," 156.

[70]Steven Simels, *Gender Chameleons: Androgyny in Rock 'n' Roll* (New York: Timbre Books, 1985), 27.

[71]Ibid., 29-30.

[72]Ibid., 30-31.

[73]Ibid., 32.

[74]Arnett, *Metalheads*, 10. See also Robert Duncan, *The Noise: Notes from a Rock 'n' Roll Era* (New York: Ticknor & Fields, 1984), 85; James Lull, "Listener's Communicative Uses of Popular Music," in *Popular Music and Communication*, ed. James Lull (Beverly Hills, CA: Sage Publications, 1987), 163.

Many individuals (Christians and non-Christians) in adopting counterculture styles are guilty of what some in the social sciences refer to as "ego screaming." Here an oppositional style functions primarily to satisfy the person's unmet "need" for recognition, rather than to make a social statement or identify one's self with all the values of the counter-culture. See Klapp, "Style Rebellion," 71, 78; Kaiser, *The Social Psychology of Clothing*, 462.

[75]Weinstein, *Heavy Metal*, 129. See also pp. 130-31.

[76]John Podhoretz, "Metallic Rock That's Designed to Shock," *U.S. News & World Report*, 7 September 1987, 50.

[77]Roy Trakin, "David Lee Roth, on the Record," *USA Today*, 4D, n.d. I am grateful to Tim Fisher for providing me with a copy of this article.

[78]David W. Cloud, *Contemporary Christian Music Under the Spotlight* (Oak Harbor, WA: Way of Life Literature, 1999), 128.

[79]C. K. Barrett, *A Commentary on the First Epistle to the Corinthians*, Harper's New Testament Commentaries (New York: Harper & Row, 1968), 256.

[80]Ibid.

[81]Gordon D. Fee, *The First Epistle to the Corinthians*, The New International Commentary on the New Testament (Grand Rapids: Eerdmans, 1987), 527.

[82]Cf. Walter Bauer, *A Greek-English Lexicon of the New Testament and Other Early Christian Literature*, trans. William F. Arndt and F. Wilbur Gingrich, 2d ed. (Chicago: University of Chicago Press, 1979), 869.

[83]Cf. Bauer, *Greek Lexicon*, 869-70.

[84]Cf. Henry George Liddell and Robert Scott, comps., *A Greek-English Lexicon*, 9th ed. (Oxford: Clarendon Press, 1996), 1964-65.

[85]Translation is mine.

[86]Henry Alford, *Acts-II Corinthians*, 1875; repr., *Alford's Greek Testament: An Exegetical Critical Commentary*, vol. 2 (Grand Rapids: Baker Book House, 1980), 568. Cf. Raymond F. Collins, *First Corinthians*, Sacra Pagina Series, ed. Daniel J. Harrington, 7 (Collegeville, MN: The Liturgical Press, 1999), 403-04, 413; Jerome Murphy-O'Connor, "Sex and Logic in 1 Corinthians 11:2-16," *Catholic Biblical Quarterly* 42 (1980): 498; Bruce K. Waltke, "1 Corinthians 11:2-16: An Interpretation," *Bibliotheca Sacra* 135, no. 537 (January-March 1978): 55.

[87]Leland Ryken, James C. Wilhoit, and Tremper Longman III, eds., "Hair," in *Dictionary of Biblical Imagery* (Downers Grove, IL: Inter-Varsity Press, 1998), 360.

[88]Ibid.

[89]Ibid., 359. The Nazirite vow should caution us from treating sartorial symbols as foolproof indexes of human motive. For example, a women with a shaven head may be signifying lesbianism, as is often the case, or she may simply be recovering from chemotherapy. Likewise I once knew a young man whose hair was becoming girlishly long, only to discover that he was too poor to have it cut.

[90]Bob Greene, "Words of Love," *Esquire*, May 1984, 12.

[91]Ibid., 13.

[92]Ibid.

[93]Ibid.

[94]Ibid.

[95]Ibid.

[96]Fee, *First Corinthians*, 512. Other causes for the shame, just as inimical to Christian conduct, have been suggested. See Collins, *First Corinthians*, 407-09; Kenneth T. Wilson, "Should Women Wear Headcoverings?" *Bibliotheca Sacra* 148, no. 592 (October-December 1991): 447-48; Murphy-O'Connor, "Sex and Logic," 487-90; Cynthia L. Thompson, "Hairstyles, Head-Coverings, and St. Paul: Portraits from Roman Corinth," *Biblical Archaeologist* 51 (June 1988): 112-13; Waltke, "1 Corinthians 11:2-16," 50.

[97]Although today the black leather look may not signal the same kind of perversion that it did in the eighties, with certain styles it can still carry overtones of defiance, machismo, and lawlessness.

[98]Savage, *Time Travel*, 384.

[99]Cf. Albert LeBlanc, "All Part of the Act: A Hundred Years of Costume in Anglo-American Popular Music," in *Dress and Popular Culture*, ed. Patricia A. Cunningham and Susan Voso Lab (Bowling Green, OH: Bowling Green State University Popular Press, 1991), 67.

[100]Cf. Weinstein, *Heavy Metal*, 30, 221.

[101]Cheryl Cline, "*Essays from* Bitch: The Women's Rock Newsletter with Bite," in *The Adoring Audience: Fan Culture and Popular Media*, ed. Lisa A. Lewis (London: Routledge, 1992), 75.

[102]Ibid., 79-80.

[103]Rabey, "Age to Age," 30.

[104]LeBlanc, "All Part of the Act," 72. Today's alternative, metal, and punk bands (secular and Christian) are less ostentatious and oppositional in their fashions, preferring the slovenly hip-hop or skate-boarder look: tennis shoes, cargo shorts, jeans, undershirts, t-shirts, button shirts (open and untucked), tank tops, muscle shirts, tattoos, earrings, and denim or leather jackets. Hair styles can range from the entirely shaven skin-head look to the peroxide mohawks of punkers and long hair of metalheads. Randall Balmer comments on the grunge look of the members of Jars of Clay: "Several of them seem to take pains to convey the impression they have spent more time with a parole officer than a youth pastor...." "Hymns on MTV," *Christianity Today*, 15 November 1999, 34.

[105]J. A. Thompson, *Handbook on Life in Bible Times* (Downers Grove, IL: Inter-Varsity Press, 1986), 97.

4

Toward the Meaning of Rock Music

Introduction

AS THE CCM CONTROVERSY penetrates the twenty-first century, the most important question still has to do with the moral capacity of music. That is, can a style of music apart from the lyrics communicate good or evil? Although other matters of concern have shared in the debate, ultimately CCM must stand or fall on the basis of the neutrality or non-neutrality of music.

Those who advocate a pro-rock position point out that music itself is incapable of communicating evil or good. Rather, like language, it is a neutral tool that can be used positively or negatively based on the intentions of the performer and the accompanying lyrics. Further, they maintain that an unpleasant reaction to a musical style is not morally based, but a matter of cultural conditioning and taste. They marshal ethnomusicological studies, changing responses to music, and other evidence to demonstrate that there is no patently sacred or profane form of music. Harold M. Best provides one of the most unequivocal expressions of this position: *"With certain exceptions, art and especially music are morally relative and inherently incapable of articulating, for want of a better term, truth speech. They are essentially neutral in their ability to express belief, creed, moral and ethical exactitudes, or even world view."*[1] (Emphasis original.) This perspective was actually institutionalized at one time into a confession known as the "Christian Rocker's Creed": "We hold these truths to be self-evident, that all music was created equal—that no instrument or style of music is in itself evil—that the diversity of musical expression which flows forth from man is but one evidence of the boundless creativity of our Heavenly Father."[2]

Below I will examine such claims and demonstrate why they are mistaken and unworthy of acceptance. It will be seen that music can, in fact, be morally charged and serve as an effective medium for conveying a variety of ideas, feelings, and behaviors, which can be either compatible or incompatible with Christian ideals. Matters relating to aesthetics will be addressed in the following chapter.

Ethnomusicology

One of CCM's most effective tools for showcasing the moral neutrality of music is evidence from ethnomusicology, the discipline of musicology that studies and compares the musical practices of different cultures.[3] The argument goes something like this: "Because different cultures and subcultures respond differently to unfamiliar forms of music, music must be relative and neutral rather than inherently good or evil."[4] Yet a proper understanding of music and how it communicates will expose the shortcomings of this position.

There are actually several reasons why musical styles are not universally understood, but none has to lead to the conclusion that music is morally neutral. One of the reasons for varying responses among individuals and groups is because musical meaning and effect are mediated through symbols and not directly injected into the mind and body like narcotics. Because music is a language of symbols, which must be learned, cultures do not always interpret forms of music identically. Manoff explains:

> Each living language has its own set of cues.... These cues originate in musical practices: for example, a chord progression, manner of singing, a type of rhythm, a way of combining timbres and melodies. Interacting with these musical phenomena are the broader cultural responses, such as feelings, ideas, body image, etc. The results of the interaction—the cues—are internalized through habit and create the basis of the living language.... All this happens within a particular culture or group.[5]

Musical symbols, which are invested with feelings and ideas, vary according to culture. This is one of the reasons why non-westerners do not always respond identically to western styles and vice versa. Meaning must be attributed to the characteristic elements of a style for the music to communicate. This is not always easy to do for someone outside a particular culture who is not familiar with what meanings (feelings, values, ideas) to attach to the musical symbols of a certain style.

Nevertheless, I would argue that there is in some sense a universal aspect to music since music often accurately expresses emotions and feelings, which are common to all mankind. John Hospers identifies how music can express emotional qualities:

> When people feel sad they exhibit certain types of behavior: they move slowly, they tend to talk in hushed tones, their movements are not jerky and abrupt or their tones strident and piercing. Now music can be said to be sad when it exhibits these same properties: sad music is normally slow, the intervals between the tones are small, the tones are not strident but hushed and soft. In short, the work of art may be said to have a specific feeling property when it has features that human beings have when they feel the same or similar emotion, mood, etc. This is the bridge between musical qualities and human qualities, which explains how music can possess properties that are literally possessed only by sentient beings.[6]

Therefore, it is arguable that on a broad anthropological level musical styles are universal—or potentially so—due to the emotional and psychological continuity of mankind and music's ability to imitate and exaggerate emotions through sound.[7] Many factors, however, can interfere with the cross-cultural understanding of music such as how emotions are interpreted, the use of musical symbols unrelated to their referent, and the representation of non-emotional entities in music. Further, many of these factors suffer from the intrusion of human depravity, which can distort the relationship between the sign and its referent or can promote an unbiblical understanding of emotions. Therefore, a case for the neutrality of music cannot be made from ethnomusicology.

Another point needs to be stressed: even if musical styles are not universally understood, like spoken language they are still capable of moral discourse within their cultural contexts. This of course is one of the chief concerns of CCM, to communicate Christ through indigenous musical styles, not those that are alien.[8] The whole matter of ethnomusicology, universality, and the semiotics of music is discussed in detail in Appendix C. Here it simply needs to be emphasized that universal meaning and moral meaning are not necessarily inseparable.[9]

Neutrality or Desensitization?

Another method of illustrating the neutrality of music, especially rock music, is to recall the public hysteria accompanying earlier rock styles and performances and then point out that people no longer have the same reaction to the music. The obvious conclusion is that factors other than the style were responsible for the reactions. Miller, for example, uses this line of reasoning to support his argument for musical neutrality, "If you watch people calmly listen to the Beatles today, you will wonder what all the fuss was about. If the problem was inherently in the style, there would be no difference in the response people have to the music today from the response they had in the sixties."[10] An earlier and almost identical example was offered by Steve Lawhead, "Watch a film of the Beatles at Shea Stadium, the stands packed with thousands of screeching, crying fans, and you wonder what all the commotion was about. Was it the music? No. If music was the mover, those bouncy songs would still drive people crazy. Put on a stack of old Beatle records and you won't get anybody to scream and tear their hair."[11]

Miller and Lawhead seem, at first, to have a valid point since there were several factors, aside from the music, that engendered Beatlemania and similar manias.[12] Yet, the only thing that this illustration proves is that music produces its effect by way of sign and referent rather than by being forced into the listener, who falls helplessly under its spell. This, however, is not an index that musical styles are morally neutral since musical symbols are known to be effective carriers of moral meaning. Consequently this type of logic suffers from the same weakness that was observed for the argument from ethnomusicology: both uncritically accept the inconsistency of human response as an automatic indication of inherent neutrality, relativism, or polysemy (multiple meanings) in musical discourse.

Further, proponents of the second view ("mania-no-more") often fail to consider the psychological phenomenon of desensitization (also "habituation," or "sensory fatigue"), which has frequently been observed by musicians and musicologists. Repeated exposure to any stimulant (direct or mediated) will eventually lead to tolerance, dissatisfaction, and burnout. The product then becoming unappealing to the user must be replaced by another more capable of exciting the dull receptors.[13] Arthur Koestler calls this process "the principle of infolding," concerning which Bernice Martin elaborates: "Each style, once all its main features have been developed naturally moves into more extreme and emphatic versions of itself until it exhausts its own logic and provokes the introduction of a counter style. Some such process has surely happened in pop music."[14] This is one of the reasons why the style of rock music did not remain static, why the Everly Brothers would be replaced by the Doobie Brothers and so on. Simon Reynolds comments, "The problem is that, as with any drug or intoxicant, tolerance builds up rapidly.... But noise hipsters...can cope with absurd levels of outrage/dissonance, and therefore require extreme after extreme in order to feel stimulated/mindblown. Burnout approaches."[15]

Rubin explains how heavy metal was a response to desensitization par excellence:

> To retain the intensity Presley had generated simply by sneering and singing the country blues, rock and roll during the seventies was obliged to turn assaultiveness up to the max. The result was called heavy metal....
> To create it then—since loud sounds are more aggressive than soft ones—make heavy metal loud. Since males are more aggressive...than females, make it male. Make it screamed rather than sung, distorted rather than pitched, lumbering rather than sprightly, insistent rather than diffuse, massed rather than single....
> In fact, all that hard rock players *really* had to do was exaggerate what they were already doing: play the riffs still louder, distorting their timbres, and the solos still faster.[16]

Likewise, Arnett estimates that

> even within popular music, vulgar art did not begin with heavy metal. The rock music of the 1960s and 1970s also exalted vulgarity. But heavy metal has reformulated the audaciousness and excess of rock for the 1980s and 1990s now that rock has become tamed and respectable....

Heavy metal came forth in part as a response to rock's new docility. Heavy metal performers made their performances and their songs outrageous enough to violate even the new, expanded boundaries of social acceptability. Increasingly sophisticated sound technology gave them the weapons they needed to create a new sound of unprecedented fierceness to accompany their fierce, defiant, angry ideology. And the adolescents of the world listened, and responded, by the millions.[17]

Joe Stuessy attributes the rapid changes in rock—indicated by increasingly harder styles, more bizarre clothing, and elaborate props—to competition within the industry: "To grab the spotlight from the current stars, a new band must play louder, have more elaborate props, cut bigger holes in their jeans, wear more spikes and chains, shout more obscenities, and bite the heads off more bats than the current groups."[18] This strategy of "one-upmanship" and the natural desensitization that Reynolds described help to explain the rapid changes in rock music and why people do not react to the Beatles or Elvis as they used to. As Stuessy puts it, "What were once vices are now habits."[19]

Negotiating Meaning

CCM's conviction that musical styles do not contain inherent moral meaning is of a piece with the deconstructive/poststructural position of many secular musicologists.[20] The lack of confidence among musicologists in inherent structures of musical meaning, such as the expressionist model earlier presented by Hospers, results in a clearly pluralistic doctrine of musical discourse. Once the link between the symbol and its referent has been ruptured, it is only a small step to the annihilation of the stability of musical codes and the creation of multiple and individualized meanings. Sheila Whiteley represents this position well:

Clearly, any meaning assigned to music does not have to depend upon the existence of external referents. As Shepherd points out, 'music is not an informationally closed mode of symbolism relevant only to "emotive, vital, sentient experiences", or "inherent psychological laws of rightness"', and whilst lyrics and song titles suggest a preferred reading, music's abstract character allows for a mapping of individual experience and meaning that provides a sense of identity and a fluidity of engagement.[21]

Likewise, Walser argues for a 'dialectic' rather than a 'linear' model of communication "in which meanings are multiple, fluid, and negotiated."[22] He states that "a C major chord has no intrinsic meaning; rather, it can signify in different ways in different discourses, where it is contextualized by other signifiers, its own history as a signifier, and the social activities in which the discourse participates."[23] McClary expresses the same sentiments:

> For music is not the universal language that it has sometimes been cracked up to be: it changes over time, and it differs with respect to geographical locale. Even at any given moment and place, it is always constituted by several competing repertories, distributed along lines of gender, age, ethnic identity, educational background, or economic class.[24]

Yet even amidst this celebration of indeterminacy there is still an important recognition of the existence of some kind of stability within music, at least within the context of culture. McClary is an ideal example of one who denies transcendent meaning in music, while affirming cultural meaning:

> Meaning is not inherent in music, but neither is it in language: both are activities that are kept afloat only because communities of people invest in them, agree collectively that their signs serve as valid currency. Music is always dependent on the conferring of social meaning—as ethnomusicologists have long recognized, the study of signification in music cannot be undertaken in isolation from the human contexts that create, transmit, and respond to it.[25]

Walser admits to the collective agreement and recognition of meaning within genre:

> By approaching musical genres as discourses, it is possible to specify not only certain formal characteristics of genres but also a range of understandings shared among musicians and fans concerning the interpretation of those characteristics.... as John Fiske puts it, "Conventions are the structural elements of genre that are shared between producers and audiences. They embody the crucial ideological concerns of the time in which they are popular and are central to the pleasures a genre offers its audience."[26]

He adds,

> Genres then come to function as horizons of expectation for readers (or listeners) and as models of compositions for authors (or musicians). Most important, Todorov argues that genres exist because societies collectively choose and codify the acts that correspond most closely to their ideologies.[27]

Perhaps Walser's insight about "preferred meaning" is the most useful:

> The fact that ideas can be fairly consistently communicated, regardless of the nuances of individual response, is what points to the importance of musical discourses as coherent systems of signification. The range of possible interpretations may be theoretically infinite, but in fact certain *preferred meanings* tend to be supported by those involved with a genre, and related variant meanings are commonly negotiated.[28] (Emphasis added.)

Likewise, Laing, another advocate of the multiple meaning approach, confesses:

> More generally, though, the need of those controlling discourses is to ensure that one particular meaning is generated and the others excluded. That meaning is referred to as the 'preferred' or 'dominant' meaning in semiology. One important way in which this is achieved is by defining the role of the listener, the audience, the receiver of the discursive message, in such a way that only the preferred meaning 'makes sense' to them. Other possible meanings are then dismissed as inessential, irrelevant or even unintelligible.[29]

Reductionism

What is important for the CCM debate in all this is that the commitment to musical indeterminacy and polysemy has permitted its Christian practitioners to retain the same musical symbols while attempting to assign new "heavenly" meanings to them. This process is variously referred to as "negotiating meaning," "discursive fusion," or "transforming codes."[30] For example Weinstein claims that Christian metal "transforms the code of heavy metal to serve the purposes of Evangelical Christian sects and denominations."[31] Robert H. Mitchell suggests that a Christian metal fan "can use the sound [of heavy metal] to express the reality of Jesus Christ."[32] Howard and Streck posit that "the meanings [of rock music] can be negotiated—even cleaned up and Christianized."[33] Walser practically illustrates what is meant by negotiating meaning or code transformation with his interpretation of Stryper's music:

> For example, the Christian heavy metal band Stryper demonstrates that the specific musical gestures of heavy metal operate within a code that communicates experiences of power and transcendent freedom because their attempt to appropriate the codes of metal is posited on the suitability of precisely such experiences for evangelism. The power is God's; the transcendent freedom represents the rewards of Christianity; the intensity is that of religious experience. Stryper appropriates and reinterprets the codes of heavy metal, using metal's means to produce different meanings. Metal's noisiness might seem incompatible with a Christian agenda, but Stryper exploits just that subversive aura to make more appealing what would otherwise seem a wholly institutional message. Stryper presents Christianity as an exciting, youth-oriented alternative; they offer their fans a chance to enjoy the pleasures of heavy metal and feel virtuous at the same time.[34]

In the process of demonstrating negotiation, Walser employs a strategy that is often used in the entertainment industry (secular and Christian) to defend some of its most disturbing practices and behavior. He resorts to reductionism, an argumentative technique that breaks down offensive or disagreeable material into elemental components that are unobjectionable; in other words, it is argument by means of gross understatement. Here Walser reduces the meaning of heavy metal to "power" and "transcendent freedom," which can be value-free entities, apart from further definition (although even here he has difficulty reconciling "metal's noisiness" with images of Christian piety).[35] The problem with this description is that the sounds of heavy metal are far more than just powerful and transcendent.

The Sound of Heavy Metal

My contention against describing heavy metal solely in terms of power and transcendence (thus minimizing its true message) can be verified with more elaborate and credible descriptions. Rock journalist Lester Bangs, despite his flair for sensationalism, leaves much in his description of heavy metal that can be supported by both experience and more scholastic evaluations:

> As its detractors have always claimed, heavy-metal rock is nothing more than a bunch of noise; it is not music, it's distortion—and that is precisely why its adherents find it appealing. Of all contemporary rock, it is the genre most closely identified with violence and aggression, rapine and carnage. Heavy metal orchestrates technological nihilism....
>
> ...For its noise is created by electric guitars, filtered through an array of warping devices from fuzz tone to wah-wah, cranked several decibels past the pain threshold, loud enough to rebound off the walls of the biggest arenas anywhere. Add the aural image of a battering ram, and you've got a pretty good picture of what heavy metal sounds like.[36]

Less rhetorical, but still convincing, is Jon Pareles:

> Heavy metal's main subject matter is simple and virtually universal. It celebrates teen-agers' newfound feelings of rebellion and sexuality. The bulk of the music is stylized and formulaic, a succession of reverberating guitar chords, macho boasts, speed-demon solos and fusillades of drums.[37]

According to George H. Lewis, "the themes of rebellion in both the words and music of heavy metal rock groups such as Motley Crue reflect and reinforce very successfully the values and feelings of pre-teen and early male adolescents...."[38] Dee Snyder (Twisted Sister) concurs: "That's why heavy metal exists. It is the only form of rock 'n' roll besides punk where the essential element of rebellion still exists...."[39] Next, Manoff comments on the music of the Blue Oyster Cult: "Raw, frenetic, purposefully distorted, this music is not meant to be pretty."[40] Stuessy adds: "There were the distorted, repetitive guitar riffs and steady duple subdivisions of the beat that were to characterize heavy metal. The vocal style and musical ambiance seemed to project attitudes of anger, defiance, and aggression."[41]

(It should be enlightening that Christians depict Christian metal in many of the same terms: "'Smashmouth' was the adjective often used to describe the intense music of Barnabas: powerful rock 'n' roll, unbridled musical aggression."[42] Likewise, the drummer for Disciple doesn't just play the drums, he "assaults [them]…with thunderous power," while "Brad's bruising guitar lashes out with blazing fury," as one sympathetic reviewer put it.[43] Another reviewer assures the reader that in their latest album the group has not veered from their customary "outspoken harshness, guitar shrieks and Nine Inch Nails-like vocals that Disciple fans love."[44])

Arnett considers heavy metal to be "inherently well suited to expressions of violence; the rough, distorted guitar sound, the rumbling bass guitar, and the pounding drums would not be effective in conveying gentleness or compassion but are exceptionally effective in portraying chaos, death, war, destruction, and other violent themes."[45] Elsewhere he remarks that "the music that accompanies these lyrics [of the song "Kill Again" by Slayer] is every bit as violent as the lyrics themselves."[46] In fact Arnett found in an analysis of both the lyrics and music of 115 heavy metal songs that one-half of them communicated anger as the dominant mood, and only fifteen percent evoked a positive emotion.[47] The anger and aggression of heavy metal were also apparent to its youthful listeners; one bragged, "It's aggressive; I just like the speed and anger of it." Another exclaimed, "I love his electric guitar…. I mean, it's *screaming*."[48] Furthermore, Arnett claims that for adolescents the actual metal concert "is the sensory equivalent of war—without the bullets—and they find it exhilarating. It is the ultimate in sheer skull-pounding, body-wracking, roaring sensation, and to them it is an ecstatic experience."[49]

According to Arnett's survey, many metalheads (forty-eight percent of males) admitted that they listened to heavy metal when they were in an angry mood: "If I get in an angry or violent mood," said one, "to tell you the truth, I'll put it in and I'll turn it up. A lot of times it reflects how I feel."[50] Another metalhead confessed, "There are just times when you get the urge to hear some thrash [metal]." This was usually when he was "extremely mad at the world, not just any person in particular."[51] Arnett's study of female metal fans yielded similar results, "If I'm in a bad mood, sometimes I listen to it. It gets me more angry, but by the time I'm done listening to it, it gets my anger out."[52]

Curiously, Christian rocker Brian Duncan verifies this with his own testimony: "I think music became a kind of salvation for me.... It was a way of expressing my frustrations about feeling trapped. If I was angry I could play rock 'n roll. That certainly expressed anger better than anything else."[53]

Like the young lady above, most of the adolescents in Arnett's study who claimed they listened to heavy metal when angry also claimed that it had a cleansing effect on them; that is, listening to heavy metal tended to purge them of their anger and calm them down.[54] Although Arnett tends to justify the music on this account,[55] this is hardly a biblical method of dealing with anger. It is not a subduing, putting away, or soothing of anger (Proverbs 29:11; Romans 12:19; Colossians 3:8) through biblical means of repentance, forgiveness, self-control, and surrender, but a violent unleashing of anger through music. One youth describes it this way: "It [heavy metal] seems to escalate the anger when I'm listening to it, pumps up the adrenaline, but at the same time it's a release of anger as well."[56] The fact that metalheads claim that moshing has the same effect of "purging" them of their anger[57] demonstrates that anger is never really conquered, but simply redirected, reprocessed, and vented through pulverizing music and dancing. The illusion of serenity and relief it creates is no permanent solution to anger, but is based on a debunked hydraulic model of human emotions. Unfortunately, this highly problematic theory is still advocated by some therapists, who encourage angry patients to beat the stuffing out of a pillow or slam into tackling dummies as a "constructive" release of their hostility.[58] Finally, it should be noted that within a small minority of individuals interviewed heavy metal increased their aggression, often resulting in vandalism and other destructive behavior. One adolescent admitted to wanting to "beat the c... out of someone" after listening to hardcore heavy metal.[59]

Distortion

The most distinctive component of heavy metal music and perhaps the major source of its transgressive appeal is the sound of the distorted electric guitar, pioneered by Jimi Hendrix and Eric Clapton.[60] Here I invoke Walser's own description of distortion to make the point that power and transcendence, as descriptions of heavy metal, are too reductive:

> Historically, such distortion has been regarded as undesirable, and generations of audio engineers have joined in the quest for perfect audio fidelity, laboring to eliminate all types of distortion while increasing power-handling capabilities. To the horror of these engineers, in the 1960s they began to receive requests from guitar players to produce devices that would deliberately add electronic distortion (in the late 1950s, guitar players had experimented with distortion by slashing their speaker cones)....
>
> Not only electronic circuitry, but also the human body produces aural distortion through excessive power. Human screams and shouts are usually accompanied by vocal distortion, as the capacities of the vocal chords are exceeded. Thus, distortion functions as a sign of extreme power and intense expression by overflowing its channels and materializing the exceptional effort that produces it. This is not to say that distortion always and everywhere functions this way; guitar distortion has become a conventional sign open to transformation and multiple meanings. Heavy metal distortion is linked semiotically with other experiences of distortion, but it is only at a particular historical moment that distortion begins to be perceived in terms of power rather than failure, intentional transgression rather than accidental overload—as music rather than noise.[61]

More pungent are comments on distortion from heavy metal record producers, such as this one from Eddie Kramer (producer for Jimi Hendrix, Led Zeppelin, Anthrax, and KISS): "Distortion is the flag-waver of the rebellious generation. Think about Hendrix, the Who, and the Stones, and you think of those wonderful distorted guitar sounds."[62] Likewise, Tom Werman of Mötley Crüe, Poison, Ted Nugent, et al., says: "Distortion is equivalent to grinding your teeth. It's anger. It's a rude sound, and it's got a wonderful texture. When I talk to guitar players about what kind of distortion we want for a part, I always vary between crushed glass and big shards of broken glass."[63] Don Gehman, Pat Benatar's producer, puts it bluntly, "Distortion is the sound of adolescence. It's anger, it's out of control."[64] Also insightful are occasional descriptions of instruments being attacked or "megawatt guitars being mutilated on stage."[65]

Beyond Reductionism

Although Walser is careful to avoid labels that stereotype heavy metal as crude and primitive, favoring morally benign terms such as "power," "transcendence," "freedom," "intensity," and "energy," occasionally even he can be found describing heavy metal in less-than-ennobling language.[66] At times he refers to the "violence of the drums,"[67] to music that is "chaotic" and "brutal," and to a "heavy distortion that charges the air with menace."[68] Dokken's guitar solo in the song "Heaven Sent" is "an articulation of frantic terror, made all the more effective by its technical impressiveness and its imitations of vocal sounds such as screams and moans."[69] Elsewhere, he describes the musical message of Poison's song "Nothin' but a Good Time" as "rebellious and aggressive" and adds that "the visual narrative and the musically coded meanings are roughly parallel; the lyrics are supported by the music that is energetic, rebellious, and flamboyant."[70] There is no reductionism here.

Likewise, at times we can even catch CCM sympathizers in incriminating descriptions of Christian rock. Patrick Kavanaugh reports that "some Christian bands are as grungy and loud as any of their secular counterparts.... Their styles are almost indescribable, but all emphasize a driving drumbeat, harmonic distortion, and very little melodic content. The vocal lines contain at least as much screaming as true singing...."[71] Best confesses, "In the case of rock styles, the music is not only stylistically static but abusively loud, assaultive, and in some cases physically hurtful. And it stays that way."[72] Corbitt once admitted,

> The [Christian rock] concert itself assaulted my senses and my sensibility. A young electrician supervising the concert suggested I wear earplugs and gave me a pair. Young people rushed to the front and began dancing under the assault of sound. The first performers on the stage, "Reality Check," could have been any rock group in the country. Dyed hair, hip-hop clothes, and earrings shouted the pop culture as loudly as their ear-shattering guitars.... "Where is Christ in all this?" I asked myself.[73]

Furthermore, if the traumatizing sound of heavy metal can simply be described as powerful, then its devotees would be satisfied as easily with a recital of tubas or organs, both instruments that produce powerful sounds. But this is unthinkable because heavy metal does not just articulate power, but excessive, obsessive, tyrannical, and delinquent power, as has been repeatedly documented. Likewise, Walser's preference for the housebroken phrase "transcendent freedom" instead of what others have described as rebellion—as even Walser admits with "Runnin' with the Devil"[74]—should be greeted with skepticism. Heavy metal is certainly transcendent, but it is far more. Transcendence can be achieved by a wide variety of musical resources outside of heavy metal, including harps, violins, and acoustic guitars. But none of these would be an appropriate substitute for the kind of transcendence that headbangers find appealing in metal music. This is because more than simply transcendence is being discharged. Heavy metal simulates, in musical terms, the kinds of feelings that individuals within the metal subculture generally experience and express at times of disillusionment, anger, rage, uninhibited autonomy, sexual potency, and parental overthrow (also civil and ultimately divine). Therefore, the power and transcendent freedom of heavy metal—though possibly appropriate for signifying other manifestations of obsessive, distorted, and delinquent power and rebellion—cannot be negotiated to represent the power of God or the freedom from sin that he offers.

Dancing

A factor that is often overlooked in claims that the meaning of rock music can be negotiated to serve the church is that of dancing. Dancing as visual art and body language is far more transparent a signifier than music[75] and more limited than music as to its external referents. Since the unmistakable sexual symbolism of rock-based dancing has already been documented, it simply needs to be asked why the (perverse) dance forms and stage histrionics have remained the same if rock's musical codes have been transformed by Christian lyrics so that they now symbolize biblical themes. Whereas one may argue that a certain combination of musical elements can take on various meanings (and I think these meanings are far more restricted than most), it is rather difficult to find a non-sexual or otherwise wholesome connotation for the flexions of rock-related aphrodisiac dancing and stage acrobatics. Although Mick Jagger may be guilty of hyperbole in the following statement, if even a tithe of what he maintains is true, CCM's case for musical negotiation is left floundering in inconsistency: "What I'm doing is a sexual thing. I dance, and all dancing is a replacement for sex."[76] It is clear then that as much as CCM may claim to have reworked the musical codes of rock, its retention of orgiastic dance forms and stage antics seriously undermines its appeal.

Limited Negotiation

Still, it is not to be denied that musical meanings are negotiable; but that negotiability should be limited to external referents that are organically related to the musical genre or composition. Stephen Davies makes this point rather convincingly: "It is not true that just any music might be used appropriately with just any text. Pizzaro's rage music in Beethoven's *Fidelio* would not be at all suitable in mood for the love duet between Leonore and Florestan."[77] This of course assumes a biblical worldview of absolutes or at least a secure point of reference for music, such as the emotions. Therefore, even though musical symbolism may be fluid, it is not arbitrary; the symbols, from a biblical perspective, cannot represent any conceivable entity, but must be limited to a range of compatible feelings, images, and artifacts.[78] For example distortion in heavy metal may theoretically find non-emotional referents similar to adolescent rage and excess, such as the wanton violence of roller derby or professional wrestling, but for symbolizing Christian themes it is entirely unsuitable because negotiation (the reassigning of symbols to new referents) must take place with symbols and referents that are compatible.

Incompatible Cues: Test Case One

The compatibility of musical symbol and referent is so crucial to proper meaning that it even proves problematic for Walser's interpretation of Christian heavy metal: "Metal's noisiness might seem incompatible with a Christian agenda, but Stryper exploits just that subversive aura to make more appealing what would otherwise seem a wholly institutional message."[79] Clearly, he has difficulty in linking the Christian worldview with distortion ("noisiness") and resolves the tension, not by denying it, but by suggesting that Stryper capitalizes on the noisiness and uses it to attract unbelievers. What Walser intimates here is that the meaning of the music could not be changed, so instead the meaning of Christianity was. The "subversive aura" of distortion, volume, and violence in heavy metal, unable to find a corresponding referent in Christianity, has been baptized into Christianity anyway and assimilated (most incompatibly) with orthodox concepts of God, the Christian life, and the gospel. From this example it is clear that the meaning of Christianity has been negotiated (or better, perverted), whereas the meaning of heavy metal has held its ground.

Test Case Two

The modification of an ideological concept under the influence of a musical code (rather than the reverse) is evident in another observation made by Walser. In the following example it is the musical symbol that remains firm, whereas the extra-musical referent (the U.S. Army) suffers a change of image and meaning to something more unruly than it is traditionally conceived to be: "Even ads for the U.S. Army ('Be All That You Can Be') featured metal guitar in a kind of subliminal seduction: military service was semiotically presented as an exciting, oppositional, youth-oriented adventure. Rebel, escape, become powerful: join the army!"[80] Thankfully, Walser's terminology here is not nearly as reductive as it is in his interpretation of Stryper. With choices such as "oppositional," "rebel," and "escape" he is much more successful in conveying the true message of heavy metal.

But more importantly, he unknowingly demonstrates that words and ideological concepts such as a military institution (and I would argue, God) can undergo a transformation of image and meaning by their association with a genre of music. The traditional concepts of military service—discipline, patriotism, sacrifice, and heroism—must now share time with escapism and rebellion due to the infusion of metal's musical codes. The same kind of transformation also takes place when two incompatible systems such as Christianity and rock music unite. It does more than just resulting in the schizophrenic "Janus-headed" creation and "peculiar hybrid" that William D. Romanowski and Carol Flake have observed.[81] CCM patrons soothe the tension and resolve the conflict of Christian rock by reinventing the meaning of Christian doctrine and lifestyle to bring it into harmony with the musical message of rock. Again something has been negotiated, but I maintain it is not the music.

Sovereignty of Lyrics?

The unyielding commitment of many Christians to lyrics, doctrine, and traditional concepts as unassailable fortresses of meaning to which musical forms and codes must prostrate in submission needs serious revision. This is, first of all, because words do not carry inherent meaning. Their meanings are assigned, learned, and nuanced within contexts such as sentences, paragraphs, chapters, and books. Further, if speech act theory has taught us anything, it is that meaning in discourse is not simply a matter of exegesis or syntactical analysis, but must be informed by the situational context of the utterance. Otherwise a statement like "Can you close the door?" would be merely a question about a person's ability to close a door rather than a polite command.

With songs the situational context of the words is expanded to include the accompanying music, tonal inflection, and body image. Therefore, the musical environment of the words and concepts will contribute significantly to their meaning, whatever influence the lyrics in turn may have on the music.[82] Walser insightfully states: "But I would argue that musical codes are the primary bearers of meaning; lyrics, like costume and performers' physical motions, help direct and inflect the interpretation of the meanings that are most powerfully delivered, those suggested by the music."[83] Simon Frith, emphasizing the priority of the music over the lyrics in rock communication, demurs:

> Sociologists of popular music have always fallen for the easy terms of lyrical analysis. Such a word-based approach is not helpful at getting at

the meaning of rock.... Most rock records make their impact musically rather than lyrically. The words, if they are noticed at all, are absorbed after the music has made its mark. The crucial variables are the sound and rhythm.[84]

Likewise, Schultze et al. contend: "The problem with trying to pin down the lyrical meaning is that rock and roll has always expressed more and meant more than its lyrics alone. The text is but one avenue to the meaning of the song."[85] In reference to the group Guns n' Roses they explain that "lyrics do not offer a reliable guide to deciphering their public image or the mood of the music itself, which can speak as loudly as any set of words."[86]

Although the process is undoubtedly dialectic, in which both the music and the words define one another, there is much to indicate that the musical meaning remains remarkably stable despite the fact that it does not communicate as specifically as the lyrics. This is why I have such problems with Best's understanding that "the Word of God is not context absorbing; it is context disturbing. It does not change with the context. Rather, the context must change because of its presence."[87] The truth, however, is that even though Scripture is God's Word, it is still transmitted through the organ of human language and submits to the rules of language, which include deriving meaning through context. Davies rightly observes that "the semantic content of spoken utterances can be affected by pitch, rhythm, tempo, accent, phrasing, attack, and decay [*sic* "delay"?]."[88]

Suppose for instance that one Christian says to another, with a charitable smile, blissful eyes, and a cheerful and sincere tone, "Beloved, let us love one another for love is from God" (1 John 4:7). Then suppose that the identical statement is made with a sinister scowl, grinding teeth, squinting eyes, and a gritty and growling voice. Could anyone, including Best, believe that the words carried the same meaning on both occasions? In the first, the meaning of the words was enhanced and complemented by the facial expression, speech accents, and tonal inflection. In the second, there is utter disillusionment and conflict because of the obvious dissonance between the learned meaning of the words, "Beloved, let us love one another...." and the ferocious attitude with which they are dispensed. It illustrates that even the Word of God attains meaning within context. Although this seems like an exaggerated example, it really is not, since this is exactly the kind of situation that occurs in hardcore Christian rock. Christopher John Farley of *Time* magazine recognizes the contradiction when describing the music of dc Talk: "There is something absurdly fun about hearing words of devotion screamed out over the rampaging guitars."[89]

Walser contributes a similar example, this time demonstrating how the distinctive elements of a musical genre can influence the meaning of the lyrics:

Before any lyrics can be comprehended, before harmonic or rhythmic patterns are established, timbre instantly signals genre and affect. Imagine this text being done by AC/DC, with raucous screaming and pounding: "I hear footsteps and there's no one there; I smell blossoms and the trees are bare." Now compare Frank Sinatra crooning it, backed by strings. The musical cues create very different effects: one is of frantic agony of paranoia; the other is the delicious disorientation of bourgeois love.[90]

James Chute borrows this equation and applies it to the music-lyric antithesis in CCM:

The music's message is clear, and adding the words of Jesus Christ to the lyrics does not make one bit of difference. Whether a metalhead is listening to Ozzy Osbourne or Stryper, the feeling he or she gets in his gut is one and the same. The music inevitably overwhelms the best intentions...of the lyrics. In the struggle between the words and the music, a struggle that has existed for centuries, music most often has the upper hand.[91]

He adds,

The contemporary Christian musicians would have us believe that changing the words changes the music's very nature, as if the power of music resides in the words alone; as if music can be completely severed from its cultural and social context and suddenly take on meanings not only removed, but contradictory to those contexts.[92]

Flake opines,

> Lowell Hart and other antirock crusaders were at least partially correct about Christian rock being a contradiction in terms. When no attempt was made to fuse form and content, the result was the creation of strange hybrid beasts that headed off in two directions at once: Christian punk, Christian new wave, Christian heavy metal.[93]

Even Michael W. Smith betrays an awareness of the music-lyric paradox in CCM; Michael McCall reports that Smith "expects some people to miss the positive spirit in his message and instead hear only the chaotic chords of his music."[94]

Priority of Music Over Lyrics

There is sufficient evidence to indicate that, at least in pop music, lyrics are of secondary importance to the music. Walser recalls:

> Like most musicians and fans, I respond more intensely to music than to words or pictures. Before I knew any lyrics, before I had seen any of the major performers, I was attracted to heavy metal by specifically musical factors. Within the context of the other kinds of music I knew, I found the "language" of heavy metal—the coherent body of musical signs and conventions that distinguished it as a genre—powerful and persuasive.[95]

Sociologists Bruce K. Friesen and Warren Helfrich echo: "Of equal importance to the lyrics are the subtle (or not so subtle) ways that the music produces an emotive interpretation of the lyrics being sung and further defines the ideational context."[96] Their convictions are supported by field studies of teenagers and their musical priorities. For instance, the 1987 Prinsky and Rosenbaum study discovered a marked preference for music over lyrics among teenagers. One student commented, "I don't listen to the words, only how the song sounds. I don't give a d...what they [lyrics] say."[97] Others admitted that they did not comprehend the lyrics and were attracted to the beat because they enjoyed dancing.[98] Likewise, in an earlier study of teenagers by P. Hirsch (1969), seventy percent reported a greater attraction to the music than to the lyrics.[99]

Of course in the heavier genres of rock, the lyrics are barely comprehensible anyway. In the words of Podhoretz, "The subject matter [of speed metal] is meant only to shock—and, besides, you can't hear the words, anyway. 'It's very aggressive music,' says Elektra Records' executive Michael Alago. 'The music is so overwhelming that the words are secondary.'"[100] McClary and Walser concur:

> Heavy metal fans, for instance, don't seem to be much concerned with verbal discourse; they go to concerts where lyrics are almost completely unintelligible, and they don't mouth the lyrics along with the songs even if they know them—they are much more likely to mime the guitar solos or make power gestures or yell.[101]

Chute challenges,

> Go to a concert by Judas Priest, Iron Maiden, or any other metal band and you might be able to understand a word here or there, but not many. Maybe some metal aficionados have all the words memorized, but don't bet on it. The words don't really matter because the message is in the music.[102]

Even CCM booster Donald P. Ellsworth, at the dawn of heavy metal mania, had this to say about using hard rock as a medium for the gospel:

> But hard rock usually requires a certain amount of textual obliteration. The volume of sound needed for hard or acid rock is that of a "mind-blowing" experience. There is little chance of communicating anything other than the total inundation of sound to the point of psychic escape from reality. The responsibility of the church is not to provide escape from reality, but to give answers to contemporary problems through legitimate, biblical means.[103]

Further, researchers find that listeners are able to negotiate the meaning of lyrics or even reject them. This is understandable since rock lyrics (including those of CCM) are often so ambiguous that they invite multiple meanings and are left in the hands of the listeners to tool to personal tastes and needs. According to McClary and Walser, "the texts of some genres of popular music are not clearly discernible by its fans... and the obscurity of the verbal dimension seems even to be part of the attraction."[104] When Eddie Van Halen was asked what his mother would think about the explicit lyrics of lead singer David Lee Roth, he replied, "I don't know what the lyrics are."[105] The infamous song by Twisted Sister "We're Not Gonna Take It," considered by many watchdog organizations to be overtly insurrectionary, is claimed by the group to have an open-ended reference. The intolerance that it promotes can be applied to any context, whether school, work, or whatever.[106] (How reassuring!) Even when the topic is suicide, more than one meaning is possible, according to Walser: "But music does not simply inflict its meaning upon helpless fans; texts become popular when people find them meaningful in the context of their own lives. That is why a wide range of responses is possible [to songs about suicide]."[107] Oddly enough this type of deconstructive approach to lyrics is actually encouraged by one CCM group, Never the Less: "But feel free to let the song mean whatever you think it means to you personally. Thats [sic] the beauty of music."[108]

Some studies reveal that listeners, especially teenagers, often failed to comprehend the deeper meaning of texts. Prinsky and Rosenbaum found that

> interpretations of lyrics were quite literal and the students rarely understood the frequent use of symbolism and sometimes complex metaphors. For example, most of the teenagers who listed the song "Digital Display" as one of their favorites discussed computers and/or romantic relationships but overlooked symbolic references to sex.[109]

Roger J. Desmond's summary of several studies on lyric comprehension that were performed in recent decades indicates a remarkable consistency in their conclusions. On the whole rock lyrics were comprehended only by about one-third of the teenagers surveyed.[110]

A final category consists of those who clearly understand harmful lyrics but claim to resist their message.[111]

This kind of evidence scarcely provides consolation for Christians, who realize that comprehended or not, negotiated or not, misunderstood or not, lyrics antithetical to a Christian worldview are clearly blasphemous and those who patronize them are playing with fire. Although they minimize dangers and disregard the spiritual forces of darkness operating in rock music, these findings nevertheless suggest that the hegemony of lyrics over music is perceived rather than actual. Further, if lyrical messages are prone to manipulation, reinterpretation, incomprehension, misunderstanding, and rejection when the music and the lyrics are compatible—as is usually the case with secular rock—how much more fragile is the stability of lyrical meaning when the musical message opposes and contradicts it, as is the case with CCM? Certainly, the Bible testifies to the importance and power of words and speech (Proverbs 18:21), as well as the ability of language to communicate. But there is no endorsement of the view that the meaning of words cannot be contradicted or that words receive meaning apart from larger contexts. On the contrary, the Bible teaches that actions that accompany words can either reinforce them or overturn them (1 John 3:18; 4:20; Titus 1:16; James 2:15-17). So then, although in some genres like folk music the lyrics supersede the music in importance,[112] in rock music the music clearly has the upper hand in meaning, significance, and attraction.

Reductionism in CCM

Like Walser, CCM advocates often engage in their own brand of reductionism, such as when Miller states: "Granted, much of rock music does generate an exciting atmosphere, but excitement is not wrong in itself.... Excitement itself is neutral, but a rock artist has the opportunity to channel that excitement toward positive or negative ends."[113] Likewise, Menconi proposes that rock music expresses such things as passion, action, energy, tension, and urgency—all of which, like excitement, are amoral elements of various emotions, feelings, and moods that can be either righteous or unrighteous. [114] Since qualities like excitement or energy are common denominators in negative feelings of rebellion, rage, and sensuality, as well as love, joy, and happiness, they are offered as the most complex levels of meaning and expression that rock is capable of. One can hardly object to such an appraisal since there is nothing evil about excitement or energy.

Music: Moral or Amoral?

Nevertheless, rock music creates much more than just excitement, energy, passion, etc., as CCM advocates would have us believe. The following data when taken collectively seriously challenges the conviction that rock music in itself only generates value-neutral qualities or states of being. The Bible, the ancients, rock musicians, sociologists, musicologists, and rock historians recognize specific attributes in music that go far beyond the reductionistic terms that CCM enthusiasts employ. They associate specific emotions, feelings, and moods with music.

The Bible

In the Bible we discover useful references to music's capacity to represent specific moods and feelings: Job 30:31, "My harp has been turned into mourning, and my flute to the sound of weeping." Jeremiah 48:36, "Therefore, my heart moans for Moab like flutes." And Isaiah 24:8, "The gaiety of tambourines ceases,...The gaiety of the harp ceases" (NASB). Also included is a non-canonical example from the Dead Sea Scrolls: "Then I will play the lyre to the sound of salvation and the harp to the sound of rejoicing [...] and the flute to the sound of praise without end" (*1QH* [*Hodayot*] 18:23).[115] Alfred Sendrey's comments on this passage are worth noting: "Here, the psalmist uses the well-known biblical pattern of associating transition from sadness to joy with the sound qualities of various musical instruments."[116]

Even so, we must go beyond Sendrey since our passages do not refer to "sound qualities," but to the type of melody that is played on the instruments. This is because the same instrument that embodies sadness in some passages personifies happiness in others. For example, the harp (*kinnōr*) in Job 30:31 is "turned into mourning" (or "reproduces the sounds/sensations of mourning"), but in Psalm 81:2 the same instrument appears in the context of joy and praise and is called the "pleasant harp [*kinnōr*]." Likewise, the flute (*'ûgāb*) in Job 30:31 is turned "into the sound of weeping" (or "reproduces the sound of weeping"), but in

Job 21:12 it accompanies rejoicing, "and they rejoice at the sound of the flute ['*ûgāb*]."

Therefore, when the Bible identifies specific emotions with musical instruments, it is not referring to their tonal qualities, but to the melodies produced on them, melodies that express those emotional qualities through sound—as *1QH* 18:23 seems to verify.

Evidence from the Scriptures ought to shed much light on the neutrality debate. Since the biblical references to music examined here reveal that music is a language in itself, capable of expressing feelings, emotions, and moods, not all of which are upright and virtuous, it is only reasonable to conclude that music has the power to communicate evil.

Ancients

Ancient Greek philosophers like Plato and Aristotle firmly recognized music's ability to shape the soul. Plato said: "Education in music is most sovereign, because more than anything else rhythm and harmony find their way to the inmost soul and take strongest hold upon it, bringing with them and imparting grace...."[117]

Aristotle, Plato's student, is even more insistent, "But rhythms and melodies contain representations of anger and mildness, and also of courage and temperance and all their opposites and the other moral qualities, that most closely correspond to the true natures of these qualities."[118] He also states:

> The same holds good about the rhythms also, for some have a more stable and others a more emotional character, and of the latter some are more vulgar in their emotional effects and others more liberal. From these considerations, therefore, it is plain that music has the power of producing a certain effect on the moral character of the soul, and if it has the power to do this, it is clear that the young must be directed to music and must be educated in it.[119]

This is, of course, not to say that Plato and Aristotle's (Pythagorean) understanding of musical composition and how it engages the passions is correct on all points or beyond criticism. I mention them simply because they are some of the earliest to acknowledge that music is not morally neutral and that it can convey specific meaning in the emotional realm. Also their influence on important figures that will be discussed later necessitates a brief overview of their philosophy of music.

Sociologists, Musicologists, Composers, and Rock Historians

The insights of sociologists, musicologists, composers, and rock historians, who contribute to our topic from their own perspective and training, are also in harmony with the previous evidence. Peter Wicke in his sociological study of rock music describes rock's capacity to communicate specific values:

> And even if involvement with rock music is a relatively independent cultural process, it is fulfilled in relation to playing styles, and stylistic forms, structures of sound and visual concepts of presentation which primarily follow the musician's value judgments and the meanings they intended. These reflect the musician's view of himself as an artist as well as the aesthetic and political claims which he connects with his music.[120]

Sociologist William Schafer writes, "It [rock] is a medium, a means of communicating emotions...the medium is the message."[121] Elsewhere he adds, "There is no separation of form and content in rock, since they are fused as a continuous experience, a package of simultaneous impressions and feelings."[122]

Music critics prior to the advent of rock music also testify concerning music's ability to communicate to the emotions. Leonard B. Meyer explains:

> From Plato down to the most recent discussions of aesthetics and the meaning of music, philosophers and critics have, with few exceptions, affirmed their belief in the ability of music to evoke emotional responses in listeners. Most of the treatises on musical composition and performance stress the importance of communication of feeling and emotion. Composers have demonstrated in their writings and by the expression marks used in their musical scores their faith in the affective power of music. And finally listeners, past and present, have reported with remarkable consistency that music does arouse feeling and emotions in them.[123]

Clyde S. Kilby finds that

> composers of music are in fact as ready as other artists to admit great human motives. Paul Hindemith declares that all the ethic[al] power of music will be at the command of the composer and he will use it "with a sense of severest moral responsibility," and Aaron Copland says that in giving meaning to life music has purpose. "I would even add," says he, "moral purpose." The old and tantalizing problem of describing the specific manner in which great music symbolizes a moral universe will encourage the Christian to a deeper search into musical meaning, rather than to the alternative of supposing musical value to reside in the shifting taste of an individual or a social group.[124]

Next, Stuessy makes this important observation: "But music too is a language. The trained musician has learned to communicate using that language. It is just as intelligible, and probably more powerful, than verbal language."[125] He adds, "We have known intuitively for centuries that music can make us feel relaxed, scared, patriotic, ambitious, mad, sad, happy, romantic, and reverent."[126]

Finally, among rock historians, Charles Brown describes the rhythmic factor in musical communication: "In music the basic beat pattern, or rhythm, tells us something about the emotional feel of different kinds of songs."[127]

Sexuality in Rock Music

Along with rebellion the sound of rock music from its very inception has been closely implicated with sexuality. Certainly the lyrics of many songs make covert, sometimes explicit, references to sex,[128] but what ought to concern Christians who tolerate or promote CCM is that sexuality in rock permeates its very musical forms and codes, whose meanings cannot be restricted to mere excitement or even passion.[129]

Rock Performers

A number of secular rock artists admit that rock music as a style is erotic or sexually oriented. Debbie Harry, lead singer of Blondie, discloses, "I've always thought that the main ingredients in rock are sex, really good stage shows and really sassy music. Sex and sass, I really think that's where it's at."[130] John Oates of Hall and Oates simply says, "Rock 'n' roll is 99% sex."[131] Frank Zappa candidly proposes, "Rock music is sex. The big beat matches the body's rhythms."[132] Jan Berry of Jan and Dean as early as 1965 stated, "The throbbing beat of rock-and-roll provides a vital sexual release for its adolescent audience."[133] Paul Stanley, guitarist-vocalist for KISS, recalls, "Then I saw The Beatles on television and I said to myself, 'I can do that'—not necessarily the same way, but to touch that same kind of nerve; that hidden, unknown erogenous zone—which is what rock and roll is all about."[134] Lastly, Neil Tennant of the Pet Shop Boys comments, "Our music is, and always has been, fueled by a strong sexual undertow. Pop music is partially about sex. The two things can't be divorced."[135]

It may be argued that dramatic statements like these are meant to generate shock-effect, publicity, and record sales and, therefore, ought not to be taken seriously. But even if sensationalism was the primary agenda (and there is certainly more involved here than that), it is obvious that these impressions were not drawn out of thin air, especially since they come from a variety of sources and time periods. Further, the same argument of sensationalism could be advanced (and has been by advocates of rock) in defense of satanic or erotic themes in the *lyrics* of rock music.[136] And yet what Christian would dismiss such disclosures as mere publicity stunts or entertainment? Moreover, these candid comments are supported by serious works of scholarship in the humanities.

Sociologists and Musicologists

Frith and McRobbie's study of sexuality in rock music provides important scholastic insights:

> Of all the mass media rock is the most explicitly concerned with sexual expression. This reflects its function as a youth cultural form: rock treats the problems of puberty, it draws on and articulates the psychological and physical tensions of adolescence, it accompanies the moment when boys and girls learn their repertoire of public sexual behavior. If rock's lyrics mostly follow the rules of romance, its musical elements, its sounds and rhythms, draw on other conventions of sexual representation,

and rock is highly charged emotionally even when its direct concern is nonsexual.... "Rock 'n' roll" was originally a synonym for sex, and the music has been a cause of moral panic since Elvis Presley first swiveled his hips in public.... For a large section of postwar youth, rock music has been the aesthetic form most closely bound up with their first sexual experiences and difficulties, and to understand rock's relationship to sexuality isn't just an academic exercise—it is a necessary part of understanding how sexual feelings and attitudes are learned.[137]

Bernice Martin's conclusion is similar:

Of all the features of social order which rock organizes, mediates and reflects, sexuality is probably the most important single element.... Most young people today discover their own sexuality in and through rock music. The symbolism of rock parallels the praxis of puberty as the young translate theoretical knowledge into experiential understanding, as they try on emotions and roles both vicariously and for real.[138]

Norma Coates is more to the point as she blends academic research with personal experience:

Conversely, and curiously, some respondents, when asked why they like the [Rolling] Stones, reply 'because they're sexy.' In this case, 'they're' does not necessarily refer to the manly beauty of Mick, Keith or even Bill or Charlie. It refers, rather, to the sound of the Stones, the totality of the mix and the beat, the way the music hits the body and the hormones instantaneously.... This sound, perhaps some of the most definitional sound of ultimately undefinable rock, is coded as unmistakably phallic, and masculine.[139]

The verdict of the authors of *Dancing in the Dark* again accords with the analysis of their secular counterparts:

The sheer sound of rock—apart from its lyrical content—acknowledged, displayed, and even celebrated incohate and unspoken pubescent fears and desires. Part of the appeal, clearly was sexual: rock put "it" all out in the open, even though this display was at first deftly sublimated and rarely verbal....[140]

Finally, I include the now-famous testimony of rock's sexuality from Allan Bloom: "Young people know that rock has the beat of sexual intercourse."[141] And, "But rock music has one appeal only, a barbaric appeal, to sexual desire—not love, not eros, but sexual desire undeveloped and untutored."[142]

Encoding Eroticism

The question that needs to be asked, however, is *how* rock music expresses sexuality. Many researchers find that sexuality in music is encoded by "mapping patterns through the medium of sound that resemble those of sexuality."[143] In rock music this usually takes the form of audibly reproducing sequences of arousal and release or the gradual escalation of desire to climax in exclusively masculine terms.[144] Frith considers this to be one of the sexual codes of heavy metal: "The music is loud, rhythmically insistent, built around techniques of arousal and release."[145] Nancy Holland applies this to other forms of rock as well,

> The usual dynamic in rock is one that reproduces the 'normal' male pattern of sexual arousal and release, as in Prince's "Darling Nikki".... The success of such songs in arousing desire in a female audience through an appeal to the patterns of male sexual response might be explained by the fact that women in our culture are taught to respond sexually in a way that mirrors male sexuality. Indeed, rock music is arguably one way in which they are taught this.[146]

Whiteley practically illustrates this feature in her musical interpretation of the Rolling Stones' "Satisfaction":

> Sexual arousal is musically encoded by the ascending sequence, the push toward the climactic 'get', the slide down to 'no' which prefaces the more languorous delivery on 'satisfaction' which is itself subjected to a more intensive sense of arousal in the repetitive fade-out.[147]

Another method of conveying sexuality in rock music is through what is often referred to as the phallic beat. McClary explains that rock music

> is typically characterized by its phallic backbeat. It is possible to try to downplay that beat, to attempt to defuse its energy—but this strategy often results in music that sounds enervated or stereotypically "feminine." It is also possible to appropriate the phallic energy of rock and to demonstrate...that boys don't have any corner on that market.[148]

Walser describes the rhythmic power of Van Halen's "Runnin' with the Devil" as "strongly gender coded, it could be called phallic...."[149] Frith and McRobbie explain that "musically, such rock takes off from the sexual frankness of the rhythm and blues but adds a cruder male physicality (hardness, control, virtuosity). [Phallic] rockers' musical skills become synonymous with their sexual skills...."[150] Elsewhere, they add, "Rock's rhythmic insistence can be heard as a sexual insistence...."[151] In *Sound Effects*, Frith stresses that "the sexuality of music is usually referred to in terms of its rhythm—it is the beat that commands a directly physical response...."[152] Further, as early as the 1960s Nik Cohn asserted, "What was new about it [rock and roll/pop] was its aggression, its sexuality, its sheer noise; and most of this came from the beat."[153] That this backbeat is the express diction of eroticism is also apparent in the immediate expectations that it triggered in two listeners who sampled Madonna's single "Justify My Love": "I expect highly sexual images from Madonna—the breathy delivery and the slow repetitive rhythm implied this;" and, "Due to the pulse of the music, I presumed the video would involve some sort of simulated sex scenes."[154]

In order to explain more specifically how rock's backbeat, or rhythm, communicates sexuality, it will be necessary to cite Richard Dyer at length:

> Rhythm, in Western music, is traditionally felt as being more physical than other musical elements such as melody, harmony, and instrumentation. This is why Western music is traditionally so dull rhythmically—nothing expresses our Puritan heritage more vividly. It is to other cultures that we have had to turn—above all to Afro-American culture—to learn about rhythm.... Infusions of black music were always seen as (and often condemned as) sexual and physical....
>
> However, rock is as influenced by black music as disco is. This then leads me to the second area of comparison between the eroticism of disco and rock. The difference between them lies in what each "hears" in black music. Rock's eroticism is thrusting, grinding—it is not whole-body, but phallic. Hence it takes from black music the insistent beat and makes it even more driving; rock's repeated phrases trap you in their relentless push, rather than releasing you in an open-ended succession of repetitions as disco does.

Most revealing perhaps is rock's instrumentation. Black music has more percussion instruments than white, and it knows how to use them to create all sorts of effects—light, soft, lively, as well as heavy, hard, and grinding. Rock, however, hears only the latter and develops the percussive qualities of essentially nonpercussive instruments to increase this, hence the twanging electric guitar and the nasal vocal delivery. One can see how, when rock 'n' roll first came in, this must have been a tremendous liberation from popular song's disembodied eroticism—here was really physical music, and not just mealy-mouthed physical, but quite clear what it was about—[phallic]. But rock confines sexuality to [the phallus] (and this is why…rock remains indelibly phallo-centric music).[155]

On the contrary disco, insists Dyer, "restores eroticism to the whole of the body and for both sexes, not just confining it to the [phallus]. It leads to the expressive, sinuous movement of disco dancing, not just that mixture of awkwardness and thrust so dismally characteristic of dancing to rock."[156]

It is apparent then that rock music encodes eroticism by reenacting through a syntax of sound-combinations and phrases the processes and sensations of sexual intercourse in males. Even so, we should remember that these sexual cues are more culturally determined than the other deviant qualities of rock, such as rebellion and excess. In other words such meanings, which seem so automatic and universal to us, are really processed and mediated through culture. According to McClary and Walser, "The rhythmic impulses of rock music are as socially constructed as are the contrapuntal intricacies of the Baroque fugue."[157] The physical, sinuous, heavily rhythmic, rapid, bouncy, and raw elements of rock certainly communicate sexuality among those who are conversant with these codes. But an individual who is not familiar with western music or rock music may not be able to readily identify these musical properties with sexuality without inculturation.[158] One reason for this is because rock music not only expresses human sexuality per se, or a culture's understanding of it, but it in turn dictates how it is to be experienced and practiced[159]—impure, crude, self-gratifying, and unrestrained.[160] (Other factors that impede cross-cultural communication have been discussed earlier and would also apply here.)

At the same time it should be emphasized that this can never be a simple matter of recycling reusable symbols that are arbitrarily connected to their referents. What we have here are musical structures that are organically related to the actual sensations of copulation in males. They are adapted to mime and exaggerate male sexuality and potency through metaphors of sound. It is true that movement toward climax alone could denote a variety of other things. But when the pulsating syncopated rhythms—"heavy, hard, and grinding"—are combined with penetrating vibrations, libidinous tonal inflections, and sensual posturing (rock, as any music, makes its impact through a sum of its parts, rather than its components in isolation), it is difficult to deny that there is any more hospitable, inviting, or authentic referent for those signs than sexuality or to deny that such components are entirely incompatible with Christian conversation. Whether sexual codes in rock music are purely cultural or cross-cultural—in a very basic sense as I would argue—it should be clear enough that they convey more than just excitement and passion and are unquestionably inappropriate for Christian expression or witness. As I have argued earlier, and maintain here, music need not be a universal language to convey morality or undergo Christian critique and even condemnation.[161]

Other Forms of Exciting Music

Finally, we should remember that other forms of music such as bluegrass, polka, campmeeting songs, and much praise and worship music are also exciting and create an exciting atmosphere.[162] If rock music simply produced, for example, excitement or energy, then any of the genres mentioned above could conceivably be used by secular rock groups to convey their counter-Christian messages effectively. After all, it would simply be channeling excitement toward a negative purpose. Any such attempt would be counterproductive, to say the least, since excitement is not the only thing that is sought for in rock music. Who could picture Johnny Rotten and the Sex Pistols trying to convey their message of nihilism and lawlessness to the melodious but exciting tune of "I'll Fly Away" (without significant modification)? Why then should we consider it acceptable for Christians to sing of the joy of salvation, which brings order and dignity, to the anarchic beat of punk rock, "a frenzied noise made up of the monotonous screeching sound of guitars played in parallel and drums being flogged mercilessly"?[163]

Based on the evidence, it is apparent that rock music conveys more than the building blocks of emotions. It communicates the very feelings, moods, and ideas that characterize fallen man at his worst. Therefore, reductionistic explanations for the objectionable attributes of rock music remain unconvincing. One would do well to consider this point since from personal experience and research I have found reductionism to be an extremely common tactic for disarming rock critics and justifying rock music. When a defense goes something like this, "Rock music is *just, merely, simply, only...*" beware, a reductive explanation may be forthcoming!

Syncopation

The syncopated rhythms of rock music have been the target of considerable criticism by CCM opponents as the most malignant element of the music.[164] But according to Lawhead,

> Syncopation is merely the accenting of a beat between the regular beats of the rhythm. You might call it misplacing the beat. It works like this: if the regular beat goes 1-2-3-4, syncopating it might make it go 1-and-2-and-3-and-4. Say it to yourself emphasizing the "and," and you will get some idea of what is happening.[165]

Whatever else syncopation is or does, it has been credited as the distinguishing feature of rock music, even in its embryonic stages. Charlie Gillett identifies this rhythmic pattern in the early rock and roll of Bill Haley:

> But the novel feature of Haley's style, its rhythm, was drawn from black music, although in Haley the rhythm dominated the arrangements much more than it did in Negro records. With Haley every other beat was heavily accented by the singers and all the instrumentalists at the expense of the relatively flexible rhythms and complex harmonies of dance music records cut for the black audience.[166]

Haley himself recognized the importance of syncopated rhythms to his music:

I felt that if I could take, say, a Dixieland tune and drop the first and third beats and accentuate the second and fourth, and add a beat the listeners could clap to as well as dance this would be what they were after. From that the rest was easy...take everyday sayings like "Crazy Man Crazy", "See You Later, Alligator", "Shake, Rattle and Roll", and apply what I have just said.[167]

According to Laing, "Syncopated rhythms of this kind accentuate the 'off beat' and in doing so draw the listener into the music to 'supply' the 'missing' first and third beats either mentally or physically, through hand-clapping, nodding or dancing."[168] Consequently, Laing considers syncopation to be essential to dance forms in rock music.[169] Elvis—less analytically than Laing—also placed the responsibility for his hip-related outbursts on the beat, "It's a beat that gets to you. If you like it and you feel it, you can't help but move to it. That's what happens to me. I can't help it."[170]

Generally speaking, CCM lobbyists have attempted to answer complaints about syncopation by pointing out that syncopation is found in many styles of music including classical and religious, which is of course true.[171] Consequently, the strategy is to pull the offensive element (syncopation) out of its rock context and expose its use in other musical genres that find no objections of sensuality from moralists. This explanation, unimpeachable from all outward appearances, falls apart, however, under closer scrutiny. The trouble is that syncopation in general has been successfully defended, rather than its role in rock music.

The problem in rock is not syncopation per se, but a syncopated beat in dominance to the harmony and melody, which it usually overwhelms.[172] To claim that syncopation in rock music is faultless by documenting its existence in other forms that are enjoyed by critics— where it is implemented in different proportions and ways than in rock music—is misleading and unsound. It is the predominance and intensity of the syncopated beat (or non-syncopated beat)[173] in combination with the comparatively negligible harmony and melody that help to give rock its effect.

Here Lawhead correctly explains why syncopation is different in rock than in other forms of music:

> However, since the rhythms of classical music are not as prominent as they are in rock, a listener may not as easily notice when syncopation comes into play. Of course, not all rock is syncopated, but since rock is a music of few elements, the beat is very close to the surface and is easily apprehended. Rock simply relies on this common musical device to perhaps a greater degree than other forms of music.[174]

Although the beat is a major feature of rock, it is not the only element. Rock receives its constitution, identity, and meaning from all its elements, which form the vital context for understanding the function and effect of the individual parts.[175] Consequently, isolating the components of rock music in other unobjectionable genres unscrupulously distances those elements from the environment that defines how they function and affect the listener and in which they must ultimately be judged. It is this crucial point that Miller entirely overlooks when he insists, "It is inconsistent to accept the beat of one style and denounce the beat of the other when the beat is essentially the same."[176]

Miller errs again by resorting to "elevator music" (Muzak) to demonstrate that the beat of rock music is blameless: "Further, 'the beat' of rock is often identical to the beat of softer music played in doctors' offices or department stores."[177] First of all, in most cases the beat of the songs is significantly minimized since Muzak's repertoire consists of popular melodies. Second, a good deal of elevator music is in fact rock, disco, even punk and heavy metal—whatever songs were or are now popular.[178] In the absence of overpowering rhythm, the melodies of some rock songs can be quite inoffensive, as evinced by Muzak. In a similar way, agreeable melodies can be distorted and perverted by adding important stylistic combinations characteristic of rock music.

So then, although syncopation per se is not blameworthy, its special role in the ensemble of rock music—as the phallic backbeat, rhythmic overkill, and primary stimulus for rock-based dancing—makes it an important contributor to the collectively offensive message of rock music. Huey Lewis and the News' single "The Heart of Rock & Roll" captures the meaning of syncopation in rock poetically and convincingly: "When they play their music, ooh that modern music, they like it with a lot of style; but it's still that same old backbeat rhythm that really, really drives 'em wild." Almost as suggestive is this description of syncopation from a review of Kathy Troccoli's *Images* in *Contemporary Christian Music* magazine: "On the first listen *Images* hits like a party record. Sequencers stutter and shake; explosive, violent drums syncopate dangerously off the beat; and untamed guitar solos writhe and snake through dense jungles of reverberation."[179]

Worldview and Music

Before this chapter on music and moral neutrality closes, it is necessary to consider the issue of worldview and music. Music, even when understood correctly as a sign system, is an articulation of a culture's worldview and so resists the concept of moral neutrality. This is because worldview is comprised of a society's values and myths—that is, how it perceives human relationships, emotions, social priorities, behavioral norms, authority, ultimate commitments, truth, self, God, goodness, and morality.[180] Whether a certain worldview, or aspects of it, agree with biblical ideals or not determines whether it is to be affirmed or rejected by Christians. In all societies there will be some values that can be welcomed and others that must be rejected or transformed. Most Christians recognize this and practice some form of resistance or affirmation with more obvious customs and traditions. For example, in America Christians endorse Mother's Day and (most) resist Halloween because they recognize the clear covenantal or anti-covenantal principles operating behind these customs.

Nevertheless, many Christians are unwilling to admit what musicologists, aestheticians, and philosophers have generally come to recognize—namely, that worldview is also expressed in the styles of music and art that a culture embraces.[181] Bruno Nettl discloses that "in each culture music will function to express a particular set of values in a particular way."[182] Elsewhere more powerfully,

> But in the end, the overriding determinant [of the nature of a culture's music] must be the special character of a culture. The way in which people live, relate to each other, see themselves in relation to their natural

and human environment, control energy, and subsist, determine the kind of music they have.[183]

According to David A. Locher, "Style organizes a worldview for a group of people who share certain meanings."[184] Walser adds, "Todorov argues that genres exist because societies collectively choose and codify the acts that correspond most closely to their ideologies. A society's discourses depend upon its linguistic (or musical) raw materials and upon its historically circumscribed ideologies."[185] With specific reference to the baby boomers, secular and Christian, Michael S. Hamilton observes:

> Once this oversized generation [baby boomers] decided that music would be the primary carrier of its symbols and values, music quickly became, in the words of George Steiner, "the new literacy of Western culture." When one chooses a musical style today, one is making a statement about whom one identifies with, what one's values are, and ultimately, who one is. As a result, music has become a divisive and fractionalizing force, Balkanizing Western culture into an ever-expanding array of subcultures—each with its own national anthem.
> ...For better or for worse, the kind of music a church offers increasingly defines the kind of person who will attend, because for this generation music is at the very center of self-understanding. Music for baby boomers is the mediator of emotions, the carrier of dreams, and the marker of social location.[186]

Understandably, then, worldview is especially evident in rock music, as Schultze et al. explain:

> More than any other contemporary cultural form, rock captures the central elements of the romantic spirit: its individuality, freedom, and rebellion, its search for adventure and originality, its exultation of emotion, physicality, and imagination, and its relish of contradictions, extremes, and paradoxes. It stands in sharp contrast to the classical spirit of integration, order, control, and rationality which makes for a stable and staid society.[187]

Romanowski makes the point even more directly,

> Contrary to the beliefs of those in the contemporary gospel music business, musical style is not neutral. Rock music, as well as other styles

CCM artists adopted, was organically wed to the socio-cultural setting in which the music was created and developed.[188]

As case in point, consider the worldview projected by acid rock, a subgenre of rock music and a predecessor of heavy metal. According to Arnett, "Acid rock, played by performers such as Jimi Hendrix, was so named because it was deemed to be an auditory representation of the experience of an acid (LSD) trip, that is, a musical depiction of what it is like to experience the effects of the hallucinogenic drug LSD."[189] It did so by rejecting "distinct chord changes in favor of blending sound much as an artist blends color on a canvas."[190]

Here Chute's earlier objection to the troublesome matrimony of CCM and western culture bears repeating, "as if music can be completely severed from its cultural and social context and suddenly take on meaning not only removed, but contradictory to those contexts."[191] Francis Schaeffer summed it up nicely when he declared, "As the music which came out of the biblical teaching of the Reformation was shaped by that world view, so the world view of modern man shapes modern music."[192]

Keeping in mind the concept of worldview as it relates to musical style not only helps us to understand how music cannot be morally neutral, but will be crucial in understanding the following chapter on rock music and aesthetics.

Endnotes

[1]Harold M. Best, *Music Through the Eyes of Faith* (San Francisco: Harper, 1993), 42, also 15.

[2]*Contemporary Christian Music*, November 1988, 12. Also Angelo De Simone, *Christian Rock: Friend or Foe* (New Haven: Selah Production Agency, 1993), 55, 84, 93.

[3]For a more complete definition of ethnomusicology consult Bruno Nettl, *The Study of Ethnomusicology: Twenty-Nine Issues and Concepts* (Urbana, IL: University of Illinois Press, 1983), 4ff.

[4]Cf. Steve Miller, *The Contemporary Christian Music Debate: Worldly Compromise or Agent of Renewal?* (Wheaton, IL: Tyndale House, 1993), 25-26; J. Nathan Corbitt, *The Sound of Harvest: Music's Mission in Church and Culture* (Grand Rapids: Baker Books, 1998), 33, 121.

[5]Tom Manoff, *Music: A Living Language* (New York: W. W. Norton & Company, 1982), 105. I wish to qualify my use of the word "language" in this book when referring to music with the caveat that there are critical differences between spoken language and musical expression. Nevertheless, I have used "language" for lack of a more convenient term and because of its standardization in musical discussions. For the differences between music and language see Stephen Davies, *Musical Meaning and Expression* (Ithaca, NY: Cornell University Press, 1994), 1-49; William Edgar, *Taking Note of Music* (London: Third Way Books, 1986), 58-64.

[6]John Hospers, "Aesthetics, Problems of," in *The Encyclopedia of Philosophy*, ed. Paul Edwards (New York: The Macmillan Company & The Free Press, 1967), 47. In much the same way Peter Kivy explains that "sadness is an expressive property of the music which the listener recognizes in it, much as I might recognize sadness as the quality of a dog's countenance or even of an abstract configuration of lines." *Music Alone: Philosophical Reflections on the Purely Musical Experience* (Ithaca, NY: Cornell University Press, 1990), 146.

[7]Cf. Jeremy S. Begbie, *Voicing Creation's Praise: Toward a Theology of the Arts* (Edinburgh: T. & T. Clark, 1991), 210.

[8]Although Corbitt, and Howard and Streck maintain that music is not inherently bad or good, they accept the idea that certain elements of a style can convey evil within the confines of a culture-specific musical discourse. Corbitt, however, fails to recognize any such elements in rock music. Corbitt, *Sound of Harvest*, 121, 153, 155, 254, 280-81, 282, 341; Jay R. Howard and John M. Streck, *Apostles of Rock: The Splintered World of Contemporary Christian Music* (Lexington, KY: The University Press of Kentucky, 1999), 18, 19.

[9]A denial of universals, however, is important to CCM in that it leads to the conclusion that musical cues are entirely arbitrary and thus potentially reassignable like letters and words in human language. This issue will be dealt with later in the chapter and in Appendix C.

[10]Miller, *Christian Music Debate*, 26.

[11]Steve Lawhead, *Rock of This Age: Real and Imagined Dangers of Rock Music* (Downers Grove, IL: Inter-Varsity, 1987), 59.

[12]See Barbara Ehrenreich, Elizabeth Hess, and Gloria Jacobs, "Beatlemania: Girls Just Want to Have Fun," in *The Adoring Audience: Fan Culture and Popular Media*, ed. Lisa A. Lewis (London: Routledge, 1992), 84-106.

[13]Cf. Emery Schubert, "Enjoyment of Negative Emotions in Music: An Associative Network Explanation," *Psychology of Music* 24, no. 1 (1996): 26; Gina Arnold, *Kiss This: Punk in the Present Tense* (New York: St. Martin's Griffin, 1997), 47, 120; Stephen C. Pepper, "Aesthetic Design," in *Introductory Readings in Aesthetics*, ed. John Hospers (New York: The Free Press, 1969), 61-66. In the case of Elvis Presley, Lawhead does recognize the

possibility of desensitization. *Rock Reconsidered: A Christian Looks at Contemporary Music* (Downers Grove, IL: Inter-Varsity, 1981), 51.

[14]Bernice Martin, "The Sacralization of Disorder: Symbolism in Rock Music," *Sociological Analysis* 40, no. 2 (1979): 119.

[15]Simon Reynolds, *Blissed Out: The Raptures of Rock* (London: Serpent's Tail, 1990), 60.

[16]Nathan Rubin, *Rock and Roll: Art and Anti-Art* (Dubuque, IA: Kendall/Hunt Publishing Co., 1993), 146. Similarly, Martin notes: "The sexual aggressiveness of Presley in the 1950s looks strangely 'classical' and indirect if one compares it with say Jim Morrison in the sixties or Alice Cooper or David Bowie in the seventies." "The Sacralization of Disorder," 119.

[17]Jeffrey Jensen Arnett, *Metalheads: Heavy Metal Music and Adolescent Alienation* (Boulder, CO: WestviewPress, 1996), 57-58. See also Philip Gordon, "Review of Tipper Gore's *Raising PG Kids in an X-Rated Society* and *Dee Snider's Teenage Survival Guide*," *Popular Music* 8, no. 1 (January 1989): 120.

[18]Joe Stuessy, *Rock and Roll: Its History and Stylistic Development* (Englewood Cliffs, NJ: Prentice Hall, 1990), 43.

[19]Ibid., 389.

[20]Cf. Robert Walser, *Running with the Devil: Power, Gender, and Madness in Heavy Metal Music* (Hanover, NH: Wesleyan University Press, 1993), 29-30, 31, 33.

[21]Sheila Whiteley, *Sexing the Groove: Popular Music and Gender* (New York: Routledge, 1997), xxxii. See also Simon Frith, "Towards an Aesthetic of Popular Music," in *Music and Society: The Politics of Composition, Performance, and Reception*, ed. Richard Leppert and Susan McClary (Cambridge: Cambridge University Press, 1987), 137. Simon Frith and Angela McRobbie, "Rock and Sexuality," in *On Record: Rock, Pop, and the Written Word*, ed. Simon Frith and Andrew Goodwin (New York: Pantheon Books, 1990), 386.

[22]Walser, *Running with the Devil*, 21. See also p. 39.

[23]Ibid., 27. See also Philip Tagg, "Musicology and the Semiotics of Popular Music," *Semiotica* 66 (1987): 286.

[24]Susan McClary, *Feminine Endings: Music, Gender, and Sexuality* (Minneapolis: University of Minnesota Press, 1991), 25.

[25]Ibid., 21.

[26]Walser, *Running with the Devil*, 28.

[27]Ibid., 29.

[28]Ibid., 33. Cf. Frith, "Towards an Aesthetic of Popular Music," 139-39.

[29]Dave Laing, *One Chord Wonders: Power and Meaning in Punk Rock* (Philadelphia: Open University Press, 1985), xii-xiii.

[30]McClary, *Feminine Endings*, 8, 102; Walser, *Running with the Devil*, 21, 33, 55; Robert Walser, "Bon Jovi's Alloy: Discursive Fusion in Top 40 Pop

Music," *OneTwoThreeFour 7* (Winter 1989): 7, 8, 17; Deena Weinstein, *Heavy Metal: A Cultural Sociology* (New York: Lexington Books, 1991), 53-54.

[31]Weinstein, *Heavy Metal*, 53-54.

[32]Robert H. Mitchell, *I Don't Like That Music* (Carol Stream, IL: Hope Publishing Co., 1993), 65.

[33]Howard and Streck, *Apostles of Rock*, 18, also p. 17.

[34]Walser, *Running with the Devil*, 55. He makes much the same appeal in his earlier article. "Bon Jovi," 17.

[35]Walser also makes no attempt to reconcile other deviant components of Stryper's heavy metal with the Bible—such as their unmistakable androgyny and phallic rock iconography.

[36]Lester Bangs, "Heavy Metal," in *The Rolling Stone Illustrated History of Rock & Roll: The Definitive History of the Most Important Artists and Their Music*, ed. Anthony De Curtis and James Henke (New York: Random House, 1992), 459-63. See also E. Ann Kaplan, *Rocking Around the Clock: Music Television, Postmodernism, and Consumer Culture* (New York: Methuen, 1987), 61.

[37]Jon Pareles, "Metallica Defies Heavy Metal Stereotypes," *Minneapolis Star Tribune*, 13 July 1988, 12 Ew.

[38]George H. Lewis, "Patterns of Meaning and Choice: Taste Cultures in Popular Music," in *Popular Music and Communication*, ed. James Lull (Beverly Hills, CA: Sage Publications, 1987), 206. See James Lull, "Listener's Communicative Uses of Popular Music," in *Popular Music and Communication*, ed. James Lull (Beverly Hills, CA: Sage Publications, 1987), 152.

[39]Charles M. Young, "Heavy Metal: In Defense of Dirtbags and Worthless Puds," *Musician*, September 1984, 42.

[40]Manoff, *Living Language*, 408.

[41]Stuessy, *Rock and Roll*, 302.

[42]Devlin Donaldson, "Barnabas: Forging Musical Horizons," *Contemporary Christian Music*, October 1998, 69. The striking contradiction here cannot be overlooked. At least one CCM proponent sees these behavior qualities as contrary to Christian maturity and holiness: "Are we not to rid ourselves of all bitterness, rage and anger, brawling and slander, along with every form of malice? Yes, yes, yes" (Charlie Peacock, *At the Crossroads: An Insider's Look at the Past, Present, and Future of Contemporary Christian Music* [Nashville: Broadman & Holman, 1999], 38). How, then, can this be reconciled with the "unbridled musical aggression" and "attitudes of anger, defiance, and aggression" characteristic of heavy metal?

[43]Scott Herrin, "Disciple Wrestling Match," *HM Electronic Magazine*, no. 78 (July/August 1999). Document available on the World Wide Web at http://www.christianmusic.org/cmp/hmmag/issue78/78ConcertReviews.htm.

[44]Val Sutton, "Disciple," *HM Electronic Magazine*, no. 78 (July/August 1999). Document available on the World Wide Web at http://www.christianmusic. org/cmp/hmmag/issue78/78Disciple.htm.

[45]Arnett, *Metalheads*, 47. See also p. 10.

[46]Ibid., 48.

[47]Ibid., 55. According to Menconi, "Adolescents struggle with feelings of anger, rebellion, sexuality, powerlessness, frustration, lack of self-worth, and depression." Al Menconi and Dave Hart, *Staying in Tune: A Sane Response to Your Child's Music* (Cincinnati, OH: The Standard Publishing Co., 1996), 114.

[48]Arnett, *Metalheads*, 66.

[49]Ibid. See also p. 57.

[50]Ibid., 19. Similar conclusions were reached by James Lull's study of new wave listeners: "College students reported that 'new wave' rock music was useful to them when they were in the mood to be 'rowdy, crazy, radical, energetic, hyped up, when they felt like fooling around, when they wanted to dance or when they were drunk or stoned.'" "Listener's Communicative Uses," 151.
Further, the connection between musical style and personality or disposition may not be accidental. The experiments of David Rawlings et al. suggest that "individuals may like sounds or pieces of music because of their social meaning. Harsh, discordant music, and the sounds of which it is typically comprised, may come to represent for certain groups a breaking from convention and an aggressive, radical and rule-defying approach to life. Indirect support for this view may be obtained by observing the names of musical pieces or groups, or by reading the lyrics of songs." "Toughmindedness and Preference for Musical Excerpts, Categories and Triads," *Psychology of Music* 23, no. 1 (1995): 63-80.

[51]Arnett, *Metalheads*, 74.

[52]Ibid., 146. It should be carefully noted that this evidence does not claim that heavy metal necessarily creates an angry mood in the listener, only that it is conducive to it. A proper understanding of music as metaphor will reject ideas that musical styles cause, without mediation, certain types of behavior. Therefore I find no conflict between the conclusions presented here and those of William Neil Gowensmith and Larry J. Bloom, who found that heavy metal did not "cause listeners to report higher levels of anger than would be expected in individuals listening to other musical styles." "The Effects of Heavy Metal Music on Arousal and Anger," *Journal of Music Therapy* 34, no. 1 (1997): 42.

[53]On the World Wide Web at http://www.cmo.com/cmo/cmo/data/bduncan. htm.

[54]Arnett, *Metalheads*, 19, 35, 146; "Adolescents and Heavy Metal Music: From the Mouths of Metalheads," *Youth & Society* 23, no. 1 (September 1991): 83, 93-94.

[55]Arnett, "Adolescents and Heavy Metal," 93-94.

[56]Arnett, *Metalheads*, 81.

[57]Ibid., 19, 35-36, 83; Arnett, "Adolescents and Heavy Metal," 84.

[58]Carol Tavris, "Anger Defused," *Psychology Today*, November 1982, 25-35; Leonard Berkowitz, "The Case for Bottling Up Rage," *Psychology Today*, July 1973, 24-31; Martin Bobgan and Deidre Bobgan, *PsychoHeresy: The Psychological Seduction of Christianity* (Santa Barbara, CA: Eastgate, 1987), 68-70. In a similar example of 'robbing Peter to pay Paul,' David Pass suggests that in a fallen world God uses music as a purgational agent to provide "a safe outlet for humanity's aggressive impulses." *Music and the Church* (Nashville: Broadman Press, 1989), 28.

[59]Arnett, "Adolescents and Heavy Metal," 83-84. See also Arnett, *Metalheads*, 56.

[60]Walser, *Running with the Devil*, 9.

[61]Ibid., 42.

[62]Chris Gill, "Dialing for Distortion: Sound Advice from 10 Top Producers," *Guitar Player*, October 1992, 86.

[63]Ibid.

[64]Ibid., 93. See also pp. 86, 92, and Rubin, *Rock and Roll*, 146.

[65]Anne Fadiman, "Heavy Metal Mania," *Life*, December 1984, 103; Malcolm Dome and Mick Wall, "World View: Metal Crusade in Global Gear," *Billboard*, 27 April 1985, HM-12.

[66]Walser's choice of benign terminology is evident throughout his book: pp. 2, 45, 49, 55, etc.

[67]Walser, *Running with the Devil*, 54.

[68]Ibid., 167.

[69]Ibid., 119.

[70]Ibid., 127. See also pp. 68, 162.

[71]Patrick Kavanaugh, *The Music of Angels: A Listener's Guide to Sacred Music from Chant to Christian Rock* (Chicago: Loyola Press, 1999), 257. Kavanaugh does not, however, consider these to be negative traits.

[72]Best, *Music*, 124.

[73]Corbitt, *Sound of Harvest*, 32. Contra De Simone (pp. 164-66), CCM fans *do* in fact deliriously rush the stage and participate in power gestures such as fist thrusts. Both occurred during the 30th Annual Dove Awards, when the Newsboys took the platform, and have been witnessed elsewhere by spectators like Corbitt.

[74]Walser, *Running with the Devil*, 52.

[75]Cf. McClary, *Feminine Endings*, 161; Best, *Music*, 60. For greater possibilities of cross-cultural interpretation in dance see Judith Lynne Hanna, *Dance,*

Sex, and Gender: Signs of Identity, Dominance, Defiance, and Desire (Chicago: University of Chicago Press, 1988), 243, 245.

[76]Sheila Whiteley, "Little Red Rooster v. the Honky Tonk Woman: Mick Jagger, Sexuality, Style and Image," in *Sexing the Groove: Popular Music and Gender*, ed. Sheila Whiteley (New York: Routledge, 1997), 76.

[77]Davies, *Musical Meaning and Expression*, 206, cf. 289.

[78]Contra Laing, *One Chord Wonders*, xii.

[79]Walser, *Running with the Devil*, 55.

[80]Ibid., 15.

[81]William D. Romanowski, "Roll Over Beethoven, Tell Martin Luther the News: American Evangelicals and Rock Music," *Journal of American Culture* 15, no. 3 (Fall 1992): 83; Carol Flake, *Redemptorama: Culture, Politics, and the New Evangelicalism* (New York: Penguin Books, 1984), 11, 22, 184.

[82]Contra Best, *Music*, 46, 54-55.

[83]Walser, *Running with the Devil*, 40-41.

[84]Simon Frith, *Sound Effects: Youth, Leisure, and the Politics of Rock 'n' Roll* (New York: Pantheon Books, 1978), 14.

[85]Quentin J. Schultze et al., *Dancing in the Dark: Youth, Popular Culture, and the Electronic Media* (Grand Rapids: Eerdmans Publishing Co., 1991), 160.

[86]Ibid., 159.

[87]Best, *Music*, 55.

[88]Davies, *Musical Meaning and Expression*, 2.

[89]Christopher John Farley, "Reborn to Be Wild," *Time*, 22 January 1996, 64.

[90]Walser, *Running with the Devil*, 41.

[91]James Chute, "What Hath Pop Wrought in Jesus' Name?" *The Milwaukee Journal*, 17 August 1986, 8E.

[92]Ibid.

[93]Flake, *Redemptorama*, 184.

[94]Michael McCall, "Smitty Gets Gritty," *Contemporary Christian Magazine*, June 1986, 19.

[95]Walser, *Running with the Devil*, xiv. See also p. 26.

[96]Bruce K. Friesen and Warren Helfrich, "Social Justice and Sexism for Adolescents: A Content Analysis of Lyrical Themes and Gender Presentations in Canadian Heavy Metal Music, 1985-1991," in *Youth Culture: Identity in a Postmodern World*, ed. Jonathan S. Epstein (Malden, MA: Blackwell Publishers, 1998), 265.

[97]Lorraine E. Prinsky and Jill Leslie Rosenbaum, "'Leer-Ics' or Lyrics: Teenage Impression of Rock 'n' Roll," *Youth & Society* 18, no. 4 (June 1987): 387.

[98]Ibid. Cf. Peacock, *At the Crossroads*, 125.

[99]Prinsky and Rosenbaum, "Leer-Ics," 387. Cf. Schultze et al., *Dancing in the Dark*, 161.

[100]John Podhoretz, "Metallic Rock That's Designed to Shock," *U.S. News & World Report*, 7 September 1987, 51. Cf. Arnett, *Metalheads*, 10.

[101]Susan McClary and Robert Walser, "Start Making Sense! Musicology Wrestles with Rock," in *On Record: Rock, Pop, and the Written Word*, ed. Simon Frith and Andrew Goodwin (New York: Pantheon, 1990), 285-86.

[102]Chute, "What Hath Pop Wrought?" 8E. See also Randall Balmer, "Hymns on MTV," *Christianity Today*, 15 November 1999, 36.

[103]Donald Paul Ellsworth, *Christian Music in Contemporary Witness: Historical Antecedents and Contemporary Practices* (Grand Rapids: Baker Book House, 1979), 139-40.

[104]McClary and Walser, "Start Making Sense," 285.

[105]Ibid., 286.

[106]Walser, *Running with the Devil*, 33.

[107]Ibid., 150. See also p.144.

[108]On the World Wide Web at http://www.angelfire.com/nt/nl/lyrics.html.

[109]Prinsky and Rosenbaum, "Leer-Ics," 387. See also pp. 388-89, 391.

[110]Roger Jon Desmond, "Adolescents and Music Lyrics: Implications of a Cognitive Perspective," *Communication Quarterly* 35, no. 3 (Summer 1987): 278.

[111]Arnett, *Metalheads*, 60-61.

[112]Chute, "What Hath Pop Wrought?" 8E; Ellsworth, *Christian Music in Contemporary Witness*, 130.

[113]Miller, *Christian Music Debate*, 26. For another example see Corbitt, *Sound of Harvest*, 275.

[114]Menconi and Hart, *Staying in Tune*, 164-65. Cf. Dean Smallwood, "Christian Rockers All Set to Jam in Jesus' Name," *Huntsville Times*, 20 September 1998, G5.

[115]Alfred Sendrey, *Music in Ancient Israel* (New York: Philosophical Library, 1969), 193. The translation of *1QH* 18:23 is mine.

[116]Ibid.

[117]Plato *The Republic* 3.401D in *The Loeb Classical Library*.

[118]Aristotle *Politics* 8.5.6 in *The Loeb Classical Library*.

[119]Aristotle *Politics* 8.5.9 in *The Loeb Classical Library*. We should keep in mind, however, that not all Greeks subscribed to such views. For example Philodemus of Gadara went in the opposite direction, claiming that music apart from the words was unable to affect the emotions. Hospers, "Aesthetics," 21.

[120]Peter Wicke, *Rock Music: Culture, Aesthetics and Sociology*, trans. Rachel Fogg (Cambridge, England: Cambridge University Press, 1990), 92.

[121]William J. Schafer, *Rock Music: Where It's Been, What It Means, Where It's Going* (Minneapolis: Augsburg Publishing House, 1972), 13.

[122]Schafer, *Rock Music*, 25.

[123]Leonard B. Meyer, *Emotion and Meaning in Music* (Chicago: University of Chicago Press, 1956), 6-7.

[124]Clyde S. Kilby, *Christianity and Aesthetics*, IVP Series in Contemporary Christian Thought, vol. 3 (Chicago: Inter-Varsity Press, 1961), 25-26.

[125]Stuessy, *Rock and Roll*, 18. Cf. Corbitt, *Sound of Harvest*, 54, 160.

[126]Stuessy, *Rock and Roll*, 394.

[127]Charles Brown, *The Art of Rock and Roll* (Englewood Cliffs, NJ: Prentice-Hall, 1983), 7.

[128]William Graebner, "The Erotic and Destructive in 1980s Rock: A Theoretical and Historical Analysis," *Tracking: Popular Music Studies* 1, no. 2 (1988): 8-20.

[129]Passion, like excitement, is an innocent reductive quality that can be directed at a wide range of objects.

[130]*Hit Parader*, September 1979; quoted in John Blanchard, Peter Anderson, and Derek Cleave, *Pop Goes the Gospel* (Welwyn, England: Evangelical Press, 1983), 32.

[131]*Circus*, 31.1.76; quoted in John Blanchard, Peter Anderson, and Derek Cleave, *Pop Goes the Gospel: Rock in the Church*, enlarged and revised (Darlington, England: Evangelical Press, 1989), 41.

[132]David A. Noebel, *Christian Rock: A Stratagem of Mephistopheles* (Manitou Springs, CO: Summit Ministries, n.d.), 6.

[133]Blanchard, Anderson, and Cleave, *Pop Goes the Gospel* (rev. ed.), 44.

[134]Elianne Halbersberg, *Heavy Metal* (Cresskill, NJ: Sharon Publications, 1985), 32.

[135]Stan Hawkins, "The Pet Shop Boys: Musicology, Masculinity and Banality," in *Sexing the Groove: Popular Music and Gender*, ed. Sheila Whiteley (New York: Routledge, 1997), 124.

[136]Yet the most common defense for such offensive material is that it merely serves as entertainment or increases record sales and the group's popularity. Cf. Arnett, *Metalheads*, 60-61; "Adolescents and Heavy Metal," 91. See also Menconi and Hart, *Staying in Tune*, 82-87.

[137]Frith and McRobbie, "Rock and Sexuality," 371.

[138]Martin, "The Sacralization of Disorder," 121.

[139]Norma Coates, "(R)Evolution Now? Rock and the Political Potential of Gender," in *Sexing the Groove: Popular Music and Gender*, ed. Sheila Whiteley (New York: Routledge, 1997), 50.

[140]Schultze et al., *Dancing in the Dark*, 150.

[141]Allan Bloom, *The Closing of the American Mind* (New York: Simon and Schuster, 1987), 73.

[142]Ibid.

[143]McClary, *Feminine Endings*, 8.

[144]Nancy J. Holland, "Purple Passion: Images of Female Desire in 'When Doves Cry,'" *Cultural Critique* 10 (Fall 1988): 96; Iain Chambers, "Popular Culture, Popular Knowledge," *OneTwoThreeFour* 2 (Summer 1985): 42.

[145]Frith, *Sound Effects*, 227. Cf. Walser, *Running with the Devil*, 76.

[146]Holland, "Purple Passion," 93. See also pp. 94, 98.

[147]Whiteley, "Red Rooster," 72. See also p. 74.

[148]McClary, *Feminine Endings*, 154.

[149]Walser, *Running with the Devil*, 49.

[150]Frith and McRobbie, "Rock and Sexuality," 374.

[151]Ibid., 388.

[152]Frith, *Sound Effects*, 240.

[153]Nik Cohn, *Rock from the Beginning* (New York: Stein and Day Publishers, 1969), 9.

[154]Sheila Whiteley, "Seduced by the Sign: An Analysis of the Textual Links Between Sound and Image in Pop Videos," in *Sexing the Groove: Popular Music and Gender*, ed. Sheila Whiteley (New York: Routledge, 1997), 265.

[155]Richard Dyer, "In Defense of Disco," in *On Record: Rock, Pop, and the Written Word*, ed. Simon Frith and Andrew Goodwin (New York: Pantheon Books, 1990), 414-15. Cf. Chambers, "Popular Culture," 148-49. For the percussive use of instruments in rock music see p. 22.

[156]Dyer, "Defense of Disco," 415.

[157]McClary and Walser, "Start Making Sense," 289. Cf. Frith and McRobbie, "Rock and Sexuality," 373.

[158]Frith and McRobbie, "Rock and Sexuality," 386.

[159]Simon Frith, "Afterthoughts," in *On Record: Rock, Pop, and the Written Word*, ed. Simon Frith and Andrew Goodwin (New York: Pantheon Books, 1990), 421; McClary, *Feminine Endings*, 53-54. Cf. Frith and McRobbie, "Rock and Sexuality," 388.

[160]Cf. Bloom, *Closing of the American Mind*, 73.

[161]It should be noted that rock music is not the only form of music that expresses sexuality. In *Feminine Endings* McClary makes a case for sexual representations in classical music, much of which is believable (pp. 37, 54, 57). Classical music has a wide range of expression, which in some composers included metaphors of sexuality. On the other hand, her feminist critique of classical music is sometimes guilty of over reading the music and intentions of the composers. The results are often avant-garde and clearly Freudian/oedipal (despite her denial, p. 68). At times they are simply absurd (pp. 163-64).

[162]It would also not be an exaggeration to claim that these styles (especially bluegrass) contain elements of passion, urgency, and tension.

[163]Wicke, *Rock Music*, 141-42.

[164]Janet LaRene, "Anti Rock and Roll Crusade," in *Twenty-Minute Fandangos and Forever Changes: A Rock Bazaar*, ed. Jonathan Eisen (New York: Ran-

dom House, 1971), 89, 90; Kimberly Smith and Lee Smith, *Oh, Be Careful Little Ears: Contemporary Christian Music...Is That in The Bible?* (Mukilteo, WA: Wine Press, 1997), 39-49.

[165]Lawhead, *Rock of This Age*, 54.

[166]Charlie Gillett, *The Sound of the City: The Rise of Rock and Roll*, rev. ed. (New York: Pantheon Books, 1983), 14.

[167]Ibid., 24.

[168]Laing, *One Chord Wonders*, 61.

[169]Ibid.

[170]Steve Turner, *Hungry for Heaven: Rock and Roll and the Search for Redemption* (London: Kingsway Publications, 1988), 35.

[171]Miller, *Christian Music Debate*, 27; Lawhead, *Rock Reconsidered*, 62; De Simone, *Christian Rock*, 118-21.

[172]Kimberly and Lee Smith, whose treatment of syncopation is one of the most nuanced and balanced of any CCM opponent, add that syncopation is misused (i.e., becomes unnatural) when it conflicts with the melody rather than complementing it. They list ragtime, flamenco, polka, and mazurka as types of music that sometimes use syncopation to complement the melody. *Oh, Be Careful Little Ears*, 44-45, 66.

[173]A non-syncopated or monad beat is used in conjunction with the dyad or syncopated beat in punk rock, with the non-syncopated rhythms (on the bass) usually dwarfing the syncopated (on the drums). Laing, *One Chord Wonders*, 61-62, 63.

[174]Lawhead, *Rock Reconsidered*, 62.

[175]Cf. Edgar, *Taking Note of Music*, 93.

[176]Miller, *Christian Music Debate*, 27.

[177]Ibid.

[178]Frith, *Sound Effects*, 270; Brown, *Rock and Roll*, 4.

[179]Mark Eischer, *"Images* Kathy Troccoli," *Contemporary Christian Music*, December 1986, 32. It is necessary to ask how this type of description could possibly appeal to the renewed spiritual nature of a Christian.

[180]Cf. Calvin M. Johansson, *Discipling Music Ministry: Twenty-First Century Directions* (Peabody, MA: Hendrickson, 1992), 31. Johansson's treatment of worldview in chapter four of the same book is highly recommended.

[181]Nettl, *Ethnomusicology*, 150, 207, 208, 212, 243; Dane L. Harwood, "Universals in Music: A Perspective from Cognitive Psychology," *Ethnomusicology* 20, no. 3 (September 1976): 530-31; Edgar, *Taking Note of Music*, 75, 76-77, 83; Frith, "Towards an Aesthetic of Popular Music," 139-40; Walser, "Bon Jovi," 8; McClary, *Feminine Endings*, 8; Corbitt, *Sound of Harvest*, 15, 33, 190, 234-35.

[182]Nettl, *Ethnomusicology*, 159.

[183]Ibid., 240.

[184]David A. Locher, "The Industrial Identity Crisis: The Failure of a Newly Forming Subculture to Identify Itself," in *Youth Culture: Identity in a Postmodern World*, ed. Jonathan S. Epstein (Malden, MA: Blackwell Publishers, 1998), 100. See George H. Lewis, "Popular Music: Symbolic Resource and Transformer of Meaning in Society," *International Review of the Aesthetics and Sociology of Music* 13, no. 2 (December 1982): 184; Lewis, "Patterns of Meaning," 201.

[185]Walser, *Running with the Devil*, 29.

[186]Michael S. Hamilton, "The Triumph of the Praise Songs: How Guitars Beat Out the Organ in the Worship Wars," *Christianity Today*, 12 July 1999, 30.

[187]Schultze et al., *Dancing in the Dark*, 164.

[188]Romanowski, "Roll Over Beethoven," 84.

[189]Arnett, *Metalheads*, 43. Cf. Menconi "Electronic instruments gave artists the ability to simulate the hazy confusion of their latest psychedelic drug trips." De Simone, however, merely complains that the "lyrics are suggestive of a psychedelic experience." Menconi and Hart, *Staying in Tune*, 56; De Simone, *Christian Rock*, 35.

[190]Robert P. Snow, "Youth, Rock 'n' Roll, and Electronic Media," *Youth & Society* 18, no. 4 (June 1987): 340-41.

[191]Chute, "What Hath Pop Wrought?" 8E.

[192]Francis A. Schaeffer, *How Should We Then Live? The Rise and Decline of Western Thought and Culture* (Old Tappan, NJ: Fleming H. Revell Co., 1976), 193. By 'music of the Reformation' Schaeffer refers specifically to Bach and his penchant for resolution.

5

Aesthetics, Music, and Morality

Introduction

IN THIS CHAPTER WE will address the question of whether rock music as a style can be criticized from an aesthetic point of view—aesthetics being the branch of philosophy that deals with the nature of beauty. That is, is rock music simply bad music that violates proper standards of musical composition? Is it crude, cheap, vulgar, and artistically inferior, as rock opponents (secular and Christian) allege?

CCM loyalists respond to such criticisms by admonishing disputants to refrain from judging styles that they dislike since they are outside the circle of those who enjoy them. Good music is considered to be simply music that creates a heightened state of being in the individual, not music that conforms to the stylistic canons of "experts" or moralists. In other words, there may be good or bad songs within a style, but there is no such thing as a bad style of music. Therefore, they feel that rock music (or any style) is perfectly legitimate for Christian amalgamation, as long as it remains within its sphere of function.

The worthiness of every type of music is evident in the definition of gospel music constructed by the Gospel Music Association: "Gospel music is music in any style whose lyric is substantially based upon historically orthodox Christian truth...."[1] Further, Brad Davis (without a thimble of support) asserts:

> Good music is music that serves its function, whether that be worship, entertainment or relaxation, without jeopardizing our relationship with God. God created Jewish temple music, just as he did Gregorian chants, Genevan tunes, oratorios, string quartets, opera, jazz, swing, be-bop, motown, rock, pop, funk, rap and who knows what's to come. He didn't create any music to be inherently bad music; and contrary to popular belief, no music is the Devil's music.[2]

A similar appeal is made by Steve Phifer, with *preference* as the key:

> The Bible says nothing about the style of music God likes. The Scriptures were written for all ages of people, eras of history, and cultures. Within a given culture, people's preferences make some styles appropriate and others ineffective or even offensive. Change the culture, and the styles change. As citizens of a higher kingdom, we cannot let our particular cultural corner of the earth condition us to think that our favorite music is the only music God likes. Personal preferences are natural and harmless unless we elevate them to the level of divine truth.
>
> God is more eclectic in His musical tastes than any human could possibly be. When it conforms to His revealed preferences of content and motivation, He enjoys all the music all God's children make in all the world. When we present music to him in the ways he prefers, God takes joy in it even if others take offense. We must respect the variety of music in the church, even if we don't enjoy it.[3]

More sustained and sophisticated aesthetic positions have been submitted by Lawhead, Miller, Corbitt, and Best. Something of their aesthetic philosophy can be discerned in the following statements. According to Lawhead, "Clearly, an entire style of music cannot be labeled good or bad; only individual pieces of music can be judged."[4] Likewise Miller, "A style should be judged only within the context of its intended function by the people for whom it was designed," and, "Truly good music must be judged within a form by those who appreciate the form, not by those from without who neither understand nor enjoy the style."[5] From Corbitt's perspective, "Our aesthetic standards of 'good and bad' (excellence) are culturally determined. Within every culture, and within each style of music, there are evaluative standards of the 'best.'"[6] Lastly, Best opines,

> The seeking out of quality must take place within musical categories, not between them. In the creational model of contrasting kinds, one does not judge the aesthetic quality of a cactus by talking about an orchid; in the narrower sense of species and species, pine trees and eucalyptus trees cannot be similarly compared. It makes sense, then, to apply these analogies to musical evaluation.[7] (Italics original.)

In effect, they are purporting that apples can only rightly be compared with other apples and not with oranges—and this by one who appreciates apples. This is similar to Aristotle's understanding of aesthetics within genre. Aristotle felt that literary genres should be examined for features within them that produce enjoyment. After standards of judgment have been developed for a genre, individual works within the genre can be evaluated by them.[8]

The following response will not be concerned with traditional aesthetic standards such as unity, complexity, variation, intensity, or uniqueness,[9] but with larger questions of morality and aesthetics, namely how aesthetics relates to the image of God in man and the Adamic nature. It will deal with questions raised, either directly or indirectly, by the CCM position on aesthetics. For example, can Christians really be forbidden to judge a style of music or art form in itself, as CCM advocates exhort? And, are we to assume that in the fall of man his sense of beauty and taste were somehow exempt from corruption?

Theological Problems

Although CCM advocates seem to have a solid case for evaluating music on the basis of preference and genre—rather than by some undefined universals of music—they have actually lapsed into serious doctrinal error. By claiming that "truly good music must be judged within a form by those who appreciate the form, not by those from without who neither understand nor enjoy the style,"[10] they end up making the human consciousness the ultimate criterion for judging music. In an unfortunate regress to secular aesthetic (and ethical) standards, CCM aestheticians essentially admit that the measure for what is good or bad in music is found within man himself, who assigns it value based on its ability to give pleasure. Human autonomy—that is, the understanding that the human moral consciousness is the final arbiter or point of reference (whether collectively or individually) in matters such as aesthetics, ethics, religion, and philosophy—is the fundamental error of modernity in that it finds its Archimedean point within itself.[11] Yet, it is to this autonomous system that CCM's aesthetic theory also subscribes. We, however, must never look within man or some principle in the universe to determine right and wrong in any matter. Rather, we must go outside of self to a transcendent God who regulates all aspects of our lives, including the exercise of our intellect, emotions, and will in all cultural spheres, even aesthetics.[12] Our ultimate point of reference must never exist within the fluctuations of self, society, or even the universe, but in God and his inscripturated revelation.[13]

Aesthetic Standards

CCM proponents have claimed repeatedly that the Bible does not prescribe standards of music, with the exception that music must be played skillfully and be appropriate to its setting and function. It may be true that the Bible does not impose musical standards in a systematic form, but this does not indicate that musical and aesthetic standards cannot be gleaned from Scripture. First, the Bible's coverage of major doctrines, such as the Godhead, is far from systematic in that it distributes its teachings in various places, literary forms, and contexts.

Second, the key to musical aesthetics does not always appear in musical texts, but in those passages that speak of attributes that comprise the image of God in man. The very ability of man to appreciate and evaluate beauty is a glorious feature of the divine image that he possesses. The ability to reason from general to specific, to conceive ideas, and to appreciate beauty are not found in even the highest animal forms, but are conspicuously characteristic of the image of God in man.[14] Further, we should remember that because these attributes of God reflect the same in us, in a finite and derived manner, we must be dependent on God for understanding their proper use. Only God is self-sufficient and does not need to go outside of himself for standards of right and wrong. Man, however, is a creature, not autonomous; his knowledge is derived and analogical;[15] he must think the thoughts of God after him and be dependent on God's revelation[16]—this being the case even before Adam's fall.

Since man's aesthetic endowment is an attribute of God, not only does it obligate him to seek his aesthetic standards from God, but it also minimizes relativism and uncertainty in the aesthetic enterprise.[17] God is absolute, not relative. He creates things for a purpose, according to his divine counsel and wisdom. He has instituted the arts and music within human culture, not to be developed according to fluctuating human passions, but analogically as a covenantal expression of his glorious nature. As Edgar puts it, "Our art is offered up to God in covenant response."[18] Divine attributes such as righteousness, love, holiness, purity, majesty, order, reason, harmony, balance, and goodness should govern our evaluation and production of music. It is undeniable that variety and creativity are characteristics of God; yet whatever variety and creativity we exercise in the arts, our workmanship must reflect divine qualities if it is to glorify God. Therefore, CCM's relativism, which denies absolute standards in music, is impossible to reconcile with the derived and analogical nature of the aesthetic impulse in man.[19]

An aside: In this matter I find myself largely in agreement with Dutch Neo-Calvinists Abraham Kuyper, Herman Bavinck, and Hans Rookmaaker. The resemblance of their aesthetic to Plato's [beauty as transcendent] has exposed them to unfair criticism.[20] Nevertheless, understanding beauty as universal, transcendent, and timeless—though Platonic—is also quite biblical, as I have explained above. Neither is their emphasis on formal beauty in art (symmetry, proportion, order, wholeness, and harmony) merely Platonic (contra Jeremy Begbie),[21] but is also evident in the few examples of artistic achievements in the Bible. For instance the tabernacle, the temple, and their furnishings exhibit symmetry, proportion, order, and harmony (Exodus 25-28; 30:1-5; 36-39; 1 Kings 6-7; 2 Chronicles 2-3). Although not art proper, since most of these items were predominately utilitarian, the artistic undertow in their design is undeniable (Exodus 26:1, 31, 36; 35:31-35; 1 Kings 6:29, 32, 35; 7:29, 36). The decorative element is especially characteristic of the priestly garments, which were specifically created "for glory and beauty" (Exodus 28:2-28, 33-34, 40). Consequently, the Neo-Calvinist's theory of beauty does have biblical support and is not riding on the coattails of Greek aesthetic ideals.

Third, we should be aware that the arts and music are extensions of the *created* world and are subject to divinely imposed limitations that define and regulate their composition and use in accordance with God's purposes. The creatureliness of music and art not only makes them finite, but also liable to corruption following the entrance of sin. Music, like the rest of creation, has been disfigured by sin beginning with the fall of our first parents. Music is not infinite; it is created, limited, and, since the Fall, subject to corruption. Unlike CCM we must not assign incorruptibility, autonomy, and self-referentiality—attributes that belong exclusively to God—to created phenomena such as art or music. This would apply to entire genres as well as to individual songs.

What Is Music?

More so, if aesthetics is a purely personal or culturally relative activity and has no biblically-based guidelines or controls (except excellence and function), not only can anything be considered good music, but potentially any pattern of sound can be accepted as music proper![22] For example, in the absence of biblical norms overriding personal tastes, random sounds like the clanging of tin cans being dragged behind a car could suffice for music. As ridiculous as this may seem, this is precisely the kind of thing that has been accepted in the past as music. Nettl projects that "only the most broadminded listener would accept as music certain sounds made by electronic machinery and by the breaking of a musical instrument, but such sounds have indeed been presented as 'music' in contemporary Western culture!"[23]

As early as 1913 Futurists such as Luigi Russolo sought to expand the boundaries of music by rejecting its traditional definitions.[24] Russolo's *L'Arte dei Rumori*, "the art of noise," included industrial noises like the sound of tramways, cars, and crowds, which the Futurists considered to be aesthetically superior to compositions of classical composers.[25] Noise as music is also what modern composer John Cage proposed in 1952 with his famous *4' 33"*. This arrangement involves little more than a pianist, who seats himself at a piano and shuts the lid, playing nothing for four minutes and thirty-three seconds. The "music" consists of incidental sounds made in the concert hall such as those of the audience whispering, coughing, shuffling their feet, or whatever.[26] Cage once remarked, "all noise seems to me to have the potential to become musical, simply by being allowed to appear in a musical work."[27] Rubin adds that "other by-products of Cage's music included the philosophy of total acceptance inherent in it—there could be neither right or wrong solutions in art created totally by chance."[28]

More than simply a playful experiment or an attempt at redefining what qualifies as music, Cage's understanding of the boundlessness of music is a reflection of his Zen Buddhist beliefs and its metaphysic of purposelessness.[29] In fact it was Cage's intention to draw others toward Buddhist philosophy by way of such "compositions"—another reminder of how music and worldview cannot easily be separated.[30] Consequently, it should be of no surprise that Cagean philosophy eventually impacted groups like Led Zeppelin, the Beatles, Pink Floyd, and Jefferson Airplane.[31]

Clearly, an abandonment of biblical parameters for aesthetics, such as the ones proposed earlier, results in the kind of absurdity exhibited by Cage and his followers. The aesthetic philosophy of CCM simply cannot be consistent with itself and make exceptions with noise music.[32] If the Bible is reticent about defining the parameters of good music in the explicit terms that CCM patrons require,[33] neither does it provide a definition for what constitutes music and non-music, in the *same* terms.

Even if one invokes the absolute/biblical criteria of quality, craftsmanship, and skill as the basis for aesthetics, these criteria—according to the CCM position—would still be relative to their genres rather than being universal.[34] From the CCM point of view, noise music would have to be judged by its own canons of what constitutes excellence, not by some external, absolute pattern.[35]

And what about those musical genres where craftsmanship, skill, and virtuosity are tantamount to high treason? It has long been recognized that punk and alternative rock "place a lot of emphasis on the unskillfulness of the musicians and the display of raw power within their performances."[36] Walser discloses that "the Ramones and the Sex

Pistols placed musical amateurism at the aesthetic core of punk rock."[37]
According to Iain Chambers, with punk rock

> the possibility of discussing 'artistic' qualities and 'musicianship' was
> brutally mauled.... a previous musical sense was rudely transformed into
> 'nonsense'. The disbelief of the pop music establishment was further
> intensified by punk's repeated invocations of a populist musical tech-
> nique: 'This is a chord. This is another. This is a third.'[38]

Christian rocker Steve Taylor recognizes the same principle in new
wave (an adaptation of punk): "And I also knew that new wave music
was, essentially, four guys getting together who couldn't play musical
instruments, and that appealed to me because I couldn't play anything
either."[39] De Simone, another CCM musician, concedes, "This [punk]
is the worst format found in rock music. The music and lyrical contents
of a song are extremely amateur[ish] and sloppy, with no respect for
musical scales."[40] Even the singing of the early punks was considered
"anti-singing."[41] Where is one to turn when good is bad and bad is
good? When genre rules, however, even skill and craftsmanship must
submit to a higher authority.

Realizing the undesirable implications of unlimited relativism, Best
espouses the sovereignty of the musical community in aesthetic appraisal rather than the individual:

> If we can agree that there is no universal aesthetic covering all music,
> we should also agree that there is not an infinity of aesthetics or aes-
> thetic subtypes, separately designed for each new twist or paraphrase.
> The final absurdity of this would be the creation of a maze of discreet,
> personalized, self-constructed aesthetics, each one intended to justify
> each thing done: This is mine; it is unique; it is different; it is separate;
> therefore it is good.... Each activity, no matter how similar it might be
> to another, is considered by its practitioners to be unique, free of value
> judgment from another quarter. Each is self-justified, therefore above
> question. These particles of pseudouniqueness are the opposite of what
> true pluralism is intended to be: a relational, nurturing intercourse of
> things, in which communities learn from each other, values are shared,
> excellence expected, and standards maintained.[42]

This certainly bears the imprint of reform, but alas, it is no real solution to the hazards of autonomy, but relativism all over again, a mere numbers game in the guise of aesthetic stewardship. Whether *one* person alone holds to an aesthetic standard or *several* makes little difference since theoretically both are forms of individualism, relativism, and human autonomy that reject the imposition of divine or transcendent standards. Best feels that an individual's aesthetic must submit to that of a community (genre), but denies that that community must submit to anything higher. But on what basis? Do numbers and agreement guarantee rightness?[43] Moreover, does Best have the privilege to judge or restrict the aesthetic canons of an individual while denying others the opportunity to do so to an entire group/genre? Although promising at first glance, I fear this is simply an attempt to climb out of the bottomless pit of musical relativism and autonomy by the creation of artificial categories.

Depravity

Not only does CCM confer ultimate authority in aesthetics to human desire and reason—indirectly denying that man's aesthetic capacity is derived from God and must function in harmony with the same attribute in God—but its relativism creates certain insufferable consequences for the doctrine of human depravity. By assuming that criticism can take place only within a genre and that a genre cannot be judged by a higher standard from without, CCM essentially divorces aesthetics from depravity.

Scripture, however, teaches that with the fall of Adam and Eve the entirety of the human person was polluted with sin (Genesis 6:5; Ephesians 4:18-19). This depravity permeates every component of the human being: the body (Romans 6:6, 12; 7:24; 8:10, 13); the mind (Romans 1:21; 2 Corinthians 3:14-15; 4:4; Ephesians 4:17-18); the will (Romans 6:17; 2 Timothy 2:25-26); and the emotions and affections (Romans 1:26-27; Galatians 5:24; and 2 Timothy 3:2-4).[44] Truly, the totality of man's nature—all the faculties of his personhood, his spirit/soul, intellect, affections, emotions, will, and conscience—have been defiled by sin.[45] In other words, no property in us has escaped the corrosive effects of sin. Although this does not mean that man is as sinful as he can be or that each individual participates in every type of sin equally, it does mean that there is no activity possible for human nature that is unmolested by sin and imperfection.

This also holds true in the sphere of aesthetics, which enlists the use of man's emotions, affections, and intellect, all of which are scarred with sin and contaminated with weakness and error.[46] The doctrine of depravity dictates that man's ability to judge what is good and pleasing to God and conformable to his virtues in the realm of aesthetics is seriously crippled. This does not simply refer to imperfection, which is evident to some degree in every human endeavor, but to the existence of sinfully distorted tastes and concepts of what is good, pleasing, and beautiful. Consequently, it is *impossible* to claim orthodoxy and yet maintain that artwork, art forms, and art appreciation cannot be inferior, cheap, and grossly perverted in that the very powers in the human psyche that combine to form the aesthetic impulse are cursed with sin and alloyed with impurity.

Despite this unsoundness in the very qualities that form the image of God in man, glimmers of the once-pristine condition of these gifts do appear even in the works of unregenerate men, whom God through common grace stimulates to produce and appreciate those things that are in accordance with his nature and goodness.[47] For this reason a non-Christian artist can paint a landscape that is truly beautiful and a testimony to the glory of God—although it is never meritorious or pleasing to God (in a redemptive sense) in that it is tainted with imperfection and produced with improper motive.

Al Menconi

A typical example of the neglect of the doctrine of depravity in CCM's aesthetic philosophy can be detected in Al Menconi's novel approach to aesthetics. Menconi attempts to draw parallels between palatal tastes and musical tastes. He reflects on how people's tastes differ when it comes to food and recalls a steak dinner where the differences were strikingly apparent: "Why didn't we all season our steaks the same? Because we each had different tastes. The ones who seasoned their steaks with salt and pepper thought I was nuts for eating mine with hot sauce."[48] He offers another example that involves spice tolerance, which varies with individuals and cultures. He has observed, for example, that southern Californians can eat much hotter food than midwesterners, and Indians (Asian) than southern Californians, and so on.[49] Then he launches into his comparison with music:

> Now let's change our focus from food to music. *Which style is best: mellow, spicy (upbeat, contemporary, rock), or somewhere in between?* Again, the answer is that one is no more correct than another. Each style of music is simply different. A person's choice of music depends on his cultural background, maturity and age, the music he grew up listening to, and his personal tastes.[50] (Emphasis original.)

Although one could think of several differences between musical tastes and palatal tastes, the following is a critical one that bypasses Menconi. Because we live in a society where food is plentiful and often wasted, we forget that in many cultures food is whatever the land yields. In such situations what may be naturally unappetizing in smell or taste has to be overcome for the sake of survival. For example a society whose most abundant food staple is fish would hardly show wisdom if they rejected fish because of its unpleasant odor. Likewise, in some societies in the interest of prudence, every edible part of an animal is consumed, such as the brain and eyes. Consequently, because food is necessary for life (unlike music) but not always initially appetizing, taste in food is given much greater latitude than it is in music.

This principle may also explain why some cultures can tolerate spicier foods than others. Historians believe that spices were added to foods when man first began to cook, although little more is known about their earliest functions;[51] their use, however, may not have originally been for flavor, if more recent examples are any indicator. For instance one of the chief duties of spices was to improve the quality of poorly preserved meats and beverages.[52] Spices were also used extensively as medicines, after which they gradually made their way to the table.[53] At times they were the stuff of primitive science and superstition—sometimes functioning as aphrodisiacs.[54] Closer to home, chile peppers—rich in vitamins—serve as health food for the average Mexican.[55] Finally, some societies that live in tropical climates believe that eating spicy foods actually has a cooling effect on their bodies. Consequently, a culture's preference for hot spices may have developed out of more practical concerns, though their present role may be solely for flavor.

Even so I submit that depravity can manifest itself even in this basic area of life, although biblically food restrictions only apply to the concepts of legitimacy and health. By legitimacy I mean that the item must be something truly edible like meat or plants, not plastic or fiberglass. Secondly, sometimes even legitimate foods eaten in excess can be unhealthy (i.e., too much salt). When our sense organs desire that which is illegitimate, the cravings that drive them can be considered corrupted.

This is evident in the acquired tastes of extremely bitter and toxic products like chewing tobacco, cigarette smoke, and liquor. No one, for example, is instinctively drawn to the flavor of chewing tobacco, as they are to say honey or whipped cream; the taste is acquired by continually suppressing the mouth's revulsion to the plant's acrid flavor. With sinful persistence the individual overcomes the body's natural warning system and acquires a taste for the tobacco. Likewise, I think that if drinkers were honest, they would admit that whisky, scotch, vodka, and the like offer only a slight improvement in taste over nail-polish remover; and yet despite this built-in emetic quality, its patrons develop a liking for it.

When it comes to hot spices, depravity can manifest itself in a unique way. Spices are of course legitimate foods, nutritious, and even the hottest do not permanently harm the body. Therefore, adding hot spices to enhance the flavor of food can be a delightful experience; but purposely torturing the mouth with XXX super hot sauces, like Mad Dog Inferno or Dave's Insanity Sauce, to experience a kind of painful pleasure is evidence of bodily abuse and depravity. I doubt that any believer would argue that the divine gift of food and the pleasure of eating ever involved this type of self-inflicted masochism; and yet in this enterprise, make no mistake about it, the pleasure is in pain. Kellye Hunter, a specialist in hot foods, reveals: "Truly, the appeal lies in their painful effects and the process of weeding out 'who can take it, and who can't.'"[56] A manufacturer of these sauces admits, "in this industry, causing pain is doing a service...causing pain is what the consumer wants."[57] Consequently, hot sauces are used in rites of passage, contests of masculinity, and other such graceless social trials.[58]

Menconi's hermeneutical mistake is one that commonly besets the CCM faithful. They conclude that evidence of preference, taste, and variety within culture and an absence of explicit restrictions in the Bible automatically indicate that God has allotted mankind absolute freedom of choice in these areas.[59] This position, however, breaches the creator-creature distinction and promotes rank relativism and autonomy. A true, covenant view of appetite, however, allows for variety and individual preference, which at the same time are divinely circumscribed and protected from unbridled liberty and caprice.[60]

Therefore, it would be justifiable to opine that "this type of food is too spicy or bitter for me, but not morally improper, injurious, or abusive to the sense organs." In the same manner it is legitimate to suggest that "an up-tempo rendition of a certain tune is too rapid for me, although it is not a perversion of musical principles." But it is illegitimate to insist that food can never be too spicy or bitter for anyone at anytime, or that a song can never be too rapid, loud, or otherwise perverted.[61] If we are to hold a consistent view of our creatureliness, finitude, and moral depravity, this must be the case, both with music and foods. Otherwise, one could presumably contend that preferring the odor of a cesspool to the fragrance of perfume is merely a matter of taste.

Finally, it needs to be realized that comparing musical tastes to culinary tastes makes for a deceptively effective alibi for CCM apologists because it is difficult to amass verifiable examples of depraved palates. But the reason for this dearth is not because the human palate is immune to the effects of depravity, but because the coefficient between bad tasting food and toxin is so high. In other words, although it is possible (biblically speaking) for someone's taste to degenerate to the level of desiring the putrefying meat of a week-old road kill, it is not likely that that taste will ever develop for the obvious reason that the rancid meat would kill the individual before he could desensitize himself to its appalling taste and smell.[62] This barrier prevents truly grotesque examples of palatal depravity from manifesting themselves. And yet where the effect of the toxin is not immediate, definite examples do exist (chewing tobacco, smoking, and liquor).

Harold Best

Despite its importance, one finds an alarming depreciation of the doctrine of depravity throughout Best's work, a direction prognosticated early in his book: "As horrible as the Fall is, do we make too much of it by trying to guess what it is all by itself, instead of talking about how God works within it and helps us overcome it, even while we continue in sin?"[63] Such groundwork leads him elsewhere to draw careless analogies between the created world and music:

> God makes things; God makes them well; God calls them good; and God has no trouble saying that one thing may be better than another. If this does not trouble God whose handiwork far outstrips ours, why should it trouble us? *Consequently, there should be nothing wrong with the discovery and disclosure of the coexistence of goodness and better-than-ness in musical and artistic practice.*[64] (Emphasis original.)

Here we encounter not only a perilous disregard for the doctrine of depravity, but an inexcusable neglect of the creator-creature distinction. The result is an incongruent simile that wrongly attributes intrinsic goodness to musical styles despite their origin in the cradle of sinful humanity.[65]

Charlie Peacock

Even those who give due credence to the Fall seem to be allergic to the idea that depravity could infiltrate the development of musical styles. Charlie Peacock, for example, is one of the most sensitive in the CCM community to the pervading influence of man's fallen nature: "The catch with being human and not God is that we're just as apt to imagine and create a mess as we are a masterpiece."[66] Elsewhere he preaches, "Because God's creations are good, they can be used for good; but there is no guarantee that we as fallen creatures will always use them for good. On the contrary, it's possible for sinful human beings to choose very poorly when using something very good."[67] And, "No enterprise in which Christians participate will be free from sin and error."[68] Despite embracing these scriptural truths, Peacock refuses to apply the doctrine of depravity to the human "enterprise" of creating music: "We must respect all forms of musical and lyrical artistry, recognizing that God delights in and makes intelligent use of the diversity of his creation."[69]

Part of the problem is that he takes the concept that music (as an art form) is good—by virtue of it being created by God—and makes it identical to man's appropriation of that art form for the invention of various musical genres, forms, and individual pieces.[70] But the two clearly must be differentiated; anything less would be another violation of the creator-creature distinction. God may be responsible for the concept of music as an entity in itself, but man, not God, is the author of the many musical styles. Although Peacock does not deny that music can be misused, he limits it to things such as "background music in a film promoting hate crimes," or the sin of limiting music to ministry settings rather than appreciating its multi-cultural uses.[71]

Another part of the problem is that the prospect of a musical style manifesting depravity is never given a fair hearing. To Peacock the issue of musical neutrality was laid to rest in musical melees of the seventies and eighties, and so it should surprise no one that he treats the inherent goodness of all musical styles as a given.[72] The chief foible, then, in Peacock's doctrine of depravity is that, although it consents that music that is already composed can be misused, it dismisses the possibility that the composition of the music itself and its institutionalization as genre are subject to the disfiguring effects of the Fall. Thus it is clearly insufficient and reductionistic.

Therefore, the critical flaw in CCM's theology of music has to do with (what I term) its prelapsarian approach to aesthetics, creativity, and freedom. As I have argued, CCM supporters endorse a theology of music that, by and large, would be credible only prior to the fall of man (prelapsarian), not after—with the exception of the final eschatological renewal. In addition to the prelapsarian heresy, and related to it, is the undermining of both the creator-creature distinction and the doctrine of depravity, as well as the error of subjecting the aesthetic standards of Christian music to the sinful template of the human moral consciousness (individually or collectively). The resulting aesthetic is one that chimes with the common proverb, "Beauty is in the eye of the beholder." From a biblical perspective, however, this is unacceptable, since the beholder's evaluation mechanisms are defective and badly in need of repair.

Theological Foundations

Such doctrinal errors are hardly surprising when one considers the feeble theological foundations of CCM, an offspring of the Jesus movement of the late sixties and early seventies.[73] The fledgling movement with its hippie converts found it difficult to part with their preference for experience over reason or their distrust of institutionalized Christianity.[74] Added to this recipe was their devotion to a counter-culture value system and icons, which they adapted to their new-found faith. Richard Quebedeaux recalls that "when young people converted in the Jesus movement, many of them simply did not give up their former habits, practices, and cultural attitudes—drinking, smoking, and characteristic dress and language. They only modified them."[75] One might add to these non-relinquishables rock and roll, along with its ideological thrust that "there are no taboos left."[76]

Further, the influence of the charismatic movement and its emphasis on direct communication with God led to a tremendous depreciation of theology and sound biblical exposition in the embryonic stages of the CCM movement.[77] According to Peacock, "CCM became the product of an environment where, not only was it acceptable to de-emphasize learning of God from his Word, [but] such foolishness was (and still is) sometimes encouraged."[78] In fact to this day Peacock admits that CCM is in need of a "comprehensive theology of music in general, and a theology of CCM artistry, industry, and audience in particular."[79]

Furthermore, Howard and Streck contend that personalized theology at the expense of solid exegesis is characteristic not only of CCM but also of evangelicalism as a whole:

> Within the modern evangelical church, articulating the principles and assumptions of the faith has largely become an activity for armchair theologians. The authority of the ministers and church councils, resting on the foundations of scholarly training in theology, biblical exegesis, history, and the like is giving way to the authority of the individual, rooted in experience. From mass organizations such as Promise Keepers...to listservs, newsgroups, and chatrooms on the Internet, the basis for much contemporary Christian theology has moved outside the church; it has moved beyond church authority, beyond privately interpreted scripture, and come to rest in private experience. Theology is now less a matter of logical argument founded on biblical exegesis than an impressionist collage emerging from the raw materials of what's available in the surrounding culture. For millions of evangelicals, contemporary Christian music is a crucial source; it is grist for the mills of their personal theologies.[80]

In light of this anti-intellectual environment, one can understand the emergence of CCM's prelapsarianism, as well as other shortcomings in its aesthetic philosophy. Moreover, these positions have been accepted and fossilized beneath the permafrost of CCM's constitution to such a degree that today when CCM does have its share of capable theologians and philosophers (e.g., Peacock and Michael Card), questioning these foundations is as unthinkable as reexamining the Nicene or Chalcedonian creeds. Consequently, aesthetic and ethic continue to be polarized in contemporary Christian thought.

Dada and Surrealism

The following examples from art and music should make it abundantly clear that aesthetics cannot be divorced from morality. History reveals that movements in art, literature, and music are pregnant with intention, design, and meaning—all of which possess moral capacity and are capable of expression and comprehension. This is especially so with art forms that have imbibed or adapted the aesthetic of Dada or Surrealism. The offspring of larger political and philosophical agendas,

Dada and Surrealism are examples of two modern literary and artistic movements that manifest intention, design, and meaning.

Most attribute the inauguration of modern art to atheist and Marxist Pablo Picasso with the unveiling of his *Les Demoiselles d' Avignon* (1906-1907), a painting that expressed the fragmentation of humanity and the world.[81] Picasso once said, "Art is not to decorate apartments. Art is a weapon of revolution and my art is revolution."[82] And so it was. Before long Picasso's cubistic revolution would gain a sizable foothold and become a catalyst for later avant-garde movements such as Dada and Surrealism.

Dada

Dada was born in 1916 in a small cafe in Zurich where a group of dissenting artists and intellectuals from war-torn Europe gathered. There, Hugo Ball, a German conscientious objector, formed the Cabaret Voltaire, a place where young artists like himself could find an avenue of expression.[83] Soon the mellow productions at the cabaret became noticeably absurd as the dadaist protest against the First World War, as well as their popularity, grew.[84] At times they would feature a bizarre jig where participants danced with stove pipes on their heads to the accompaniment of dog yapping or the cacophonous banging of tin cans. These performances quickly spread throughout Zurich, consisting of "wild 'Cubist' dances, shouted simultaneous recitations, noise music…and obscenities hurled at the audience."[85] It was at about this time that Ball and Richard Huelsenbeck appropriately expressed the irrationalism of the movement with *dada*, French baby-talk for "hobbyhorse," which was selected accidentally while thumbing through a French dictionary.[86]

Georges Ribemont-Dessaignes, a French dadaist, explains that "the activity of Dada was a permanent revolt of the individual against art, against morality, against society. The means were manifestoes, poems, writings of various kinds, paintings, sculptures, exhibitions, and a few public demonstrations of clearly subversive character."[87] George Grosz remembers,

> Nothing was holy to us. Our movement [Dada] was neither mystical, communistic nor anarchistic. All of these movements had some sort of program, but ours was completely nihilistic. We spat on everything, including ourselves. Our symbol was nothingness, a vacuum, a void.[88]

Ergo their anti-aesthetic doctrine could be summed up as "Nothing exists. All is appearance and convention. There is no difference between a beautiful work and an ugly work. Nothing is good and nothing is bad. There is no difference between...a limousine and a jalopy."[89] Heulsenbeck, likewise, remarks, "We loathed every form of art that merely imitated nature and we admired, instead, the Cubists and Picasso," further recommending that "art should altogether get a sound thrashing, and Dada stands for the thrashing with all the vehemence of its limited nature."[90]

Marcel Duchamp illustrated the absurdity of art by confiscating any object from everyday life and signing his name to it—whether a bicycle wheel, snow shovel, or urinal.[91] Decades later (1962), when Dada was welcomed as art rather than rejected as anti-art, Duchamp complained, "When I discovered ready-mades I thought to discourage aesthetics. In Neo-Dada they have taken my ready-mades and found aesthetic beauty in them. I threw the bottle rack and the urinal into their faces as a challenge and now they admire them for their aesthetic beauty."[92]

(This can only be an example of aesthetic desensitization and depravity within western civilization, as is further evident in the lamentations of a pop artist in 1963: "It was hard to get a painting that was despicable enough so that no one would hang it—everybody was hanging everything. It was almost acceptable to hang a dripping paint rag...."[93] Jack D. Flam inserts, "The Dada-inspired questioning of the borderline between art and non-art,...had become an essential part of the modern sensibility."[94] Similarly, Bruce Altshuler estimates, "In addition to the impossibility of shocking the middle class, always a desideratum of the historical avant-garde, an artistic underground seemed untenable because there was no escaping media attention and the public's voracious appetite for the new."[95])

Although Dada as art is quite beyond all description, Calvin Tomkins succeeds in retelling one of the movement's most famous displays:

It was held in a glassed-in courtyard behind a café, which could only be reached through a public urinal. Inside, paying visitors saw Fatagaga and other drawings on the walls; an aquarium filled with red liquid, with a woman's head of hair floating on top and an arm protruding from below the surface; a wooden sculpture to which [Max] Ernst had chained a hatchet in case anyone wished to destroy it; and a young girl (live) in a white communion dress who recited obscene poetry. In no time at all someone smashed the aquarium, and the floor was awash with red water.[96]

Next, Kurt Schwitters outlines the ideal of his "Merz" art, whose aesthetic was similar to Dada's:

Take a dentist's drill, a meat grinder, a car-track scraper, take buses and pleasure cars, bicycles, tandems and their tires, also war-time ersatz tires and deform them. Take lights and deform them as brutally as you can. Make locomotives crash into one another.... For all I care, take man-traps, automatic pistols, infernal machines, the tinfish and the funnel, all of course in an artistically deformed condition.[97]

From Zurich, Dada spread to Berlin, Cologne, Paris and Hanover. Though it expired in Paris in 1921, the die was already cast; Dada's aesthetic of freedom and meaninglessness would be a vital impetus to later art forms such as Surrealism, Abstract Expressionism, and Pop Art.[98] We should remember that although the movement began as a protest against the carnage of World War I, it burgeoned into a fierce attack against all the hallowed spheres and values of western society, including literature and art.[99]

Surrealism

Surrealism, in some sense the stepchild of Dada, was spawned by the subliminal experiments of poet André Breton, who in 1919 put himself into a trance-like state and recorded every thought and image that entered his subconscious.[100] Counting the experiment a success, Breton moved on to specify the canons of the movement—one over which he would exercise almost sole regency for nearly forty years. In 1924 he produced his well-known *Manifeste de surréalisme* in which he defined Surrealism as, "pure psychic automatism, by which it is intended to express, verbally, in writing, or by other means, the true function of thought—thought dictated in the absence of all control exercised by reason and outside all esthetic or moral preoccupations."[101] He would later write, "Surreality depends on our wish for a complete disorientation of everything."[102]

By uniting subconscious thought with the visible world and placing familiar objects in unnatural and irrational combinations, Breton produced a hallucinatory art that sought to unmask the shallowness of conscious western thought. Surrealism also set out to subvert reason, God, conscience, and aesthetics, and made generous use of erotic symbolism.[103] As Hebdige recollects, "Breton's manifestos (1924 and 1929) established the basic premise of Surrealism: that a new 'surreality' would emerge through the subversion of common sense, the collapse of prevalent logical categories and oppositions...and the celebration of the abnormal and forbidden."[104]

Representative of the surrealistic aesthetic is Salvador Dali's 1938 *Rainy Taxi*, which Altshuler briefly depicts:

> Inside an old vehicle sat two mannequins, the driver with shark's head and dark goggles, and his passenger, a disheveled woman covered with live Burgundian snails. Lettuce surrounded the passenger and sustained the snails, vines entwined the doors, and the interior was completely drenched by rain that fell from the ceiling.[105]

Although Surrealism dissipated around 1940, its influence continues until the present day. David A. Noebel bemoans the degree to which modern art has distorted man's sense of beauty. He tells of "a prestigious university [which], after spending $3 million on an art building, accepted as art 18 plates of horse manure (chips)."[106] Another sample of modern art comes from Duchampian Walter De Maria, who in 1969 filled an entire New York art gallery (3,600 square feet) with evenly distributed dirt! Commenting favorably on De Maria's *Earth Room*, reviewer Roberta Smith describes its "aesthetic" effect: "Any item presented dramatically out of context or in excessive amounts creates a certain fascination and often its own kind of formal beauty."[107] She also remarks, "It [the *Earth Room*] is an elegant desecration, a defiling of the traditional container of contemporary art objects, which ends up being a celebration of esthetic experience."[108]

Throughout history clay has been used to create beautiful pottery and sculptures, but in the hands of Peter Voulkos, ceramics have become a monument to decay and destruction in the spirit of Abstract Expressionism.[109] One such "masterpiece," *Big Missoula* (1995), is described by a reviewer as

> wheel-thrown in four parts, it is a massive elephant's foot of a form. Reeling under its heavy accretion of raw, random patches, scrubby edges, cracks and lumps, stroke and splatter, its outside hide is scarred, its big lip scraped and broken. Inside, the piece has a satiny skin. Scaled like a coat of armor of many disparate pieces clinging crazily to the central cylinder, balancing tier on tier of ragged, ruffled edges...[110]

His other creations exhibit a similar fascination with the destructive power of the natural elements on clay—grotesque forms, randomly slapped together, amorphous, deformed, gouged, dilapidated, and thoroughly ravaged. His 1960 *Gallas Rock*, still on display at the Frederick S. Wight Galleries of UCLA, is, in the most charitable of terms, a painfully ugly structure composed of "over 100 thrown and slab pieces attached to a series of central core cylinders."[111] It resembles a pile of weather-beaten stones slowly crumbling at the base of an abandoned quarry.

Finally, consider James Hyde's 1996 *Radius*, a tossed salad of pigment and paper housed in an eight foot glass case. At every turn the optic nerve is assaulted with eruptions of paint blindly splattered in ungeometric and disproportionate combinations. To this already acrid sight, crumpled scraps of paper are fortuitously attached, giving it the appearance of a sewage lagoon, swirling with oil and debris.[112]

At this point it should be clear that Dada and Surrealism (and the art forms they engendered) had a definite ideological ax to grind; their purposes were anything but amoral. (Neither was the expression of their agenda limited to content, but was evident in the formal properties of their art.) Indeed, the dadaist and surrealistic aesthetic was one of irrationalism, fragmentation, disintegration, satire, and shock. According to their own admission it was patently anti-aesthetic.

Our examination of the ingredients and purposes of Dada and Surrealism raises some important questions. For example, can Christians communicate a consistently Christian message through art forms that have adopted the aesthetic and stylistic canons of Dada or Surrealism? More specifically, should Christians be allowed to imitate any artistic, literary, or musical style that expresses absurdity, nihilism, and chaos, for the purpose of communicating the gospel? I think most Christians would agree that neither of these questions should be answered in the affirmative.

More so, what would happen if we applied CCM's aesthetic philosophy to the art forms we have just mentioned? Would it be unfair for Christians to condemn displays of horse manure or galleries of dirt (or the art forms and aesthetic that sponsored them), since CCM's aesthetic ambassadors insist that musical styles (and presumably art styles as well) should only be appraised from within by those who appreciate the styles, rather than by outsiders and adversaries? After all, this is precisely what Roberta Smith, who favorably critiqued De Maria's dirt display, did.[113] So then, because aesthetic philosophies and art forms that subscribe to them are morally conditioned, Christians must not be forbidden to pass judgment on them. In fact, as Christians we are obligated to judge them.

Punk Rock

We are now faced with a critical question: Can the characteristic components of Dada and Surrealism—nihilism, meaninglessness, irrationalism, shock, and absurdity—be expressed in a genre of music? The answer is "yes," and the best example is punk rock.[114] Although punk rock has declined in popularity since its heyday, it is worth examining because it makes a vital contribution to understanding intention, design, and meaning in musical genre. Punk's social, political, and moral ideologies have been documented and self-consciously defined by its originators and propagators to a greater degree than other varieties of rock music. Consequently, it forms a priceless archive of first-hand information for verifying the aesthetic and ideological motivations behind a rock genre.

Punk Origins

It is generally agreed that punk rock evolved out of a series of underground anti-art experiments conducted in New York during the 1960-70s by avant-garde artists who incorporated whatever was considered to be useless, trivial, and obscene into their craft.[115] (According to Wicke the term "punk" is vernacular for "muck, trash, rubbish, even whore.")[116] "Using the most shocking representation possible of what was worthless," says Wicke, "the New York punk artists tried to question a value system whose other side they thus displayed."[117] Moreover, it was out of International Situationism, an anti-art philosophy inspired by Dada and Surrealism, that Malcolm McLaren, the revolutionary manager of the New York Dolls (a transvestite band), developed the anti-music sound of punk and marketed it in Great Britain through the punk rock group the Sex Pistols.[118] There, during the 1970s, punk became a graphic social expression of boredom and anarchy within a teenage culture that was suffering from high unemployment and disillusionment.[119]

Dada and Punk

The dadaist underpinnings of punk philosophy have been recognized since the birth of the movement and by all estimates are quite beyond dispute. Apart from self-disclosures by McLaren and Bernie Rhodes (manager of the Clash) to this effect, the harmonious assessment of rock authorities as to the dadaist leanings of punk is telling.[120] Brown, for example, agrees with Wicke and others in relating that "essentially, punk philosophy is dadaist or antiart."[121] More meaningful is Arnold's comparison of punk rock to Marcel Duchamp's "masterpiece," a urinal named *Fountain*; she considers punk rock to be "Duchamp's *Fountain* all over again, only with electric guitars."[122]

Philosophically, punk is very similar to Dada, sharing with it a preoccupation with death, perversion, loathsomeness, and chaos.[123] John Street discloses that "McLaren and his cohorts were only interested in the disruption of the existing order;... The point was not to create a new world, just to mess up the old one."[124] Chambers explains how this philosophical similarity translated into stylistic similarity:

> The Dadaist logic of sucking in the trivia, the rubbish and the cast-offs of the world and then stamping a new meaning on the chaotic assemblage was there in both punk's music and sartorial regime. Earlier subcultural styles, like earlier musics, were 'cut-up', mixed and re-signified [sic].[125]

Another way in which punk mirrors Dada is by sharing its mission to inflict its audiences with shock and outrage.[126] Something of this shock philosophy can be discerned in the names of many punk rock groups: Black Flag, the Circle Jerks, the Germs, the Subhumans, Ruin, Bad Religion, Rancid, the Dead Kennedys, Bikini Kill, the Rhythm Pigs, the Stranglers, the Damned, the Idiots, Ringworm, and Jack Killed Jill.[127] (But, as we shall soon see, punk rock achieved its shock-effect not only through banal and obscene titles and lyrics, but also by overturning the aesthetic and stylistic norms of pop music at the time.)[128]

An impression of the dadaist aesthetic in punk can be captured if we compare the following description of the Sex Pistols to an earlier account of dadaist performances at the Cabaret Voltaire:

> They [the Sex Pistols] sing 'No Fun', and a song called 'Anarchy in the UK'; people get up and dance on stage, pour beer over each other, while the singer insults the audience and goads them to jump on one another. Two girls are dressed in a bin-liner and tied up to one another with a dog chain; the boy next to me has his face obscured by a Cambridge Rapist mask while cameras hover, kids jump and wrestle by the stage as the noise mounts. The singer, Johnny Rotten, wears a dirty white shirt ripped and festooned with stickers saying 'I survived the Texas Chainsaw Massacre'....[129] (Italics original.)

But far from simply *matching* the debasement of the dadaists, in some respects the punks actually *surpassed* them, as Rubin explains:

> Nihilism carried the Sex Pistols far beyond the dadaists, who destroyed traditional means of making art but took part in community life, wore suits, lectured wittily, and hunted mushrooms as John Cage did. But, whereas Cage (and Little Richard) invested in anti-art, the Pistols

plumbed the depths of anti-culture, assaulting attitudes about clothing, language, the Queen, and human decency. By letting their hair stand up in every direction, they questioned the need to be decorous. By using indecorous language on television, they questioned the need to be civil. By spitting on passerbys, they questioned civilization itself. (Punk fans colored their hair pink, green, yellow and purple, or in multiple hues. They dressed in black or gray, wore bondage pants tied together at the knees and stuck safety-pins in their cheeks....)[130]

So then, the dadaist influence on punk is incontrovertible; as Craig O'Hara remarks, "the comparison [between punk and Dada] is valid, though Punks generally show a distaste for dadaist art."[131]

Punk Aesthetics

Punk rock provides a sterling example of how music can incarnate and articulate rebellion. Because the rock sound, for various reasons, was becoming too sophisticated and amiable, punk actually set out to subvert whatever virtuosity rock had achieved.[132] As the rock and roll of Bill Haley rebelled against the aesthetic norms of its era, so punk outdid its sire and gave it a black eye. Brown admits, "Punk was a form of rebellion, like other styles of rock; it turned against all other musical forms of the 1970s."[133] Kristine McKenna feels that "punk's *raison de'être* was the subversion of the status quo,"[134] while Laing considers it "part of a reaction against the centrality of progressive rock in its various forms."[135] Laing boils down the revolution to three factors: (1) a rejection of the prevailing methods and institutions of pop music for new approaches; (2) a defiance of the aesthetic standards of pop music; and (3) the adoption of revolutionary themes and lyrics for the new music.[136] Punk's remonstrance against the stylistic elements of rock music in the 1970s came in the form of electric guitar distortion (adopted from heavy metal); willful incompetence for virtuosity; a recidivism to primal rhythms for the finesse of the melody line; a confusion of syncopated and non-syncopated rhythms, with the non-syncopated dominating; repetition instead of variety, and blurring instead of distinction.[137]

Wicke explains in detail the repristination of rock music through the punk invasion:

> The polished sound structures of a rock 'art' concerned with 'content' were now opposed by a challenging dilettantism which only had to sound loud, aggressive and chaotic to be accepted as rock music. No more technical apparatus,...no more stars fingering runs on guitar or keyboards at breakneck speed with contorted faces...: just simple, brutal rhythmic patterns with three guitars and drums, to whose accompaniment the musicians screamed out their view of their situation in selected obscene street slang.... Once again rock had the inimitable self-made music flair of the early sixties, just more aggressive, louder, shriller, more hectic and full of cynicism.... And behind the whole thing was the incessant repetition of one message: NO FUTURE.[138]

Interestingly, on the very eve of punk rock (1976), Mick Farren recognized how the taming down of rock music was alien to its heritage:

> From the blues onwards, the essential core of the music has been the rough side of humanity. It's a core of rebellion, sexuality, assertion and even violence. All the things that have always been unacceptable to a ruling establishment. Once that vigorous, horny-handed core is extracted from rock 'n' roll, you're left with little more than muzak.[139]

Just as perceptive is Mick Jagger:

> The best rock & roll music encapsulates a certain high energy—an angriness—whether on record or on stage. That is, rock & roll is only rock & roll if it's not safe. You know, one of the things I hate is what rock & roll has become in a lot of people's hands: a safe viable vehicle for pop. Oh, it's inevitable, I suppose, but I don't like that sort of music. It's like rock & roll—the best kind, that is the real thing—is always brash. That's the reason for punk. I mean, what was punk about? Violence and energy—and that's really what rock & roll's all about.[140]

Clearly, Farren and Jagger have homed in on the authentic spirit of rock and roll and how its domestication cuts the very nerve of rock's original charter: to incinerate western bourgeois values, music, and aesthetics with a revolution of anti-aesthetic sound.[141] It was this subversive element that punk (and heavy metal) restored to rock music.

Christians should observe that nothing that could be remotely considered spiritually uplifting is offered by punk rockers, fans, writers, and sociologists concerning the nature and meaning of the punk sound. For example, it is said that the Ramones "did not smash their instruments, they attacked with their weapons of sound. Their onslaught so intense they could overwhelm and exhaust an audience."[142] Likewise, the Clash have been described as *"four men with brutally cut hair..., tigers let out of a cage. [They] Bark into a microphone, start making pummelling, industrial noise. The noise...coalesces with the speed and my internal explosions into a perfect chaos."*[143] (Italics original.) Chambers sees punk as "a harsh accumulation of the previous forms of white rebellious noise.... Sartorial cut-up is matched by sonorial cut-up."[144] Arnold, who earlier likened the punk sound to a musical latrine, also refers to it as a "cacophonous noise" that drives dogs and cats into hiding.[145] Savage boasts that the Stranglers "are talented enough to translate their aggression and studied venom into direct musical terms: an instantly recognizable sound...that scrapes under your skin and lodges there, even better than an irritant."[146] To Laing, punk launched an all out assault on the growing complexities and virtuosity of rock with "sounds [that] were distorted, dirtied and destroyed, so that their meanings were mangled."[147]

Brett Gurewitz, founder of Epitaph Records (a punk label), flatly insists that "punk rock music is rock 'n' roll, and rock 'n' roll is rebellion.... that...[expletive] music spoke to them because it brought out the rebelliousness in it.... It's visceral, it's sexual, it's primal, it's rock 'n' roll."[148] O'Hara admits, "Rebellion is one of the few undeniable characteristics of Punk. It is implicit in the meaning of Punk and its music and lyrics."[149] Hebdige contributes a sociologist's description of punk: "Typically, a barrage of guitars with volume and treble turned to maximum accompanied by the occasional saxophone would pursue relentless (un)melodic lines against a turbulent background of cacophonous drumming and screaming vocals."[150] McKenna considers the performances of the Germs as "nothing more than willfully invoked chaos."[151] Equally revealing are punk slogans like, "We make noise 'cos its our choice,"[152] and McLaren's memorable taunt that the Sex Pistols were "into chaos, not music."[153]

But more. Wicke provides a grizzly description of the music and philosophy of the Sex Pistols:

> This anarchist credo was literally spat out by Sex Pistols' lead singer Johnny Rotten in a barely articulated scream. The whole thing was accompanied by a frenzied noise made up of the monotonous screeching sound of guitars played in parallel and drums being flogged mercilessly. Undisguised anger hammered the short phrases of a minimalist two-chord aesthetic into the heads of their listeners.[154]

An account of the punk sound by Keith Morris is almost as incriminating:

> Throw in a bass and a guitar, miscellaneous amplifiers, speakers, a makeshift drum kit, a cheap public-address system, and a Radio Shack microphone, cram this in a dimly lit room, and watch them plug in and blow up! There wasn't room for or tolerance of the "mellow," "laid-back," "go with the flow" friendly vibe typically associated with California. Here it was all attack, volume, ringing ears, sweat, anger, intensity, and hard work.[155]

Finally, I forward what is probably the most incisive observation I have yet to encounter regarding the conflicting worldviews of rock music and Christianity. In an interview in 1983 McLaren reminded everyone that "we live in a Christian society concerned with order: rock 'n' roll was always concerned with *dis*order. Punk rock promoted blatantly the word *chaos*. Cash from Chaos."[156] Punk then is quite unmistakably a brand of music that was designed not to be listened to but "to be hit by."[157]

Consequently, I fail to comprehend how Peacock manages to reconcile punk rock with his theology of music as articulated here: "In music I see God's handiwork, his order, his design, and I give him thanks and praise for creating it and for giving me the skill to write and produce it."[158] Likewise, how utterly reductionistic it is for Undercover (a Calvary Chapel based punk rock band) to campaign: "We don't have to justify playing loud and fast. The content of our music is the gospel of Jesus Christ."[159]

Over twenty years later punk rock still commands a substantial following—credited primarily to a punk resurgence in the early nineties—but as a whole the movement has waned from its early momentum and has ironically become part of the status quo that it originally set out to destroy.[160] Further, the focus of punk seems to have shifted from communication through style to communication through content.[161] Consequently, punks are now more active in speaking out directly on (liberal) social, political, and environmental issues.[162] Some punk analysts consider this to be a maturing of punk, while others feel the movement is simply in a temporary coma awaiting its rebirth so that it can once again prowl the earth and stain the pages of musical history.[163]

Conclusion

Punk rock is the translation of the degenerative values of Dada and Surrealism into musical terms. It not only offers an outstanding example of the desensitization process, but demonstrates intention, design, and meaning in a musical genre in well-documented and graphic ways. Moreover, it forever transfers the concept of musical bottom-feeding from the arena of theoretical possibility to that of certified reality. Therefore, is the Christian wrong for passing judgment on the punk genre as being unfit for the Christian message? Is this musical form beyond criticism—despite it being called "trash aesthetics" by more than one rock journalist[164]—simply because there are many who have acquired a taste for it and appreciate it? Even though the answer is obvious, none of the anti-aesthetic features of punk has prevented Christians from adopting it or its milder cousin, new wave.

In fact Christian punk accounts for a surprising share of CCM patrons and has been well received within the ranks of the CCM industry. The Christian Music Place Artist's Directory alone listed over eighty punk rock groups, and there is every reason to believe that this is a very conservative estimate of the actual total. Further, many of these groups perform at Christian rock festivals like Cornerstone, which for 1999 promised, "There's metal coming from one tent, ska from another, rap from another and plenty of punk everywhere, loud and fast."[165]

Not only have the music, wardrobe, and dancing of punk been adopted *in toto*, but Christian punkers also exhibit the punk aesthetic and attitude in more direct ways.

Aesthetically, they often refer to their music as "noise," and their singing as "screaming"—sometimes using the term "rawk" instead of "rock" to underscore the *raw*ness of the sound.[166] Chaotic music is considered a virtue, of course, and many groups are applauded for shunning art- and pop-punk and adhering to the more terrorizing old school punk of the Sex Pistols, Clash, Subhumans, and Social Distortion.[167] Dadaist/punk anti-aesthetics is also evident in compliments like this one for the group the Blamed: "The whole thing [sound] is big and ugly, and sometimes ugly can be a truly beautiful thing."[168]

The offensive punk attitude, always evident in the music, sometimes becomes obvious in other ways. For example Justin of Duckie rudely sticks his tongue out at the camera when photographed.[169] The pedigree for Matt May, bass guitarist for Never the Less, reads as follows: "Matt was born to be in a Punk Rock band. His mother said it best: 'Matt, your [*sic*] just naturally offensive!'"[170] Even more in line with punk philosophy is the group's drummer, Ryan Shields, whose duties are listed as "Drums, background vocals, and trying to get people pi... off at the band."[171] Trevor Garvey, the lead vocalist, betrays the same attitude and reveals the source, "The first punk band I heard was Bad Religion [a blasphemous, atheistic group]. I loved how they were so pi... off, and yet had such great melodies to sing to. I figured If [*sic*] I am ever in a band it will be like that one."[172] And yet this kind of language is actually mild compared to Pat Nobody of Nobody Special, who expresses the idea of unconventional courage with a vulgar locker room term for testicles.[173]

When choosing a name, Christian punk groups often match the shock philosophy of the early punks. The most distasteful are One Bad Pig, Crashdog, Quality Scrub, Blenderhead, Dead Pharisees (à la Dead Kennedys?), Ninety Pound Wuss, Residue, Luti-kriss, Mindrage, and the Blamed (à la the Damned?). This banality is sometimes evident in song titles like "I Scream Sunday," "Up the Nose" (One Bad Pig), and "You Make Me Puke" by Lust Control, whose first album was entitled

This Is a Condom Nation.[174] Other semblances with punk philosophy, such as violence and moshing, were discussed in chapter two.

CCM diehards who may wish to draw the line with punk rock are forced by their own sweeping statements on the amorality of music to suppress any judgment since, after all, it is only a matter of taste. Nevertheless, as has been repeatedly demonstrated, there can be no cleavage between aesthetics and morality in music or art because man's aesthetic instinct has been infected with sin and waywardness.

We should not assume at this point, because of our especially close look at the anti-Christian components of punk rock, that other forms of rock are now admissible. Punk is simply an extreme version of a larger genre that is already unsuitable through similar, though less-volatile, characteristics and origins. It is because of the desensitization process that earlier rock forms seem so inoffensive, not because they are aesthetically irreproachable. Just a few years prior to the entrance of punk, Cohn used the same terms to describe the music of the Rolling Stones:

> All that counted was sound and the murderous mood it made. All din and mad atmosphere. Really it was nothing but beat, smashed and crunched and hammered home like some amazing stampede. The words were lost and the song was lost. You were only left with chaos, beautiful anarchy. You drowned in noise.[175]

Indeed, most rock forms express rebellion within their own musical contexts, as is evident in one of the first rock and roll songs, Bill Haley's "Rock Around the Clock," which according to Wicke "is consciously unbalanced and noisy, literally every bar seems to signal rebellion."[176]

In closing, one has to wonder whether there can be any serious discussion of aesthetics within CCM when members of their own guild affectionately describe their music as "smashmouth" or "music to melt your face off;"[177] refer to their bands as "cheesy, in-your-face, sarcastic American rock band[s]" or "tone deaf;" [178] speak of praising God "'til your ears bleed;"[179] and create record labels like Morphine, Worthless, Screaming Giant, Grrr (simulating a dog growl), and Tooth & Nail, which offers an album entitled *Songs from the Penalty Box*, picturing a snarling hockey player with a missing front tooth and featuring groups like Ninety Pound Wuss.[180] Can any thinking person consider this a stewardship of the arts?

Or, can anyone watch the members of One Bad Pig crank up chain-saws or bludgeon the stage with their guitars (literally!) and not recognize that they are making statements as bold and emphatic as those of Duchamp and Breton about the nature of beauty, the parameters of music, and the imperial sovereignty of the individual conscience in matters of aesthetics? As ambassadors of Cage and McLaren, whose philosophy they exhale with every maddening scream and twisted chord—sounds more appropriately studied by seismologists than musicologists—this band carries punk's message of nihilism to the far reaches of their domain, resounding the anthem of their dadaist mentors that "there is no difference between a beautiful work and an ugly work. Nothing is good and nothing is bad. There is no difference between...a limousine and a jalopy."

It is hoped that through this chapter the reader will have come to realize that CCM's doctrine of aesthetics is anything but orthodox. Rather, it has repeatedly proven itself to be theologically reckless by essentially maintaining that man can only be creative but never *dis-creative*, that his sense of beauty has been insulated from the Fall, and by according "genre" a level of impunity unparalleled with any other human activity or commodity. The resulting aesthetic is one that is incurably relativistic, secularly based, and similar to the "whatever-turns-you-on" philosophy of many modern artists and musicologists, who in their unwillingness to pass judgment on any genre of music are forced to accept the obviously unacceptable.[181]

Endnotes

[1]Steve Rabey, "What Makes Music 'Christian?'" *Contemporary Christian Music*, May 1999, 55.

[2]Brad Davis, "Hot Pink Refrigerators," *Reformed Perspective*, April 1994, 17.

[3]Steve Phifer, "God's Favorite Music," *Pentecostal Evangel*, 24 April 1994, 6. See also Karen A. DeMol, "Sound Stewardship: How Should Christians Think About Music?" *Pro Rege* 26, no. 3 (March 1998): 14-16.

[4]Steve Lawhead, *Rock of This Age: Real and Imagined Dangers of Rock Music* (Downers Grove, IL: Inter-Varsity, 1987), 117.

[5]Steve Miller, *The Contemporary Christian Music Debate: Worldly Compromise or Agent of Renewal?* (Wheaton, IL: Tyndale House, 1993), 52, 55.

[6]J. Nathan Corbitt, *The Sound of Harvest: Music's Mission in Church and Culture* (Grand Rapids: Baker Books, 1998), 248. See also p. 254, as well as David B. Pass, *Music and the Church* (Nashville: Broadman Press, 1989), 31, 44.

[7]Harold M. Best, *Music Through the Eyes of Faith* (San Francisco: Harper, 1993), 92. Best's analogy with the created world confuses the issue. The crucial question is not whether the standards of one genre should be imposed upon another, but whether there are any overarching divine or inherent standards of correctness and beauty that regulate all musical production. It is true that standards of one class of music should not govern those of another, but this does not mean that all genres and functions of music are automatically legitimate. Further, unlike the created world, musical genres convey worldviews, have moral capacity, and can be the result of a perverted sense of beauty.

[8]John Hospers, "Aesthetics, Problems of," in *The Encyclopedia of Philosophy*, ed. Paul Edwards (New York: The Macmillan Company & The Free Press, 1967), 20.

[9]See Monroe C. Beardsley, "Reasons in Aesthetic Judgments," in *Introductory Readings in Aesthetics*, ed. John Hospers (New York: The Free Press, 1969), 245-53; Lawhead, *Rock of This Age*, 117-19.

[10]Miller, *Christian Music Debate*, 55. Cf. Lawhead, *Rock of This Age*, 119.

[11]For example see Curt J. Ducasse, "The Subjectivity of Aesthetic Value," in *Introductory Readings in Aesthetics*, ed. John Hospers (New York: The Free Press, 1969), 282-307; Clive Bell, "Significant Form," in *Introductory Readings in Aesthetics*, ed. John Hospers (New York: The Free Press, 1969), 88.

[12]Herman Bavinck, *Our Reasonable Faith: A Survey of Christian Doctrine*, trans. Henry Zylstra (Grand Rapids: Baker Book House, 1956), 489.

[13]Cf. Clyde S. Kilby, *Christianity and Aesthetics*, IVP Series in Contemporary Christian Thought, vol. 3 (Chicago: Inter-Varsity Press, 1961), 22-24.

[14]Bavinck, *Our Reasonable Faith*, 212. Theologians would call this the "broader image" that was distorted but not lost in the fall.

[15]Cornelius Van Til, *Christian Apologetics* (Phillipsburg, NJ: Presbyterian and Reformed Publishing Co., 1976), 9.

[16]Cornelius Van Til, *Christian Theistic Ethics*, In Defense of Biblical Christianity, vol. 3 (Phillipsburg, NJ: Presbyterian and Reformed Publishing Co., 1980), 23.

[17]Cf. William Edgar, *Taking Note of Music* (London: Third Way Books, 1986), 44-45; Kilby, *Christianity and Aesthetics*, 22-24.

[18]Edgar, *Taking Note of Music*, 98.

[19]For a secular case for objectivity in aesthetics see T. E. Jessop, "The Objectivity of Aesthetic Value," in *Introductory Readings in Aesthetics*, ed. John Hospers (New York: The Free Press, 1969), 271-81.

[20]Jeremy S. Begbie, *Voicing Creation's Praise: Toward a Theology of the Arts* (Edinburgh: T. & T. Clark, 1991), 155-60; Calvin Seerveld, "In Search of the Aesthetic," Unpublished Paper, Philadelphia, January 1976.

[21]Begbie, *Creation's Praise*, 156.

[22]Cf. Corbitt, who feels that the definition of music itself is culture bound. *Sound of Harvest*, 33-34, 294.

[23]Bruno Nettl, "On the Question of Universals," *The World of Music* 19, no. 1/2 (1977): 3. See also Beardsley, "Reasons in Aesthetic Judgments," 274.

[24]John D. Erickson, "The Cultural Politics of Dada," in *Crisis and the Arts: The History of Dada*, ed. Stephen C. Foster, vol. 1: *Dada the Coordinates of Cultural Politics* (New York: G. K. Hall & Co., 1996), 27; Roy Allen, "Aesthetic Transformations: The Origins of Dada," in *Crisis and the Arts: The History of Dada*, ed. Stephen C. Foster, vol. 1: *Dada the Coordinates of Cultural Politics* (New York: G. K. Hall & Co., 1996), 77; Bruce Altshuler, *The Avant-Garde in Exhibition: New Art in the 20th Century* (New York: Harry N. Abrams, 1994), 33. Futurism was an avant-garde artistic movement that influenced Dada. For Futurism see Christine Poggi, *Defiance of Painting: Cubism, Futurism, and the Invention of Collage* (New Haven: Yale University Press, 1992).

[25]Edgar, *Taking Note of Music*, 7; Georges Ribemont-Dessaignes, "History of Dada," in *The Dada Painters and Poets: An Anthology*, ed. Robert Motherwell, 2d ed. (Boston: G. K. Hall & Co., 1981), 117; Michael Erlhoff, "Performances," in *Crisis and the Arts: The History of Dada*, ed. Stephen C. Foster, vol. 1: *Dada the Coordinates of Cultural Politics* (New York: G. K. Hall & Co., 1996), 158; Poggi, *Defiance of Painting*, 185-86.

[26]Edgar, *Taking Note of Music*, 56; Nathan Rubin, *Rock and Roll: Art and Anti-Art* (Dubuque, IA: Kendall/Hunt Publishing Co., 1993), 160.

[27]Jean-Jacques Nattiez, *Music and Discourse: Toward a Semiology of Music*, trans. Carolyn Abbate (Princeton, NJ: Princeton University Press, 1990), 52.

[28]Rubin, *Rock and Roll*, 160.

[29]Edgar, *Taking Note of Music*, 56; Rubin, *Rock and Roll*, 159.

[30]Edgar, *Taking Note of Music*, 56.

[31]Rubin, *Rock and Roll*, 162.

[32]An unwillingness to apply any appreciable biblical standards to music is evident in the aesthetic of most CCM promoters, such as Dave Hart: "Where the church gets into trouble is when it assumes that God follows the Church's standards and traditions. Appearance, volume, style, and culture, are not spiritual standards. They are man made standards." Al Menconi, "A Serious Look at Christian Heavy Metal: 'Vengeance Is Mine,' Saith the Lord—Or Is It?" *Media Update*, January-February 1989, 13.

[33]See Robert H. Mitchell, *I Don't Like That Music* (Carol Stream, IL: Hope Publishing Co., 1993), 36.

[34]For example, DeMol, "Sound Stewardship," 14-16; Lawhead, *Rock of This Age*, 117-19; Corbitt, *Sound of Harvest*, 248, 256.

[35]Cf. Corbitt, *Sound of Harvest*, 248, 256.

[36] Santiago-Lucerna, "'Frances Farmer Will Have Her Revenge on Seattle:' Pan-Capitalism and Alternative Rock," in *Youth Culture: Identity in a Postmodern World*, ed. Jonathan S. Epstein (Malden, MA: Blackwell Publishers, 1998), 190. Cf. Dave Laing, *One Chord Wonders: Power and Meaning in Punk Rock* (Philadelphia: Open University Press, 1985), 60; James Lull, "Listener's Communicative Uses of Popular Music," in *Popular Music and Communication*, ed. James Lull (Beverly Hills, CA: Sage Publications, 1987), 166.

[37]Robert Walser, *Running with the Devil: Power, Gender, and Madness in Heavy Metal Music* (Hanover, NH: Wesleyan University Press, 1993), 14. Cf. Patrick Gray, "Rock as a Chaos Model Ritual," *Popular Music and Society* 7, no. 2 (1980): 81; Al Menconi and Dave Hart, *Staying in Tune: A Sane Response to Your Child's Music* (Cincinnati, OH: The Standard Publishing Co., 1996), 62.

[38]Iain Chambers, "Popular Culture, Popular Knowledge," *OneTwoThreeFour* 2 (Summer 1985): 177.

[39]Steve Rabey, *The Heart of Rock and Roll* (Old Tappan, NJ: Fleming H. Revell, 1986), 75.

[40]Angelo De Simone, *Christian Rock: Friend or Foe* (New Haven: Selah Production Agency, 1993), 36. De Simone's admission here, as well as his understanding that Christian music should be joyful, pleasant, beautiful, and skillfully and professionally executed, seem quite inconsistent with his relentless position that all musical styles are derived from God, a matter of personal taste, and beyond judgment (pp. 15, 24, 25, 27, 59, 93, 94).

[41]Chambers, "Popular Culture," 178. See also John Street, *Rebel Rock: The Politics of Popular Music* (Oxford: Basil Blackwell, 1986), 176.

[42]Best, *Music*, 93-94.

[43]In this respect Curt J. Ducasse's relativism, which considers the individual's aesthetic consciousness as sovereign, is far more consistent with its own profession. For if there are no universal, transcendent, intuitive, self-evident, and divinely imposed standards of beauty and goodness then indeed "numbers mean nothing at all." "The Subjectivity of Aesthetic Value," 307.

[44]Millard J. Erickson, *Christian Theology* (Grand Rapids: Baker Book House, 1983), 628-29.

[45]I will not debate the implications of the fall on the human will. Calvinists and conservative Arminians agree on the doctrine of depravity, with the exception of the human will. Calvinists hold that the will, being corrupted by sin, is unable to respond to the free offer of grace in Christ, while conserva-

tive Arminians feel that although the will was at one time unable to respond, through what is known as prevenient grace or common grace the ability to choose was restored to man by God, enabling man to receive or reject the free offer of salvation. This controversy does not affect our discussion on aesthetics since there is sufficient agreement on both sides regarding the corruption of the other aspects of man.

[46]Cf. Edgar, *Taking Note of Music*, 56.

[47]John Murray, *Collected Writings of John Murray*, Select Lectures in Systematic Theology, vol. 2 (Edinburgh: Banner of Truth Trust, 1977), 102.

[48]Menconi and Hart, *Staying in Tune*, 160.

[49]Ibid., 159-60.

[50]Ibid., 161.

[51]J. O. Swahn, *The Lore of Spices: Their History, Nature, and Uses Around the World* (New York: Barnes & Noble, 1991), 12.

[52]Ibid., 15, 43, 38, 103.

[53]Ibid., 22, 24, 27, 32-33, 36, 42, 52, 56, 102, 144, 146, 148.

[54]Ibid., 26, 27, 97.

[55]On the World Wide Web at http://www.firegirl.com/eating.html; Swahn, *The Lore of Spices*, 176.

[56]Kellye Hunter, "Playing with Fire: The Risks and Benefits of Selling Super Hot Sauces," *Fiery Foods Magazine Online.* Document available on the World Wide Web at http://www.fiery-foods.com/zine-industry/playing.html.

[57]Ibid. Indeed many consumers 'want it.' David Ashley discloses that "one in seven hot shop customers comes through the door wanting the hottest thing that the store has to offer." Hunter, "Playing with Fire."

[58]Ibid.

[59]On p. 161 Menconi leaves no doubt that there is no limit to how "spicy our musical steak" can be. Likewise Michael S. Hamilton, "The Triumph of the Praise Songs: How Guitars Beat Out the Organ in the Worship Wars," *Christianity Today*, 12 July 1999, 35.

[60]The doctrine of depravity here does not contradict 1 Timothy 4:3-4, which most likely refers to Jewish dietary regulations.

[61]Yes, even spiciness has its limits: Although capsaicin, the ingredient in chile peppers that gives them their fiery flavor, causes desensitization so that one can build up tolerance and eat hotter and hotter peppers, it is possible to mix capsaicin in such high concentrations that it can blister the tongue, mouth, or any other part of the body. Consequently it is the main ingredient in pepper spray, a mace used in law enforcement and on bears, where the capsaicin is about three times more potent than in the hottest chile sauces. The potential for harm is also evident in the warning labels of some chile sauces: "Use at your own risk," "Use only one drop at a time;" some retailers will only sell a super hot brand called Dave's Private Reserve, if the customer signs a clearance waiver. Lastly, capsaicin causes constriction of the esophagus and bron-

chial tubes and can cause seizures in some individuals. Correspondence from Paul W. Bosland, of The Chile Pepper Institute, August 12, 1999; Hunter, "Playing with Fire."

[62]Menconi unknowingly verifies this in an earlier chapter: "Healthy people do not knowingly drink poison or consume the moldy, green stuff that grows in the back of their refrigerators. It's poison! It will make us deathly ill! And it probably won't taste too good either!" Menconi and Hart, *Staying in Tune*, 147.

[63]Best, *Music*, 17. Best's mistake is not one of awareness, but of underrating the effects of the fall and restricting its application. His earlier writings indicate that he is keenly conscious of the fall and its disfiguring effects on aesthetics, "What he [man] creates is often bent in its content, purpose, and direction. Man's ability to criticize and judge art is just as fallen as his other faculties." "There is More to Redemption Than Meets the Ear," *Christianity Today*, 26 July 1974, 13.

[64]Best, *Music*, 104-05. Similarly Pass, *Music and the Church*, 44.

[65]If depravity is depreciated by Best, it is entirely ignored by Corbitt. Music is seen as a gift from God granted to all mankind, but there is no hint of the effects of the fall on aesthetics or music. The concept of depravity has been bartered away for diversity. See Corbitt, *Sound of Harvest*, 33, 248.

[66]Charlie Peacock, *At the Crossroads: An Insider's Look at the Past, Present, and Future of Contemporary Christian Music* (Nashville: Broadman & Holman, 1999), 26.

[67]Ibid., 92.

[68]Ibid., 37.

[69]Ibid., 202.

[70]Ibid., 86, 92-96.

[71]Ibid., 96, 97.

[72]Ibid., 62, 202.

[73]Ibid., 41, 67. Gospel folk and rock actually began in the early sixties in England and took its cue from similar innovations in liberal Protestant music. Typical of the more than two thousand evangelistic "beat groups" in the mid-sixties was the Salvation Army's Joystrings, which performed in British coffee houses, bars, and night clubs. The degree to which the Jesus movement across the Atlantic was influenced by its British counterpart is not clear, but Ellsworth feels that even if entirely on its own the marriage of rock and gospel would have eventually taken place in the U.S. Donald Paul Ellsworth, *Christian Music in Contemporary Witness: Historical Antecedents and Contemporary Practices* (Grand Rapids: Baker Book House, 1979), 110, 111, 114-15, 123, 125, 126, 128, 129; Donald P. Hustad, "Music Speaks... But What Language?" *Christianity Today*, 6 May 1977, 16.

[74]Peacock, *At the Crossroads*, 41-42; Ronald M. Enroth, Edward E. Ericson, Jr., and C. Breckinridge Peters, *The Jesus People: Old-Time Religion in the Age of Aquarius* (Grand Rapids: Eerdmans, 1972), 164-65, 171-72, 174-75.

[75]Richard Quebedeaux, *The Worldly Evangelicals* (San Francisco: Harper & Row, 1978), 118. Cf. Hamilton, "The Triumph of the Praise Songs," 32.

[76]Quebedeaux, *The Worldly Evangelicals*, 118. The diversity of the movement, however, demands that such generalizations be nuanced. Some sects like Bethel Tabernacle could be quite proscriptive, forbidding such things as miniskirts, hugging between members of the opposite sex, and even the use of Jesus rock for evangelism. Enroth, Ericson, and Peters, *The Jesus People*, 97.

[77]Peacock, *At the Crossroads*, 43-45; Enroth, Ericson, and Peters, *The Jesus People*, 167, 176. Most of the Jesus People were charismatic, and those who weren't were tolerant of their charismatic brethren. Enroth, Ericson, and Peters, *The Jesus People*, 16, 112.

[78]Peacock, *At the Crossroads*, 51.

[79]Ibid., 70.

[80]Jay R. Howard and John M. Streck, *Apostles of Rock: The Splintered World of Contemporary Christian Music* (Lexington, KY: The University Press of Kentucky, 1999), 218-19.

[81]Francis A. Schaeffer, *How Should We Then Live? The Rise and Decline of Western Thought and Culture* (Old Tappan, NJ: Fleming H. Revell Co., 1976), 184, 187.

[82]David A. Noebel, *Christian Rock: A Stratagem of Mephistopheles* (Manitou Springs, CO: Summit Ministries, n.d.), 9.

[83]Richard Huelsenbeck, "En Avant Dada: A History of Dadaism," in *The Dada Painters and Poets: An Anthology*, ed. Robert Motherwell, 2d ed. (Boston: G. K. Hall & Co., 1981), 23-24; Calvin Tomkins, *The World of Marcel Duchamp 1887-* (New York: Time, 1966), 56.

[84]Tomkins, *Marcel Duchamp*, 56.

[85]Ibid., 57.

[86]Huelsenbeck, "En Avant Dada," 24.

[87]Ribemont-Dessaignes, "History of Dada," 102. See also Schaeffer, *How Should We Live*, 188.

[88]Dick Hebdige, *Subculture: The Meaning of Style* (London: Routledge, 1979), 106.

[89]Albert Gleizes, "The Dada Case," in *The Dada Painters and Poets: An Anthology*, ed. Robert Motherwell, 2d ed. (Boston: G. K. Hall & Co., 1981), 302.

[90]Richard Huelsenbeck, "Dada Lives!" in *The Dada Painters and Poets: An Anthology*, ed. Robert Motherwell, 2d ed. (Boston: G. K. Hall & Co., 1981), 279; Huelsenbeck, "En Avant Dada," 44.

[91]Schaeffer, *How Should We Live*, 188, 190.

[92]Jack D. Flam, "Foreword," in *The Dada Painters and Poets: An Anthology*, ed. Robert Motherwell, 2d ed. (Boston: G. K. Hall & Co., 1981), xiii.

[93]Ibid.

[94]Ibid.

[95]Altshuler, *The Avant-Garde in Exhibition*, 9.

[96]Tomkins, *Marcel Duchamp*, 63.

[97]Kurt Schwitters, "Merz," in *The Dada Painters and Poets: An Anthology*, ed. Robert Motherwell, 2d ed. (Boston: G. K. Hall & Co., 1981), 63.

[98]Tomkins, *Marcel Duchamp*, 66.

[99]Ibid.; Flam, "Foreword," xii.

[100]Tomkins, *Marcel Duchamp*, 95, 96.

[101]Ibid., 98.

[102]Altshuler, *The Avant-Garde in Exhibition*, 122.

[103]Noebel, *Christian Rock*, 9.

[104]Hebdige, *Subculture*, 105.

[105]Altshuler, *The Avant-Garde in Exhibition*, 122-24.

[106]Noebel, *Christian Rock*, 9.

[107]Roberta Smith, "De Maria: Elements," *Art in America*, May/June 1978, 104.

[108]Ibid.

[109]Rose Slivka, "The Dynamics of Destruction," *Art in America*, January 1999, 85.

[110]Ibid.

[111]Ibid., 88.

[112]See Raphael Rubinstein, "Abstraction Out of Bounds," *Art in America*, November 1997, 110. Begbie (pp. 213-14) argues that disorder in modern art should not be maligned as crude and meaningless since it can serve as social commentary on the ravages of sin. In one sense I must admit that even something as unpleasant as the Holocaust Museum (Jerusalem) functions as an effective reminder that nothing of the sort must ever happen again. But at the same time who would consider piles of human hair or gold fillings to be art or aesthetic? Further, one would be hard pressed to prove from Scripture that one of the purposes for the arts is to invoke horror, confusion, and fragmentation by its very form, even if simply for moral critique. Instead, contrary to Scripture, such an approach abuses man's creativity in order to *dis*-create, and when it is honored as art it glorifies the very evil it hopes to expose.

[113]Smith, "Elements," 103-05.

[114]Dada's involvement in music is certainly as old as Dada itself. We recall that the earliest performances at the Cabaret Voltaire included cubist dances, dog barking, and noise music. Dada, along with Zen Buddhism, also had a major impact on John Cage and his noise music. Elsewhere, the irrationalism of Dada can be discerned in John Lennon's "I Am the Walrus," with its confusing blend of "goo goo joob," "oom pah oom pah," "everybody's got

one," and "sit you down, Father; rest you." Musically this is more apparent in "Strawberry Fields Forever," an alchemy of "muffled trumpet fanfares, purposeless drumming, organ like sounds with reversed articulation—materials brought together as if by chance which reveal unsuspected compatibilities." Rubin, *Rock and Roll*, 82, 159-60.

[115]Peter Wicke, *Rock Music: Culture, Aesthetics and Sociology*, trans. Rachel Fogg (Cambridge, England: Cambridge University Press, 1990), 138; Laing, *One Chord Wonders*, 11.

[116]Wicke, *Rock Music*, 138. See also Laing, *One Chord Wonders*, 41-42.

[117]Wicke, *Rock Music*, 138-39.

[118]Ibid., 136; Laing, *One Chord Wonders*, 23-24, 126; Craig O'Hara, *The Philosophy of Punk: More Than Noise!!* (Edinburgh: AK Press, 1995), 10-11. For Situationism see Chambers, "Popular Culture," 249; Street, *Rebel Rock*, 175.

[119]Wicke, *Rock Music*, 136; O'Hara, *Philosophy of Punk*, 11.

[120]Chambers, "Popular Culture," 181.

[121]Charles Brown, *The Art of Rock and Roll* (Englewood Cliffs, NJ: Prentice-Hall, 1983), 242.

[122]Gina Arnold, *Kiss This: Punk in the Present Tense* (New York: St. Martin's Griffin, 1997), xi.

[123]See Harold G. Levine and Steven H. Stumpf, "Statements of Fear through Cultural Symbols: Punk Rock as a Reflective Subculture," *Youth & Society* 14, no. 4 (June 1983): 430.

[124]Street, *Rebel Rock*, 175.

[125]Chambers, "Popular Culture," 183.

[126]Laing, *One Chord Wonders*, 76-78.

[127]See Levine and Stumpf, "Statements of Fear," 431.

[128]Laing, *One Chord Wonders*, 78.

[129]Jon Savage, *Time Travel: Pop, Media and Sexuality 1976-96* (London: Chatto & Windus, 1996), 127-28.

[130]Rubin, *Rock and Roll*, 179.

[131]O'Hara, *Philosophy of Punk*, 16. O'Hara (pp. 16-17) points out that punk has a greater affinity to Futurism, an avant-garde movement similar to Dada.

[132]Wicke, *Rock Music*, 137.

[133]Brown, *Rock and Roll*, 241.

[134]Kristine McKenna, "Burned Bridges & Vials of Blood," in *Make the Music Go Bang! The Early L.A. Punk Scene*, ed. Don Snowden (New York: St. Martin's Griffin, 1997), 43.

[135]Laing, *One Chord Wonders*, 13.

[136]Ibid., 14. One might include here punk's ambition to do away with barriers between the performer and the audience, and a return to a more grassroots philosophy of audience and entertainer. Laing, *One Chord Wonders*, 84; O'Hara, *Philosophy of Punk*, 17.

[137]Laing, *One Chord Wonders*, 60-63.

[138]Wicke, *Rock Music*, 137. Cf. Santiago-Lucerna, "Alternative," 191-92.

[139]Steve Turner, *Hungry for Heaven: Rock and Roll and the Search for Redemption* (London: Kingsway Publications, 1988), 139.

[140]Mikal Gilmore, "Mick Jagger," *Rolling Stone*, 5 November-10 December 1987, 34.

[141]Cf. Rubin, *Rock and Roll*, 124.

[142]"Ramones," All the Stuff (and More) vol. 1 Sire Records 1990, 7.

[143]Savage, *Time Travel*, 126.

[144]Chambers, "Popular Culture," 10.

[145]Arnold, *Kiss This*, xii.

[146]Savage, *Time Travel*, 26.

[147]Laing, *One Chord Wonders*, 26.

[148]Arnold, *Kiss This*, 104.

[149]O'Hara, *Philosophy of Punk*, 23.

[150]Hebdige, *Subculture*, 109. See Levine and Stumpf, "Statements of Fear," 423.

[151]McKenna, "Burned Bridges," 44.

[152]Santiago-Lucerna, "Alternative," 192.

[153]Laing, *One Chord Wonders*, 97.

[154]Wicke, *Rock Music*, 141-42.

[155]Keith Morris, "Bring on the Guinea Pigs," in *Make the Music Go Bang! The Early L.A. Punk Scene*, ed. Don Snowden (New York: St. Martin's Griffin, 1997), 50.

[156]Savage, *Time Travel*, 151.

[157]Claude Bessy, "Less Than Total Recall, by What's His Face," in *Make the Music Go Bang! The Early L.A. Punk Scene*, ed. Don Snowden (New York: St. Martin's Griffin, 1997), 173.

[158]Peacock, *At the Crossroads*, 96.

[159]Dan Peters, Steve Peters, and Cher Merrill, *What About Christian Rock?* (Minneapolis: Bethany House, 1986), 140.

[160]Arnold, *Kiss This*, xii, 71; Menconi and Hart, *Staying in Tune*, 74.

[161]O'Hara, *Philosophy of Punk*, 22.

[162]Ibid., 105, 109.

[163]Ibid., 5; Arnold, *Kiss This*, 205.

[164]Chambers, "Popular Culture," 248. According to Lawrence Grossberg, "Rather than seeking to become art or to trash aesthetic pleasures, rock and roll constructs an aesthetics of trash (for example, this is the dominant way in which punk and postpunk were received)." Lawrence Grossberg, "Rock and Roll in Search of an Audience," in *Popular Music and Communication*, ed. James Lull (Beverly Hills, CA: Sage Publications, 1987), 194.

[165]*Contemporary Christian Music*, February, 1999.

[166]For "noise" see the web sites of One 21 (www.accnorwalk.com/~ivan/main. html.), Duckie (users.erols.com/iluvduckie/DUCKiE!!.html.); for "screaming" see the bands Lust Control (www.geocities.com/SunsetStrip/Lounge/ 4892/interview.html.), One Bad Pig (www.algonet.se/~kosher/obp.), the Blamed (tlem.netcentral.net/reviews/9504/frail_rev.html.); for "rawk" see the Underdog Conspiracy (www.sunflower.org/~dabeys/un/unbio.htm.).

[167]Such grassroots Christian punk groups would include Nobody Special, Spudgun, and Upside Down Room.

[168]Todd Brown, *"TleM Review* of *Frail* by The Blamed." Document available on the World Wide Web at tlem.netcentral.net/reviews /9504/frail_rev.html.

[169]On the World Wide Web at http://users.erols.com/iluvduckie/happypix. html.

[170]On the World Wide Web at http://www.angelfire.com/nt/nl/mattpics.html.

[171]On the World Wide Web at http://www.angelfire.com/nt/nl/ryanpics.html.

[172]On the World Wide Web at http://www.angelfire.com/nt/nl/trevpics.html.

[173]On the World Wide Web at http://www.rio.com/~wretched/ns2.html.

[174]Like the metal bands discussed in chapter two, these groups claim biblical referents for their names and song titles, but the double entendre and its connection to punk philosophy is unmistakable. Thus, for example, the Dead Pharisees can claim that their name *means* "dead to the law and alive with Christ" (Romans 7:6; Ephesians 2:5), but its *public* appeal is clearly punk, and probably a parody of the Dead Kennedys. With an album named *Mummified Priest* and a web page bookended with skulls, this group (whose oldest member is but nineteen) treats death with a sort of cinematic enchantment and insensitivity unheard of in the Bible, but quite popular among the morbidly minded headbangers of this generation. If the only purpose behind such a name was to express death to the law and life in Christ, it could have been accomplished much more tastefully and accurately than "Dead Pharisees." See on the World Wide Web at http://www. mosqui-tonet.com/~pharisee/about.html.

[175]Nik Cohn, *AwopBopaLooBopaLopBamBoom: Pop from the Beginning* (London: Paladin, 1970), 157; quoted in Bernice Martin, "The Sacralization of Disorder: Symbolism in Rock Music," *Sociological Analysis* 40, no. 2 (1979): 104.

[176]Wicke, *Rock Music*, 45.

[177]Devlin Donaldson, "Barnabas: Forging Musical Horizons," *Contemporary Christian Music*, October 1998, 69; David S. Hart, "Heavy Metal Thunder," *Contemporary Christian Music*, January 1988, 18.

[178]Brian Quincy Newcomb, "On Her Majesty's Secret Service," *Contemporary Christian Music*, March 1999, 37; Lou Carlozo, "Super Tone Deaf," *Contemporary Christian Music*, February 1999, 18.

[179]Steve Rabey, "Age to Age," *Contemporary Christian Music*, July 1998, 32.

[180]*Contemporary Christian Music*, July, 1998. Tooth & Nail Records is not a marginal Christian label but quite popular and influential, signing groups like the Supertones and MxPx.

[181]Ideal examples of this kind of secular thinking would be Clive Bell and Curt Ducasse. Bell, "Significant Form," 88; Ducasse, "The Subjectivity of Aesthetic Value."

6

Rock Music and Psychological Studies

Introduction

CCM ADVERSARIES OFTEN CITE psychological studies to prove that rock music is mentally and physically harmful to human beings and other life forms. Until Steve Miller such criticisms failed to receive adequate treatment by the CCM faithful, often being dismissed as apocryphal, amateurish, or inconclusive.[1] Miller, however, considers evidence from psychology to be a serious threat and goes to great lengths to personally investigate the damaging studies. Corbitt contributes his own version, which can be considered an updating of Miller's findings, though not any kind of an advancement or paradigm shift; his stance is also less apologetic.[2] Consequently, I will concentrate on Miller's assessment since it represents the most developed endeavor of this type.[3]

John Diamond

In his examination Miller focuses on the experiments of John Diamond, which have been marshaled by many CCM opponents to demonstrate that rock music causes physical damage by weakening the muscles. Miller attempts to discredit Diamond's approach by disclosing the unorthodox methodology of his experiments on muscle groups and the inconsistency of his conclusions.[4] Perhaps his most effective refutation comes from incidences in practical life, such as when he argues that popular music is used in weight rooms to increase motivation and that in one case it assisted a college student to break a sit-up record.[5]

Since it is inherently problematic, I will not attempt to defend behavioral kinesiology or Diamond's hypothesis concerning rock music's muscle-weakening effects—although it is worth mentioning that some researchers seem to hold to a similar notion that "rock music with its repetitive beat tends to produce a reduction in skeletal muscle tension, resulting in reduced motor activity."[6] Regardless of the fidelity of Diamond's experiments, the muscle strength that music produces or reduces should not be a major criterion for evaluating the benefits or drawbacks of a musical genre, since according to differing circumstances both muscle weakness and stimulation can be desirable. Despite the genuine weaknesses that Miller points out in Diamond's method, what is suggested by the experiments and supported by other observations and studies is that music can affect living organisms, including human beings, in significant and often consistent ways.

Miller's Method

Before Miller takes the offensive with research that hopes to debunk Diamond's theories, he informs his readers that "the following study will apply equally to other assertions that popular music styles cause psychological harm."[7] Intending to capitalize on the weakness of Diamond's method, Miller attempts to baptize all studies detrimental to rock music with the same stigma. This, however, is questionable for at least three reasons. First, the constitution and fabric of other studies and experiments are of a different vintage than Diamond's. They use different approaches, subjects, and methods and have different outcomes than Diamond's. Second, as will be shown, Miller's own findings have significant drawbacks at times and are not as conclusive as they first seem.

Third, though Miller shows a wise suspicion about the viability of psychological studies, he himself assigns them an authoritative role by relying on information favorable to him—most of which has to do with the "familiarity hypothesis"—to debunk anti-rock studies. We should realize that the "familiarity and individual-preference hypothesis," as helpful and corrective as it may be, is also subject to revision, reinterpretation, and refinement. Therefore, Miller's all-inclusive approach is simply unsatisfactory. He needs to deal with all the opposing studies individually, or at least in larger classifications and subgroups, instead of implicating them with the ignominy of Diamond's approach.

Finally, in claiming that "studies sensationalized by critics have been weighed in the balance and found wanting,"[8] we should take note that Miller essentially deals with only two studies out of several. Further, it will be demonstrated that Miller is successful in discrediting only one of the two studies that he chooses to deal with.

The Factor of Preference

Music and Motion

Miller first cites a 1979 study in *Perceptual and Motor Skills* titled "Effects of Familiarity of Music on Vigilant Performance." He uses it to undermine Diamond's opinion that rock music is physically disabling. Miller states that "the object of the N.C. State study was to ascertain what effect music might have on the maintenance of vigilance."[9] This, however, is not entirely correct. The researchers were well aware of studies showing that music increased vigilance in task performance.[10]

The experiment really focuses on the conclusion of a 1976 study (Corhan and Gounard) that suggested that "vigilance performance is best when background stimulation is discontinuous and contains elements of uncertainty, as in rock music, which was more diversified, vigorous, and changeable than easy-listening music."[11] Craig W. Fontaine and Norman D. Schwalm, the authors of our article, actually disprove Corhan and Gounard's thesis that the unpredictable and harsh properties of rock music assist in vigilance, recommending on the contrary that it was not the musical style but the familiarity that caused improvement. They claim that their study "questions Corhan and Gounard's (1976) premise that vigorous rock music should be associated with better performance than easy-listening music due to its physical properties of discontinuity and uncertainty."[12] They conclude that psychological factors like familiarity may override the physiological effects of music. So then Fontaine and Schwalm demonstrate that it was not the turbulent composition of rock music that contributed to the improved performance (referring especially to Corhan and Gounard), but its familiarity to the listeners.

Miller gleans from this article that rock music is not harmful in task performance in order to challenge Diamond's position. In this he succeeds; at the same time though, it needs to be understood that the researchers nowhere deny that styles of music can affect us physically. Rather, the study suggests that psychological factors, in some cases, may be more important than physical ones.[13] (The whole matter of musical preference—a key factor in this study—will be addressed later in this chapter.)

Another study commandeered by Miller discusses the effect of background music on physical performance by testing the hand-to-eye coordination of subjects exposed to different listening environments.[14] The four groups were no music, classical, jazz, and popular. The conclusion reached was that music did not significantly affect performance in any of the four groups, although it should be noted that the popular music group ranked lowest of all. In that the experiment itself lasted only four minutes and fifty-seven seconds, we should heed the warning of the researchers who admitted, "Present findings should not be considered conclusive," and, "caution should be taken when interpreting short-term results."[15]

Miller also makes brief mention of a University of Illinois experiment that drew the general conclusion that familiar popular music increased output and performance by subjects tested.[16]

Likewise, Corbitt cites a 1994 study in the *Journal of the American Medical Association* on how music affected surgeons.[17] Corbitt's description makes it appear as if the experiment was conducted while the surgeons were in surgery, when in reality it did not involve surgery at all but consisted of mathematical subtraction tests, which were intended to create stress and measure task performance.[18] Three conditions were imposed upon the surgeons: no music, preferred music, and Pachelbel's *Canon in D*, an orchestral piece commonly used for stress reduction.[19] The results demonstrated that the surgeons performed their arithmetic tasks fastest and most accurately when listening to the music they preferred. The preferred music also resulted in the greatest degree of stress reduction (as measured by skin conductance, blood pressure, and pulse). The *Canon in D* did not yield the benefits of the preferred music, but still ranked above the control, no music, in both the performance and stress categories.[20] An important factor in this experiment is that the vast majority of the music selected by the surgeons was classical (92%), with only two choosing jazz and two Irish folk instrumentals.[21]

This again tends to show that preference is important in evaluating the overall effects of music. We might add here a more recent observation by Mary E. Saurman (1995) that carries the familiarity view as far as heavy metal, demonstrating that in one case it assisted in relaxing a woman (a heavy metal fan) during childbirth.[22]

Relaxation

Another study that Miller cites seems to indicate that preference and not musical style was the crucial variable in relaxation.[23] This experiment was unlike the ones previously mentioned in that the musical styles were limited to no music, soothing classical, stimulating classical, romantic, atonal, and easy listening. Further, the "subjects were not allowed to choose the kind of music they heard."[24] Therefore, when Miller quotes the researchers as saying that "the most important factor in relaxation was the degree of liking for the music," we should remember that "liking" does not refer as before to one's favorite style of music, but to preferring a style within a limited selection of music that was chosen beforehand for the study, without the input or recommendation of the subjects.[25] Consequently, those who enjoyed the music to which they were exposed (without choice) tended to achieve relaxation, while those who did not, found relaxation much more difficult. Moreover, Miller fails to mention an important outcome of the experiment: the atonal (off key), cacophonous music of Schoenberg was "liked significantly less and led to significantly less relaxation than did other types of music."[26] Rock music was not a factor in the study.

What this experiment demonstrates, then, is that of the five styles of music available, "the majority of the subjects in the music groups said that music helped them relax."[27] The reason that this study is of little value to CCM is because rock styles were not employed and because the study reveals that, apart from personal preference, the

subjects, for the most part, enjoyed classical and easy listening offerings and were assisted in relaxation by them.[28]

In a final appeal to the primacy of personal preference in judging
the effects of musical style, Miller presents the results of a thorough
evaluation by Suzanne B. Hanser on music and stress reduction.[29]
Hanser's article, assessing the available studies on this topic, comes to
the conclusion that individual preference is a key ingredient in successful relaxation.[30]

Since Hanser's study echoes the findings of current research, to one
degree or another, we will now deal with the factor of preference in
music and its relation to relaxation and performance. We have seen that
some of the studies project that musical preference is able to bypass, in
many cases, the possible physiological and psychological effects of
various styles of music to the degree that preference may increase
performance and relaxation, or at least not hinder it. This factor, however, does not prove that rock music is physically or psychologically
harmless. It simply means that preference may be able to temporarily
override the physiological and psychological consequences of a style.
Even the apparent sedative effects of heavy metal music on its patrons,
though surprising, are not as conclusive (or groundbreaking) as they
first appear. Verle L. Bell, a psychiatrist who has dealt with his share of
addicts, acknowledges, "Many addicts affirm that the [rock] music
actually calms them and they feel better." Yet he maintains that
"adrenaline addicts go into withdrawal or become immersed in the
available music. They get some 'relief' from listening, but no pleasure."[31]

Neither is this phenomenon limited to music. For example, it is
well known that smoking is physically destructive to a person's health,
yet those addicted to nicotine will claim that smoking actually helps to
calm their nerves.[32] Smokers often brag that they perform better when
smoking. So then, although pleasure may temporarily mitigate the
psychological or physical effects of harmful substances, this does not
necessarily make activities like listening to rock music inconsequential;
nor does it mean that detrimental aftereffects have not occurred at a
deeper physical and psychological level, whatever the effects may be.

The series of studies that Miller uses to make his point bears this out in that all of the conclusions were based on short-term analyses. The longest period of time during which the subjects were exposed to the music was forty-five minutes,[33] with the shortest being only four minutes and fifty-seven seconds.[34] None of these experiments were able to evaluate the long-term effects of rock music on mental and physical health, which I feel must be an important consideration in any evaluation of this type. In this vein it should also be remembered that these experiments were not repeated to see whether the initial outcome could consistently be reproduced. Therefore, Miller's collection of studies is itself inconclusive.

'Of Mice and Men'

Rock opponents may have been disheartened to learn that Richard Lipkin's 1988 article in *Insight* magazine, "Jarring Music Takes Toll on Mice," was stripped of validity by Miller.[35] In the article Lipkin summarized the results and implications of an experiment published in the *Bulletin of the New Jersey Academy of Science* entitled "Neural Plasticity of *Mus musculus* in Response to Disharmonic Sound." In the experiment researchers exposed mice to two styles of music, classical and non-rhythmic drum beating, to determine the effects of various acoustical stimuli on their brains. The experiment revealed that the mice exposed to the non-synchronized rhythms "experienced hyperactivity, learning disability and memory degradation" as well as significant neurological deformities.[36]

Miller alleges, however, that Lipkin misrepresented portions of the experiment by linking the chaotic drum beats to rock music. He feels that Lipkin was mistaken because in the actual experiment "the mice were never exposed to a rock beat" and because "rock music was neither used nor even mentioned in the study."[37] According to Miller, Lipkin's error was unfortunately apprehended and disseminated by zealous critics who failed to verify his reporting with the original study. They then spuriously campaigned that learning disabilities and brain tissue damage in mice were caused by rock music, whereas Miller is certain that "they used nothing of the sort."[38]

Nevertheless, before rock critics jettison the findings of this experiment, they should be advised of certain facts that Miller overlooked. First, after reading both the *Insight* article and the original study, I am certain that Lipkin had access to firsthand information beyond that of the nine page article in the *Bulletin of the New Jersey Academy of Science*. The citations, as well as other information in Lipkin's story, were not found in the original article. An example of this is when Lipkin discloses that "the inspiration for the experiment came to the scientists about a decade ago, when they began hearing charges of conservative critics that rock music was ruining the brains of America's youth."[39]

I verified the accuracy of Lipkin's reporting by contacting Dr. Grevasia Schreckenberg, one of the authors of the original article. Schreckenberg affirmed that the selection of chaotic drumming (patterned after voodoo ceremonial drumming) was related to rock music, it being "the idea of Dr. Bird [the other author] that some 'Heavy Metal' of the 1980ties [*sic*] would fit that category."[40] The experiment was, after all, as Lipkin had stated, motivated and oriented toward the rhythmic effects of certain rock forms. Yet, by limiting himself to the journal article, Miller bypassed this important factor. So then, Miller was actually the one who was misled, since he measured the accuracy of Lipkin's reporting against the journal article alone, not realizing that Lipkin used other legitimate sources.

Whether or not voodoo-like drumming is similar to certain rock styles should not be of foremost interest. What should be of primary concern is the fact that a certain form of music did proven damage to mice. The point is that most CCM advocates not only believe that rock music is neutral and psychologically inconsequential, but that all musical forms are legitimate and beyond judgment. They are trapped in the liability of all musical amoralists in that they are forced to defend even the most grotesque and irrational musical styles as long as they are appreciated by some. The pervasiveness of this view will not allow musical relativists to make exceptions, even in the case of the chaotic drumming used in this experiment, which after all can be considered a form of music.

In conclusion then, the experiment does not necessarily prove that rock music hinders learning or alters brain tissue in humans. Yet, it does show that a form of chaotic drum beating, related to voodoo-ceremonial drumming, caused hyperactivity, learning disabilities, and some brain damage in Swiss albino mice. Music can affect living organisms negatively. Despite the fact that this was a pilot study, the two researchers felt that it was possible that such music could have negative effects on human beings as well. Harvey H. Bird remarks, "What we are seeing here is the effects of disharmonious music on mammalian brains. And insofar as human beings have mammalian brains, we cannot preclude the possibility that disharmony may affect human brains as well."[41]

Next, Miller turns to an article in the *Indian Journal of Applied Psychology* to further defuse the results of Lipkin's story.[42] He summarizes the study by explaining that "both styles of music [rock and classical] aided the learning process in the early stages and hindered it in the latter stages. Further, both styles helped the rats to maintain their learned response after they had been exposed to stress."[43] There are, however, elements of this study that Miller did not disclose. The object of the research was to verify the genuineness of the researchers' hypothesis that "musical stimulation shall [*sic*] influence the organizational behavior of albino rats in different orders and sequences."[44] Therefore, twelve albino rats were given learning exercises in three different audio environments: no sound, classical music, and rock music. The results were based on five criteria: number of errors, number of bar presses, activity level, latency (time span between bar presses), and latency after exposure to shock.[45]

In assessing their study the researchers tended to group the rats listening to classical and rock music together against the control or non-music group. Yet, in some categories there were appreciable differences between the two musical groups. Of the five categories used, only in the area of activity level did the classical group rank significantly below the rock group.[46] That is, rats listening to classical music had fewer bar presses. In other categories, however—such as errors committed—the rats exposed to rock music scored lower than did the classical and non-music group.[47] Also, in latency after shock treatment, the classical group outperformed the non-music and rock group, which fared better than the non-music group.[48] Therefore, if we distinguish between the rock and classical test groups, we discover that the classical group fared slightly better than the rock.

Rock Music: A New Herbicide

In the late 1960s a series of experiments was conducted on plants that demonstrated the beneficial and destructive powers of music. These experiments, which yielded extremely consistent results over a period of two years, have unfortunately been disparaged by rock enthusiasts as unscientific and sophomoric and have been consigned to fable-like status. Among Christians, Lawhead maligned it as a "vaguely constructed" experiment (which he thought was a possible hoax) that demonstrated nothing about plants or human beings.[49] Even careful researchers like Howard and Streck discard it as apocryphal, "an apparently undocumented experiment."[50]

Because of such skepticism, I decided that the report was worth a thorough investigation. Immediately, I discovered that such experiments did take place and were documented in *Empire Magazine* of the *Denver Post*, June 21, 1970. The experimenter was Dorothy Retallack, a forty-three-year-old biology student at Temple Buell College in Denver, Colorado.[51] The experiments that she conducted, exposing plants to different musical styles, were part of a science project required for her biology class.

In 1968 Retallack, in a series of eleven experiments, exposed several species of plants to different styles of music. Her professor, Francis F. Broman, assures us that "Dorothy worked under strict scientific controls from the first, and we did everything possible to insure accurate, unbiased results."[52] Usually groups of five different plants were placed in environmentally controlled chambers that assured identical temperatures, lighting, and air supply for the control and test groups. Further, all the plants were potted in identical soil and were given equal amounts of water at the same time. The only variable was the type of music.[53]

In one experiment Retallack exposed one set of plants (petunias and zinnias) to rock music played on station KIMN and another set to semi-classical music and hymns originating from station KLIR. All other factors being equal, including the volume, "the petunias listening to KIMN [rock station] refused to bloom. Those on KLIR [semi-classical and hymns] developed six beautiful blooms."[54] Further, the petunias surrounded by rock music leaned away from the speaker "showing very erratic growth."[55] At the same time the petunias treated with classical sounds grew toward the speaker.[56] The zinnias had a similar reaction. More telling is the fact that after one month all the plants listening to rock music died!

At this point skeptics will insist that other variables could have been responsible for the startling results. Indeed, Retallack was immediately inundated by accusations of this nature from students and faculty at the college. Retallack satisfied each of her critics by reproducing the experiment according to the stricter controls that they recommended. Some skeptics insisted that the voices of the disk jockeys on the two types of radio stations may have caused the different outcomes. In response Retallack duplicated the experiments, this time using taped music without the variable of the announcer's voice. The outcome was the same. Soothing music benefited the plants while rock music killed them.[57]

Others suggested that results such as the plants leaning away from the rock music could be attributed to her handling of the plants. To meet this objection Retallack "turned the flower pots so the plants leaned toward the speaker. A few days later the plants had reversed position and were again trying to get away from the rock sound."[58]

Another cynic felt that Retallack's emotions influenced the experiments since she was the only one who maintained the plants and their environment. Nevertheless, when the experiment was repeated, this time with the help of an impartial custodian who knew nothing of the study, the outcome was identical.[59]

Retallack did not stop simply with the results of these experiments. She supported the findings with "weekly measurements of plant growth, root system changes, and leaf discoloration."[60] Further, even after her science project was completed, she continued her experiments at school with findings that supported her original studies. These later experiments also verified that "soothing melodies seemed to make the plants flourish. Loud and discordant sounds made them droop, then die."[61]

In a final experiment, which the *Empire Magazine* recorded on film, rock music and other forms of dissonant music were tested on bean, squash, corn, morning glory, and coleus. Again, using strict controls, one group was exposed to the hard rock of Led Zeppelin and Vanilla Fudge and another to the dissonant and atonal sounds of contemporary avant-garde music. The control group was isolated from all music and sound. Within ten days the rock plants were found leaning away from the speaker, as were those listening to the avant-garde music—though to a lesser degree. Three weeks after the experiment had commenced, reporter Olga Curtis described the condition of the plants:

> The plants in the acid rock chamber were dying. The squash had almost fallen over. The morning glory, instead of crawling up as is natural, had sagged and were stretched over four pots, in the direction away from the music. Corn stalks sagged in the middle. The beans were stunted and tilted far away from the speaker. All the plants showed browning leaves except the crimson coleus.[62]

Furthermore, the article records that the plants exposed to the rock music were leaning sixty degrees away from the speaker. Even more striking is the fact that after unpotting, Retallack discovered that the roots were also traveling away from the speaker! The plants in the control group (no music) were six and a half inches taller than the rock group and had vibrant fulsome roots. The control group also outperformed those treated with avant-garde music, which managed slightly better than the rock group. Better than all these was a group that was exposed to soothing devotional music in an earlier experiment. These, as expected, grew toward the speaker, produced healthy shoots and roots and grew two inches taller than the control group of the later study.[63]

I have described these experiments in detail in order to head off the usual censures of quackery, bias, and error. The consistency and rigorous controls of Retallack's experiments are difficult to assail. Moreover, they are partially supported by similar experiments on plants and animals.[64]

Many will doubtless complain that plant and animal experiments should not determine the suitability of rock music for human beings. Even though skepticism of this sort is not unwarranted, in that plants and animals are in many ways different from human beings, we should still take these studies seriously. First, mankind does have certain biological similarities to other created beings. Second, the significance of these experiments lies in the fact that plants, and in most cases animals, do not come with preconditioned tastes in music, a factor that makes it difficult to determine the fidelity of similar studies on human beings.[65] David Tame stresses that "if music can be shown to affect plants, then such effects have to be due to the objective influence of the tones directly upon the cells and processes of the life-form."[66] Therefore, there should be reason for concern. As Retallack herself puts it, "If rock music has an adverse effect on plants, is the rock music listened to so long and so often by the younger generation partly responsible for their erratic, chaotic behavior?"[67] With this in mind, we turn to a more recent study on human beings.

Links to Bad Behavior

Impressions by the staff of a state mental health hospital that clients seemed to behave less appropriately when hard rock or rap music was played, in contrast to easy listening and country, prompted a controlled study of this phenomenon.[68] The experiment consisted of controlling the type of music played in a communal enclosure and recording the behavior of mental patients during their stay in the patio. The music was provided by two FM stations, one an all rock/rap format and the other an easy listening/country and western station.[69] The rock/rap music was played for a period of twenty-one days, followed by twenty-one days of easy listening/country music. Afterwards, the rock/rap station was played again for another eighteen days.[70]

The results indicated a significant difference in inappropriate behavior between the rock/rap periods and those of easy listening/country, confirming the earlier suspicions of the hospital staff.[71] The investigators state:

> The evidence for the effect of music conditions on observed inappropriate behaviors is compelling; when hard rock and rap music were played 5 hours per day, the average number of observed and scoreable inappropriate behaviors per day (17.7) was almost twice that of the experimental period (9.0) during which easy listening and country and western music were played.[72]

On a percentage scale the misbehaviors recorded during the rock/rap sessions averaged almost one hundred percent higher than those during the easy listening/country ones.

The researchers admit to the limitations of the experiment, however, especially noting that "no controls for lyric content or rhythm variations were exercised."[73] Although the experiment was geared toward the effects of different musical styles, the researchers feel that future studies would be necessary to determine whether the lyrics themselves may have had a mediating effect.[74]

Despite this drawback and other variables, the experiment still merits consideration.[75] To begin with, the differences in the behavior recorded were striking, with rock/rap coming out the loser by an almost two-to-one margin. Also, we must ask whether the lyrical content of country and western music is that much of an improvement over hard rock and rap or to what degree the lyrics caused the misbehavior—even at a subliminal level.[76] (Chapter four disclosed the preference for music over lyrics in pop music.) It is probable that it was a combination of both the lyrics and the music, but it is highly unlikely, under the circumstances just described and the moral ethos of rock music, that the musical form was an innocent bystander.

An aside: Neither this experiment nor any other should lead to the conclusion that rock music directly causes deviant behavior, in the sense of a hypnotic or irresistible coercion.[77] Music communicates by way of symbols, which suggest and influence behavior rather than automatically generate it. Further, variables may affect the results of such investigations, as CCM proponents would be the first to point out. I feel, however, that studies like these lend support to research in other fields that this variety of music communicates feelings and images of aggression and violence, which in turn may encourage destructive behavior.

Hearing Damage

It is difficult to comprehend how Miller could entitle a chapter "Charges of Health Threats" and disregard the hearing damage often caused by listening to rock music. Far more disappointing is Menconi, who, through a breathtaking array of misapplied Scriptures, concludes that there ought to be no limits to the volume of music:

> *But exactly how loud is too loud? Is soft music more biblical than loud music? At what volume does it go from being spiritual to unspiritual?*
> ...I have found dozens of instructions to sing loudly, play musical instruments loudly, and generally make a loud noise to praise God.[78] (Italics original.)

In a textbook example of private interpretation, Menconi attempts to garner support for the deafening sound of today's electronically amplified rock music from the primitive instruments and singing of Hebrews (usually in the open air), who at their most intense volume levels could never approach the modern object to which they are likened. Much more reckless are the Hebrew word studies that he uses to prove his point:

> The other two, *ranan* and *ruwa*, indicate that the singing should be loud....
> Just how loud? The root of *ranan* suggests that the singing should be a loud, raspy, harsh-sounding shrill. The root of *ruwa* suggests that the singing should split the ears with sound! So the next time we start to criticize a Christian band for being too loud, we should remember Scripture.[79]

First of all, if *ranan* (properly *rānan*) suggests anything by its root, it is a "ringing cry," and this based on an onomatopoeic interpretation of the word's origin.[80] By onomatopoeic I mean that the pronunciation of the word resembles the actual sound of the activity. Here it is thought that the double nasalization of *rānan* crudely imitates the ringing sound sometimes achieved in loud sustained vocalization. Although it is impossible to prove conclusively, this interpretation is probably correct; but to proceed from there to Menconi's imperative "that the singing should be a loud, raspy, harsh-sounding shrill" is clearly the product of over-imaginative exegesis.[81] Rather, most scholars agree that in the context of music the sense of *rānan* is simply that of jubilant singing or shouting.[82]

His understanding of the significance of the root meaning of *ruwa* (properly *rûaʻ*) is even more at fault. The root meaning of *rûaʻ* does *not* suggest "that singing should split the ears with sound," but rather the awakening of emotions, and so may have originally meant "to frighten, surprise, delight, excite pleasure, or arouse wonder."[83] Even so, the best way to derive a verb's sense is not through its etymology, but through the context in which it was used at the time of writing. The primary meaning of *rûaʻ* in the Old Testament is simply "'to raise a noise,' by shouting or with an instrument,"[84] and in the context of music it takes on shades of meaning very similar to *rānan*, i.e., a loud, joyful shout.[85]

So then, Israelite music does not support the high decibel levels that accompany rock music. Of course, any music or sound elevated to unhealthy levels is likely to cause hearing damage. This, however, is no reprieve for rock fans since one of the indispensable ingredients and signifiers of most rock forms is excessive volume. In fact high volume interpenetrates rock music to such a degree that loud music and rock music are often synonymous in popular thinking. Rock music, especially in heavier styles, makes its impact through punishing sounds that traumatize the auditory receptors,[86] making its aural assault as violent and reckless to the eardrums as its style of composition to good tonal art. This is because rock music is designed to dominate the listener, and the high volume helps to facilitate this end. Robert Duncan observes,

> And of course it was loudness that appealed to the fans. Now rock 'n' roll had always liked *loud*, in part because *loud* was unlikable and in part because *loud* could hold its own in the cacophony of modern city life. But mainly rock 'n' roll liked *loud* because loud meant passion, *loud*

meant the pent anger of the age, and loud rock 'n' roll thus became an acting out of that anger....[87]

In fact some hard rock albums explicitly encourage their listeners to "PLAY THIS MUSIC LOUD," if they are to appreciate its full impact.[88] Consequently, rock fans find it difficult to enjoy their music at low or normal sound levels, especially in concert settings.

As a result, proven hearing damage has occurred in individuals from listening frequently to rock music at high volumes, as several writers have documented. Noebel estimates that "many of America's youth could well be deaf by the age of 25 and others [would suffer] with hearing losses of a substantial nature."[89] John Blanchard cites British studies that demonstrate how decibel levels at many rock concerts far exceed the recommended levels of safety.[90] He adds:

> An ear, nose and throat specialist in the United States estimates that about 40% of students entering university have hearing defects caused by listening to rock music; twenty-five years ago, in pre-rock days, the figure was 1%. In a study carried out on 505 British students in higher education, Hanson and Fearn discovered that "statistically significant hearing losses were found in the group that admitted frequent attendance at pop music entertainment." Other studies by Ronald Fearn...suggested that up to one million young people in Britain suffered some degree of hearing loss caused by listening to loud music and that many have hearing problems normally associated with sixty-five to seventy-year-olds.[91]

Tom Allen warns,

> Most ear doctors say that we should not listen to anything above 90 decibels on the sound scale. Many rock music groups, both secular and Christian, play at the 120-125 decibel level! (Keep in mind that the SST Concorde Supersonic jet hits just over 130 decibels when leaving Washington's Dulles Airport).[92]

James Lull adds, "Parents and audiologists have warned teenagers for years that high-volume concerts will cause permanent hearing loss. The warnings have had little impact on listening behavior."[93] As we have already seen, they have also had little impact on the listening behavior of Christians.

It should be emphasized that hardcore Christian concerts are no more charitable to the ears than secular ones. There is essentially no difference in the equipment and volume levels of comparative secular and Christian rock bands. Patrick Kavanaugh, referring to Christian groups like Blindside, Skillet, and the Crucified, says, "the volume at concerts usually stays above one hundred decibels."[94] Consequently, like their secular counterparts, Christian rock bands must also wear earplugs for hearing protection during concerts.

For several reasons then, any serious treatment of rock music and health threats cannot afford to neglect the issue of volume and hearing damage.

Conclusion

When we assess Miller's defense, we learn that none of his studies successfully vindicates rock music from allegations of psychological and physical damage. As explained earlier, none of the experiments on musical style and preference lasted more than forty-five minutes, and none were repeated, whereas most of the experiments that were cited against rock were much longer in duration. It was also explained that the advantages to short-term performance that familiar music offers are not guarantees that the music is actually beneficial or harmless.

At the same time we must accept Miller's challenge to move beyond secondhand reports and refrain from accepting psychological studies at face value.[95] Yet, even though many of these studies have variables and are not conclusive, because a sufficient number of them suggest that music affects living organisms—including human beings—negatively and positively, there is enough reason for concern. Further, because music is apprehended through biological organs and tissues (often delicate), which are created, finite, and capable of injury and abuse, music must have at the very least biological controls. This is most apparent in the volume of rock music, as we just saw. More so, rock musicians recognize this limitation when they (non-Christians and Christians!) boast that their music is loud enough to make the ears bleed or cause a headache.[96] Also, since rock is electronically amplified music, it has greater potential to penetrate the human body. Arnett testifies that at a heavy metal concert, "on occasion you can actually feel your ribcage vibrating."[97] The simple point is that an unlimited view of musical parameters does not comport with a finite view of its receptacle, the human body. One would think that even the most ardent relativist would concede this point. But if Menconi's attitude, "If it's too loud, you're too old,"[98] is any example, don't count on it.

Endnotes

[1]Steve Lawhead, *Rock of This Age: Real and Imagined Dangers of Rock Music* (Downers Grove, IL: Inter-Varsity, 1987), 54-60. Even so I feel that Lawhead represents one of the more advanced early critiques of psychological studies on music.

[2]J. Nathan Corbitt, *The Sound of Harvest: Music's Mission in Church and Culture* (Grand Rapids: Baker Books, 1998), 144-49.

[3]It should be noted from the outset that using the term "psychological" to describe the kinds of experiments that have partaken in the CCM debate is somewhat misleading, since many studies deal primarily with physiological aspects like blood pressure and respiration, and brain, cell, and motor function.

[4]Steve Miller, *The Contemporary Christian Music Debate: Worldly Compromise or Agent of Renewal?* (Wheaton, IL: Tyndale House, 1993), 9-10, 11.

[5]Ibid., 12. Likewise, Corbitt reports that strongly rhythmic music like rock speeds injury rehabilitation "because it stimulates movement and masks minor pain." *Sound of Harvest,* 149.

[6]Frances F. Cripe, "Rock Music as Therapy for Children with Attention Deficit Disorder: An Exploratory Study," *Journal of Music Therapy* 23 (1986): 34.

[7]Miller, *Christian Music Debate,* 13.

[8]Ibid., 20.

[9]Ibid., 13.

[10]Craig W. Fontaine and Norman D. Schwalm, "Effects of Familiarity of Music on Vigilant Performance," *Perceptual and Motor Skills* 49 (1979): 71.

[11]Ibid.

[12]Ibid., 73-74.

[13]Ibid., 74.

[14]David W. Sogin, "Effects of Three Different Musical Styles of Background Music on Coding by College-Age Students," *Perceptual and Motor Skills* 67 (1988): 275-80.

[15]Ibid., 279.

[16]Miller, *Christian Music Debate*, 15; Leon K. Miller and Michael Schyb, "Facilitation and Interference by Background Music," *Journal of Music Therapy* 26 (1989): 42-54.

[17]Corbitt, *Sound of Harvest*, 149.

[18]Karen Allen and Jim Blascovich, "Effects of Music on Cardiovascular Reactivity Among Surgeons," *Journal of the American Medical Association* 272, no. 11 (September 1994): 882.

[19]Ibid.

[20]Ibid., 882, 883-84.

[21]Ibid., 884.

[22]Mary E. Saurman, "The Effect of Music on Blood Pressure and Heart Rate," *EM News* 4, no. 3 (August 1995): 1-2. Saurman's conclusions are of limited value since no apparent distinction was made between the music and the lyrics, or comprehension of lyrics. As a possible explanation for how this type of music could assist in relaxation see Makoto Iwanaga, "The Effects of Repetitive Exposure to Music on Subjective and Physiological Responses," *Journal of Music Therapy* 33, no. 3 (1996): 228.

[23]Miller, *Christian Music Debate*, 16-17; Valerie N. Stratton and Annette H. Zalanowski, "The Relationship Between Music, Degree of Liking, and Self-Reported Relaxation," *Journal of Music Therapy* 21 (1984): 182-92.

[24]Stratton and Zalanowski, "Music and Relaxation," 190.

[25]Ibid., 187.

[26]Ibid., 189.

[27]Ibid., 191.

[28]Ibid.

[29]Suzanne B. Hanser, "Controversy in Music Listening/Stress Reduction Research," *The Arts in Psychotherapy* 15 (1988): 211-17.

[30]Ibid., 213-14.

[31]Verle L. Bell, "How the Rock Beat Creates an Addiction," in *How to Conquer the Addiction of Rock Music* (Oak Brook, IL: Institute in Basic Life Principles, 1993), 84.

[32]Ibid.

[33]Fontaine and Schwalm, "Familiarity of Music," 72.

[34]Sogin, "Styles of Background Music," 277. The studies that were short term were Miller and Schyb, (40 min.), Fontaine and Schwalm (45 min.), Sogin (4 min., 57 sec.), and Stratton and Zalanowski (15 min.).

[35]Miller, *Christian Music Debate*, 15-16.

[36]Grevasia M. Schreckenberg and Harvey H. Bird, "Neural Plasticity of *Mus Musculus* in Response to Disharmonic Sound," *Bulletin of The New Jersey Academy of Science* 32, no. 2 (Fall 1987): 77.

[37]Miller, *Christian Music Debate*, 15; Richard Lipkin, "Jarring Music Takes Toll on Mice," *Insight*, 4 April 1988, 58.

[38]Miller, *Christian Music Debate*, 16.

[39]Lipkin, "Jarring Music," 58.

[40]Correspondence from Dr. Grevasia Schreckenberg, Lakewood, NJ, June 16, 1995.

[41]Lipkin, "Jarring Music," 58.

[42]Catherine Joseph and A. K. Pal, "Effect of Music on the Behavioral Organization of Albino Rats Using the Operant Conditioning Technique," *Indian Journal of Applied Psychology* 19 (July 1982): 77-84.

[43]Miller, *Christian Music Debate*, 16.

[44]Joseph and Pal, "Effect of Music on Albino Rats," 78.

[45]Ibid., 79-83.

[46]We should note that in the activity level and latency category the researchers considered the differences among the three groups to be statistically insignificant, although the rock group ranked better than the other two. Joseph and Pal, "Effect of Music on Albino Rats," 81-82.

[47]Ibid., 79. We should also note that the classical group was slightly less successful than the non-music group in errors committed.

[48]Ibid., 83.

[49]Lawhead, *Rock of This Age*, 55-56. Likewise Angelo De Simone, *Christian Rock: Friend or Foe* (New Haven: Selah Production Agency, 1993), 51-52.

[50]Jay R. Howard and John M. Streck, *Apostles of Rock: The Splintered World of Contemporary Christian Music* (Lexington, KY: The University Press of Kentucky, 1999), 36.

[51]Olga Curtis, "Music That Kills Plants," *Denver Post*, 21 June 1970, 8M.

[52]Ibid., 9M.

[53]Ibid. This is precisely what De Simone, who never bothered to read the article, upbraids in such experiments: "I strongly believe that even if these 'experiments' were conducted under the most professional conditions, by professional scientists, the results would have been the same no matter what kind of music the scientists used—rock, country, jazz, or even classical music—as long as the experiments were conducted under exactly the same conditions, circumstances, and volume outputs." *Christian Rock*, 52.

[54]Curtis, "Music That Kills Plants," 9M.

[55]Ibid.

[56]Ibid.

[57]Ibid.

[58]Ibid.

[59]Ibid., 9-10M.

[60]Ibid., 10M.

[61]Ibid., 11M.

[62]Ibid.

[63]Ibid.

[64]David Tame, *The Secret Power of Music: A Study of the Influence of Music on Man and Society, from the Time of the Ancient Civilizations to the Present* (Wellingbrough, Northamptonshire: Turnstone Press Limited, 1984), 141-45.

[65]Ibid., 144.

[66]Ibid., 142.

[67]Curtis, "Music That Kills Plants," 11M.

[68]Clarke S. Harris, Richard J. Bradley, and Sharon K. Titus, "A Comparison of the Effects of Hard Rock and Easy Listening on the Frequency of Observed Inappropriate Behaviors: Control of Environmental Antecedents in a Large Public Area," *Journal of Music Therapy* 29, no. 1 (Spring 1992): 6-17. Unlike the previous studies surveyed in this chapter, this is the only one that has a purely psychological and behavioral orientation (rather than physiological).

[69]Ibid., 10.

[70]Ibid., 10-11.

[71]Ibid., 11.

[72]Ibid., 12.

[73]Ibid., 15.

[74]Ibid.

[75]For other variables see pp. 14-15.

[76]Cf. Al Menconi and Dave Hart, *Staying in Tune: A Sane Response to Your Child's Music* (Cincinnati, OH: The Standard Publishing Co., 1996), 104-05; De Simone, *Christian Rock*, 56.

[77]Cf. William Neil Gowensmith and Larry J. Bloom, "The Effects of Heavy Metal Music on Arousal and Anger," *Journal of Music Therapy* 34, no. 1 (1997): 33-45.

[78]Menconi and Hart, *Staying in Tune*, 162. Mitchell displays a similar disregard for human limitations and hearing damage. Though he admits that some pop music does produce "sheer painful volume," he still maintains that it is appropriate for some listeners. De Simone, however, does recognize the danger of hearing loss due to loud music. Robert H. Mitchell, *I Don't Like That Music* (Carol Stream, IL: Hope Publishing Co., 1993), 62; De Simone, *Christian Rock*, 51.

[79]Menconi and Hart, *Staying in Tune*, 162.

[80]Francis Brown, S. R. Driver, and Charles A. Briggs, *The New Brown-Driver-Briggs-Gesenius Hebrew and English Lexicon* (Peabody, MA: Hendrickson, 1979), 943.

[81]Menconi fails to document either of his word studies. He also makes the common mistake of trying to ascertain the meaning and significance of a word from its origin rather than its immediate context and current usage. This is commonly known as the etymological or root fallacy. Moisés Silva illustrates the pitfalls of this approach with an example from the English language:

Who can resist the charm of finding out that the word *gossip* comes from *godsib* ("related to God"), used of godparents in the Middle Ages, and that the current meaning of the word arose from the chatter—not always edifying—typical at christenings in those days?... For some reason, however, most of us go on to infer that such a discovery gives us a better understanding of the *present* meaning of the word. And that is where our troubles begin.

...It should be quite apparent that the vast majority of English speakers today, being quite unaware of the history behind *gossip*, use the word without any reference to christenings, the concept of godparenting, or anything of the sort. (Moisés Silva, *God, Language and Scripture: Reading the Bible in the Light of General Linguistics*, Foundations of Contemporary Interpretation, vol. 4 [Grand Rapids: Zondervan Publishing Co., 1990], 87.)

[82]R. Laird Harris, Gleason L. Archer, Jr., and Bruce K. Waltke, *Theological Wordbook of the Old Testament*, vol. 2 (Chicago: Moody Press, 1980), 851; Ludwig Koehler and Walter Baumgartner, *The Hebrew and Aramaic Lexicon of the Old Testament*, vol. 3, trans. M. E. J. Richardson (Leiden: E. J. Brill, 1996), 1247-48; Norman E. Wagner, "*Rinnah* in the Psalter," *Vetus Testamentum* 10 (1960): 435-41; Ernst Jenni and Claus Westermann, *Theological Lexicon of the Old Testament*, trans. Mark E. Biddle (Peabody, MA: Hendrickson, 1997), 1240.

[83]Koehler and Baumgartner, *Hebrew and Aramaic Lexicon*, 1206. Also L. Kopf, "Arabische Etymologien und Parallelen zum Bibelwörterbuch," *Vetus Testamentum* 8 (1958): 203-04.

[84]Harris, Archer, and Waltke, *Theological Wordbook of the Old Testament*, 839.

[85]Tremper Longman III, "*rw*'," in *New International Dictionary of Old Testament Theology and Exegesis*, ed. Willem A. VanGemeren, vol. 3 (Grand Rapids: Zondervan, 1997), 1082; Harris, Archer, and Waltke, *Theological Wordbook of the Old Testament*, 839; Brown, Driver, and Briggs, *Hebrew Lexicon*, 929.

[86]Robert P. Snow, "Youth, Rock 'n' Roll, and Electronic Media," *Youth & Society* 18, no. 4 (June 1987): 334-35; Elianne Halbersberg, *Heavy Metal* (Cresskill, NJ: Sharon Publications, 1985), 32; Nathan Rubin, *Rock and Roll: Art and Anti-Art* (Dubuque, IA: Kendall/Hunt Publishing Co., 1993), 146; Robert Walser, *Running with the Devil: Power, Gender, and Madness in Heavy Metal Music* (Hanover, NH: Wesleyan University Press, 1993), 9.

[87]Robert Duncan, *The Noise: Notes from a Rock 'n' Roll Era* (New York: Ticknor & Fields, 1984), 46. See also p. 47.

[88]James Lull, "Listener's Communicative Uses of Popular Music," in *Popular Music and Communication*, ed. James Lull (Beverly Hills, CA: Sage Publications, 1987), 147-48.

[89]David A. Noebel, *The Marxist Minstrels* (Tulsa: American Christian College Press, 1974), 69. Cf. William Edgar, *Taking Note of Music* (London: Third Way Books, 1986), 7.

[90]John Blanchard, Peter Anderson, and Derek Cleave, *Pop Goes the Gospel: Rock in the Church*, 1983, enlarged and revised (Darlington, England: Evangelical Press, 1989), 24-27.

[91]Ibid., 25-26.

[92]Tom Allen, *Rock 'n' Roll, the Bible and the Mind* (Beaverlodge, AB, Canada: Horizon House Publishers, 1982), 156; quoted in Frank Garlock and Kurt Woetzel, *Music in the Balance* (Greenville, SC: Majesty Music, 1992), 154.

[93]Lull, "Listener's Communicative Uses," 148.

[94]Patrick Kavanaugh, *The Music of Angels: A Listener's Guide to Sacred Music from Chant to Christian Rock* (Chicago: Loyola Press, 1999), 257.

[95]For the potential pitfalls of purely experimental research see Roland S. Persson and Colin Robson, "The Limits of Experimentation: On Researching Music and Musical Settings," *Psychology of Music* 23, no. 1 (1995): 39-47.

[96]Cf. Steve Turner, *Hungry for Heaven: Rock and Roll and the Search for Redemption* (London: Kingsway Publications, 1988), 102; Steve Rabey, "Age to Age," *Contemporary Christian Music*, July 1998, 32; David S. Hart, "Heavy Metal Thunder," *Contemporary Christian Music*, January 1988, 18.

[97]Jeffrey Jensen Arnett, *Metalheads: Heavy Metal Music and Adolescent Alienation* (Boulder, CO: WestviewPress, 1996), 10.

[98]Al Menconi, "What's Wrong with Christian Music? An Open Letter to Contemporary Christian Musicians," *Contemporary Christian Music*, June 1987, 19.

7

On the History of Ecclesiastical Music and CCM

Introduction

IN THE ONGOING CCM debate, examples of secular influence in church music have probably caused conservatives more vexation than any other apology for CCM. In fact, it has become the main rallying point, even fortress, for CCM when it seeks to exonerate itself from criticisms of worldliness. Some form of this argument appears in most books that defend CCM, and even untutored CCM patrons often respond to objections with statements like, "Martin Luther used barroom tunes, and the Wesleys used the popular music of the day in their hymnody."

No recent writer has exploited the potential of this argument more than Steve Miller.[1] In fact, within the three chapters that he dedicates to this topic, Miller is able to effectively overwhelm and immobilize CCM opponents who accept his historiography uncritically. He does so by (selectively) following the music of the church from its inception to the present day and showing that throughout the history of Christianity church music has borrowed heavily from its surrounding culture and used the music for spiritual benefit.

Perhaps more troubling to musical purists is his disclosure of the history of ecclesiastical resistance to musical forms that today we consider harmless. Miller (and others) understand the current opposition to CCM to be nothing new, but part of a process of change, resistance, and renovation. He seeks to illustrate a historical pattern of separation, integration, conflict, and renewal and proposes that this is exactly what is taking place today.[2] Although he does not insist that history must repeat itself, he believes that in this case it has, and attempts to prove so by pointing out the many similarities between the current debate and musical controversies of the past. Consequently, he encourages his readers not to resist the musical changes that will eventually overcome them. Here Miller is clearly on the offensive and very persistent in making his point. Because of its potential impact, I will specifically critique Miller's version of this argument in this chapter.

The Apostolic and Ancient Church

Our first task will be to deal with Miller's disclosure that the early church adopted pagan musical styles. He explains,

> The cultural milieu of the early church was primarily Greek rather than Hebrew.... Greek thought and art forms dominated those early centuries.... and the ancient hymn writers set their lyrics to music with its stylistic roots in pagan Greek culture rather than biblical Hebrew culture.[3]

This news would not be a fatal blow even if it were accurate since most CCM critics do not claim that all styles of secular music are unsuitable. What is more, the evidence simply does not support Miller here, proving rather the opposite. It seems that Miller's source, *The History and Use of Hymns and Hymn Tunes* by David Breed, has betrayed him. Breed's book is simply incorrect in this area and is dwarfed by newer more exhaustive works (such as Sendrey's) that offer more reliable evidence.

Leading experts are in agreement that, though there is some evidence that Hellenistic poetic meters entered into some Christian hymnody at a later period, the vast majority of early Christian hymnody was distinctly Jewish and originated in the synagogue.[4] This fact is also evident in the New Testament where Paul commands the Colossians to sing psalms, hymns, and spiritual songs (Colossians 3:16), which is probably a reference to the music of the synagogue.[5] Sendrey states:

> But reports of the Early Church Fathers about the meetings of the first Christians comprise numerous references to the paramount importance attached by the new religion to psalm-singing, as practiced in the traditional, i.e., Jewish manner.... As a matter of fact, the first Christian songs have been either ancient synagogal chants, or were based upon Jewish "tunes," which were familiar to everybody at those times.[6]

By the end of the second century a discernibly hostile view toward pagan musical forms and instruments had developed. Beginning with the ascetic Tatian, continuing in the third and fourth centuries with Tertullian and Chrysostom, and persisting with Ambrose and Augustine, critical attitudes toward secular music gathered momentum and were solidly entrenched in the life of the ancient church.[7] James McKinnon feels that the reason for their antagonism (often excessive and unjustified) was due to the influence of Greco-Roman and Jewish moralism, which carried much the same tone. He admits that "there is hardly a major church father from the fourth century who does not inveigh against pagan musical practice in the strongest language."[8]

For example, even Clement of Alexandria, who made use of some Greek meters, clearly distinguished between the sacred and profane as he "warns the Christians of the chromatic (i.e., orgiastic) and burlesque melodies of the heathens and commands them to return to the traditional, diatonic psalmody of David."[9] Suzanne Haïk-Vantoura adds that "he [Clement] praised the liturgical music of the ancient Hebrews.... 'The songs of the Hebrews were of regular and harmonious cadence; their melodies simple and serious.'"[10] Clement's testimony of the ennobling character of Christian music and his efforts to resist pagan melodies is conveniently summed up by Sendrey: "In a moralizing tendency, CLEMENT OF ALEXANDRIA shows a deep cleavage between the music of the heathen revelers at their wild feasts, and the ardent, dignified singing of the Christians at their banquets."[11] Therefore, quite to the contrary of Miller's version, we find that the early church, for the most part, not only resisted secular tunes, but preserved the tunes and singing of the synagogue.

Ephraem Syrus

Next we turn to Miller's example of Ephraem Syrus, a beloved father of the Syrian church.[12] Miller is correct in saying that Ephraem imitated the form of Gnostic hymn writers in order to counter their heresies with orthodox teaching. Yet there are certain underlying facts that will enlighten us concerning the nature of this imitation and the musical form, known as the *madrāšâ*. First, though Gnostics, Bardaisan and his son Harmonios produced melodies that could hardly be considered pagan in character. In fact, the fifth-century historian Sozomen reports that the dictions of the *madrāšâ* were elegant, and the melodies charmed the Syrians.[13] Around the same period of time, the musically conservative Theodoret of Cyrus adds this important comment about the character of their music and Ephraem's use of it:

> And since Harmonios, the son of Bardesanes, had composed some songs long ago, and by mixing the sweetness of melody with his impiety had beguiled his audience and led them to their destruction, Ephraem took the music for his song mixed in his own piety, and thus presented his listeners with a remedy both exceedingly sweet and beneficial.[14]

Moreover, the *madrāšâ* was characterized by alliteration, rhyme, parallelism, and word play[15]—all of which, with the exception of rhyme, are also characteristic of Hebrew poetry. Likewise, Sendrey suggests that the psalter of Bardaisan and Harmonios was sung to the lyre in Jewish fashion.[16] Further, we discover that the versification of Ephraem's hymns was not metric but tonic, where accented syllables alternate with unaccented ones—a configuration also thought to be of Semitic origin.[17] Dimitri Conomos inserts, "They [the music of Bardaisan and Harmonios] included 150 psalms, in a pentasyllabic meter, reportedly modeled on those of David.... In retribution, St. Ephrem composed other psalms based on the same meter and with equivalent verse structure."[18]

Finally, we should carefully consider the insight of James McKinnon, who points out that due to Ephraem's popularity, his achievements were considerably sensationalized by later historians: "By the sixth century his biography had become richly ornamented with legend and his oeuvre interlarded with *spuria*."[19] This, along with the evidence presented above, casts tremendous doubt on the validity of using Ephraem's example as support for CCM, with the exception that Ephraem does betray a level of pragmatism in his approach.

Hilary of Poitiers

Miller, again depending on Breed, offers St. Hilary, Bishop of Poitiers, as Ephraem's counterpart in the Western (Latin-speaking) church. According to Breed, Hilary imitated the singing of the Arians to promote true Christianity.[20] Although this is more or less true, Miller's use of it is again misleading.

St. Hilary of Poitiers (315-367 A.D.) was an unyielding champion of orthodoxy and the first Latin hymn writer. He was one of the outstanding church fathers of the fourth century and an accomplished scholar, learned in both Latin and Greek. His primary contributions to music were his Latin hymnody and his allegorical commentary on the Psalms.[21] It was perhaps during his exile in the East that he was introduced to religious poetry by Greek Christians. It may also have been at this time that Hilary became familiar with the Arian method of disseminating doctrine through music and sought to imitate it for the orthodox faith.[22]

Further, Hilary considered himself a musical pioneer and an innovator in the class of King David.[23] Being familiar with the best of classical Latin poetry, Hilary chose to put his themes to the poetic meters of the finest Latin poet-moralists, such as Horace (65-8 B.C.) and Ovid (43-18 B.C.-A.D.), after substantially modifying them. As a mnemonic aid Hilary enhanced his poetry with acrostics, commonly associated with Lamentations and other Old Testament verse.[24] A. J. Mason explains that "Hilary was an explorer and a pioneer. 'He was the first who ever burst' into the untried region of Latin Christian hymnody."[25] He also feels that Hilary was pragmatic in that he used a metrical system that was popular at the time.[26]

Nevertheless, there was also a conservative bent to Hilary. He shared with the other fourth-century Latin fathers a revulsion toward pagan musical practice and instruments. In his *Instructio psalmorum*, an allegorical commentary on musical instruments, he exposes his musical discretion:

> Instead, it is an instrument [psaltery] built in the shape of the Lord's body and made without any inward or outward curve, an instrument moved and struck from above and brought to life to sing of supernal and

heavenly teaching, not one that sounds with a base and terrestrial spirit, as do the other earthly instruments.[27]

How do we explain this contradictory attitude toward secular music forms? McKinnon seems to find the answer, not only in Hilary's case but also the other fathers, in their cautious acceptance of music as an academic discipline.[28] As much as the ancient church disdained its pagan culture, it felt free to employ the insights and benefits of classical education through the seven liberal arts. As such, music was classified as a mathematical discipline along with arithmetic, geometry, and astronomy. According to McKinnon, "the *ars musica* is most characteristically a matter of number, in particular the fractions defining the intervals of the tonal system and the ratios underlying the rhythmical and metrical systems."[29]

In that classical canons of poetic meter were treated in an academic and mathematical sense, we can understand why Hilary would employ them in his hymns while sharing the same attitude of criticism toward pagan music held by the other fathers. Indeed, Hilary is consistent in that metrical changes in poetry are at most an insignificant form of secularization. The adaptation is as much linguistic as it is cultural. With respect to the inconsistency of the fathers, McKinnon advises that "everything [academic/mathematical study of music] is dealt with in a manner so far removed from everyday music that there is no real contradiction in the fact that the church fathers accepted it while rejecting pagan musical practice."[30] Therefore, I conclude that only in an indirect sense can Hilary be used as a precedent for the current controversy.

Conclusion

The music of the early church did not have its "stylistic roots in pagan Greek culture rather than biblical Hebrew culture," as Miller opines. Rather, the preponderance of the evidence points to an extremely conservative hymnody that originated in the synagogue. In fact, the relative resiliency of the Jewish form is so apparent in early church history that the Gregorian chant, which came much later, is said to have striking similarities to the synagogal chant.[31]

The evidence also shows the sensitivity (even over-sensitivity) of the ancient church fathers toward the music of their culture. Their negative attitude toward pagan musical forms is one of the most characteristic and striking features of any anthology of patristic writings on music—a fact barely acknowledged by Miller.[32]

It is true, however, that Ephraem, Hilary, and others did to some degree fall under the spell of pragmatism.[33] We should keep in mind that the church fathers were not immune to this unbiblical tendency. The acclaimed early church father and scholar Origen was committed to an allegorical mode of interpretation, in part, because he wished to make the Bible acceptable to the Greeks, who associated divine inspiration with allegorical meaning.[34] Further, Origen felt that proficiency in the allegorical method would elevate the Scriptures in the perception of non-Christian literary critics, who considered the Bible to be crude and inferior by the standards of classical literature.[35] Even prior to Origen, Clement of Alexandria was under the impression that Christianity, when understood through the grid of Greek philosophy, would attract the philosophically minded of the pagan world. Although we should not underrate the overall contributions of these men, we should realize that their pragmatic motivations were partially responsible for introducing systems of thought and interpretation that were largely incorrect and would plague the church for centuries to come.

Martin Luther

As Miller continues his journey through history, he pauses for a long look at Martin Luther, the pioneer of the Protestant Reformation.[36] Luther has been a favorite weapon in the arsenal of CCM apologists due to his innovations in evangelical hymnody and his use of secular material.[37] The boast that much of our hymnody includes secular melodies is largely based on the musical practices of the Reformation period.

Through a series of select quotations from Luther, as well as citations from his biographers, Miller tries to depict Luther as one who is operating in the same spirit of musical innovation as that represented by CCM. Of course, much of what he reports about Luther is accurate. For example, he is correct in disclosing that Luther wished to simplify the hymnody and make it understandable and meaningful to the average person. He is also accurate in stating that Luther was sensitive to the youth and wished to facilitate their participation in music. Moreover, Luther also felt that music should be used in proclaiming the gospel.[38]

Nevertheless, the overall impression of Luther that comes forth is skewed in favor of CCM's own doctrine. One of Miller's citations will suffice: "'For the youth's sake,' wrote Luther, 'we must read, sing, preach, write, and compose verse, and whenever it was helpful and beneficial I would let all the bells peal, and the organs thunder, and everything sound that could sound.'"[39] If we carelessly project twentieth-century musical practices and interpretations upon this citation, it is possible to agree with Miller's portrayal of Luther. Therefore, a fresh examination of Luther's musical ideology and practice is called for to see whether it accords with the popularized version.

Luther's Purpose

In that the propagation of Protestant doctrine was probably Luther's foremost purpose in writing and promoting evangelical hymnody, he sought nothing less than "that the words of the Scriptures should be placed in the mouth of every member of the congregation."[40] If we question why such a task was considered novel, we should remember that in Luther's day singing was limited (in most cases) to the clergy, while the congregation listened.[41]

More so, with few exceptions the masses, liturgy, and hymns of the Catholic church were conducted in Latin, a language unintelligible to the majority of the German peasantry. When reading Miller's citations of Luther such as, "It is best that such a service be planned for the young and for the unlearned folk who come to church," and, "Please omit all new-fangled court expressions, for to win popularity a song must be in the most simple and common language,"[42] we must interpret them in light of this serious language/literacy problem that existed in Luther's day. It was for the sake of comprehensibility that Luther wished to avoid the ornate Gothic expressions of the Latin hymns when translating them into German.[43]

Further, Luther was aware that in translation the accents and speech rhythms of the Latin language would never be entirely suitable for German inflection. Therefore, he saw the need for fresh melodies that would do justice to the German language:

> But I would very much like to have a true German character. For to translate the Latin text and retain the Latin tone or notes has my sanction, though it does not sound polished or well done. Both the text and notes, accent, melody, and manner of rendering ought to grow out of the true mother tongue and its inflection, otherwise all of it becomes an imitation, in the manner of apes.[44]

If these reasons were not sufficient for Luther, he would add that even if the current songs were understandable, their venomous content of "un-Christian fables and lies" was enough to destroy their value and demand replacement.[45]

In a sense Luther's prolific hymn writing was motivated by the same concern that compelled him to translate the Bible into German. He wished to give the people the Bible as well as Christian music in the vernacular. This intention is clearly visible in a letter to George Spalatin,

> [Our] plan is to follow the example of the prophets and ancient fathers of the church, and to compose psalms for the people [in the] vernacular, that is, spiritual songs, so that the Word of God may be among the people also in the form of music. Therefore, we are searching everywhere for poets.[46]

As we focus on Luther's primary intention for producing an evangelical hymnody, we must recognize that he saw other benefits in music. He considered music to be a gift from God that repels the devil, who causes "saddening cares and disquieting worries"[47]—perhaps depending on 1 Samuel 16:18-23. Moreover, his impression of music as a relaxant and device for upbuilding the character of youth[48] smacks of Platonic and Aristotelian musical theory, which attributes similar powers to music. At times he refers to music as a "mistress and governess of those human emotions…which as masters govern men or more often overwhelm them."[49] He also heralds,

> For whether you wish to comfort the sad, to terrify the happy, to encourage the despairing, to humble the proud, to calm the passionate, or to appease those full of hate—and who could number all these masters of the human heart, namely, the emotions, inclinations, and affections that impel men to evil or good?—what more effective means than music could you find?[50]

The Platonic element, unmistakable here, can be further supported by his medieval liberal arts training, which exposed him to substantial portions of Plato and Aristotle.[51] Consequently, it would be no exaggeration to brand Luther's position on music as Platonic—likewise John Calvin's[52]—making it highly unlikely that he would subscribe to present-day amorality theories.

Finally, it should be pointed out that while commenting in his "Preface to the Wittenberg Hymnal" (1524), Luther reveals another purpose for his hymn-writing that is directly related to the youth:

> And these songs were arranged in four parts to give the young—who should at any rate be trained in music and other fine arts—something to wean them away from love ballads and carnal songs and to teach them something of value in their place, thus combining the good with the pleasing, as is proper for youth.[53]

A four-part arrangement would be ideal for boy's choirs and would allow them robust participation in spiritual music that would replace their desire for sordid secular songs.[54]

Sources of Luther's Hymnody

During his busy lifetime, Luther composed thirty-seven chorales: fifteen of them were original melodies; thirteen were melodies from Latin hymns; four were melodies from German hymns and *Leisen* (religious German folksongs); two were pilgrims' songs; two were of unknown origin; and one was parodied from a secular folksong.[55] Luther depended heavily on the Scriptures, older Latin hymns, liturgical music, and the *Leisen* for the lyrics of his songs.[56]

Although Luther took the entire melody from only one secular song—"I Came From an Alien Country" for "From Heaven on High, I Come to You"—his own compositions reveal the infiltration of elements belonging to the style of contemporary folksong.[57] Clearly, the abundance of new texts written, in contrast to the paucity of melodies available, was a major catalyst for turning to secular music. Nevertheless, the difference between the secular and sacred at the time was not easily distinguishable in that music in the medieval period had predominantly ecclesiastical origins and orientation.[58] As Edwin Liemohn explains, "Those who taught and those who studied [music] were associated with the work of the church and many melodies written for secular texts were produced by the same men who wrote melodies for church use."[59] This secular-sacred connection can be seen in the similarity of the secular folksong with the *Leisen* (religious folksong),[60] a topic that merits a closer look.

The *Leisen* and Folksong

Luther adapted many elements from the folksong and *Leisen* in composing his chorales. Folk music is essentially the nonprofessional, improvised music of common people, which is perpetuated orally and expresses basic human experiences such as love, joy, fear, and sadness.[61] Whereas secular folksongs center on man's needs and experiences from a nonreligious perspective, religious folksongs (such as *Leisen*) are intended to express man's spiritual needs and experiences.[62] Understandably then, the difference between the two (secular and sacred folksong) is not significant.[63] Consequently, Luther felt free to borrow elements from both and adapt them to his original creations.

The Meistersinger

In addition to folksong, the serious more sophisticated music of the day, represented in the compositions of the well-trained Meistersingers and Minnesingers (today's art-song), also influenced Luther.[64] The Meistersinger, as Robert L. Harrell explains, was "a middle-class literary and musical movement of the fifteenth and sixteenth centuries which kept alive the folksong tradition of the traveling bards and also the aristocratic tradition of the Minnesinger of the twelfth to fourteenth centuries."[65]

The Minnesingers themselves were dependent on the French troubadours and trouveres for their material, who in turn were influenced by the medieval church. Gustave Reese explains the musical environment of the troubadours:

> The music of the Church was doubtless enriched by the music of the people; but it was very likely more influential than influenced. For the troubadour to model his songs directly on ecclesiastical melodies was both natural and easy. He heard music in the churches, and he attended churches frequently.... As we have noted... there was no sharp line of demarcation between sacred and secular music.[66]

In some cases the recycling process from sacred to secular and back to sacred was shorter than the above sequence. The sacred melody to the Lutheran chorale "To God Alone Be Honor on High," was parodied from a Meistersinger melody that itself was taken from the plainsong "Gloria." In this instance the church was simply reclaiming lost property.[67]

Luther's dependence on the Meistersinger is indicative of his good taste and his selectivity in that he carefully matched the text and the melody and made whatever adaptations necessary to align the music to the sacred text.[68] This is all the more true when we consider the variety of music available to Luther such as satires and drinking songs,[69] none of which contributed to his hymnody.[70]

It is perhaps in his selectivity of rhythm that we notice the seldom-acknowledged conservatism of Luther. In order for the congregation to sing in unison, a song had to contain some form of rhythm.[71] The plainsong (Gregorian chant), however, lacked the necessary rhythm. On the other hand, dance songs and drinking songs produced a rhythm far too intense and definite for Luther's purposes. Therefore, it is believed that in developing his chorales, Luther managed to discard dance songs altogether and limit the rhythm in other songs.[72] Harrell is quite convinced of this point: "Strongly rhythmic dance music also existed in Luther's day. The rhythms from these songs do not appear in Luther's music; rather, the rhythmic basis of the chorales lies in the word accents instead of dance rhythms."[73] And again, "The nature of the rhythms in the chorales, being based on the rhythms and accents of the words, is different from that of rhythms found in dance songs, which need a much more insistent and pronounced rhythm to enable the dancer to keep time."[74]

Ulrich S. Leupold, an authority on Luther, adds this in support of Luther's discrimination,

> Rollicking drinking songs were available in the 16th century too. Luther steered clear of them. He never considered music a mere tool that could be employed regardless of its original association but was careful to match text and tune, so that each text would have its own proper tune and so that both would complement each other.[75]

Likewise, Peter C. Lutkin remarks: "But whatever their source, these justly famous tunes are marked by devotional earnestness and great dignity.... The emotional element in music was scarcely yet developed, and even the love song of Luther's time was a serious and weighty affair."[76]

The example of Luther's only parody, "From Heaven On High I Come to You," provides an interesting example of both Luther's re-sourcefulness and discretion. The melody to this chorale was originally annexed from the popular folksong "I Come From an Alien Country,"[77] and first appeared in the 1535 edition of Klug's hymnal.[78] Neverthe-less, the same chorale ("From Heaven on High") in the Leipzig hymnal four years later was accompanied by an *original* tune from Luther, not the borrowed one.[79] The plot thickens as the secular tune, which was rejected in the 1530s and '40s, reappears as the melody for Luther's "From Heaven Came the Angelic Host" after his death.

What, then, explains the use, removal, and reuse of this secular tune? It is quite commonly accepted that the tune that Luther originally borrowed ("I Come From an Alien Country") was also popular at the time in taverns and dance halls.[80] Therefore, many feel that, because the tune's use in worldly haunts would sully the sacred text and bring secular associations inappropriate to worship, Luther replaced it with an original one.[81] The reinstatement of the tune to another chorale, "From Heaven Came the Angelic Host," after it would have lost its popularity in the dance halls as well as its worldly associations, sup-ports this position.[82] Moreover, Luther's desire to disassociate the youth from worldly love ballads for something pure and noble (as mentioned earlier) would also explain why he would abandon the borrowed melody so quickly.

Conclusion

As we have seen, Martin Luther was both eclectic and scrupulous at the same time. Millar Patrick phrases it this way,

> He was not content to accept anything uncritically; he was jealous of congruity between the theme of the verse and the spirit of the music. He carefully tested the propriety for their purpose of the melodies he considered, and where necessary molded them into suitability.[83]

Luther did not conceive of music as a neutral object that could be fully exploited in the propagation of the gospel. Rather, he demonstrates a rare sensitivity in the field, insisting that in the cohabitation of text and tune there must be congruence. In some cases he retained or modified secular elements, and in others he rejected them altogether. Yet, in all instances he endeavored to act with discrimination. Best's comments, though lengthy, leave us with some important closing thoughts:

> A misuse of history has overemphasized borrowing. A case in point is Luther's comment (when he was criticized for borrowing a drinking song) that the devil should not have all the good tunes. But Luther's position must be seen in the fuller context of his convictions about music. Borrowing to him was only a small part of a rich means of expression. When he borrowed, he borrowed excellence only and left mediocrity to the devil. A skilled musician and a composer, he looked with the greatest admiration to the best music of his time, that of the composer Josquin des Préz. If Luther's total position were injected into the contemporary discussion of church music, it would make him very unpopular.
>
> And if he were here today, he would have to reckon with new factors. He would have to examine the practice of borrowing in the light of a distance between the Church and secular culture unlike anything he had to face. He would have to confront an unprecedented proliferation of musical styles from both within and without Western culture, and he would have to face the Church with its preference for provincial witness. He would undoubtedly recognize that a large part of our musical experience is depersonalized, issuing electronically from walls, ceilings and

earphones as a background for everything from shopping to worshipping.[84]

The Wesleys

Introduction

Like his predecessors, Miller has capitalized on the hymn writing of the beloved Wesleys, Charles and John, as an example of the successful integration of secular musical forms into Christian hymnody.[85] He brings out the well-known fact that Charles Wesley employed secular tunes and popular styles of the day in his prolific hymn-writing in order to make an appeal for CCM's openness to secular styles. For example he asserts,

> Wesley had no qualms about combining the sacred and the secular when it came to the tunes that would carry the biblical message. "It was Wesley's practice to seize upon any song of the theater or the street the moment it became popular and make it carry some newly written hymn into the homes of the people."[86]

It must be insisted, however, that any plausible examination of Charles Wesley and the impact of his hymns should include his brother, John. Although John lacked the poetic genius of Charles and composed few hymns, he was, nevertheless, an ardent music critic and had much to say about the character of Methodist hymnody. Indeed, Charles did write most of the hymns, but John compiled the hymnals with characteristic precision, editing and revising them to include only the best.[87] This was necessary because in the sheer abundance of Charles' hymn writing (6,500) he produced much that was chaff; in Routley's assessment, "We must accept the fact that the generous and hospitable Gospel of the Wesleys allowed a good deal of bogus music to slip in."[88] Patrick writes,

> Charles had no discriminative faculty with regard to his own hymns, but John in revising and winnowing them showed remarkable judgment. The verdict he once passed on some of them might apply to them in mass— "some bad, some mean, some most excellently good."[89]

In fact, as Timothy Dudley-Smith puts it, "Without John's editorial excellence, and the humility [of Charles] to submit to it, Charles would have been much less as a hymn writer for today."[90] Therefore, we must be careful not to evaluate Charles' overall work in isolation from the prudent oversight of his brother.

John Wesley

Far from being an inclusivist, John Wesley was quite the music critic and surprisingly dogmatic at times. The evidence reveals that John, like Calvin and Luther, was a clear platonist when it came to music; that is, he did not believe that music was morally neutral! For this we turn to his tract, "Thoughts on the Power of Music," written in 1779:

> By the *power of music*, I mean its power to affect the hearers, to raise various passions in the human mind. Of this we have very surprising accounts in ancient history. We are told, the ancient Greek musicians in particular were able to excite whatever passions they pleased: to inspire love or hate, joy or sorrow, hope or fear, courage, fury or despair; yea, to raise these one after another, and to vary the passion just according to the variation of the music.[91]

Moreover, in his *Journal* (October 22, 1768) John espoused some pointedly negative views concerning polyphony, for which he also found support from the ancients,

> I was much surprised in reading an essay on music, wrote by one who is a thorough master of the subject, to find that the music of the ancients was as simple as that of the Methodists; that their music wholly consisted of *melody*, or the arrangement of single notes;... He [Charles Avison] farther observes that as the singing [of] different words by different persons at the very same time necessarily prevents attention to the sense, so it frequently destroys melody for the sake of harmony; meantime it destroys the very end of music, which is to affect the passions.[92]

An entry in his *Journal* on August 9, 1768 reveals John's scrutiny and intolerance of Methodist musical practice on one occasion,

> I began reading prayers at six, but was disgusted with the *manner* of singing: (1) twelve or fourteen persons kept it to themselves, and quite

shut out of the congregation; (2) these repeated the same words, contrary to all sense and reason, six, eight, or ten times over; (3) according to the shocking custom of modern music, different persons sung different words at one and the same moment—an intolerable insult on common sense and utterly incompatible with any devotion.[93]

John found support for his views from Johann Christoph Pepusch, who arranged music for *The Beggar's Opera*. Pepusch at eighty-one lamented with him that the art of music had been lost since the days of the ancients and that the present masters had no "fixed principles."[94] Although it cannot be determined with certainty that John's musical convictions were shared by Charles, we can safely say that John's views were reflected in the Methodist hymns and hymnals through his editorial activity. According to Louis F. Benson,

> Wesley gave the same forethought and attention to the musical as to the literary side of Methodist Song, keeping its direction in his own hands. His equipment for this undertaking was his sound musical feeling, a very limited technical knowledge, and an unusual practical sense. Perceiving the importance of the Hymn Tune to the purpose he had in view, he provided a body of "authorized" hymn tunes, and expected that none other should be sung by his followers. His cardinal principle was that the tunes should invite the participation of all the people; and, next should keep within the limits of sobriety and reverence.[95]

This means that any blanket statements about Charles Wesley having "no qualms" stand only until they are glazed with John's inquisition and censorship, who in a musical sense "was a thoroughgoing conservative."[96]

In what may be more meaningful to the CCM controversy, I forward this important observation about John's attitude toward secular music from Steven Darsey:

> His [John's] point about the Lancashire hornpipe gives insight into Wesley's views on the inherent religious character of music. The hornpipe would have been well known to Wesley as a popular dance form. By stating that some tunes have no more religion than these hornpipes [*Minutes of Conference*, 1768], Wesley implies that some tunes were inherently sacred and others inherently secular, and thus some were appropriate for worship and others were not.[97]

Darsey's conclusions can be supported by the fact that in his later years (seventy-eight), John again makes a distinction between the sacred and the secular, as well as repeating his disapproval of polyphony:

> I came just in time to put a stop to a bad custom which was creeping in here: A few men, who had fine voices sang a Psalm which no one knew, in a tune fit for an opera, wherein three, four, or five, persons, sung different words at the same time! What an insult upon common sense! What a burlesque upon public worship! No custom can excuse such a mixture of profaneness and absurdity.[98]

The Music of the Times

Before we proceed into a deeper investigation of the Wesleyan hymnological renewal, the musical practices of early eighteenth-century England need to be probed. This period was characterized by the Handelian opera and oratorio. Newly available advances in the printing of music made the music of the opera available to the general public,[99] and since there were no copyrights to restrict borrowing, it was freely practiced and even considered a complement. In contrast, the Church of England limited itself to metrical psalm singing, stubbornly holding to the works of Thomas Sternhold and John Hopkins. The melodies were lifeless, regimented, and unable to stir the soul, reflecting the spiritual condition of Protestant Christianity at the time.[100] The evangelical revival in England, with its stress on personal faith in Christ, naturally demanded lyrics and melodies that were consistent with the new emphasis. The source for the tunes that went with these new lyrics was primarily the Handelian opera and compositions from lesser opera composers such as John Frederick Lampe.

George Frideric Handel

German-born George Frideric Handel was the most popular musician in England at the time and is celebrated to the present day as one of the greatest composers of all time, due largely to his gift for melody.[101] Between 1745 and 1784 as many as forty-eight Handelian operas were performed and became well known.[102] It is not enough to say that Charles Wesley was quite appreciative of masters such as

Handel, since Handel himself, twenty-two years his senior, also took an interest in Charles and desired to compose hymns for him.[103] Although only three hymn tunes were directly composed by Handel for the Wesleys,[104] the Methodists used many tunes and choruses from Handel's operas. One of the first was the Jericho Tune from the opera *Riccardo Primo*, which John included in his foundery collection. This tune was indicative of the type of music that was selected from the oratorio and opera, namely tunes with religious themes from religiously-based performances. As John Wilson explains, "They [the tunes] were intended, it is true, to be 'entertainment'; but they were on religious themes, and that fact would allay any criticism of the borrowing."[105]

John Frederick Lampe

In his treatment of the Wesleys, Miller correctly relates that Charles' "compilation, *Hymns on the Great Festivals and Other Occasions*, contained twenty-four tunes by a German composer of comic opera."[106] Nevertheless, he neglects to mention that the composer was a Christian at the time. Lampe, like Handel, was born in Germany and was one in a class of secondary composers for the English stage. It is certain that Lampe, a friend of both John and Charles, was converted before providing the tunes for Charles' words in the 1746 hymnal that Miller was referring to. For verification we turn to John's *Journal*, November 29, 1745: "I spent an hour with Mr. Lampe, who had been a Deist for many years, till it pleased God, by the *Earnest Appeal*, to bring him to a better mind."[107] Lampe composed minimally for the opera after that and died five years later in Edinburgh.

The Wesleys' Purpose

We can now be detained with the important question of why the Wesleys used essentially secular music in their hymnody. The all-too-common answer is that they wished to win unbelievers through music that appealed to them. There is also the tendency to assume that the Wesleys were concerned only with the content of the music and not the style. I propose, however, that—due to the puritanical demeanor of the

Wesleys, as well as John's suspicion of current musical practice—this version is inaccurate and in need of amendment. The following discussion reexamines the evidence and takes into consideration the pietistic leanings of the Wesleys along with other important facts, both of which lead to more balanced and credible conclusions.

The best place to begin is with Erik Routley who discerns that "his [Charles'] purpose in writing them was threefold: to provide a body of Christian teaching, to provide material for public praise, and to objectify his rich personal faith."[108] Is it possible to understand, within these three purposes, why Charles set his lyrics to secular tunes? Although there is no single answer, the following reasons should prove enlightening.

Reasons for Secular Tunes

Unlike his predecessors, Charles employed various metrical forms in his hymns such as iambic, trochaic, dactylic, anapests, and couplets.[109] In addition many of his hymns added refrains and extensions to the metrical structure. These differences necessitated a change from, or adaptation of, the older psalm tunes, which could not support the newer structures.[110] The tunes, however, from the Handelian opera and oratorio suited this new format and were generously employed by Charles. So then, we have unmasked at least one reason for Charles' use of secular tunes: the need to find suitable melodies for his newer metrical structures.

To explain his second intention, we need a brief background into the formative influences of the Wesleys. Prior to their conversions, both Charles and John had spent considerable time with a group of German evangelicals known as the Moravians. In addition to admiring the Moravians' courage and devotion to Christ, both the Wesleys were captivated with the exuberant hymnody and singing of this group.[111] James Sallee describes the Moravian influence:

> The Wesleys' association with the Moravians during the trip and then in Georgia had an important influence on what was to become Wesleyan hymnody. Its immediate effect was to introduce to congregations an enthusiastic type of hymn singing quite foreign to the sober singing of the metrical psalms.[112]

Routley then makes an important connection between the singing of the Moravians (German pietists) and the music of the opera used by Charles:

> The true genesis of this style [Lampe's] is in German pietism, which used a highly decorative style in its devotional lyrics...; this decorative style reached its highest pitch of grace and discipline in the sacred lyrics of J.S. Bach published in the Schemelli *Chorale Book* of 1736, and it was a departure from the more restrained and severe style of Crüger and his school. It developed over the period 1670-1740, and it was this section of German piety which especially influenced the Wesleys. In itself, the music was probably hardly known to John and Charles Wesley personally, but this was the style of music associated with the evangelical religion in Germany, and it found its way at once into Methodism through the agency of the German-born Lampe. That was its religious origin, but we repeat that in any case this musical texture was common to sacred and secular music, and this musical material was that which, in their own ways, Handel, Bach and Haydn applied to their special purposes.[113]

It is quite evident then, according to Routely, that the Wesleys' approval of opera music was conditioned by their prior predilection for Moravian singing. What is more significant is that Routley traces the roots of the operatic style back to the music of the German evangelicals, whose style influenced German composers such as Lampe and Handel. Technically, then, the Wesleys were only introducing a style that was already, more or less, church property and "was common to sacred and secular music."[114]

In summary, the evidence points to two main reasons for the use of secular tunes in the hymnody: (1) The Wesleys were dissatisfied with the regimented metrical psalms sung by the Anglican church and were unable to express the newfound joy and intimacy of the evangelical faith with the lyrics or *meters* of these psalms. The new and various meters for the hymns demanded metrical structures different from those of the psalms, and these were found in the style or in the actual tunes of the popular music of the day; and (2) there is good reason to assume that the Wesleys used the popular music of the day (opera) because it was (whether they realized it or not) stylistically consistent with the spirited hymnody of the Moravians, which they had come to love and considered excellent in quality.

So then, there is simply not the kind of firsthand evidence—and much to the contrary—to conclude that the Wesleys were intentionally committed to appropriating secular styles for evangelizing and acclimating a pagan culture to Christianity. It is true, however, that Charles composed invitation songs that called sinners to salvation and that many have credited Methodist singing with a significant role in their conversion.[115]

Opposition

In most cases opposition to the Wesleys was also unlike the modern resistance to CCM. It was based predominately on the Anglican Church's predisposition to condemn those who dissented from their traditions and doctrines.[116] So when the Wesleys' evangelical emphasis was being scorned by the Church of England, their departure from the psalms became another reason for the church to repudiate the Methodists. M. F. Marshall states, "Thus, hymn singing, which Dissenters and Methodists practiced, came to stand for all that was wrong with non-orthodox faith."[117]

Early attacks against Methodist hymnody by Anglicans such as John Scot (1740) claimed that the compositions were irrational and based on an inaccurate concept of God that was expressed in words and melodies that stirred the emotions.[118] John responded by reminding them that "when it is seasonable to sing praise to GOD they do it with the spirit and with understanding also…in psalms and hymns which are both sense and poetry."[119] There were also later criticisms of Methodist music (1840s) such as those of Vincent Novello, a cultivated church musician, who referred to the music of the Methodists and Dissenters as light and trivial.[120] Furthermore, J. A. La Trobe in the late eighteenth century expressed objections to certain parodies of drinking songs contained in the Methodist hymnal.[121] Some of the criticisms, then (such as the previous two), may have been warranted, as even John did not approve of the exuberance of some of the later Methodist music.[122]

Further, modern hymnologists William J. Reynolds and Milburn Price certify that

> the character and quality of the Methodist tunes of the late eighteenth century declined. Trivial tunes became widely used, and the overly florid style that became so popular greatly weakened the strength of the Methodist hymn singing as the nineteenth century approached.[123]

Therefore, we can draw three conclusions about the opposition to Methodist hymns: (1) the resistance came mainly from the Anglican church, whose criticism of Methodist music was born out of a more significant resentment of the Methodists' evangelical emphasis; (2) as we saw earlier, much backlash was averted due to the religious themes of the borrowed tunes;[124] and (3) some of the later objections to the music may have been justified, as they were shared not only by critics of the time, but on occasion by John himself, as well as current writers.

Despite the criticisms of their contemporaries, some have testified to the aesthetically pleasing nature of their music: "The song of the Methodists is the most beautiful I ever heard. Their fine psalms have exceedingly beautiful melodies composed by great masters. They sing in a proper way, with devotion, serene mind and charm."[125] Indeed, Wesleyan hymns were delivered with the most profound and searching lyrics accompanied by singable melodies that can be described as thoughtful, noble, and devout.[126] Is it any wonder that such was the quality of the hymns and singing when we consider how carefully the words and tunes were selected and how stringently their singing was policed? John Wesley wrote in the preface to *Sacred Melody*, 1761, "Sing them exactly as they are printed here, without altering or mending them at all; and if you have learned to sing them otherwise, unlearn it as soon as you can."[127]

Conclusion

So then, when these facts are taken into account, the example of the Wesleys does far more to undermine CCM's position than it does to buttress it. John, who must be factored into the overall success of the Wesleyan hymnological revolution, was a far cry from the musical amoralists of today. As Darsey insists, "Clearly, Wesley was critically selective about the tunes he used for worship and he would not, contrary to today's popular notion, have considered raiding the bars indiscriminately for hymn tunes;"[128] he adds that "Wesley would not permit a hymn to be sung simply because it was popular. He would not permit hymns to be sung that did not measure up to his standards."[129]

Furthermore, it has been clarified that the factors that guided the Wesleys in using the popular music of the day were different from those that motivate CCM today. Likewise, the musical environment and the ethos of the tunes that the Wesleys selected were unquestionably different from rock styles. Finally, the nature of the criticism of Methodist hymnody is also largely out of cadence with the current opposition to CCM. I close with an urgent admonition from Darsey, who expresses my sentiments exactly: "No reasonable interpretation of the facts can justify in the name of John Wesley the freewheeling use of nearly any song that strikes the fancy of modern worship."[130]

Ira D. Sankey

We will now be occupied with Miller's treatment of Ira Sankey and the gospel hymn. Ira D. Sankey accompanied D. L. Moody as his song leader during Moody's evangelistic campaigns and popularized the gospel hymn, represented by such favorites as "The Sweet By and By," "Sweet Hour of Prayer," and "Rescue the Perishing." Miller informs us that "his style of song could be described as a popular folk hymnody," and gives two testimonies stating that Sankey's success was due to the fact that his music was delivered in a popular style.[131]

I am interested here only in liberating the *form* of Sankey's gospel hymn from incorrect implications suggested by Miller. This should not be construed as an endorsement of Moody and Sankey's understanding and overemphasis of the gospel song as an evangelistic tool. Both were convinced that the gospel should be preached from the pulpit and choir loft.[132] Like many, they were plagued by pragmatism, a mentality that gripped the United States after the Civil War in both religious and secular spheres.

As we take soundings of Sankey's style and music, we discover that Sankey did not invent the gospel hymn. Sallee explains:

> This does not mean the gospel hymn did not exist before these men [Sankey and Moody], but it was popularized and received its greatest impetus as an aid in mass evangelism at the Moody-Sankey revival meetings. The convergent efforts of many authors, composers, and compilers produced what Moody and Sankey called the gospel hymn.[133]

Moreover, Sankey's solo style (one of his distinguishing characteristics) was already in use by evangelist Richard Weaver and Philip Phillips (a singing evangelist), whose method of singing the gospel was well known.[134] As a matter of fact, while in England Sankey borrowed songs from Phillips' *Hallowed Songs*.[135]

If intentions carry any weight, Sankey's own comments concerning the nature of his singing imply that he did not intend to contextualize his message through stylistic imitation: "There is no art or conscious design to it [his singing]. I never touch a song that does not speak to me in every word and phrase. Before I sing I must feel, and the hymn must be of such a kind that I know I can send home what I feel into the hearts of those who listen."[136]

An examination of the secular elements of Sankey's method and style is now in order. First, Sankey was a soloist, which though uncommon and unwelcome in some religious settings, was certainly not new (Richard Weaver) nor a violation of Scripture. Second, Sankey used a small reed Esty organ for accompaniment, which, along with other accompanying instruments, was tabooed by some at the time as worldly.[137] Yet his choice of the small organ actually reveals his own reservations about the role of music proper in the song service, as we will see momentarily.

Some consider a third secular element to be Sankey's style of singing, which centered on the lyrics rather than the music.[138] As Mel R. Wilhoit explains, Sankey "often paused at the ends of phrases, apparently to allow the meaning of each line to sink in; within each phrase he freely employed rubato, stretching some words and rushing others, to emphasize the text."[139] This may, however, have had more to do with

Sankey's convictions on the proper ratio of music and singing than with imitation or popular influence. According to Helen F. Rothwell,

> While Mr. Sankey admired the large organ, he felt that people did not sing so well with it. Its loud tones, he believed, drowned the voices, and people tended just to sit and listen without singing. For that reason he favored the use of a small organ, especially in his solo work. He always insisted that the organist play softly, for it was the singing and not the music which he sought to emphasize in all his services. For that reason he felt that instrumental music, other than necessary to keep the correct key, was not essential in the house of God.[140]

But of what manner were the tunes that the English found so compelling? The gospel song was actually a developed version of the American Sunday school song, which featured an elegant, graceful form that was initially influenced by the music of Stephen Foster.[141] Wilhoit writes, "This [style] consisted of diatonic but tuneful melodies in a homophonic texture with simple harmonies and slow harmonic rhythm. One of the most telling features was the popular verse/chorus format."[142] Although there was an earlier secular influence, its outcome was aesthetically productive and in no way detrimental to or unworthy of the Christian message—though some at the time decidedly disagreed.[143] Curiously, Wilhoit also informs us that the gospel song, popularized by Sankey, actually impacted secular music at various levels.[144]

Thus we may posit that Sankey's melodies, though similar to popular song, can never be described as worldly or unsuitable for edification. They are stirring, yet simple; joyous, yet modest; sprightly, yet devout, to which their present-day resiliency testifies. Miller would like to attribute Sankey's success to his use of the musical idiom of the people. In accordance with my research, I would like to propose that it was not the "secularity" of the style per se, but the simplicity and singability of the tunes (which is characteristic of folk music) that made them so attractive.[145] We have no real evidence that musical contextualization, as it is practiced in today's Christian music industry, was intended by Sankey. As William C. Rice explains, "Sankey's tunes were sentimental and very simple; their appeal came from their folklike unpretentiousness...."[146]

Conclusion

Although the Moody-Sankey innovations are still quite distant from current philosophies and practices, they do share the concept that music should be used as a tool in evangelism. Quite apart from the issue of style, the Moody-Sankey commitment to harness the power of music for evangelism, and its apparent success, is similar to CCM's and therefore provides them with a small measure of support from recent history.[147] Thus we are left with a mixed bag. On the one hand, the style is perfectly acceptable and edifying, but, on the other, their policies have contributed to the current misunderstanding of music and evangelism. Miller would like to exploit both (argument from style and method) for his purpose; yet in this case he is only entitled to one.

William Booth

William Booth, founder of the Salvation Army, presents us with an authentic forerunner of the current utilitarian view of music, as Miller delights in showing. Booth combined Christian lyrics with secular tunes to evangelize the masses. Although Booth was not concerned with the secular associations of the tunes he impounded, his critics found it extremely troublesome, fearing that "the familiar tunes would remind people of their sinful days."[148]

In Booth, Miller has hooked a true pragmatist like himself. He wastes no time in loading the pages with quotations from Booth that can be used to support the most radical forms of musical contextualization:

> Not allowed to sing that tune or this tune? Indeed! Secular music, do you say? Belongs to the devil does it? Well, if it did, I would plunder him of it, for he has no right to a single note of the whole gamut. He's a thief!... Every note and every strain and every harmony is divine, and belongs to us.[149]

In the context of much of the nineteenth-century musical milieu of Booth, such a statement is understandable,[150] but it is doubtful that he would have held the same opinion had he sampled a few airs of Mötley Crüe or the Dead Kennedys. Nevertheless, Miller finally finds in Booth the historical support that most closely approximates his understanding of music and ministry.

Evaluation

As we conclude, it should be emphasized that this close scrutiny of Miller's historiography was not intended to prove him wrong in every case. Although on some topics—such as the ancient church—Miller's treatment is highly suspect, on others like Sankey and more so Booth, he shoots closer to the bull's-eye. Neither should the examination imply agreement on my part with all of the methods and motivations of the men under review; it was not my intention to create plaster saints who were untouched by compromise or always impeccable in their actions. What I have attempted to do is to show that there is a marked difference between the innovations and changes that occurred during these historical junctures and what is taking place today. I have acknowledged that men like Ephraem, Hilary, Luther, and the Wesleys utilized their musical environment, while maintaining that the reasons for their borrowing, the nature of the borrowed product, and their selectivity and adaptation do little to support the CCM position, and in some instances disable it.

Calvin, Zwingli, Watts, Leavitt, and others have not been discussed since Miller's assessment of their role in the history of ecclesiastical music is less problematic.[151] Yes, Calvin permitted only the psalms for worship and forbade musical instruments, Zwingli had organs destroyed, and the Moravians banned the fiddle.[152] Further, it is an unflattering reflection on the church that hymns found their way into its liturgy with such fight and fury.

Lastly, it is not to be denied that forms of popular music were introduced into gospel hymnody at any point in the modern age of the church. Although the examples of rejecting musical innovations and change are an embarrassment to conservatives, we should not imagine that today's objection toward CCM is simply a repetition of Miller's historical pattern, as will be demonstrated. At the same time, we should treat these incidents as warnings against harboring unscriptural attitudes toward music and be challenged to refrain from baseless accusations.

A Haunting Past

Some in Christendom have committed atrocities that were far more serious than organ-banning. Should the injustice of Galileo's persecution in the seventeenth century prevent us from challenging Darwinism today? Should the execution of twenty innocent people at the Salem witch trials in 1692 force us to stop reproving occultic and New Age teachers today?

These incidences are not as scarce as one might think; prior to Galileo's ruthless inquisition before Pope Urban VIII in 1632, many early sixteenth-century Europeans rejected Copernicus' heliocentric model of the universe. Although as a whole Protestants were hospitable to Copernicus' ideas, Luther dismissed him cynically, and Philipp Melanchthon, Luther's understudy, felt it necessary to refute him from the Bible.[153]

Far more tragic is the legacy of witch-hunts in Europe and Great Britain, which make the Salem incident seem minor by comparison. It is estimated that within a century (1580-1680), Scotland (a Protestant nation) executed 3,400 people for witchcraft.[154] Some suggest that in Europe and the British Isles, well over 300,000 people were sent to the gallows and flames during the seventeenth century alone.[155] These needless deaths took place under the sanction of Catholic and Protestant magistrates. And what were the signs of possible witchcraft? Such "obviously" demonic manifestations as a wart on the chest, talking to one's self, or having one's cow go dry.

It is quite evident that a record of presumptuous actions in other sectors has not prevented the church from its prophetic activities. No one would think of giving ground in either of these areas because of previous failings. Overreactions of the past should not neutralize genuine concerns of the present. Most conservatives do not oppose CCM because it is new, different, and carries different musical cues than they are accustomed to, or even because it has its origin in the world. They are convinced that clear moral principles are involved in the style of the music itself, and have attempted to support their claims with both biblical and secular evidence. Although some examples of resistance will follow in the shadow of the past, many of the objections presented today are based on biblical principles and research.

Is There a Difference?

There are many important differences between the current debate and the examples from church history, which will reveal that CCM is not the repetition of a predictable historical cycle. First, on a functional level, CCM has already distinguished itself from earlier movements by developing into a highly lucrative industry (almost $1 billion a year) that provides for the *entertainment*, as well as ministry, needs of its consumers. Peacock cautions CCM zealots against carelessly identifying the current movement with others in the evolution of church music: "Anyone trying to fit contemporary Christian music on the whole into this continuum will have a very difficult time making a case for their position."[156] The reason he provides is that

> CCM mirrors the larger industry of which it's a part—the mainstream music business. On the whole, contemporary Christian music is really just pop music that attempts to satisfy the musical and lyrical needs of its original community while reaching outward to new listeners.[157]

Second, it should be remembered that what is often targeted as the secular style borrowed by the church is really folk music. Folk music can be defined as the music of untrained composers, which is orally transmitted, fluid in form, and represents the basic human experiences of a community.[158] Since folk music is a broad classification—which includes cradle songs, drinking songs, work songs, love songs, patriotic songs, dancing songs,[159] as well as *religious* songs—it is not as radical an intrusion into uncharted waters as one might think. As noted earlier, the difference between the German religious folksong, the *Leisen*, and the secular German folksong was not appreciable.[160] It also needs to be stressed that throughout much of church history, the distinction between secular and sacred music was not nearly as sharp as it is today. The church was one of the major institutions over society and often influenced its music.[161]

Third, the current controversy involves more than just musical forms, but often includes counter-culture accessories and practices such as unwholesome and immodest clothing, orgiastic dancing, and sexually-suggestive body language. None of these elements entered into previous church controversies; the issues were focused on musical style alone rather than music and the visual symbolism of a self-admitted counter-culture.

Fourth, although certain styles of music and musical instruments were upbraided by overzealous Christians in the past, there are no records to my knowledge of testimonies about the subversive character and intent of a musical style that the church adopted in the past by its secular pioneers. Yet, as I have documented earlier and will do so again, rock music's own performers have shocked us with statements that sound as if they belong on the lips of fundamentalists. For example, Allen Lanier of the Blue Oyster Cult says, "Rock and roll brings out violent emotions. There's a lot of violence, a lot of aggression in the music."[162] Mick Jagger warns, "Rock and roll is not a tender medium; it's raunchy and macho. There's no such thing as a secure family-oriented rock and roll song."[163] David Bowie insists, "Rock 'n' roll will destroy you. It lets in lower elements and shadows. *Rock has always been the devil's music.*"[164] (Emphasis original.)

Fifth, the conservative position against rock music has been supported through studies performed by reputable researchers in the social sciences, as well as a blue ribbon panel of historians and musicologists, most of whom have no religious agenda or bias against rock music. In fact many of them actually advocate it. This, then, is another element that is missing in Miller's journey through history.

The Legacy of Contemporary Christianity

The final element in Miller's schema is renewal. In that the Jesus movement (a group diverse in conviction and emphasis) has been considered by many to be a renewal associated with CCM, a few comments are in order. It is not to be denied that the movement's desire to reach the hippie culture, which was by and large rejected by the traditional church, was commendable and that many were genuinely converted. Indeed, it served as a rude awakening to isolationist conservatives, who were unwilling to dirty their hands to reach the unlovely. Whereas many conservatives preached what amounts to "clean yourself up before you receive Christ," the Jesus movement said more biblically, "Come as you are."[165]

The problem, however, was that "come as you are" more often meant "remain as you are," at least as far as music, language, clothing, and social habits were concerned. Counter-culture symbolism went unchecked, and modesty and decency were cast to the wind by many segments of the movement like Calvary Chapel, which sometimes baptized female converts in string bikinis before hundreds of onlookers at Corona del Mar State Beach.[166] Such baptisms customarily included an earnest embrace by the pastor and the baptized, whether male or female, clothed or barely so.[167] But this new unfettered and feeling-based approach to the Christian life sometimes resulted in more serious moral ensnarements. Ronald M. Enroth et al., who studied the movement firsthand, lament:

> It is dismaying, though not surprising, to hear of Jesus People who have relapsed into drugs and illicit sex. We have heard of young people reading the Bible while high on drugs and unmarried couples first praying, then sleeping together. Entire ministries, communal and other, have fallen apart because of such relapses. It is particularly disastrous when leaders slip, for new converts find their faith severely shaken in these situations. But if there is no rational check upon the emotions, this kind of backsliding is predictable. The combination of devotion and libertinism is rooted in a dualistic view of man that separates value from the concrete times and places of human existence. If true salvation lies in the soul, one can be indifferent to the actions of the body.[168]

As often happens in highly experiential religion, there were a sobering number of dropouts and burnouts among the Jesus People: "For them the Jesus trip has proven futile and unsatisfying as the drug trip and other trips that they tried in the past," say Enroth et al. "Jesus has been, for them, no more than a temporary emotional high that passed with time."[169]

Whether one considers the movement to be a genuine renewal or not will depend on one's theological perspective and definition of renewal. I suppose it is possible that for all its flaws—and only a few were mentioned—the Jesus movement could be considered a renewal, but frankly, I doubt it. The long term effects of the Protestant Reformation, the English evangelical revival, and the Great Awakenings were both spiritually and theologically profound;[170] this is precisely why I have such reservations about labeling the Jesus movement a renewal.[171] In one sense we can appreciate and learn from their missionary zeal and desire for a meaningful relationship with God; yet, in another we must come to grips with their theological assets, which were dreadfully inadequate (and purposely so), causing them to overlook important principles of depravity, culture, ideology, syncretism, authority, and sometimes common sense—the repercussions of which haunt us to this day in the form of CCM, their firstborn.

With its start in the Jesus movement, CCM has been with us for over thirty years, coinciding with a period of western evangelical history that exhibits many troubling trends and directions. Menconi, for instance, estimates that "seventy percent or more children raised by Christian parents never live for Jesus Christ as adults."[172] Some of this can be blamed on the weakening of authority structures in the family and the epidemic divorce rate within evangelicalism—one of the most publicly embarrassing outcomes of our rapprochement with modernity.

Moreover, there is every indication that the world has proselytized the church in several critical areas, including theological liberalism, feminism, pragmatism, pop psychology, materialism, and music and entertainment. Sadly, today's evangelical church resembles a spoiled teenager with an unlimited expense account and no sales resistance.

When it comes to doctrine, the situation is just as dismal. Our era has been beset with tremendous doctrinal confusion, toleration of heresies, and New Age mysticism. At the heels of such acquiescence (and perhaps because of it) has come the ecumenical movement, which threatens to undo the Reformation in the interest of social and political reform—which is fast becoming the church's main agenda. In fact there is no shortage within the CCM community of those who have kissed the Pope's slipper. As early as the 1970s, Annie Herring, lead singer and songwriter for the Second Chapter of Acts, is reported to have "combined the enthusiasm of the charismatic movement with the rich interior life of a Catholic mystic."[173] More recently, the alliance of Michael Card and Catholic John Michael Talbot was warmly received by some of the most influential members of the CCM industry.[174] Even more inexcusable was the delegation of CCM artists who performed for Catholic youth during the Pope's 1999 visit to St. Louis. The Ws, Audio Adrenaline, Jennifer Knapp, dc Talk, the Supertones, and Rebecca St. James willingly participated in this Catholic event and praised the Pope for his ministry to the youth.[175] It apparently does not occur to these musicians that the same Pope when venturing south of the border denounces evangelicalism as a Protestant cult and warns Catholics against its deluding influence.

In his widely acclaimed book *Evangelicalism: The Coming Generation*, James Davison Hunter documents the seismic shift away from traditionally held beliefs among modern evangelicals in key areas such as biblical inerrancy, the final state of unbelievers, evolution, and morality. For example, in the early to mid-eighties, only about forty percent of evangelical collegians and seminarians still held to the doctrine of the inerrancy of Scripture, while (according to the Roper Theology Faculty Survey, 1982) roughly sixty-one percent of evangelical theologians did.[176]

Further, the penetration of neo-orthodox theology—with its understanding of the Bible, not as the Word of God, but as that which becomes the Word of God when combined with the faith of the reader—into evangelicalism is evident to Hunter in a more subjectivist approach to biblical interpretation.[177] To neo-orthodoxy the events recorded in the Bible are not as important as the theological teaching that is conveyed by them. Ergo, the veracity of biblical history is seriously jeopardized. For instance when it comes to the origin of the world, almost seventeen percent of evangelical college and seminary students (a small but telling number according to Hunter) betrayed neo-orthodox influence by stating that the creation account in Genesis was to be taken symbolically rather than literally.[178] Although in most cases orthodoxy is still maintained, equivocation on theological issues that were once unquestionable is noteworthy. In Hunter's words, "There is less sharpness, less boldness, and, accordingly, a measure of opaqueness in their theological vision that did not exist in previous generations (at least to their present extent)."[179]

In terms of the Great Commission and the eternal fate of unbelievers, as many as one-third of evangelical academicians felt that unbelievers who die without ever hearing the gospel can still enter into heaven. This reflects a disturbing decline from the convictions of previous generations of evangelicals, well over ninety percent of whom believed that the state of all unbelievers—informed or not—was eternal damnation.[180] According to Hunter, "For a substantial minority of the coming generation [of evangelicals], there appears to be a middle ground that did not, for all practical purposes, exist for previous generations."[181]

When it comes to activities that were once considered entirely incompatible with consistent Christian witness and lifestyle, this generation of evangelicals again demonstrates a serious departure from older values. It is no longer unusual for even students at the most prestigious evangelical seminaries to frequent bars and dance in nightclubs till all hours of the night. Consider also the fact that a mere seven percent of evangelical collegians felt it was always morally wrong to attend R-rated movies.[182] (For those who are unaware, R-rated movies contain considerable amounts of profanity, nudity, sex [heterosexual and homosexual], and violence.) Incredibly, at one of the most doctrinally conservative seminaries in the United States, smoking by students, faculty, and staff is actually permitted, and that on the very campus! And why should this surprise anyone? Hunter's statistics reveal that as early as 1982 those evangelicals who disapproved of cigarette smoking and using tobacco products at all times had dropped to a shocking fifty-one percent from 1961 (at seventy-one percent) and 1951 (at ninety-three percent)—and this despite a greater public awareness of the dangers of smoking.[183] Even in the area of smoking marijuana, where one would expect an almost unanimous evangelical opposition, one finds an intolerable number of holdouts—a whopping thirty percent in 1982—who were unwilling to say that smoking marijuana was wrong in every circumstance.[184]

Younger Christians possibly fare worse. Sexual promiscuity is no longer uncommon among our youth, even at Christian colleges. Christian crisis pregnancy clinics provide services for a distressing number of young Christian women. Those who manage to wait until marriage have already engaged in appalling levels of physical intimacy and foreplay (necking, petting, fondling, and caressing)—which one or two generations earlier would have resulted in a trip to the woodshed.[185] Both male and female teens are under the impression that modesty is out of fashion and so have abandoned it altogether. Scenic necklines, fig leaves for skirts, and splits in every imaginable place are now acceptable attire for Christian women (teens and adults), even in church.

Youth ministry, if it is to be tolerated, *must* involve some form of entertainment—whether sports, rock music, drama, or comedy. Simply preaching Christ and him crucified has sent many a youth pastor into early retirement or forced them to cave in to the "pizza and Petra" model in demand by today's youth. Before we surrender to the sloppy notion that nothing more can be expected of human beings at this early level of maturity and emotional development, we should consider the response to the gospel in other parts of the globe. Missionaries to Eastern Europe and elsewhere continue to bring reports of young people who remain for hours to hear the Word of God and even plead for more after the service has ended.

Hunter finds that this striking abandonment of traditionally held Christian codes of moral conduct began in the 1960s. Since that time, he reports, "the moral boundaries separating Christian conduct from worldly conduct have been substantially undermined."[186] He describes the shift in toleration as a "process...in which 'sin' is being redefined."[187] He adds:

> Clearly some norms have not changed. Evangelicals still adhere to prohibitions against premarital, extramarital, and homosexual relations. But

even here, the attitude toward those prohibitions has noticeably softened. In brief, the symbolic boundaries which previously defined moral propriety for conservative Protestantism have lost a measure of clarity. Many of the distinctions separating Christian conduct from "worldly conduct" have been challenged if not altogether undermined. Even the words *worldly* and *worldliness* have, within a generation, lost most of their traditional meaning.[188]

From Hunter's point of view, evangelicalism's divestment of earlier convictions for a more relativistic disposition toward morality and participation in culture has resulted in a weakening of its cohesiveness and an erosion of its identity as a morally distinct community.[189] Further, the fact that the evangelical reappraisal of sin, morality, and Christian liberty is a mere subset of similar attitudes within a declining secular culture suggests that this new direction is not, in most cases, the outworking of sound biblical doctrine, but rather the result of postmodern influences.

This is not to say that CCM is responsible for this steady disintegration. It does, however, show that the permissiveness and leniency of CCM in the realm of music parallels the general trajectory of this generation of evangelicals in other important issues. More importantly though, it casts serious doubt on the optimistic assessment of CCM propagandists regarding the condition of evangelicalism since the advent of CCM.[190]

Endnotes

[1]De Simone also covers the topic briefly (pp. 110-17). Preceding him and Miller were Harold Myra and Dean Merrill, and Donald P. Ellsworth, who is less radical in his conclusions and applications than Miller.

[2]Steve Miller, *The Contemporary Christian Music Debate: Worldly* Compromise or Agent of Renewal? (Wheaton, IL: Tyndale House, 1993), 142-43.

[3]Ibid., 109.

[4]Gerald Abraham, *The Concise Oxford History of Music* (Oxford, England: Oxford University Press, 1988), 40; Everett Ferguson, "Did They Sing Hymns?" *Christian History* 12, no. 37: 14; Alfred Sendrey, *Music in Ancient Israel* (New York: Philosophical Library, 1969), 183; Edward Foley, *Foundations of Christian Music: The Music of Pre-Constantinian Christianity*, American Essays in Liturgy, ed. Edward Foley (Collegeville, MN: The Liturgical Press, 1996), 58, 81-82.

[5]Sendrey, *Music in Ancient Israel*, 64, 190.

[6]Ibid., 189-90.

[7]James McKinnon, *Music in Early Christian Literature* (Cambridge, England: Cambridge University Press, 1987), 2.

[8]Ibid.

[9]Sendrey, *Music in Ancient Israel*, 317.

[10]Suzanne Haïk-Vantoura, *The Music of the Bible Revealed: The Deciphering of Millenary Notation*, trans. Dennis Weber (Berkeley, CA: Bibal Press, 1991), 141.

[11]Sendrey, *Music in Ancient Israel*, 203.

[12]Miller, *Christian Music Debate*, 109; Donald Paul Ellsworth, *Christian Music in Contemporary Witness: Historical Antecedents and Contemporary Practices* (Grand Rapids: Baker Book House, 1979), 31-32.

[13]Sozomen, *Ecclesiastical History* III, 16, in Philip Schaff and Henry Wace, eds., *A Select Library of Nicene and Post-Nicene Fathers of the Christian Church* (New York: Christian Literature Co., 1890), 296.

[14]Theodoret of Cyrus, *Ecclesiastical History* IV, 29, 1-3, in McKinnon, *Music in Early Christian Literature*, 105.

[15]Kathleen E. McVey, trans. and ed., *Ephrem the Syrian: Hymns*, The Classics of Western Spirituality (New York: Paulist Press, 1989), 26.

[16]Sendrey, *Music in Ancient Israel*, 197.

[17]Haïk-Vantoura, *Music of the Bible*, 247, 257.

[18]Dimitri Conomos, "Bardaisan," in *The New Grove Dictionary of Music and Musicians*, ed. Stanley Sadie, vol. 2 (London: Macmillan Publishers Limited, 1980), 150. Ephraem's sensitivity to the appropriateness of the borrowed style can be supported by his overall disposition toward pagan music, which is similar to that of the other early church fathers: "Where cithara playing and dancing and hand-clapping take place, there is the deluding of men and the ruin of women and the sorrow of angels and a feast for the devil." Ephraem, *Über die Enthaltung von weltlichen Lustbarkeiten* 5 (BKV, Kempten 1870), Zingerle I, 414; quoted in Johannes Quasten, *Music and Worship in Pagan and Christian Antiquity*, trans. Boniface Ramsey (Washington, D.C.: National Association of Pastoral Musicians, 1983), 134.

[19]McKinnon, *Music in Early Christian Literature*, 92.

[20]Miller, *Christian Music Debate*, 109.

[21]McKinnon, *Music in Early Christian Literature*, 121.

[22]A. J. Mason, "The First Latin Christian Poet," *Journal of Theological Studies* 5 (1904): 422.

[23]Ibid.

[24]Ibid., 422-23. Mason reminds us that the acrostic form also appears in Latin poetry.

[25]Ibid., 425.

[26]Ibid.

[27]St. Hilary, *Instructio psalmorum* 7, in McKinnon, *Music in Early Christian Literature*, 123.

[28]McKinnon, *Music in Early Christian Literature*, 4.

[29]Ibid.

[30]Ibid.

[31]Sendrey, *Music in Ancient Israel*, 228; Haïk-Vantoura, *Music of the Bible*, 143.

[32]Miller, *Christian Music Debate*, 109-10.

[33]Basil the Great (329-379 A.D.) held similar ideals on the persuasive effects of music. Ellsworth, *Christian Music in Contemporary Witness*, 33.

[34]Moisés Silva, *Has the Church Misread the Bible? The History of Interpretation in Light of Current Issues*, Foundations of Contemporary Interpretation, vol. 1 (Grand Rapids: Zondervan Publishing Co., 1987), 58-59.

[35]Joseph W. Trigg, *Biblical Interpretation* (Wilmington, DE: Michael Glazier, 1988), 25.

[36]Miller, *Christian Music Debate*, 111-15.

[37]See Robert H. Mitchell, *I Don't Like That Music* (Carol Stream, IL: Hope Publishing Co., 1993), 26.

[38]Carl F. Schalk, *Luther on Music: Paradigms of Praise* (St. Louis: Concordia Publishing House, 1988), 34, 37, 38; Ellsworth, *Christian Music in Contemporary Witness*, 49-50.

[39]Miller, *Christian Music Debate*, 114.

[40]Erik Routley, *Church Music and Theology* (London: SCM Press, 1959), 61.

[41]William J. Reynolds and Milburn Price, *A Survey of Christian Hymnody* (Carol Stream, IL: Hope Publishing Co., 1987), 15; Robert Lomas Harrell, "A Comparison of Secular Elements in the Chorales of Martin Luther with Rock Elements in Church Music of the 1960's and 1970's" (M.A. Thesis, Bob Jones University, 1975), 28.

[42]Miller, *Christian Music Debate*, 113.

[43]Ulrich S. Leupold, ed., *Luther's Works* (Philadelphia: Fortress Press, 1965), 54; Martin Luther, "To George Spalatin," trans. Gottfried G. Krodel, in *Luther's Works*, ed. Gottfried G. Krodel and Helmut Lehmann, vol. 49: *Letters II*, American (Philadelphia: Muhlenberg, 1972), 69.

[44]Martin Luther, "Against the Heavenly Prophets in the Matter of Images and Sacraments," trans. Bernhard Erling, in *Luther's Works*, ed. Conrad Bergendoff and Helmut Lehmann, vol. 40: *Church and Ministry II*, American (Philadelphia: Muhlenberg, 1958), 141.

[45]Martin Luther, "Concerning the Order of Public Worship," trans. Paul Zeller Strodach, in *Luther's Works*, ed. Ulrich S. Leupold and Helmut Lehmann, vol. 53: *Liturgy and Hymns*, American (Philadelphia: Muhlenberg, 1965), 11.

[46]Ibid., 68; Harrell, "Secular Elements," 7.

[47]Martin Luther, "To Louis Senfl," trans. Gottfried G. Krodel, in *Luther's Works*, ed. Gottfried G. Krodel and Helmut Lehmann, vol. 49: *Letters II*,

American (Philadelphia: Muhlenberg, 1972), 428; Preserved Smith, *Life and Letters of Martin Luther* (London: John Murray, 1911), 347.

[48]Smith, *Life and Letters of Luther*, 347.

[49]Martin Luther, "Preface to Georg Rhau's *Symphoniae Iucundae*," trans. Ulrich S. Leupold, in *Luther's Works*, ed. Ulrich S. Leupold and Helmut Lehmann, vol. 53: *Liturgy and Hymns*, American (Philadelphia: Muhlenberg, 1965), 323.

[50]Ibid.

[51]Schalk, *Luther on Music*, 14, 18, 32, 33. His understanding of the benefits of music in developing good behavior is also credited to the Greeks: "If I had children and could manage it, I would have them study not only languages and history, but also singing and music…. The ancient Greeks trained their children in these disciplines; yet they grew up to be people of wondrous ability, subsequently fit for everything." Martin Luther, "To the Councilmen of All Cities in Germany that They Establish and Maintain Christian Schools," trans. Albert T. W. Steinhaeuser, in *Luther's Works*, ed. Walter I. Brandt and Helmut Lehmann, vol. 45: *The Christian Society*, American (Philadelphia: Muhlenberg, 1962), 369-70.

[52]Regarding music, Calvin once said: "There is scarcely anything in the world which is more capable of turning or moving this way and that the morals of men, as Plato prudently considered it. And in fact we experience that it has a secret and almost incredible power to arouse hearts in one way or another." Charles Garside, Jr., "The Origins of Calvin's Theology of Music: 1536-1543," in *Transactions of the American Philosophical Society* (Philadelphia: The American Philosophical Society, August 1979), 22.

[53]Martin Luther, "Preface to the Wittenberg Hymnal," trans. Paul Zeller Strodach, in *Luther's Works*, ed. Ulrich S. Leupold and Helmut Lehmann, vol. 53: *Liturgy and Hymns*, American (Philadelphia: Muhlenberg, 1965), 316.

[54]Cf. Leupold, *Luther's Works*, 315.

[55]Harrell, "Secular Elements," 33, 42.

[56]Ibid., 29.

[57]Ibid., 33.

[58]Edwin Liemohn, *The Chorale* (Philadelphia: Muhlenberg Press, 1963), 12.

[59]Ibid., 12-13.

[60]Ibid., 13.

[61]Harrell, "Secular Elements," 31-32, 71.

[62]Ibid., 32.

[63]Cf. Liemohn, *The Chorale*, 13.

[64]Harrell, "Secular Elements," 69-70; Erik Routley, *Christian Hymns Observed* (Princeton: Prestige Publications, 1982), 18.

[65]Harrell, "Secular Elements," 34.

[66]Gustave Reese, *Music in the Middle Ages* (New York: W. W. Norton & Company, 1940), 218; Ellsworth, *Christian Music in Contemporary Witness*, 38-39; Friedrich Blume, *Protestant Church Music* (New York: W. W. Norton & Company, 1974), 29.

[67]Harrell, "Secular Elements," 35.

[68]Ibid., 36, 46; Millar Patrick, *The Story of the Church's Song* (Richmond, VA: John Knox Press, 1962), 74.

[69]Maurice Frost, ed., *Historical Companion to Hymns Ancient and Modern*, rev. ed. (London: William Clowes and Sons, 1962), 71; Ulrich S. Leupold, "Learning from Luther? Some Observations on Luther's Hymns," *Journal of Church Music* 8 (July-August 1966): 5.

[70]Harrell, "Secular Elements," 36; Leupold, "Learning from Luther?" 5.

[71]Harrell, "Secular Elements," 43.

[72]Ibid., 43-44.

[73]Ibid., 36.

[74]Ibid., 71-72. Nevertheless, it is important to realize that Luther was not against dancing per se. On the contrary, he felt that when done decently and properly it was an acceptable means by which young men and women could meet and learn social graces—provided that it was sufficiently supervised. This does not mean, however, that Luther considered dance songs to be appropriate for sacred use. Smith, *Life and Letters of Luther*, 350.

[75]Leupold, "Learning from Luther?" 5.

[76]Peter Christian Lutkin, *Music in the Church*, 1910 reprint (New York: AMS Press, 1970).

[77]Patrick, *Church's Song*, 74.

[78]Harrell, "Secular Elements," 37.

[79]Ibid.; Liemohn, *The Chorale*, 13.

[80]Liemohn, *The Chorale*, 13; Paul Nettl, *Luther and Music*, trans. Frida Best and Ralph Wood (Philadelphia: Muhlenberg Press, 1948), 48; Albert Schweitzer, *J. S. Bach*, trans. Ernest Newmann (Leipzig: Breitkopf & Hrtel, 1911), 18.

[81]Harrell, "Secular Elements," 39; Liemohn, *The Chorale*, 13; Schweitzer, *J. S. Bach*, 18. Paul Nettl's view is similar: He feels that Luther composed a new tune because "he was embarrassed to hear the tune of his Christmas hymn sung in inns and dance halls." Leupold does not even take its secular use into consideration, feeling that Luther replaced the tune because it was "somewhat too insipid." Nettl, *Luther and Music*, 48; Leupold, *Luther's Works*, 4.

[82]Harrell, "Secular Elements," 39.

[83]Patrick, *Church's Song*, 74.

[84]Harold M. Best, "There is More to Redemption Than Meets the Ear," *Christianity Today*, 26 July 1974, 16. I recommend chapter 12, "The Truth about Luther" (pp. 163-71), in Tim Fisher's *The Battle for Christian Music*

(Greenville, SC: Sacred Music Services, 1992), as an excellent supplement to my research on Luther.

[85]Miller, *Christian Music Debate*, 124-27.

[86]Ibid., 126.

[87]William J. Reynolds, "Three Hymnals That Shaped Today's Worship," *Christian History* 10, no. 31: 36; Patrick, *Church's Song*, 132.

[88]Erik Routley, *The Music of Christian Hymnody: A Study of the Development of the Hymn Since the Reformation, with Special Reference to English Protestantism* (London: Independent Press, 1957), 96.

[89]Patrick, *Church's Song*, 131-32. As Patrick indicates, many of his hymns were quickly composed and transient, serving as either immediate propaganda, invective, or satire. On one occasion (1746) Charles hastily parodied a lewd dance song, "Nancy Dawson," which was brayed by a group of unruly drunks trying to disrupt his preaching. When the brawlers returned, the Methodists sang the same tune to lyrics that extolled the use of music for good and not evil in an effort to drown out the sound of the drunks. The tune has survived to this day in the children's song "Here We Go Round the Mulberry Bush." Timothy Dudley-Smith, "Why Wesley Still Dominates Our Hymnbook," *Christian History* 10, no. 31: 10.

[90]Dudley-Smith, "Why Wesley Still Dominates," 13.

[91]John Wesley, "Thoughts on the Power of Music," in Franz Hildebrandt and Oliver A. Beckerlegge, eds., *The Works of John Wesley*, vol. 7: *A Collection of Hymns for the Use of the People Called Methodists* (Nashville: Abingdon Press, 1983), 766.

[92]W. Reginald Ward and Richard P. Heitzenrater, eds., *The Works of John Wesley*, vol. 22: *Journal and Diaries V (1765-75)* (Nashville: Abingdon Press, 1993), 161-62. The author of the essay, Charles Avison, in 1752 wrote the book *Expression in Music* to which Wesley refers.

[93]Ibid., 152.

[94]John Wesley, *Journal*, June 13, 1748 in W. Reginald Ward and Richard P. Heitzenrater, eds., *The Works of John Wesley*, vol. 20: *Journal and Diaries III (1743-54)* (Nashville: Abingdon Press, 1991), 228-29.

[95]Louis F. Benson, *The English Hymn: Its Development and Use in Worship* (Philadelphia: The Presbyterian Board of Publication, 1915), 239. Cf. Reynolds and Price, *Christian Hymnody*, 49.

[96]Erik Routley, *The Musical Wesleys* (London: Herbert Jenkins, 1968), 8.

[97]Steven Darsey, "John Wesley as Hymn and Tune Editor: The Evidence of Charles Wesley's 'Jesu, Lover of My Soul' and Martin Madan's Hotham," *The Hymn* 47 (January 1996): 20. Cf. Benson, *English Hymn*, 239.

[98]John Wesley, *Journal*, April 8, 1781 in W. Reginald Ward and Richard P. Heitzenrater, eds., *The Works of John Wesley*, vol. 23: *Journal and Diaries VI (1776-86)* (Nashville: Abingdon Press, 1995), 198.

[99]Robin A. Leaver, "The Hymn Explosion," *Christian History* 10, no. 31: 17.

[100]Kevin A. Miller, "Silent String," *Christian History* 10, no. 31: 4.

[101]Routley, *Musical Wesleys*, 78-79.

[102]Ibid., 122.

[103]John Wilson, "Handel and the Hymn Tune: I, Handel's Tunes for Charles Wesley's Hymns," *The Hymn* 36 (October 1985): 19.

[104]Ibid., 20.

[105]John Wilson, "Handel and the Hymn Tune: II, Some Hymn Tune Arrangements," *The Hymn* 37 (January 1986): 26.

[106]Miller, *Christian Music Debate*, 125-26.

[107]Ward and Heitzenrater, *Journal and Diaries III*, 106.

[108]Routley, *Musical Wesleys*, 30.

[109]Dudley-Smith, "Why Wesley Still Dominates," 12.

[110]Leaver, "The Hymn Explosion," 17.

[111]Patrick, *Church's Song*, 130.

[112]James Sallee, *A History of Evangelistic Hymnody* (Grand Rapids: Baker Book House, 1978), 13. Cf. Andrew Wilson-Dickson, *The Story of Christian Music: From Gregorian Chant to Black Gospel an Authoritative Illustrated Guide to All the Major Traditions of Music for Worship* (Oxford: Lion, 1992), 116.

[113]Routley, *Musical Wesleys*, 37. See also p. 35 where Routley discusses Charles' use of German meters.

[114]Ibid.

[115]Ellsworth, *Christian Music in Contemporary Witness*, 69, 71, 72-73; Elwyn A. Wienandt, *Opinions on Church Music: Comments and Reports from Four-and-a Half Centuries* (Waco, TX: Baylor University Press, 1974), 101.

[116]Madeleine Forell Marshall, "Irrational Music Sung by a Mob of Extremists?" *Christian History* 10, no. 31: 35.

[117]Ibid.

[118]John Scot, 'A Fine Picture of Enthusiasm,' in Marshall, "Irrational Music," 35.

[119]Marshall, "Irrational Music," 35.

[120]Routley, *Musical Wesleys*, 121.

[121]Ibid., 117.

[122]Ibid., 8.

[123]Reynolds and Price, *Christian Hymnody*, 50-51.

[124]Wilson, "Handel and the Hymn Tune II," 26.

[125]James Townsend, "Radicals in Times of Revolution," *Christian History* 10, no. 31: 8. Cf. Benson, *English Hymn*, 239.

[126]Dudley-Smith, "Why Wesley Still Dominates," 12; Reynolds and Price, *Christian Hymnody*, 52.

[127]Reynolds and Price, *Christian Hymnody*, 52.

[128]Darsey, "Wesley as Hymn and Tune Editor," 20.

[129]Ibid., 18.

[130]Ibid., 24.

[131]Miller, *Christian Music Debate*, 131-32.

[132]Helen F. Rothwell, *Ira D. Sankey a Great Song Leader* (Fort Pierce, FL: Faith Baptist Church Publications, 1995), 6, 8, 13, 36. Moody never did choose a song because of its artistic virtues, but because of its ability to engage the feelings and stir the emotions of the crowd. He judged music by its impact on the listener. Consequently he favored the gospel song, which was simple enough for the musically untrained masses and delightfully appealing in its melody. Robert M. Stevenson, *Patterns of Protestant Church Music* (Durham, NC: Duke University Press, 1953), 160-61.

[133]Sallee, *Evangelistic Hymnody*, 54.

[134]Ibid., 58-59.

[135]Ibid., 54.

[136]Mel R. Wilhoit, "'Sing Me a Sankey': Ira D. Sankey and Congregational Song," *The Hymn* 42 (January 1991): 14. Cf. Rothwell, "In every instance Mr. Sankey made his music subservient to the words, which he enunciated with utmost clearness. His chief concern was to lead men to a definite surrender to Christ. At no time did he permit himself to be motivated by a desire for self display or for mere gratification of his hearers' curiosity." *Ira D. Sankey*, 29.

[137]Sallee, *Evangelistic Hymnody*, 60-61; Rothwell, *Ira D. Sankey*, 3.

[138]Wilhoit, "Sing Me a Sankey," 14; Rothwell, *Ira D. Sankey*, 28-29.

[139]Wilhoit, "Sing Me a Sankey," 14.

[140]Rothwell, *Ira D. Sankey*, 32.

[141]Wilhoit, "Sing Me a Sankey," 16.

[142]Ibid.

[143]H. M. Poteat disparagingly compared the gospel song to "blues, jazz, waltzes, [and] ragtime," and *Vanity Fair* considered Sankey's tunes and singing as the kind that would be at home in music halls. Ellsworth, *Christian Music in Contemporary Witness*, 97; Wilhoit, "Sing Me a Sankey," 14-15.

[144]Wilhoit, "Sing Me a Sankey," 17.

[145]Cf. Rothwell, *Ira D. Sankey*, 24, 34. Wilhoit sees "simplicity and immediacy of impact" as important characteristics of the Sunday school song style. "Sing Me a Sankey," 16.

[146]William C. Rice, *A Concise History of Church Music* (New York: Abingdon Press, 1964), 80.

[147]Rothwell preaches that testimonies of salvation attributable to Sankey's singing the gospel "ran into the hundreds, all proving the marvelous power of sacred song to lead men to salvation." *Ira D. Sankey*, 30.

[148]Miller, *Christian Music Debate*, 136.

[149]Ibid., 137.

[150]Cf. Wilson-Dickson, *The Story of Christian Music*, 140.

[151]One should not come away from Miller's survey with the impression that other important figures were not involved in the evolution of church music. For more exhaustive coverage consult Ellsworth, *Christian Music in Contemporary Witness*.

[152]For Calvin I highly recommend Charles Garside, Jr., who documents Calvin's strong Platonic leanings (on the power of music), Augustinian influence (on the need for music to possess gravity and majesty, and the importance of the text), as well as other dimensions of his philosophy of music. Further, contrary to the impression given by Miller (pp. 116-17) no one sought to maintain the distinction between sacred and secular tunes or to match the tune to the sacred text more than Calvin. Garside, "Calvin's Theology of Music," 20-29.

Also it should be understood that the organ's demise in Genevan churches was "because it prevented the congregation from active participation in worship" and not because of its secular associations. Wilson-Dickson, *The Story of Christian Music*, 77.

[153]Lewis W. Spitz, *The Renaissance and Reformation Movements*, vol. 2, rev. ed. (St. Louis, MO: Concordia Publishing House, 1987), 586.

[154]Robert M. Bartlett, *The Faith of the Pilgrims* (New York: United Church Press, 1978), 214.

[155]Ola Elizabeth Winslow, *Samuel Sewall of Boston* (New York: Macmillan, 1964), 114; quoted in Bartlett, *Faith of the Pilgrims*, 214-15.

[156]Charlie Peacock, *At the Crossroads: An Insider's Look at the Past, Present, and Future of Contemporary Christian Music* (Nashville: Broadman & Holman, 1999), 118. See also pp. 77-78.

[157]Ibid.

[158]*Harvard Dictionary of Music*, 2d ed., s.v. "Folk Music."

[159]Ibid.

[160]Liemohn, *The Chorale*, 13.

[161]William Edgar, *Taking Note of Music* (London: Third Way Books, 1986), 21; Blume, *Protestant Church Music*, 29; Reese, *Music in the Middle Ages*, 218; Routley, *Musical Wesleys*, 37; Ellsworth, *Christian Music in Contemporary Witness*, 35, 38, 189; Best, "More to Redemption," 16.

[162]*Super Rock*, June 1978; quoted in John Blanchard, Peter Anderson, and Derek Cleave, *Pop Goes the Gospel: Rock in the Church*, 1983, enlarged and revised (Darlington, England: Evangelical Press, 1989), 82.

[163]John Street, *Rebel Rock: The Politics of Popular Music* (Oxford: Basil Blackwell, 1986), 132.

[164]*Rolling Stone*, 12 February 1976; quoted in Blanchard, Anderson, and Cleave, *Pop Goes the Gospel*, 73.

[165]Cf. Ronald M. Enroth, Edward E. Ericson, Jr., and C. Breckinridge Peters, *The Jesus People: Old-Time Religion in the Age of Aquarius* (Grand Rapids: Eerdmans, 1972), 84-85.

[166]Enroth, Ericson, and Peters, *The Jesus People*, 91, 92.

[167]Ibid., 89. Careless physical contact and hugging between members of the opposite sex, as an expression of love, was characteristic of Calvary Chapel and was criticized by a more conservative faction of the Jesus movement, Bethel Tabernacle. Enroth, Ericson, and Peters, *The Jesus People*, 88, 89, 97.

[168]Ibid., 166-67.

[169]Ibid., 243.

[170]See Sydney F. Ahlstrom, *A Religious History of the American People* (New Haven: Yale University Press, 1972), 280ff, 415ff.

[171]Cf. Enroth, Ericson, and Peters, *The Jesus People*, 238-39. Those who take the position that it was a renewal ought to keep in mind that the expansion of the kingdom in the Jesus movement (or others like Promise Keepers, or the recent Pensacola meetings) should not be taken as God's rubber stamp of approval on all of the theology and practices involved. No movement has been without its problems or unscriptural practices, including the Reformation. The reflections of Enroth et al. in this regard are most fitting: "Simply because the Holy Spirit may be considered to be present with the movement does not guarantee that only good results can possibly come. In other revivals the work of Christ in the world has been befouled by the tragic errors of the corrupt human instruments, and there is no guarantee that it will not happen again." *The Jesus People*, 246, cf. 241.

[172]Al Menconi and Dave Hart, *Staying in Tune: A Sane Response to Your Child's Music* (Cincinnati, OH: The Standard Publishing Co., 1996), 144. Cf. William D. Romanowski, "Roll Over Beethoven, Tell Martin Luther the News: American Evangelicals and Rock Music," *Journal of American Culture* 15, no. 3 (Fall 1992): 85.

[173]Steve Rabey, "Age to Age," *Contemporary Christian Music*, July 1998, 21.

[174]Steve Rabey, "Brother to Brother," *Contemporary Christian Music*, July 1996, 44-46. Although Rabey's article does not explicitly endorse ecumenism, it is definitely slanted in that direction.

[175]Brian Quincy Newcomb, "Pope Visits St. Louis: Christian Artists Headline Catholic Youth Events," *Contemporary Christian Music*, April 1999, 12-13. Newcomb's article is anything but negative. He ignores crucial doctrinal differences between Catholics and evangelicals, even referring to the Pope as "His Holiness." A spot in *Contemporary Christian Music* (December 1998, p. 26) also puts a positive spin on the Pope's invitation to the Supertones, as does a report in July of the same year (p. 100) that mentions Kathy Troccoli's meeting with the Pope. (Troccoli recently rejoined the Catholic church, the church of her upbringing.) For a much more thorough investigation of CCM's sympathies toward Rome see David W. Cloud, *Contemporary Christian Music Under the Spotlight* (Oak Harbor, WA: Way of Life Literature, 1999), 47-58, 373, 399.

[176]James Davison Hunter, *Evangelicalism: The Coming Generation* (Chicago: University of Chicago Press, 1987), 23, 31. Unless otherwise specified, surveys cited by Hunter were administered to Christian college and seminary students between 1982 and 1985. Although the statistics are over a decade old, there is every reason to believe that the situation is much worse today, something that even Hunter foresaw (p. 49).

[177]Ibid., 26.

[178]Ibid., 27.

[179]Ibid., 46.

[180]Ibid., 35.

[181]Ibid., 47.

[182]Ibid., 58-59. Even when the same question was asked concerning X-rated movies only sixty-nine percent of evangelical college students and sixty-four percent of seminary students were willing to insist that it was always morally wrong to attend such movies (p. 61).

[183]Ibid.

[184]Ibid., 59-60. Cf. Richard Quebedeaux, *The Worldly Evangelicals* (San Francisco: Harper & Row, 1978), 119.

[185]This is also reflected in Hunter's survey, who found that in 1982 only twenty-three percent of evangelicals surveyed *disapproved* of casual petting (down from forty-eight percent in 1961), and only forty-five percent disapproved of heavy petting (down from eighty-one percent in 1961).

[186]Hunter, *Evangelicalism*, 58.

[187]Ibid., 62.

[188]Ibid., 63.

[189]Ibid., 64.

[190]At the same time it is also important to admit that some progress has been made during this quarter-century. We have certainly witnessed advances in Christian missions, evangelism, creationism, Christian education, intolerance of racism, among other things.

8
Conclusion

FROM TIME TO TIME paradigm shifts take place in important areas of life such as science, philosophy, the arts, and religion. These reorientations become major forces of change, not only within their own parameters, but also within society as a whole. Further, their influence may continue for centuries until they are replaced. We can think of the Copernican Revolution, the Protestant Reformation, Kant's *Critique of Pure Reason*, the Newtonian principle of inertia, and Derrida's deconstruction, to name a few. None of these revolutions was content to impact its own sector, but penetrated beyond its academic discipline and eventually touched the grassroots of western culture.

There is no question that throughout history Christianity has been involved in these paradigm shifts, either as a catalyst or participant, both to its benefit and detriment. The situation is no different today. Secular paradigms of human autonomy, inherited from the Enlightenment, continue to infect the body of Christ. Pluralism, the handmaid of postmodernism, is one of the most harmful societal myths that has attached itself to the western church. The church reflects the world's fascination with individual freedom and creativity. It promotes privatization of convictions and tolerance of diversity in doctrine and life. "I'll do it my way, thank you, and you do it yours," is as much a motto of the believing church as it is the world's.[1] No one will deny that the Bible teaches the freedom of the believer and diversity to some degree. Yet my impression is that evangelicalism as a whole is overly dedicated to these concepts, as well as to the destruction of its chief nemeses, "pietism," "legalism," and "asceticism."[2]

Human autonomy has waged one of its most successful campaigns against biblical doctrine (anthropology to be specific) by making the elevation of self acceptable in Christian circles. In a formalized and calculated way, through the organ of Christian psychology, the dark

Augustinian view of man has quickly given way to a positive Maslowian one, which wrongheadedly considers individual self-worth and self-esteem as critical factors in discipleship and sanctification.[3] Schuller's manifesto that "the core of sin is a lack of self-esteem,"[4] and that the church's mission is to remedy problems of low self-esteem—as outlandish as it is—is steadfastly gaining currency among leading evangelicals.[5] Hunter admits that "modern Evangelicals have accorded the self a level of attention and legitimacy unknown in previous generations. Traditional assumptions about the self have undergone a fundamental assault."[6] More so the obsession of evangelicals with self-importance reverberates into their selection of churches and Christian subcultures. Hamilton finds that

> the generation that reorganized family around the ideal of self-fulfillment has done the same with religion. Surveys consistently show that baby boomers—whether evangelical or liberal, Protestant or Catholic—attend church not out of loyalty, duty, obligation, or gratitude, but only if it meets their needs.[7]

All this to say that the problem of CCM is much deeper than convincing fellow believers to change their musical habits. The root of the problem lies in three areas: (1) a defective understanding of the nature of God; (2) pragmatism; and (3) worldliness.

The Nature of God

The sometimes-passionate, even militant, tone of this book reflects my belief that our very perception of the nature of the Godhead is at stake in the CCM debate. The immanence (nearness) of God and his incarnational activity as taught in the Bible have been seriously distorted to the point where Christians today are under the impression that Jesus Christ can be shaped or tailored into almost any personality type and lifestyle that suits their preference. And why not? Industrialized western society offers its consumers choice if nothing else. Our supermarkets, car dealerships, and screen savers are bright beacons to the fact that we are a people of choice and variety. As we customize our cars, suits, and houses, so we have customized Christ. David Wilkerson coined it perfectly when he complained that we have created an "all-American Jesus." It is very similar to the hamburger commercial that promises that you "can have it your way." "Christianity your way" is the anthem of the day. Whatever currently happens to be popular is carelessly laminated on to Christ, no matter how irreverent or vulgar.

Nowhere is this more apparent than in CCM, which furnishes us with such profane slogans as "Jesus rocks," Bryan Duncan's "holy rock and roll," and Carman's "Holy Ghost hop." One of the most unfortunate and enduring examples of this kind of hyper-incarnationalism is the recasting of Jesus Christ as a Marlon Brando wanna-be and true Christianity as a religion of rebellion in the spirit of rock and roll. Since the examples are countless, only a few can be mentioned, like Stryper's *Against the Law*; the popular witness-wear promoting Jesus as a "Rebel with a cause;" the metal fanzine *Baptized Rebellion*; and Mark Stuart (Audio Adrenaline), who remarks, "Christianity is about rebellion. Jesus Christ is the biggest rebel to ever walk the face of the earth. He turned the world upside down and was crucified for his rebellion. Rock 'n' roll is about the same thing—rebellion."[8] It is hardly a mystery that some CCM concerts boast so many initial converts.[9] Who wouldn't accept a Christ who fits them like a surgical glove?

Our society's addiction to pleasure, amusement, and entertainment is likewise celebrated in the church. It is painfully evident that Christians in the West are comfortably able to conceive of the Godhead and Christianity through the prism of entertainment. After all, much ministry today, evangelistic or not, is entertainment or based on entertainment-type formats. Even in the pulpit, many pastors and evangelists are unable to finish a sermon without intermittent infusions of (rehearsed) humor to keep the congregation amused and attentive. Much more disturbing are baiting tactics such as an advertisement for Campus Crusade for Christ's Prime Time meetings that promised: "Prime Time, a mix between Saturday Night Live and Church." Likewise, the huge Second Baptist Church of Houston Texas has gone to the trouble of consulting experts at Walt Disney World in its effort to attract the public through entertainment.[10] Donald A. Carson's comments on this topic are significant:

When church music directors never fail to tell their choirs to "go back-stage" to get ready, it is not hard to discern the tentacles of the entertainment industry controlling our vocabulary and our thoughts. When serious Christian journals publish articles with titles like "Will There Be Baseball in Heaven?" one can be quite certain that the author has not thought very deeply on Revelation 4-5, 21-22. When churches advertise themselves in the newspaper with lines like, "We feature entertaining worship"—an exact quote, I am afraid—one scarcely knows whether to laugh or weep.[11]

Along the same lines, to much of the unbelieving world Christ is advanced as a heavenly celebrity in search of earthly groupies—represented in the world by his apostles of entertainment, who in no-uncertain-terms are celebrities themselves. When rock stars, super Christian athletes, beauty contestants, and the Power Team are offered to star-struck boomers and busters as incentives to accept the Christian faith, how can we imagine that the Godhead itself is not trivialized and cheapened by the glitz of Hollywood and Nashville?

But more than being an unscriptural and man-centered approach to evangelism, the preoccupation with Christian celebrities may be symptomatic of something more serious, as CCM journalist James Long insightfully suggests:

Is it possible that our insatiable thirst for celebrity Christianity rises from the insecurity of our own faith? We're not quite convinced, so our hidden doubts must be dispelled, and our belief buttressed by the testimony of more credible voices—credible because of celebrity; he or she is looked up to by a skeptical world.[12]

Sobering words from within the CCM juggernaut... In any case, it is becoming increasingly apparent that the church has surrendered itself to extending a pop-Jesus to a pop-culture. As a result much of mainstream evangelicalism believes in and preaches—as one writer put it—a "Jesus who is the way, the truth, and the life of the party."[13]

We cannot, try as we may, hold such views and consider ourselves theologically orthodox.[14] Even CCM fans have confessed this to a limited degree. The September 1988 issue of *Contemporary Christian Music* magazine advertised a poster called "Jesus the Surfer," which pictured a tan, muscular "Jesus" with the face of a *Tiger Beat* heart-throb, in a flimsy loincloth—concealing little more than his groin—clutching a surfboard. The image was so disturbing that even subscribers to the magazine voiced their objections in a later issue:

> I was shocked by the ad for the "Jesus the Surfer" poster.... It looked more like something I would expect to find in *Mad* magazine than in *CCM*. At a time when the secular media is telling us that Jesus was a sinner, this ad tells the reader that Jesus willed that there was no media to capture his likeness so that we could "picture Him as one of our own." The ad implies that Jesus is whoever we want Him to be; that we create The Creator. I believe that this ad is in poor taste. Jesus was not a Hawaiian Surfer or an American for that matter, He was a Jew who lived in Roman occupied Israel. Why is that so hard for some people to accept? What's next? "Jesus the Skateboarder?," "Jesus the Volleyball Player?" Let's stick to the biblical facts. (Leon Carey, *CCM*, November, 1988, p. 6)

Bravo! But why stop there? What about "Jesus the Rocker," the favorite persona of the sinless Lamb of God within the CCM subculture? What is more contemptible, Jesus as a volleyball player or as a rump-shaking Messiah, jitterbugging to a medley of seditious sounds, and executing formalized gestures of copulation on his guitar? If "Jesus really rocks," then we must radically redefine the holiness of the second person of the Trinity to accommodate every pagan accretion that CCM has absorbed into its Christology. I honestly feel that this is how the oxymoron of "Christian" rock is resolved in the hearts of many Christians who believe that they are biblical. The conventional terms of orthodoxy are retained, but they are filled with new content.[15]

This may explain how Best is able to absolve the undeniable vulgarity of CCM:

> This does not mean that there is no crudeness or cheapness [in CCM], for a good part of popular culture is crude, rough-edged, raucous, overly loud, tattered and unkempt. But we must keep in mind that crudeness can be a style, within which both moral and immoral actions may take place [?!?!?!].[16]

This kind of mentality, coupled with an almost institutionalized fear of legalism, has led to a very low view of the holiness of God and Christian sanctification.

How else could we explain how the Gospel Music Association (GMA), which professes to be Christian, could invite country music singer Barbara Mandrell to host the 1993 Dove Awards? One of Mandrell's biggest recordings extols adultery. The hit single "If Loving You is Wrong, I Don't Want to be Right" (1979, ABC Records), describes the struggles of an adulteress who successfully defeats the voice of conscience and the counsel of friends and family in order to justify her affair with a married man. The woman in this song is so committed to her paramour that she concedes, "If I can't see you when I want, I'll see you when I can;" she is so intoxicated with the pleasure of the moment that she 'doesn't care what her people say,' and so selfish that even the thought of her lover's wife and two children cannot discourage her from 'hungering for the gentleness of his touch.' All of this is interlaced with the persistent refrain, "If lovin' you is wrong, I don't want to be right."

In addition Mandrell has recently made cameo appearances on the steamy NBC soap opera *Sunset Beach*. The advertisement shows her leering lustfully at a well-chiseled Adonis naked from the waist up. More puzzling than the GMA is Mandrell herself, who considers herself a devout Christian and has recorded two gospel albums![17]

An aside: The GMA's disregard for *essential* Christian truths and orthodoxy is equally egregious. During the 1999 Dove Awards the group of the year was announced by Della Reese and Sandi Patti. Reese, a member of the Science of Mind cult and star of CBS' *Touched by an Angel*—a blasphemous drama that denies the gospel by espousing a pluralistic view of religion and salvation—was passed off as a Christian before a national audience. The program was hosted by John Tesh, former co-host of *Entertainment Tonight*, who himself (along with Patti) endorses *Touched by an Angel*.[18]

Lament with me over the switch hitting Rev. Al Green, pastor of the Full Gospel Tabernacle Church, gospel singer, but also a recent inductee into the Rock and Roll Hall of Fame and according to *The*

Philadelphia Inquirer, "the world's most sensual R&B singer."[19] Green regularly performs at casinos where he sings "his old sensual, secular hits,"[20] songs that he himself concedes aid in seducing women: "Man, if you really want to get the girl, put on some Al Green and you are surefire not to miss."[21] He even tells of couples who credit his songs for leading to the conception of their children.[22] Despite this Green is listed in The Christian Music Place Artist's Directory.

Lastly, how else could we explain a Campus Crusade for Christ (CCC) skit at a beach outreach, which included making lewd and promiscuous remarks at women? This is not an exaggeration. A popular device, fully authorized by CCC to draw crowds at the seashore, consisted of a rehearsed football game where the quarterback at the ingathering of a crowd would sound off "36, 24, 36." The rest of the actor/players responding to this cue would rise from their ready positions, look around, and ask, "Where?" Then the quarterback would point to the most attractively figured and scantily-clad woman in the crowd and shout, "Over there!" Next, all the men on the team would also point to the woman and make lewd cat calls and wolf whistles at her. After the spectators finished laughing, the men would proudly announce, "Hey we're just a group of young Christians who are here to have a good time and to share the gospel." Finally, all the crusaders would unsheathe the Four Spiritual Laws, tucked in their swimming trunks, and share the gospel.

This must frighten us. Certainly these men were not what we would call nominal or Sunday Christians. They were mainstream evangelicals and zealous witnesses who had sacrificed a great deal to be part of this summer outreach. This phenomenon can only be the result of a radical redefinition of one of the most important attributes of God, his holiness. As mentioned earlier, several factors have contributed to this redefinition, including distortions of the doctrine of God's immanence and incarnation, as well as a syncretism of cultural and biblical standards.[23]

Pragmatism

This book is certainly not the first to warn about the infiltration of pragmatism into the praxis of ministry and evangelism.[24] To some, the current obsession with seeker-sensitive approaches and market-driven ministry is the climax of the pragmatic theology and methodology of evangelist Charles G. Finney.[25] Whether this reconstruction is accurate or not is not for us to decide here. What is sufficiently clear is that pragmatism with its modest beginnings has now penetrated the very core of ministerial practice and threatens to undo the church's very identity and mission,[26] as well as God's sovereignly ordained plan of salvation that resides in the counter-order of the cross.

Christians have believed the notion that what keeps the American public out of church is the church's inability to keep up with the times.[27] Faced with an unchurched and biblically illiterate society of boomers, busters, and Xers, we are now advised that if churches are to grow, they must reorient their methods and practice in order to make the unchurched feel welcome and secure and to meet felt needs. This includes more than just offering them a variety of musical styles. It means emphasizing those aspects of the gospel message that are acceptable, in demand, and inoffensive to today's seeker until they are ready to digest deeper and more complete truths. In order to be relevant, then, topics such as stress management, building relationships, and low self-esteem are offered to the seeking public. It also means communicating such messages through short low-key sermonettes that won't deplete the limited attention span of a society whose cognitive abilities have largely evaporated in front of the television set. Of course, for such a sermonette to be really effective, it first must be primed with a skit so that, as one seeker put it, "if the message doesn't speak to you, the drama will."[28]

The motivating factor in all these strategies is simply that they work, or work far better than traditional approaches to evangelism— which is, of course, the essence of pragmatism. Once again we witness the church capitulating to the spirit of the age, since baby busters themselves are devoted to the philosophy that "if something works, it must be right."[29] Mark Jonah, director of music ministries at Grant Memorial Baptist Church in Winnipeg, says of the seeker-sensitive approach at his church, "It worked, because people were saved as a result."[30] An *early* Harold Best foresaw this problem and protested, "That's what's getting worse to me about evangelicalism—the whole matter of behavioral control, crowd manipulation, and market research. That's grabbing us more and more. Our emphasis is on mass evangelism, not biblical evangelism;"[31] and, "Given today's preference for shallow entertainment, how does the Church reconcile the Nielsen ratings with the scandal of the Cross?"[32]

According to the pragmatic approach, success is inevitably measured by quantity and visible results. Yet, one does not glean such principles from Scripture. In the Beatitudes Christ unrepentantly gainsays the human plumb line of success and well-being with a revolutionary blueprint that violates the visible standards of prosperity. The Beatitudes are anything but pragmatic. They ask us to distrust our own wisdom and accept by faith a system that is wholly alien to our way of thinking. If the underlying principles of the Beatitudes were applied to evangelism, they would convey something of the idea that faithfulness in proclaiming the Word of God will result in spiritual fruit and a heavenly reward. They would not promise earthly success and multitudes of decision cards—although they would not exclude them either.[33]

Pragmatic measures are justified on the insistence that they are in harmony with Scripture—simply neutral tools that can be used positively or negatively. Philip Kenneson, however, traces this dualism of form and content, common in religious thinking, to a neo-Kantian philosophy that also carries the same distinction.[34] Since the folly of such logic from a musical point of view was already discussed, I will add this comment by Kenneson, who covers the issue from a wider vantage point:

> Such an instrumentalist view of technique is not limited to church marketers. This does not, however, make such a view any less mistaken, for it fails to acknowledge that all technique—including all management strategies and marketing tactics—is value-laden. These activities are not simply neutral instruments which leave everything as it is; rather, by

framing certain issues in particular ways these activities help *constitute* the very problems and conditions about which they purport to be neutral.[35]

For all its lambasting of conservative isolationism and fear of the academy, for all its complaining about the mossback mentality of traditionalists, CCM has been unwilling for its own part to release its white-knuckle grip on its patented method-message polarity so that it might profit from the better fruit of modern reflection and research. Howard and Streck's comments are searing:

> While scholars like Harold Innis, Marshall McLuhan, Walter Ong, and Eric Havelock have long been exploring the profound influence that particular media forms have on the messages they carry, the cultures that contain them, the social organizations that produce them, and the thought patterns that emerge from their use, evangelicals have largely ignored such thinking.... Focused on what they are trying to say, evangelicals have spent little time thinking seriously about how to say it—and, perhaps more important, about the environment in which it will be said. Evangelical culture, therefore, is left largely without an intellectual basis for critiquing media institutions or evaluating the influence the media have on the messages sent. Absent [of] any theoretical understanding of culture and/or the media, evangelicals thus blindly assume the neutrality of media and use them uncritically.[36]

Unfortunately, CCM's collapse in this critical area of thinking, so readily apparent to others, is anything but obvious to them.

Moreover, Howard and Streck seriously question CCM's overused out-pitch that attempts to sweep all of its questionable and secular practices under the rug of the 'individual's heart attitude toward God':

> The conclusions drawn are framed in individualistic terms that ignore completely the social structures of the industry. The attitude is pervasive in Christian music.... In the same issue, *Contemporary Christian Music* publisher and original editor John W. Styll wonders whether God is pleased with the industry. He then proceeds to sidestep the question by reducing the industry to its constituent individuals, concluding that individuals' attitudes are more important than their activities and that "our hearts mean more to God than our habits." It is difficult to critique an industry and the structures it has developed if only the attitudes of individuals' hearts—something further argued to be beyond the measure of

humankind—are deemed important. The approach ignores the possibility that "anti-Christian" practices have been embedded into the structures of the industry. Thus hard questions often go unasked, as well as unanswered.[37]

Toward a Biblical Solution

The antidote to pragmatism, however, is not stern traditionalism. In developing a biblical position on evangelism and culture, several factors need to be considered. To begin with, I think that the label "seeker-sensitive" is a misnomer that inaccurately describes the philosophy underwriting the approach. Aside from the fact that "seeker" is a questionable term to use of an unregenerate person (Romans 3:10-18), I have no reservations about being *sensitive* to things that may be legitimately misunderstood by members of our society. As I have argued earlier, this is the kind of accommodation that Paul had in mind in 1 Corinthians 9:19-23, preventative and defensive. Ergo the term "sensitive" would properly define such strategy. The present model of seeker-sensitive services, however, goes beyond biblical sensitivity and operates on the principle of *appeal*, by bending its knee to a legion of societal addictions and pleasures.

So then, practically speaking 'becoming all things to all men' in a defensive sense would include sensitivity to such basic matters as language and terminology. In a post-Christian era it can no longer be taken for granted that non-Christians are aware that the Bible has an Old and New Testament—many haven't the foggiest notion. More so, theologically technical or even Sunday school terminology must either be replaced or explained by the sensitive preacher who aims to accurately communicate the gospel to his unbelieving listeners. Rather than scrapping modern and classic hymnody for CCM, time should be given to explain to the non-Christian visitor the theological significance and spiritual value of each hymn. Carson, I think rightly, suggests the "guest service," a service time that is especially contoured with unbelievers in mind. Such meetings aim to remove unnecessary barriers between unbelievers and the gospel without sacrificing solid worship and preaching.[38]

In terms of offensive strategy, the Bible teaches that God's plan of salvation involves his servants and their ministerial gifts. Yet, a proper handling of 1 Corinthians 1-2 will lead us to understand that the means that God has ordained always conform to the pattern of the cross, a pattern that delights in subverting human logic and expectations with the paradox of a crucified Savior. If such a plan included the use of appealing methods, then there would always be the possibility that a rival religion that duplicated or surpassed those measures could allure the individual away from his "commitment."[39] As already documented, however, this is not God's plan of operation. Rather, God has invested the power of the gospel in the weakness and unpretentiousness of preaching, thus ensuring that only the working of his Spirit can be credited with the conversion of a sinner (1 Corinthians 2:4). This likewise provides a great level of assurance that one's motivation for accepting the gospel will be unadulterated and not based on secondary allurements.

From a theoretical perspective, Peacock's censure against pragmatism and worldliness chimes with the one just presented: "The world accepts as true that which feels right, or that which works or gets the job done. In the world's way of thinking, subjectivism and pragmatism replace the truth requirement of Christianity."[40] "Instead of living under the lie of pragmatism, thinking that whatever works must be good," he writes, "we are a people set free to start at good, and whether good choices cause us to fail or succeed by the world's standards of success is of no importance;"[41] and, "Pragmatism is a worldview which mirrors the world's ways of thinking. We don't want it. It's poison."[42] Incredibly, he even questions CCM's unparalleled separation of form and content: "Modern techniques, methods, systems, and technologies are only tools to us—or are they?"[43] Elsewhere more powerfully, "Have we viewed the world's systems, techniques, and methods as simple, neutral tools to spread the good news? Have we missed the idea that even the simplest of tools, a hammer, for example, comes with an ideological bias?"[44]

Likewise, his understanding of the theology of the cross is profound. He explains that the Dove Awards, in attempting to boost their ratings with superstar hosts and appear "cool," has violated the cardinal principle of life from death and success from failure invested in the counter-order of the cross.[45] He even suggests, "Let's give it up. Let's rethink the whole affair."[46] Amen and amen!

Nevertheless, as was the case with his doctrine of depravity, his applications here are unduly truncated. For example, why should the theology of the cross be limited to toning down the Dove Awards or even eliminating them? If Paul argued that "cleverness of speech" emptied the cross of its power (1 Corinthians 1:17), how will crowd-appealing methods such as rock concerts escape the same criticism? Further, I cannot fathom how Peacock is able to decry pragmatism and overlook entertainment evangelism in its various permutations, especially CCM. After all, the repeated mantra of its practitioners is that straight preaching isn't reaching the kids, but methods like CCM are. Recall for a moment the "do-what-works" rationale that undergirds the mission of CCM, as is honestly articulated by John Cooper of Skillet: "To do that [reach a secular audience], Christian rock groups have to appeal to the tastes of young fans. If that means turning the amplifiers up to 11 and moshing on stage, that's the way it will be."[47] Is this not pragmatism? Is this not "poison"?

Lastly, his comments on method and ideology are just as restricted. Again I am mystified at how Peacock could claim that something as utilitarian and lifeless as a hammer may be ideologically influenced and yet dismiss the same possibility for musical styles, which have the nature of language and can communicate human feelings, attitudes, and emotions.[48]

I conclude this section with David Hazard's timely admonition: "What [Oswald] Chambers points out is an adage that might be emblazoned on the lintels and doorposts of every ministry, Christian business and talk show studio: We must never confuse our desire for people to accept the gospel with creating a gospel that is acceptable to people."[49]

Worldliness

This will probably be the most objectionable portion of this critique to CCM advocates, but there is really no way to avoid it. If my assessment of the moral ethos of the rock style is correct—and I believe it is—then I have no alternative but to charge its Christian patrons and propagators with the sin of worldliness. In an earlier chapter worldliness was described as "patterns of thinking, modes of behavior, attitudes, philosophies, outlooks, grids of evaluation, affections, gratifications, priorities, and value systems that are sinful and a manifestation of the world's perverted understanding of what is true, good, and brings lasting happiness." Since these elements are undoubtedly present in rock music (if not characteristic of it) to one degree or another, the only appeal it can have to Christians is to their carnal Adamic nature.

I do not bring this charge recklessly, but on weighty evidence that has been amassed throughout this book and others. Further, spokesmen within the industry, like Peacock, have recognized this, even if it is only with respect to marketing philosophy and the definition of success, "Since so much of the CCM industry is directly copied from the ideas, systems, philosophies, and methods of the world, I believe that worldliness is present in CCM."[50] He continues, "This is how the world contributes to our darkness. It is sin to allow these incongruent ideas to set the agenda, but I believe that with very few exceptions we have done just that. This is why I believe worldliness is indeed present within CCM."[51]

I hope that the reader considers this to be a serious matter; Romans 8:7-8 warns that "the carnal mind is at enmity with God, for it is not subject to the law of God, for indeed it cannot not be; and those who are in the flesh cannot please God." According to Peacock, "any amount of worldliness is too much."[52] The rectification of this problem will be the focus of the following section.

Application

Since our faith has never been a matter of words alone, but of deeds that act on the commandments of our Lord, it is necessary to challenge the reader to action. Those who have supported this position all along should inform other believers of this tremendously important issue, with a spirit of meekness and love. They should take advantage of available resources to correct the popular myths of music and its use in church. Also, depending on one's position in the local church, one may be able to teach biblical principles on music in Sunday school, evening classes, or to youth groups. Further, books such as this can be recommended to Christian book stores and offered to church libraries and Christian schools, colleges, and seminaries. It should, of course, go without saying that CCM concerts or radio stations should never be supported either directly or indirectly.

There may be other readers who have been convicted by the Holy Spirit to relinquish their association with CCM. Richard Peck's suggestions in *Rock: Making Musical Choices* are helpful here. His first recommendation is fundamental. No attempt to rid one's self of CCM will succeed without total reliance on God.[53] The departure from rock music is not an easy one, for it not only means discarding a musical style that firmly grips its listeners, but changing one's perspective on issues that go deeper than music. Deliverance from CCM, like any other form of bondage, will fail if it is attempted in one's own power. Therefore, prayer, contrition, and even fasting should accompany any such commitment.

Expanding on this concept Peck advises, "Fill your mind with Scripture."[54] Not only will this help in combating the temptation to retreat to old listening habits, but it will also do much to correct unbiblical concepts of the nature of the Godhead, which so often ensnare those within the CCM subculture. Peck is also on the mark in advising that anyone attempting to replace CCM with a different musical style will have to exercise much patience.[55] Detoxification is seldom an overnight process. Therefore, musical tastes must be given time to change.

Finally, I suggest that sources that can restimulate the desire for rock music during the detoxification process (and afterward) should be avoided. Television is a major source of rock music—even hard rock—for the American public.[56] Those who would never choose to listen to rock music of their own accord are exposed to enormous amounts of it through television. Background and theme music for commercials, action scenes, and sporting events are often a variety of rock. In fact, even educational programming is not beyond using rock music for background accompaniment.[57] (By the way, parents should not be surprised when their children enjoy listening to rock music at an early age since even moderate television viewing can skew their tastes toward rock.)[58]

It is my sincere desire that the reader will come away from this book with a clearer understanding of the issues surrounding the CCM debate. Moreover, I hope that the reader will appreciate why it is so necessary to respond to CCM's most recent defenders. Their principles and perspectives on music will be reproduced by countless Christian youth, youth pastors, disk jockeys, and other CCM enthusiasts, who will accept their teaching at face value. It has been the intention of this book to critique these doctrines and offer a more scriptural outlook toward the rapidly changing landscape of modern music and culture. May God assist each and every one of us as we endeavor to do his will by proclaiming and practicing biblical principles in the area of music.

Endnotes

[1]See Harold M. Best, *Music Through the Eyes of Faith* (San Francisco: Harper, 1993), 53.

[2]Cf. James Davison Hunter, *Evangelicalism: The Coming Generation* (Chicago: University of Chicago Press, 1987), 71-75.

[3]Cf. Hunter, *Evangelicalism*, 65-71. Hunter discerns that "there is,...a very clear parallel between Evangelicals and non-Evangelicals in their attitudes about self" (p. 66).

[4]Robert H. Schuller, *Self-Esteem: The New Reformation* (Waco, TX: Word Books, 1982), 98.

[5]Hunter, *Evangelicalism*, 71.

[6]Ibid. Cf. Donald A. Carson, *The Gagging of God: Christianity Confronts Pluralism* (Grand Rapids: Zondervan, 1996), 467.

[7]Michael S. Hamilton, "The Triumph of the Praise Songs: How Guitars Beat Out the Organ in the Worship Wars," *Christianity Today*, 12 July 1999, 30.

[8]Troy Moon, "Audio Adrenaline Vocalist: Christian Rock Differs Little from Secular Rock Music," *Pensacola News Journal*, 1 March 1998, Life: 6E.

[9]Even here the conversion rates are not as high as sometimes projected. Recent critics, from within the movement and without, have contended that in most cases CCM has ended up preaching to the choir rather than the unconverted. Charlie Peacock, *At the Crossroads: An Insider's Look at the Past, Present, and Future of Contemporary Christian Music* (Nashville: Broadman & Holman, 1999), 184, 189-90; Mark Joseph, *The Rock and Roll Rebellion:*

Why People of Faith Abandoned Rock Music—And Why They're Coming Back (Nashville: Broadman & Holman, 1999), 5, 6, 12, 61, 186, 191, 195; William D. Romanowski, "Roll Over Beethoven, Tell Martin Luther the News: American Evangelicals and Rock Music," *Journal of American Culture* 15, no. 3 (Fall 1992): 84; Jay R. Howard and John M. Streck, *Apostles of Rock: The Splintered World of Contemporary* Christian Music (Lexington, KY: The University Press of Kentucky, 1999), 16.

[10]Marc Spiegler, "Scouting for Souls," *American Demographics*, March 1996, 44.

[11]Carson, *Gagging of God*, 466.

[12]James Long, "Mirror Christianity," *Contemporary Christian Music*, May 1995, 71.

[13]David Landegent, "Having a Good Time is Not What Counts," *The Banner*, 15 May 1995, 19.

[14]My charges are not as excessive as they appear. Howard and Streck make a similar proposal regarding differing concepts of God *within* the CCM subculture. They argue that "Separational and Transformational CCM create two very different Gods, one benign and one unfathomable." Further, "These distinct Gods lead to distinct approaches to the Christian life." *Apostles of Rock*, 118.

[15]Howard and Streck, who disagree with the "oxymoron" criticism of Carol Flake (as well as Romanowski and myself) are, nevertheless, correct in assuming that this paradoxical tension does not exist for patrons of CCM. (*Apostles of Rock*, 18-19.) But the reason for the peaceful coexistence is not because the meaning of the music has changed, but because the meaning of holiness and the Christian life have. Remember Mark Stuart, "Christianity is about rebellion.... Rock 'n' roll is about the same thing—rebellion," evidence of a deepening awareness among CCM musicians that it is easier to re-conceive and re-mythologize Christianity than it is to negotiate the codes of rock music.

[16]Best, *Music*, 178-79.

[17]Sandy Smith, "Halos and Hay Bales," *Country America*, June 1994, 43. Patrick Kavanaugh also praises Mandrell for "her sincere faith [, which] shines through all her work, especially her gospel album, *He Set My Life to Music*." *The Music of Angels: A Listener's Guide to* Sacred Music from Chant to Christian Rock (Chicago: Loyola Press, 1999), 268.

[18]Lindy Warren, "Piano Man," *Contemporary Christian Music*, November 1998, 40. Recently CCM artists (Jaci Velasquez, Fred Hammond, Amy Grant) collaborated with Reese on the new *Touched by an Angel: The Album*, which received a favorable endorsement from *Contemporary Christian Music* magazine. Melissa Riddle, "Heartbreak Hotel," *Contemporary Christian Music*, May 1999, 45-46.

[19]Karen Heller, "The Sacred and the Sensual," *The Philadelphia Inquirer*, 26 May 1999, D1.

[20]Ibid.

[21]Ibid., D10.

[22]Ibid.

[23]For some insights on the hyper-immanent theology of modern evangelicals see Howard and Streck, *Apostles of Rock*, 96.

[24]Douglas D. Webster, *Selling Jesus: What's Wrong with Marketing the Church?* (Downers Grove, IL: Inter-Varsity Press, 1992); John Seel, *Evangelical Forfeit: Can We Recover?* (Grand Rapids: Baker Books, 1993); John F. MacArthur, Jr., *Ashamed of the Gospel: When the Church Becomes Like the World* (Wheaton, IL: Crossway Books, 1993). For a response to Bill Hybels' defense of his methods see Appendix D.

[25]Cf. MacArthur, *Ashamed of the Gospel*, 227-35.

[26]Philip C. Kenneson, "Selling [Out] the Church in the Marketplace of Desire," *Modern Theology* 9, no. 4 (October 1993): 328ff.

[27]Ibid., 339.

[28]Jan Johnson, "How Can We Welcome the Next Generation into the Church? Getting the Gospel to the Baby Busters," *Moody*, May 1995, 52.

[29]Ibid., 51.

[30]Bramwell Ryan, "Where Are They Now?" *Faith Today*, September/October 1995, 17.

[31]Harold M. Best, "Music: Offerings of Creativity. An Interview with Harold Best" (interview by Cheryl Forbes), *Christianity Today*, 6 May 1977, 15.

[32]Ibid., 16.

[33]It is true that at times large numbers can be an indication of God's blessing; Jesus promised that his kingdom would have small beginnings but would someday grow to incredible proportions (Mark 4:30-32).

[34]Kenneson, "Selling [Out] the Church," 327.

[35]Ibid., 325-26.

[36]Howard and Streck, *Apostles of Rock*, 128.

[37]Ibid., 216-17. One of those hard unasked questions they feel is "How does the medium of rock music affect the nature of the Christian message presented?" (p. 263). In all fairness, however, although this question is not asked introspectively within CCM, it is answered when the industry is engaged in apologetics with its detractors. Those answers were discussed and critiqued earlier in the book.

[38]Carson, *Gagging of God*, 512.

[39]Jeff Lamp, "Gospel and Rhetoric in 1 Corinthians 1-4: Ruminations Over Implications for Christian Apologetics," paper presented at the 47th Annual Meeting of the Evangelical Theological Society, November, Philadelphia, PA, 1995, 15; Raymond C. Ortlund, "The Power of the Gospel in the Church Today," *Trinity Journal* 18 (1997): 7.

[40]Peacock, *At the Crossroads*, 7.

[41]Ibid., 37.

[42]Ibid., 92.

[43]Ibid., 153.

[44]Ibid., 158.

[45]Ibid., 154-55.

[46]Ibid., 155.

[47]Dean Smallwood, "Christian Rockers All Set to Jam in Jesus' Name," *Huntsville Times*, 20 September 1998, G5.

[48]Peacock's statement that "music is not a neutral container for the dissemination of ideas" (p. 124) has nothing to do with the belief that musical styles by themselves can communicate concepts of good and evil. The context reveals that he is speaking of music in any style being used for good or evil depending on its lyrical accompaniment.

[49]David Hazard, "Holy Hype: Marketing the Gospel in the '80s," *Eternity*, December 1985, 41.

[50]Peacock, *At the Crossroads*, 157.

[51]Ibid., 157-58.

[52]Ibid., 158.

[53]Richard Peck, *Rock: Making Musical Choices* (Greenville, SC: Bob Jones University Press, 1985), 114.

[54]Ibid., 114-15.

[55]Ibid., 115-16.

[56]Cf. Robert Walser, *Running with the Devil: Power, Gender, and Madness in Heavy Metal Music* (Hanover, NH: Wesleyan University Press, 1993), 15.

[57]I was once viewing a documentary on the development of a famous World War II fighter aircraft, when suddenly hard rock instrumentals were played in the background to accentuate the acrobatic maneuvers of the plane in flight.

[58]For additional information on the proper response to CCM, I suggest reading chapters 9 and 10 in John Blanchard, Peter Anderson, and Derek Cleave, *Pop Goes the Gospel: Rock in the Church*, 1983, enlarged and revised (Darlington, England: Evangelical Press, 1989).

Appendix A

The Meaning of *kērugma* in 1 Corinthians 1:21

IT WILL BE ARGUED here that *kērugma*, "preaching," in the context of 1 Corinthians 1:21 refers not only to the content of the message, but also to the method of its delivery. We begin with J. S. Ruef:

> The R.S.V. translation here is misleading. The Greek text is literally through the folly of 'the preaching' (N.E.B. has 'Gospel'). The Greek word is *kerygma* and refers not only to what is preached but to the act of preaching itself. The activity of the church is as much a part of God's folly as the saving act of Christ's death. Paul will make this point rather strongly in vv. 26 ff.[1]

Duane Litfin adds:

> Commentators typically—and rightly—give due attention to the content aspect of Paul's argument throughout this section [1 Corinthians 1:17-2:5], but seldom give sufficient attention to matters of form. Yet the question of form constitutes the *raison d'être* of this section and cannot be ignored without leaving a distorted image of the Apostle's argument.... The matter of form is thus a crucial link in the chain. Without it Paul's argument loses much of its weight.[2]

Semantics

When attempting to discover the meaning of a word, we should realize that in any context it can carry only one sense out of the several that may appear in a dictionary or lexicon.[3] For example, the noun "fly" has eight different meanings listed in the *Webster's New Collegiate Dictionary*, 1981. In a single sentence it can carry only one of those meanings, unless a word play or pun is intended. When we investigate the sense of *kērugma* in standard Greek lexicons (e.g., BAGD), we discover that it basically has only one sense, translated by the English equivalents "proclamation" and "preaching."[4] Unfortunately *kērugma* in 1 Corinthians 1:21 does not have an exact English equivalent that would capture the separate nuances of its meaning. Here, the aspects of *kērugma* include both the act of preaching and the message that is preached.[5] But this is not an instance of word loading, that is giving more than one sense to a word in one context, since the message and the method are not two separate senses but different aspects of one sense. More so, the context dictates that both aspects were in the apostle's mind. Therefore, it is appropriate to take them in tandem and translate *kērugma* in 1 Corinthians 1:21 with an English term like "message preached" (NASB, NKJV). Litfin explains:

> In using the word κήρυγμα [*kērugma*], Paul has intentionally chosen a term which *collapses form and content into one* [emphasis added]. He wants to preserve both before the reader's eyes. In fact, in terms of his present argument matters of form take precedence. The complaints against Paul had to do essentially with the form of his preaching, not its content. Hence the point of this passage is to justify that form. In the immediate context the issue of form introduces this section…and,…issues of form conclude it…. For all these reasons it is critically important not to wash the issue of form out of κήρυγμα [*kērugma*] in 1.21. To do so not only ignores the obvious verbal origin and aspect of this substantive but also by-passes a crucial, arguably *the* crucial element in the Apostle's present argument.[6]

Therefore, there is considerable contextual basis for the contention that in 1 Corinthians 1:21 the "foolishness of the *kērugma*" refers to both the message and the method.

Contextual Evidence

Expanding on Litfin, we should consider various contextual elements that vouch for both aspects being included in this occurrence of *kērugma*. That Paul in 1:18-31 was referring to more than the message of the cross is apparent from 1:17, which states that his proclamation of the gospel (*euaggelizō*) was not with "cleverness of speech"[7] (NASB), a method of address that would invalidate the message of the cross. According to Burton L. Mack, "When Paul explained to the Corinthians that he did not preach the gospel 'with *eloquent wisdom*, lest the cross of Christ be emptied of its power' (1 Cor. 1:17), he made the contrast by reference to a style of rhetoric familiar to his listeners."[8]

Unfortunately, most English translations put v. 17 and v. 18 under different headings, which tends to conceal the strong logical connection between these two verses, which are linked by the causal conjunction *gar*, "for." Verse 18 actually explains why the cross of Christ is invalidated through cleverness of speech,[9] because "the message of the cross is foolishness" (to those who perish), and to present a "foolish" message in an appealing, eloquent form, according to Paul, contradicts and nullifies its theme.[10] It is clear then that the concept of method, introduced in 1:17, is *presupposed* and developed in the following section in conjunction with the message of the cross.[11]

Signs and Wisdom

From the topic of method in 1:17, Paul flows into the character of the message (vv. 18-31), without, however, abandoning his instruction on style, on which he will again focus more specifically in 2:1-4. This can readily be seen in 1:22 where Paul answers the demand of the Jews for a sign and the Greeks for wisdom with a reference to both method ("we preach") and message ("Christ crucified"). Paul, as in vv. 17-18, shows in vv. 22-23 that the message and method are inseparable. The Jews, who were awaiting a powerful and victorious political Messiah, were also expecting miraculous signs to follow that would befit their concept of Messiah. The Greeks, on the other hand, were seeking for wisdom accompanied by a form of oratory (already mentioned in 1:17). But Paul gives them neither the message nor the method that would suit that type of message. Rather Paul says we "preach" (*kērussomen*) Christ crucified, addressing both the method and the message.[12]

With 1:17 clearly referring to method and v. 18 securely binding content to form, we must consider *kērussein*, "to preach," in v. 23 as referring to the method, one that was contrary to the expectations of the Jews and Greeks. Lastly, Litfin contributes this important insight to the discussion:

> The verbs Paul uses to describe his public speaking, such as εὐαγγελίζω [*euaggelizō*], κηρύσσω [*kērussō*], καταγγέλλω [*kataggellō*], and

μαρτυρέω [*martureō*], are decidedly non-rhetorical. No self-respecting orator could have used such verbs to describe his own *modus operandi*. Indeed, even though they deal with the subject of public speaking such verbs play no significant role in the rhetorical literature. This is understandable because these verbs describe a form of speaking which is at its core the antithesis of rhetorical behavior.[13]

Other Available Words

The unlikelihood that Paul meant only the message of the cross by *kērugma* is also apparent by the fact that he had at his disposal three more serviceable words to convey that meaning. He probably would have used *logos*, which can mean "message" as it probably does in 1:18 and 2:4.[14] In fact in 2:4 he juxtaposes *logos* with *kērugma*, "my message and my preaching," probably indicating a distinction in meaning between the two rather than creating emphasis through synonyms.[15] He also had available *euaggelion*, "gospel," or even *stauros*, "cross" (1:17, meaning, "message of the cross").

Weak Things

Finally, references in 1:27-29 to God choosing weak, foolish, and base things could, without much difficulty, include the method of preaching. Fee is correct in pointing out that vv. 26-29 refer to the Corinthians themselves;[16] but the use of neuter adjectives,[17] describing *things* as foolish and weak, permits Paul's reference here to be wider than just his audience.[18] At the very least it validates, through the social status of the Christians in Corinth, the counter-order of the cross and Paul's philosophy of evangelism, as Litfin explains:

> Paul's purpose in mentioning the make-up of the Corinthian congregation is to use it to illustrate his central principle: God uses what the world considers unimpressive so that in the end there can be no question as to who has accomplished the result—no man can boast. This is the principle Paul has used to justify his *modus operandi* as a preacher and it is crucial that the Corinthians grasp it.[19]

Conclusion

For these reasons I feel that *tēs mōrias tou kērugmatos*, "the foolishness of the message preached," refers to both the method of preaching as well as its message. Nevertheless, as much as it has been argued that *kērugma* in 1 Corinthians 1:21 cannot be restricted to the message of the gospel, it is just as important to recognize that the method cannot be isolated as the only aspect of the word's meaning (as in "foolishness of preaching") since the context also refers to the message of Christ and his crucifixion (1:18). Also, it is quite evident that preaching itself cannot save unless its content is the gospel. So then, both the idea of the method and the message are conveyed in the Greek phrase. The two complement each other: neither the message of a crucified Lord nor the forthright and authoritative method of public address known as "preaching" held much appeal then or now.[20]

Endnotes

[1]J. S. Ruef, *Paul's First Letter to Corinth*, The Pelican New Testament Commentaries (Middlesex, England: Penguin Books, 1971), 13. See also Canon Leon Morris, *The First Epistle of Paul to the Corinthians: An Introduction and Commentary*, Tyndale New Testament Commentaries (Leicester, England: Inter-Varsity Press, 1987), 45.

[2]Duane Litfin, *St. Paul's Theology of Proclamation: 1 Corinthians 1-4 and Greco-Roman Rhetoric* (Cambridge, England: Cambridge University Press, 1994), 201.

[3]Moisés Silva, *Biblical Words and Their Meaning: An Introduction to Lexical Semantics* (Grand Rapids: Zondervan Publishing Co., 1983), 148-56.

[4]Walter Bauer, *A Greek-English Lexicon of the New Testament and Other Early Christian Literature*, trans. William F. Arndt and F. Wilbur Gingrich, 2d ed. (Chicago: University of Chicago Press, 1979), 430-31.

[5]Litfin, *Paul's Theology of Proclamation*, 198; Robert H. Mounce, *The Essential Nature of New Testament Preaching* (Grand Rapids: Eerdmans Publishing Co., 1960), 55.

[6]Litfin, *Paul's Theology of Proclamation*, 198-99. Cf. Mounce, *New Testament Preaching*, 55.

[7]It is also translated "eloquent speech," and "skillful rhetoric."

[8]Burton L. Mack, *Rhetoric and the New Testament* (Minneapolis: Fortress Press, 1990), 9.

[9]Cf. Gordon D. Fee, *The First Epistle to the Corinthians*, The New International Commentary on the New Testament (Grand Rapids: Eerdmans, 1987), 68; Henry Alford, *Acts-II Corinthians*, 1875; repr., *Alford's Greek Testament: An Exegetical Critical Commentary*, vol. 2 (Grand Rapids: Baker Book House, 1980), 479.

[10]Cf. Fee, *First Corinthians*, 68.

[11]Cf. Litfin, *Paul's Theology of Proclamation*, 188, 190, 199.

[12]Cf. Litfin, *Paul's Theology of Proclamation*, 200. Actually *kērussō* occurs twice, if we count its elliptical use in v. 24.

[13]Litfin, *Paul's Theology of Proclamation*, 195-96.

[14]Contra Litfin, who feels it refers to preaching. *Paul's Theology of Proclamation*, 194, 205.

[15]Cf. Fee, *First Corinthians*, 51. Here *kērugma* emphasizes the act of preaching.

[16]Fee, *First Corinthians*, 67.

[17]It is perfectly legitimate, however, to use the neuter to refer to persons.

[18]Frédéric Godet, *Commentary on the First Epistle of St. Paul to the Corinthians*, trans. A. Cusin (Edinburgh: T. & T. Clark, 1886), 128.

[19]Litfin, *Paul's Theology of Proclamation*, 203.

[20]Cf. Litfin, *Paul's Theology of Proclamation*, 197, 200.

Appendix B

David's Dance Before the Lord

WHEN ROCK-RELATED DANCE styles need biblical justification, more times than not CCM devotees turn to David's exuberant dancing in 2 Samuel 6. According to them, David was rudely reprimanded by his overscrupulous wife for praising God in the form of a culturally relevant and morally neutral dance. They allege that modern criticisms are of a piece with Michal's objections and reflect narrow legalism rather than biblical discernment. The Peters brothers' version says it best:

> In 2 Samuel 6:16, David offended his wife, who saw him dancing, singing and rejoicing before the Lord as the ark was brought to Jerusalem. Apparently, Michal was offended because David's worship looked too much like the pagan Canaanites' worship. She called him shameless and vulgar (which sounds like some letters we've received describing Christian artists!)
> No matter how outlandish David might have looked, however, his heart motives were right before the Lord. He was using the same cultural style of dancing and singing as his pagan peers, but he was offering it righteously to the one true God. The style was not intrinsically evil, and his intentions for its use were proper. It was Michal, on the other hand, whom God punished.[1]

Upon closer examination, however, such interpretations show themselves to be quite superficial since they fail to consider the larger context of 2 Samuel as well as the canonical context, which must include the interpretation of this event in 1 Chronicles 15. A careful look at important factors pertaining to this issue should dispel the common and unfortunate notion that David's dance was pagan in style.

The New Cart

First, we should realize that David's dance comes in the wake of a severe punishment meted out by the Lord against Uzzah for grabbing hold of the ark of the covenant (2 Samuel 6:6-7). Uzzah's irreverence seems to be the culmination of the more fundamental error of copying the Philistines. The narrative informs us that the Israelites transported the ark on a new cart (2 Samuel 6:3) rather than on the shoulders of the Kohathites (Levites) as commanded in Numbers 4:5-6, 15. It will be recalled that in 1 Samuel 6 the Philistines returned the ark to Israel on a new cart drawn by two cows (1 Samuel 6:7ff). The connection between the Philistine episode in 1 Samuel 6 and the transport of the ark to Jerusalem in 2 Samuel 6 is unmistakable.[2] The "new cart" is the key, a phrase that only occurs in these two chapters and invites connection and interpretation.

The point to be drawn from this distant literary hookup is that David and company violated God's Word and chose rather to follow a pagan method. Further, it is likely that pragmatism was the motivation for imitating the Philistines since the Philistines' method was successful—both for themselves, in getting rid of the ark, and for the Israelites in getting it back. In either case it was not just a problem of disobeying the injunction in Numbers 4, but also of following the methodology of the uncircumcised enemies of the Lord. If it was simply a matter of failing to carry the ark according to the regulations in Numbers 4, it would hardly have been necessary to mention that it was carried on a *new* cart, i.e., in Philistine style.

The folly of the attempt (which was clearly one of form and not content) is confirmed when the Lord's anger is unleashed against Uzzah and by David's later correction to the proper procedures outlined in the Pentateuch. The rectification is most apparent in 1 Chronicles 15:2: "Then David said, 'No one is to carry the ark of God except the Levites, for the Lord has chosen them to carry the ark of the Lord and to minister to him forever.'" Therefore, the incident of the new cart and Uzzah's death—which demonstrates God's displeasure with pagan forms of worship—must be kept in mind in order to prevent private interpretations about David's dancing (as Canaanite).

David's Dance

Something else that often gets overlooked in this discussion is that Michal's main invective was not against David's style of dance, but the

fact that it caused him to expose himself to the maidens: "How dignified was the king of Israel today, who exposed himself today before the
eyes of the maids of his servants, as one of the worthless fellows
shamelessly exposes himself" (2 Samuel 6:20). That this is the primary
issue is supported by the Chronicler's version of the story, which takes
definite steps to restore a pious image to David (see below).[3]

Dancing is of course involved in Michal's disapproval, but there is
nothing in the text, outside of Michal's insinuations, that indicates that
David's dance was orgiastic or otherwise pagan in character. The two
verbs for dance selected here occur only in this chapter and so necessitate that their meanings be reconstructed by way of context and cog-
nates. The first verb $m^e kark\bar{e}r$ is a participle of $k\bar{a}rar$. Evidence from
other Semitic languages suggests that the primary meaning of this verb
is one of rotation or circular motion. Hence many scholars feel it refers
to a whirling dance or pirouette.[4] The second verb, $p\bar{a}zaz$, denotes
either a leaping or skipping movement, but because it only occurs once,
it is impossible—as with the former example—to be certain of the
exact meaning.[5] What is crucial to note is that there is nothing within
the meanings of these verbs that necessitates a vulgar, sensual, or
maniacal dance, such as would be expected from Israel's Canaanite
neighbors. When Canaanite dancing is described in 1 Kings 18:26, an
altogether different verb, $p\bar{a}sah$, is used, conveying a different type of
movement (limping).[6] In 1 Kings 18:26 we are told that the priests of
Baal danced by limping around the altar, probably to induce Baal to
send fire on the offering. Significantly, this is not the manner of dancing attributed to David nor is that verb ($p\bar{a}sah$) ever used to describe
Israelite dancing.

We are also informed that David's dance was exuberant, "with all
his might" (2 Samuel 6:13), as an expression of David's love for the
Lord and his joy over the occasion. It is important to recognize that
David's dance, though exuberant, could have been done decently, even
gracefully, without expressions of sensuality, transgression, and abandonment so characteristic of rock-based dancing. Further, the self-
abasement that Michal and David refer to, "How dignified was the king
of Israel today," and, "I will be more abased than this and will be

humble in my own eyes," does not necessitate that the dance was perverse or erotic, since even if it was done decently it would have been the kind of act that would have greatly humbled a king by lowering him to the level of the common people.[7]

Even so, some scholars have gone beyond the evidence and have considered the dance to be orgiastic and reflective of a Canaanite fertility rite. J. R. Porter is most often cited: "There are good grounds for holding that it [David's dance] was also of a fertility and orgiastic character, and that it was a prelude to the sacred marriage."[8] Ronald F. Youngblood, however, responds:

> Such extreme interpretations, however, do not tally with David's own explanation of his actions in vv. 21-22. Far from the kind of "vulgar fellow"…who would be an exhibitionist in the sight of the slave girls of his "servants," David makes it clear that he is very much concerned about how the Lord evaluates his actions.[9]

Point of View

Troubling, however, is Michal's description of David's dance as something just short of a striptease, i.e., in the manner of the "worthless fellows" (2 Samuel 6:20). The lack of a forceful denial from David also gives the impression that David felt her description to be accurate, though he obviously took exception with her critical tone. There are several reasons, however, why Michal's description should be met with suspicion.

First, it is important to discern the point of view from which David's behavior is reported. It is given by Michal rather than by David or the narrator: "How dignified was the king of Israel today, who exposed himself today before the eyes of the maids of his servants, as one of the worthless fellows shamelessly exposes himself" (2 Samuel 6:20). We have every reason to believe that the ideological perspective of Michal was not shared by the narrator (whose perspective is authoritative), whereas David's certainly was. Through various literary strategies, biblical narrators guide readers as to how they are to perceive the ideological viewpoint of a character, and whether or not the perspective of the character is that of the narrator.

David

As a participant in the story David has been restored from his previous failure with the ark (2 Samuel 6:1-10) to a place where his outlook now chimes with the narrator's: God blessed the household of Obed Edom (2 Samuel 6:11-12); David learned his lesson (implied in v. 13) and successfully transferred the ark to the capital city with sacrifices, great celebration, and, most importantly, without incident (6:12-20); he generously provided food for all Israel (6:19) and was returning to bless his household when Michal came to meet him (6:20). Consequently, David's side of the story is the one that we as readers are to find more convincing.

Michal

On the other hand, Michal is thrice vilified by the narrator as "the daughter of Saul" (6:16, 20, 23). This is more significant because the normal title for a married woman like Michal would *not* have been "daughter of Saul," but "wife of David," as in 1 Samuel 19:11 when Michal tried to protect David from Saul.[10] D. J. A. Clines concludes, "Michal is not behaving as David's wife (contrast 1 Sam xix) but as his opponent: she is acting like a true daughter of Saul, and the narrator has spelled this out by writing 'Michal daughter of Saul' in two places where her criticism of David is expressed (vv. 16, 20)."[11]

Further, Michal is framed as one who is infected with the same type of jealousy, insecurity, and paranoid delusions as her father.[12] David's response to her implies that he understood her pious indignation to be in actuality an expression of hostility for the loss of her father's throne to him, rather than a concern for modesty: "It was before the Lord, who chose me above your father and all his household" (6:21). Hebrew narrative seldom provides direct information about the intentions and motives of a character.[13] It more often does so by a variety of indirect means, as is probably the case here where we are to regard David's response to Michal as an insight into the true motive behind her complaint: David's neglect of Michal; the loss of her father's throne to David; her jealously over the attention David was receiving; and no doubt the heart-wrenching forced separation from her second husband Paltiel earlier sanctioned by David (2 Samuel 3:13-16).[14]

Moreover, Robert Alter does well to notice that "the narrator tells us exactly what Michal is feeling [in v. 16] but not why."[15] He continues:

> Michal's subsequent words to David seize on the immediate occasion, the leaping and cavorting [dancing], as the particular reason for her anger, but the biblical writer knows as well as any psychologically-minded modern that one's emotional reaction to an immediate stimulus can have a complicated prehistory; and by suppressing any causal explanation in his initial statement ["she despised him in her heart"] of Michal's scorn, he beautifully suggests the "overdetermined" nature of her contemptuous ire, how it bears the weight of everything that has not been said but obliquely intimated about the relation between Michal and David.[16]

Therefore, it would be a mistake to come away from vv. 16 and 20 with the conclusion that Michal was primarily at odds with David's manner of dance. It is likely that she was no more puritanical about his dancing than he was.

A final clue to the (un)trustworthiness of Michal's point of view is the reversal of her role from serving as David's ally to becoming his enemy. This is strongly hinted in 2 Samuel 6:16 where Michal looked out her window and despised David, whereas earlier in 1 Samuel 19:12 she lowered David through the window and rescued him. The same phrase $b^{e'}ad$ $hahallôn$, "through the window," is used in both places and acts as connective tissue to call attention to the previous passage so that implications may be drawn from it.[17]

These factors make Michal's description unworthy of full acceptance. As we have seen, there is quite a difference between the credibility of Michal, an anti-hero, and that of the narrator or David, whose statements carry full weight.[18]

David's Denial: "It Was Before the Lord"

Another important fact that is neglected in this episode is that David did (implicitly) deny Michal's charges after all. According to Youngblood, when David insisted that "it was before the Lord," he was in a sense saying it was "not before the slave girls."[19] Further by the phrase "before the Lord" David probably meant in front of the ark of the covenant.[20]

The ark of the covenant was the symbol of God's presence and the place where God met with Moses and spoke to him (Exodus 25:22). The presence of the Lord was so closely connected with it that the term "before the Lord" in appropriate contexts was almost identical to "before the ark" or its synonym "testimony."[21] The best example of this is Exodus 16:33-34: "And Moses said to Aaron, 'Take a jar and put a full omer of manna in it and leave it *before the Lord* to be preserved throughout your generations.' Just as the Lord commanded Moses, so Aaron left it *before the testimony*, to be preserved."[22] Notice how "before the Lord" in v. 33 becomes "before the testimony" in v. 34.[23]

In that the ark spent most of its time in the holy of holies, when ministry took place near the entrance of the holy of holies, such as on the altar of incense, it was often said to be "before the Lord." Leviticus 4:18 provides an excellent example, "And he shall apply some of the blood upon the horns of the altar *that is before the Lord*, which [altar] is in the tent of meeting."[24] More enlightening is the fact that the relative clause "that is before the Lord" is *restrictive* and distinguishes this altar from the brazen altar, which in this chapter is called "the altar of the burnt offering" or simply "the altar" (4:18, 19). It distinguishes it by specifying its *location* ("before the Lord") as opposed to the brazen altar, which was at the entrance of the tent of meeting.[25]

Yet even the area in front of the tent of meeting was associated with the presence of the Lord in that it was the place where the Lord would meet with Moses and the Israelites: Exodus 29:42-43, "It shall be a continual burnt offering throughout your generations at the entrance of the tent of meeting *before the Lord*, where I will meet with you to speak to you there. And there I will meet with the children of Israel." Also Exodus 29:11: "And you shall slaughter the bull *before the Lord* at the entrance of the tent of meeting." Because of this association, the area in front of the tent was sometimes simply referred to as "before the Lord," without mentioning the entrance of the tent of meeting, as in Leviticus 9:2-3:

And he [Moses] said to Aaron, "Take for yourself a male calf as a sin offering and a ram as a burnt offering, without defect, and offer them *before the Lord*. Then you shall speak to the children of Israel, 'Take a male goat as a sin offering, and a calf and a lamb, both yearlings, without defect, as a burnt offering, and an ox and a ram as peace offerings, to sacrifice them *before the Lord*.'"

That "before the Lord" was an indication of a place where they should go (as well as to God's presence) is verified by Leviticus 9:5, where the narrator describes the execution of the command that was just given by specifying the place where they went, "So they took what Moses had commanded to the *front of the tent* of meeting and the whole congregation came near and stood *before the Lord*."

Even when the ark is outside its resting place, as in 2 Samuel 6, we encounter the same type of interchangeability between the terms "before the ark (of the Lord)" and "before the Lord." Consider Joshua 6:7-8,

And he said to the people, "Proceed on and go around the city, and let the armed men pass on *before the ark of the Lord*." So it happened, that, when Joshua had spoken to the people, the seven priests carrying the seven trumpets of the rams' horns *before the Lord* passed on and blew the trumpets; and the *ark of the covenant of the Lord* came behind them.[26]

A more convincing example comes directly from 2 Samuel 6 and 1 Chronicles 13, which record the death of Uzzah. In 2 Samuel 6:7 it states that "he [Uzzah] died there by the ark of God," but in 1 Chronicles 13:10, "by the ark of God" is almost imperceptibly changed to "before God": "he [Uzzah] died there *before God*." Both are referring to the location of Uzzah's death, but in Chronicles there is an emphasis on the divine presence.

So then, we can see that the phrase "before the Lord" can indeed indicate a place—though it is never merely locative.[27] In addition to the example of 2 Samuel 6:7 and 1 Chronicles 13:10, the connection between the ark and the presence of the Lord in 2 Samuel 6 is rather strong. In 6:2 the Lord's relationship to the ark is clearly defined: "...the ark of God, which is called by the Name, the name of the Lord of Hosts who dwells between the cherubim." Elsewhere in this chapter (and the book of Samuel), the relationship between the ark and the Lord's presence is also evident.[28]

Thus, David was most likely referring to the *location* of his worship, which was in front of the ark rather than in front of the maidens, and then by extension to his intent. (At the very least it means that it was not *intended* to be before the maidens, but in front of the Lord/ark.) The fact that David's reference was primarily locational can be corroborated by the narrator's own commentary: "And David danced with all his might before the Lord" (6:14); and especially 6:16, "she [Michal] saw him whirling and leaping before the Lord." Here the locative aspect is more evident in that the narrator is describing the scene as Michal witnessed it: what David was doing and *where* he was doing it. Christians tend to bypass the locative intention of this statement, feeling rather that it refers to the attitude of David's heart. It is necessary, however, to recognize that the prepositional phrase here answers the question, "where?" and then by implication, "how?", i.e., as a sincere act of worship.

Chronicles

The most convincing reason to reject CCM's interpretation of David's dance is because of the specific changes and omissions made by the Chronicler (author of Chronicles), who has labored (for the most part) to preserve untarnished the character of both David and Solomon in his history.[29] From his rewriting of the incident, it is quite apparent that the Chronicler finds the dance episode in Samuel somewhat disturbing and so reinterprets the Samuel tradition in order to protect David's reputation and align it with his *almost* idealized version of David elsewhere.[30] The main problem he detects is Michal's charge of shameful exposure and so reports that David was wearing both a linen ephod and a long robe of fine linen, 1 Chronicles 15:27.[31] The ephod refers to a shorter apron-like garment and the robe probably to a long vestment worn underneath the ephod similar to the one described in Exodus 28:31ff.[32] The author of Samuel had only mentioned the ephod and not the robe, which (robe) would have implied that David's entire body was covered during the dance. It is possible that he felt his readers would assume the presence of the robe since the two items may have been considered part of the same wardrobe, as was the case for the high priestly vestments of Aaron (Exodus 28:4, 31; 29:5; Leviticus 8:7).

More so, the Chronicler employs an interpretive technique similar to ones later used in intertestamental and rabbinic exegesis.[33] In 1 Chronicles 15:27 he introduces a word that sounds similar to a key verb in 2 Samuel 6 but contains a different meaning (a figure known as *paronomasia*). He plays on the participle *m^{e}karkēr*, "to whirl" (2 Samuel 6:14), by replacing it with *m^{e}kurbāl*, "to be clothed" (1 Chronicles 15:27), both extremely rare verbs and sure to catch the reader's attention.[34] Sara Japhet agrees that this is no coincidence: "The choice of the word *m^{e}kurbāl* ('clothed'), to replace *m^{e}karkēr* ('danced'), is again demonstrative of the Chronicler's method; the graphical similarity of the two words is striking."[35] In doing so, the Chronicler is taking a term that could support Michal's version of the dance and replacing it with something that salvages David's reputation. In other words, the Chronicler removes the problematic verb for "dance," by which David allegedly exposed himself, and supplies in its place a verb that conveys the exact opposite, that David wore a long robe that would have concealed him even in an exuberant dance.

To further eliminate possible censure of David's dancing, the Chronicler dispenses with the two rare verbs for dancing used in 2 Samuel 6 (*kārar* and *pāzaz*) and replaces them with two familiar ones, *rāqad*, "skip-dance" and *śāḥaq*, "dance, celebrate" (1 Chronicles 15:29), verbs that would not have carried the same exotic connotations that *kārar* and *pāzaz* may have attained.[36] Further, he leaves out the fact that David danced "with all his might" (1 Chronicles 15:29), a phrase that could also lead to dishonorable and mistaken conclusions about the manner of the dance—conclusions all-too-common among liberal scholars.[37] For many of the same reasons, the Chronicler also omits the incident between Michal and David (2 Samuel 6:20-23).

So then, far from denying or whitewashing the Samuel account, the Chronicler puts it in proper perspective and attempts to arrest the false and unbecoming impressions that may have been gleaned from his much older source (1-2 Samuel). Therefore, along with the other considerations discussed—which exonerate David's dance from inappropriateness or pagan connotations—we should follow the inspired Chronicler's perspective on these events, which provides no support for Christians adopting rock-related dance styles.

Endnotes

[1] Dan Peters, Steve Peters, and Cher Merrill, *What About Christian Rock?* (Minneapolis: Bethany House, 1986), 153. Likewise Angelo De Simone, *Christian Rock: Friend or Foe* (New Haven: Selah Production Agency, 1993), 191-92, 199.

[2] Also, in the episode that immediately precedes we are told that the Philistines made war with David (2 Samuel 5:17-25).

[3] An important point to remember in this entire discussion is that even if David had exposed himself, it would have been accidental and not intentional.

[4] Mayer I. Gruber, "Ten Dance-Derived Expressions in the Hebrew Bible," *Biblica* 62 (1981): 338-39; David S. Dockery, "*krr*," in *New International Dictionary of Old Testament Theology and Exegesis*, ed. Willem A. VanGemeren, vol. 2 (Grand Rapids: Zondervan, 1997), 728.

[5] Francis Brown, S. R. Driver, and Charles A. Briggs, *The New Brown-Driver-Briggs-Gesenius Hebrew and English Lexicon* (Peabody, MA: Hendrickson, 1979), 808; Gruber, "Dance-Derived Expressions," 340.

[6] Brown, Driver, and Briggs, *Hebrew Lexicon*, 820; Gruber, "Dance-Derived Expressions," 340-41.

[7] David's abasement here does not refer to contempt or disgrace, but to "pious modesty." P. Kyle McCarter, Jr., *II Samuel: A New Translation with Introduction, Notes and Commentary*, The Anchor Bible (Garden City, NY: Doubleday & Company, 1984), 187.

[8] J. R. Porter, "The Interpretation of 2 Samuel VI and Psalm CXXXII," *Journal of Theological Studies* 5 (1954): 166; R. A. Carlson, *David, the Chosen King: A Traditio-Historical Approach to the Second Book of Samuel* (Stockholm: Almqvist & Wiksell, 1964), 95.

[9] Ronald F. Youngblood, "1, 2 Samuel," in *The Expositor's Bible Commentary*, vol. 3: *Deuteronomy-2 Samuel* (Grand Rapids: Zondervan, 1992), 877. Cf. A. A. Anderson, *2 Samuel*, Word Biblical Commentary, vol. 11 (Waco, TX: Word Books, 1989), 105-06.

[10] D. J. A. Clines, "X, X *Ben* Y, *Ben* Y: Personal Names in Hebrew Narrative Style," *Vetus Testamentum* 22 (1972): 270-71, 272.

[11] Ibid. 272.

[12]Cf. Youngblood, "Samuel," 874; C. F. Keil and F. Delitzsch, *Biblical Commentary on the Books of Samuel*, trans. James Martin (Grand Rapids: Eerdmans, 1971), 336-37.

[13]Shimon Bar-Efrat, *Narrative Art in the Bible*, trans. Dorothea Shefer-Vanson, Journal for the Study of the Old Testament Supplement Series, vol. 70 (Sheffield: The Almond Press, 1989), 18; Tremper Longman III, *Literary Approaches to Biblical Interpretation*, Foundations of Contemporary Interpretation, vol. 3 (Grand Rapids: Zondervan, 1987), 89.

[14]Robert Alter, *The Art of Biblical Narrative* (New York: Basic Books, 1981), 123.

[15]Ibid.

[16]Ibid.

[17]Cf. Youngblood, "Samuel," 875.

[18]For example, the narrator's report of Saul prophesying before Samuel and lying naked in exhaustion is not to be doubted: "And he also stripped off his clothes and likewise prophesied before Samuel and lay naked all that day and night" (1 Samuel 19:24).

[19]Youngblood, "Samuel," 877.

[20]Cf. Youngblood, "Samuel," 874; Anderson, *2 Samuel*, 106.

[21]The "testimony" (i.e., the tablets containing the Ten Commandments) can refer to the ark of the covenant. In Exodus 25:16 the Lord tells Moses to put the testimony into the ark, and beginning in 25:22 the ark is referred to as the "ark of the testimony" or the "ark in which the testimony resides." Consequently, the phrase "ark of the testimony" was sometimes abbreviated to simply "the testimony," Exodus 30:36.

[22]Likewise see Numbers 17:7, 10.

[23]For confirmation we turn to Hebrews 9:4, where we learn that indeed the jar of manna was placed in the ark.

[24]See also Exodus 28:12; 29-30; 30:8; Leviticus 16:12, 18; 24:3; 1 Kings 8:64.

[25]The altar of incense is clearly referred to as "the altar of fragrant incense, which is before the Lord" in 4:7. In this passage the relative clause is nonrestrictive; otherwise, it would imply that there was more than one altar of incense.

[26]The variant "ark" prior to "Lord" in the Peshitta, Targums, and Vulgate was probably due to scribal harmonization. Harmonization would be expected in a chapter where "before the ark of the Lord" appears three times and seems to establish a pattern. Therefore the Masoretic Text's reading "before the Lord," which is shorter and more difficult, is to be preferred. Cf. NASB, NKJV, RSV, AV, and NIV.

[27]Of course this does not mean that the phrase "before the Lord" always refers to something done before the ark or at the entrance to the tabernacle: 1 Kings 2:4; 1 Chronicles 22:8; Psalms 95:6; 96:12; 98:6, 8; 102:1, 28; 116:9.

[28]Cf. 1 Samuel 4:3-5, 21; 5:3-4, 7; 6:19; 2 Samuel 6:7, 11; 15:25.

[29]Roddy Braun, *1 Chronicles*, Word Biblical Commentary, vol. 14 (Waco, TX: Word Books, 1986), xxxiii; Raymond B. Dillard, *2 Chronicles*, Word Biblical Commentary, vol. 15 (Waco, TX: Word Books, 1987), 2.

[30]Cf. Edward Lewis Curtis and Albert Alonzo Madsen, *A Critical and Exegetical Commentary on the Book of Chronicles*, The International Critical Commentary (New York: Charles Scribner's Sons, 1910), 218; Porter, "2 Samuel VI," 167.

[31]Contra De Simone who maintains that David was almost naked when he danced before the Lord. *Christian Rock*, 191, 199.

[32]Cf. Youngblood, "Samuel," 873-74.

[33]Michael Fishbane, "Use, Authority and Interpretation of Mikra at Qumran," in *Mikra: Text, Translation, Reading and Interpretation of the Hebrew Bible in Ancient Judaism and Early Christianity*, ed. Martin Jan Mulder and Harry Sysling (Minneapolis: Fortress Press, 1990), 375.

[34]Cf. Sara Japhet, *I and II Chronicles: A Commentary*, The Old Testament Library (Louisville, KY: Westminster/John Knox Press, 1993), 307.

[35]Japhet, *I and II Chronicles*, 306. He also goes to the trouble of using the Pual participle of *krbl* in order to add the preformative m^e, to match the same preformative in $m^e karkēr$.

[36]It may also be that he chose *rāqad* and *śāḥaq* because *kārar* and *pāzaz* were so uncommon that their meanings may have been lost to post-exilic readers. The surrounding changes, however, indicate that the replacement was motivated by a fear of misunderstanding rather than lack of understanding.

[37]For example Gnana Robinson, *Let Us Be Like the Nations: A Commentary on the Books of 1 and 2 Samuel*, International Theological Commentary (Grand Rapids: Eerdmans, 1993), 181, 184; Porter, "2 Samuel VI," 166.

Appendix C

Expression in Music

Universals in Music

THE SEARCH FOR UNIVERSALS in music has experienced many fluctuations since the emergence of ethnomusicology as a discipline in the latter part of the nineteenth century.[1] For instance, in the earlier decades of this century the focus in comparative musicology had shifted to musical diversity—a reversal of the convictions of most musicologists in the nineteenth and early twentieth centuries.[2] In the late 1960s, however, interests returned to seeking cross-cultural or universal properties in music.[3] Today the pendulum has swung more over to the side of diversity, with most musicologists unwilling to concede the existence of any substantial universals in music.[4] This is because throughout this century comparative studies of music in non-western cultures have revealed that, in many cases, musical codes and conventions are unable to transcend culture, thus putting the doctrine of music as a universal language in serious jeopardy.[5] Susan McClary's comments typify the current denial of universals in music:

> But if some aspects of the codes prove stable [between seventeenth-century operas and modern music], it is not because music is a "universal language," but rather because certain social attitudes concerning gender have remained relatively constant throughout that stretch of [western] history.[6]

Far more disappointing is the espousal of the same philosophy by Christians such as Harold Best: "There is no way to explain this phenomenon [different responses to a tune] other than that music, as music, is completely relative."[7] It is not likely that this sentiment will change any time soon, especially while the philosophical atmosphere continues to be charged with the indeterminacy of postmodernism and its denial of absolutes.

Nevertheless, it should be noted that universals have been recognized to one degree or another even by skeptics of the position.[8] When universals in music are sought, ethnomusicologists come up with a variety of components. For instance, Bruno Nettl suggests very basic features like variety, redundancy, and similar melodic intervals and progressions. He also observes that "all [cultures] have rhythmic structure based on distinction among note lengths and among dynamic stresses."[9]

Emotions

I propose, however, that in the search for universals the lowest common denominator should be sought in human feelings and emotions. Although music may signify things other than emotions, the biblical witness as well as the conviction of many musicologists, psychologists, and scholars lends credibility to the thesis that the connection between music and emotions is universal and a solid point of departure for a biblical view of musical semiotics (the theory of signs and symbols). Deryck Cooke, for instance, concludes, "We may say then that, whatever else the mysterious art known as music may eventually be found to express, it is primarily and basically a language of the emotions...."[10] William Edgar also finds that "almost every culture, from the ancients to modern people, agrees that whatever else it can mean, music means emotion."[11] Furthermore, he relays that "the Bible is in accord with this consensus. Of the more than six hundred references to music in the Scripture, the majority connect it with some kind of emotional experience. The natural passage of thought between feelings and sounds is most remarkable."[12]

Next, John Blacking demonstrates the importance of emotions in musical universals:

> If human beings can never share feelings, the discovery of universal music traits would not reveal much about the nature of *music*: the octave, certain patterns of rhythm and melody, and any other structures that might be found universally, could not be given musical significance, since without evidence that feelings can be and are shared, two people could not even be said to share a sentiment through their common attitude to the same music, let alone be affected similarly by the same pat-

terns of sound. Without the possibility of truly shared experiences, music must remain one of many cultural artifacts whose forms and effects are consequences of social and cultural convention or the idiosyncratic choice of individuals....[13]

Of similar conviction is Stephen Davies, "Because I hold that expressive behaviors owe as much to our common humanity as to our various cultures and that music is expressive in being experienced as like human action, I think that there is a common expressive element found in the musics of different cultures."[14]

More so, universals can be evident in the actual practice of music. According to Blacking,

...musicians reared in mutually incomprehensible cultural traditions may use a common device which, because it is based on a universal mental structure, may resonate with listeners unfamiliar with the cultural or musical idiom. To do this, they must reach beyond the conventions of their particular society to the universal mental processes of the species.[15]

The reason that musical universals can be anchored in feelings and emotions is because emotions are generally alike in people of all races and cultures. Children throughout the world feel the same physical and emotional sensations when they cry. Likewise, people of every variety experience fear—in a biological sense—in the same way: change of heart rate, adrenaline flow, blood pressure, muscle tension, even facial expression. Although speaking of sadness, Davies' point is essentially the same, "Chinese sad-lookingness is much the same as French sad-lookingness."[16] The identical thing could be said of happiness and anger.

Kinds of Emotions

At this time it may be useful to distinguish between primary emotions and higher emotions. Primary emotions would include states such as happiness, sadness, fear, and anger. These are emotions that have detectable physical and behavioral manifestations and are most hospitable to musical expression.[17] Higher emotions consist of feelings that are subsets, and sometimes combinations, of these broader categories.[18]

Conditions such as hope, anxiety, jealousy, and shame generally do not betray external features that distinguish them from similar feelings (e.g., anxiety from nervousness), and usually cannot be known apart from access to the inner thoughts of the person.[19] In turn, these are considered less capable of musical expression, and by some incapable.[20] Although Davies doubts the expressive potential of higher emotions, he admits,

> It might indeed be the case that not all "higher" emotions are equally "high." For at least some of the Platonic attitudes [higher emotions], it could be that the dynamics of their progression, or of the behaviors by which they are expressed, are distinctive enough that music might,...provide a context for their successful expression.[21]

But even if higher emotions cannot be articulated with distinguishing precision, it is still the case that certain types of music would be more compatible or less compatible with the moods that accompany these higher emotions. Hope, for example, would be compatible with joyful music, rather than sad or angry. The joyful music could be further refined to match the dynamics of hope perhaps by slowing the tempo and adding elements of tension.[22] Likewise, themes of jealousy—a mixture of sadness, fear, even anger—would be absurd in the setting of a joyful, uplifting melody.[23] So then, even if higher emotions cannot claim the expressive potential of primary ones, their musical context is by no means arbitrary.[24]

In the Image of God

The relationship between music and emotions gains greater stability when the source of all human feelings and emotions is exposed. Human personality and emotions are imprints of the Divine, derived miniatures of the unsearchable personhood of the Trinity, rather than self-generated or the social adaptations of a developing species.[25] Therefore, it is not enough to point out that the emotional attributes of God are communicated in the Bible in anthropomorphic language as a condescension to our limited understanding, since it is also the case that our emotional makeup is *theomorphic*, that is, created and fashioned in God's image. Our ability to feel, will, reason, and desire is reflective of the same components of personality in our Creator. God is a personal being and genuinely feels love, sorrow, joy, and hatred.[26] We, as creatures made in his image, possess a likeness of those emotions. Even those feelings that are not shared by God, such as *eros*, are still bestowed by him and, therefore, can be considered reliable points of reference. Consequently, in human emotions we have the potential for a fixed referent in music and the hope of some kind of universality.

The question, however, remains as to how these emotions are transmitted in music. If the relation between the musical sign (signifier) and the emotional state that it represents (signified) is arbitrary, as it is with words and their referents, then the possibility of assigning new meaning to those symbols is very real. In the following discussion I will attempt to wrestle with such questions and to chart a course toward a biblical view of semiotics in music.

A Semiology of Music

The Hypodermic Model

Today it is generally accepted that music communicates through a system of audible symbols rather than directly.[27] Nevertheless, most people assume that music affects them without mediation because the association of feelings and experiences with musical sounds seems so intuitive and natural.[28] This often leads to the conclusion that the power of music is direct and irresistible. Sometimes referred to as the "hypodermic" model of musical communication, this position assumes that music is downloaded into the listener's psyche and renders him helpless to resist its effects.[29] Thus, according to this view, music operates directly, rather than through symbols, and has the same effects on everyone whether they want it to or not. Edgar convincingly explains why this model misrepresents the process of musical meaning:

> Music's relation to emotion is not so much a matter of the physical properties of the sounds touching our own psychophysiological natures. The meaning of music for emotion is not primarily in its acoustical properties isolated from the symbolic presentation. Of course various types of music seek to affect us through such means as heavy drumming, loudness and amplification, etc. But the effects of these depend not so

much on some biological processes unleashed within the human organism as on deeper psychological factors. Music is movement. It is closely associated with human experience in time and space.[30]

Further, an example from the Bible clearly exposes the weakness of the hypodermic model. If music affected us without mediation and interpretation, then Saul would not have been successful in resisting the soothing musical therapy of David recorded in 1 Samuel 18:10-11 and 19:9-10:

> Now it came about on the next day that an evil spirit from God rushed upon Saul, and he raved inside his house, while David was playing music with his hand, as times before. And there was a spear in Saul's hand. And Saul hurled the spear for he thought, "I will pin David to the wall" (1 Samuel 18:10-11).

It is evident that David's instrumentals were unable to relieve Saul on these occasions (through no fault of the music). Although the narrative lacks detail at this point, it is logical to assume that Saul was able to block out and resist the power of the music—since music is mediated through a network of symbols—and, contrary to the intended effect and message of the music, tried to murder David in cold blood.

Although discrediting the hypodermic model may seem like a surrender to the CCM position, which insists that moral attributes reside in words rather than in music, this is by no means the case. Simply because music primarily communicates and affects through a sign-referent system does not diminish its ability to manipulate our emotions or to encourage and stimulate behavior in powerful ways. Both Edgar and Gilbert Rouget, who actively oppose the hypodermic model, are convinced that music as symbol and referent can affect emotions and influence behavior in ways that are as potent, if not more potent, than direct coercion. Edgar maintains that "Rouget, far from denying this power, shows that the ability of music to accompany trance-inducement is in a way greater because of its sign value than if it only worked physiologically."[31] Speaking for himself concerning the power of various kinds of symbols in rock videos, Edgar explains that symbols "are far more powerful than just the use of acoustical devices. They are metaphors and allusions to evil in the medium of ordered sound, a medium which articulates meaning at a deep level."[32]

Further, the capability of music to convey meaning and influence behavior via the semiotic model (symbol-referent) is evident in the success of the Muzak service, which has documented its ability to manipulate the behavior of shoppers, waiting room patients, factory workers, and others through various types of music.[33] The power of music, even as symbol and referent, is convincingly demonstrated by one of the most vigorous opponents of the hypodermic model, Robert Walser:

> At the end of an Iron Maiden concert I attended in 1988, light, happy, Muzak-style music came through the house PA system to accompany the crowd's exit. I didn't recognize the tune, but it was very close to "It's a Small World".... This vapid music, so incongruous after Iron Maiden's powerful show, was clearly intended to disperse the energy of the concert, promoting orderly exit and calm reintegration with the world outside. It succeeded remarkably: fifteen thousand screaming, sweating, straining heavy metal fans were transformed into a group as sedate as any homeward-bound symphony orchestra fans.[34]

At this point it is necessary to stress that a rejection of the hypodermic model is not a denial that music, especially electronic music, can directly affect living organisms, including people, in positive and negative ways—as was discussed in an earlier chapter. Musicologists and social scientists furnish evidence that music can in certain instances penetrate human beings *directly*, in biological rather than strictly psychological ways. Even fans without medical training acknowledge this: "If it's [heavy metal] really loud, [it] kind of affects your heartbeat and stuff."[35] Arnett states that "on occasion [at a heavy metal concert] you can actually feel your ribcage vibrating."[36] Another sociologist, Robert Snow, observes that "in the 1960s, sound technology enabled groups to crank up the volume so that you could actually feel the music pulsate throughout your body. This wasn't a latent function, it was by design."[37] James Lull echoes, "Nearly every young person in the United States at some point hears a pop music concert live, and comes into thrilling contact with sound so loud and compelling that it seemingly 'takes over' the body."[38] Even Davies, who rejects the hypodermic model, concedes that "music might trigger some responses simply by being heard. For example, it might affect in a predictable manner the heartbeat or the rate of respiration; it might trigger muscular twitches."[39] The point is that, although music cannot control our behavior directly, it can in some cases affect us physically, forcing us to respect its capacity to penetrate and even harm the body, the temple of the Holy Spirit.

In conclusion then, even though the hypodermic model as a whole ought to be discarded for some variation of the semiotic model, the idea that music effectively communicates feelings and moral meaning and influences behavior through symbols should be retained.

Semiotic Model: Music as Symbol and Referent

As mentioned earlier, musical meaning is mediated through a system of audible symbols and syntax that represent extramusical realities, such as emotions, experiences, events, and even material objects.[40] Moreover, connections between audible symbols and their referents are forged within cultures where the members of society participate with the musicians in assigning meaning and value to the symbols.[41] Philip Tagg offers a concise explanation of the sign value of music:

> Here we regard music as a symbolic system, as that form of interhuman communication which distinguishes itself from others in that individually and collectively experiential affective states and processes are conceived and transmitted as humanly organized nonverbal sound structures to those creating these sounds themselves and/or to others who have acquired the mainly intuitive cultural skill of 'decoding the meaning' of these sounds in the form of adequate affective response.[42]

Divisions in Musical Semiology

Musicologists generally divide themselves into two camps when it comes to their conviction of what musical symbols refer to.[43] Formalism holds to the idea that music is a closed system that refers only to elements within itself. According to this position, musical meaning exists entirely within the structure of a composition or genre of music and not outside it. That is, whatever meaning can be attributed to a piece of music must be derived strictly from the internal relationship of its musical components, a kind of musical self-definition through the interplay and opposition of its parts. Consequently, the formalist view opposes the idea that music refers outside of itself to non-musical entities such as events, objects, emotions, and pictures.[44] The opposite view contends that the sounds of music and their arrangement refer to various extramusical phenomena including emotions. Both Edgar and Jean-Jacques Nattiez are correct in rejecting either extreme, arguing that music generates meaning both from within its structures and from the extramusical world that it represents in sound.[45] In what follows, however, I will focus only on how music functions as a system of sign and external referent by interacting with two varieties of signification, the bioacoustic and iconic.[46]

Bioacoustic Signification

Briefly, what is meant by the phrase "bioacoustic signification" is simply that musical signs and syntax have some sort of natural or analogical relationship to their extramusical referent, whereas in the iconic system the relationship is purely arbitrary. Music communicates bioacoustically by arranging sounds in patterns of movement through time and by regulating the volume and dynamics of those sounds in order to resemble the same qualities in human emotions or the behavior that accompanies them.[47] The most useful explanation of the bioacoustic model is furnished by John Hospers:

> When people feel sad they exhibit certain types of behavior: they move slowly, they tend to talk in hushed tones, their movements are not jerky and abrupt or their tones strident and piercing. Now music can be said to be sad when it exhibits these same properties: sad music is normally slow, the intervals between the tones are small, the tones are not strident but hushed and soft. In short, the work of art may be said to have a specific feeling property when it has features that human beings have when they feel the same or similar emotion, mood, etc. This is the bridge between musical qualities and human qualities, which explains how music can possess properties that are literally possessed only by sentient beings.[48]

A slightly more technical description of this model comes from R. Francès:

> The kinship between rhythmic and melodic pattern in music, and the patterns of gestures that accompany behavior, represents one of the basic elements of music's expressive language...the basic psychological states (calm, excitation, tension, relaxation, exaltation, despair) normally translate themselves as gestural forms that have a given rhythm, as tendencies and ascents, as modalities for organizing fragmentary forms within global forms...the transposition of these rhythms, tendencies, and modalities of movement into the sound-structure of music constitutes music's basic expressive language.[49]

Further, various experiments have been conducted to determine how emotions translate into music. Alf Gabrielsson and Patrik N. Juslin summarize the results:

> "Serious" and "solemn" music was said to be slow, low-pitched, avoid irregular rhythms and dissonant harmonies. "Sad" music is likewise slow and low-pitched, further apt to be in a minor mode, and to contain dissonance. "Happy" music is fast, high-pitched, in a major mode, and contains little dissonance. "Exciting" music is fast, loud, and apt to contain dissonance.[50]

The bioacoustic model is most readily associated with Susanne K. Langer, one of its senior advocates: "The function of music is not stimulation of feeling, but expression of it; and furthermore, not the symptomatic expression of feelings that beset the composer but a symbolic expression of the forms of sentience as he understands them."[51] It should be noted, however, that her conviction grows colder as emotions become more specific: "For *what music can actually reflect is only the morphology of feeling*; and it is quite plausible that some sad and some happy conditions may have a very similar morphology."[52]

Leonard B. Meyer is convinced that of the two methods of signification, the bioacoustic and iconic, the bioacoustic is dominant:

> However important associations formed by contiguity [iconic system] may be, their role in connotative signification [standardized associations between sign and referent] is a relatively minor one. Most connotations

arise as the result of similarities which exist between our experience of music, on the one hand, and our experience of concepts, objects, activities, qualities, and states of mind found in the extramusical world, on the other. Generally associations formed by contiguity [iconic function] modify and delimit those formed by similarity.

...Both music and life are experienced as dynamic processes—as motions differentiated both in shape and in quality. Such motions may be fast or slow, continuous or disjointed, precise or ambiguous, calm or violent and so forth. Even experiences without literal, phenomenal motion are somehow associated with activity. Sunlight, the pyramids, a smoothly polished stone, a jagged line—each, depending partly upon our attitude toward it, is felt to exhibit some characteristic quality of motion and of sound.[53]

Further, Meyer opines that the bioacoustic system not only communicates consistently within culture, but may be universal:

The question is whether the processes of association are the same in different cultures; whether similar musical processes and structures give rise to similar or analogous connotations in different cultures. A modest sampling of the evidence indicates [that] these processes are cross-cultural.[54]

David Lidov suggests something similar:

Still unlike mathematics or speech,...a sense persists of strong and precise and intimate correspondences between the details of music and bodily properties: gestures, tensions, and postures as well as such psychosomatic (or neuro-chemical) properties as states of consciousness, moods, and emotions. Those correspondences which involve kinesthesia in a direct and simple way appear ubiquitous.[55]

Philip Tagg seems to agree with the universality of the bioacoustic system, though not its primacy:

Cross-cultural 'universals' of musical code are rare and mainly bioacoustic, in other words, relations between human and musical pulse, between degrees of human bodily rates of movement, excitement, etcetera.... Most other aspects of musical structure (pitch, timbre, texture, concepts of consonance and dissonance, etcetera) share far fewer common connections to extramusical phenomena from one culture to another.[56]

Similarly, Julian Thayer's research, like the early studies of Kate Hevner, finds pitch and tempo to be crucial to the manner in which music signifies emotional meaning to its listeners.[57] Even the normal heartbeat of seventy to eighty beats per minute is suggested as a point of reference by which human beings measure the speed of musical tempo.[58] It is probably correct to assume then that among those musicologists who believe that music can refer externally, there is some degree of agreement (with varying levels of conviction) as to the legitimacy of the bioacoustic version as a system of musical signification.[59]

The viability of the bioacoustic model is supported by a recent study by Gabrielsson and Juslin, which discovered that musicians who were asked to encode various emotions through music were fairly consistent in their use of tempo, volume, timbre, timing, intonation, etc., in the expression of individual emotions,[60] supporting earlier studies that also found "reasonable agreement as to the broad characterizations of emotional expression in music."[61] For example, sadness involved using a slow tempo, low to moderate volume, and soft contrasts between long and short notes.[62] Further, they discovered that "listeners were generally successful in decoding the intended expression."[63] Finally, it was learned that primary emotions such as happiness, sadness, and anger were easier to express than higher ones like solemnity.[64]

Iconic Signification

I have chosen Lidov's term "iconic" to represent the semiotic system in which there is no necessary or essential link between the symbol and its referent. As Lidov puts it,

> In composition, the shapes of melody, chord progressions, and rhythmic patterns may be icons. These shapes are understood as images of movement or of somatic states governing movement, but they are not direct copies, causes, or consequences of these. They require interpretation.[65]

Of this version of musical signification there is little disagreement among those who adopt the non-formalist position. Although they vary in their terminology, (externalist) musicologists maintain that in many cases—some in every case—the connection between the musical symbol and its referent is purely conventional, artificial, and culture specific. Nettl urges: "There is no intrinsic relationship between ascending melodic contour and going to heaven, but if this is the way a group of people agree to represent the Ascension, then a symbol has been created."[66] Meyer, who is sympathetic to the bioacoustic mode, here reflects on the culture specific aspect of the iconic system (his "contiguity"):

> Such associations by contiguity are culture bound. A particular raga will not, for example, evoke the appropriate associations in a western listener unless he has learned its "meaning." The sound of the organ will not arouse religious associations in the members of a primitive tribe which has not been visited by missionaries—if such a tribe exists. Because contiguity creates associations which are contingent rather than necessary, they are subject to change and modification. Old associations die out and new ones arise.[67]

Consequently, this position is most often embraced by the nonuniversalist school of music. If the relationship between musical symbols and their referents is not analogical, then cross-cultural communication is seriously hampered. Edgar sums up the position nicely: "The way music *means*, emotionally, is primarily musical. It is through the many devices in the 'world' created by knowing use of many different compositional elements (which vary greatly from culture to culture) that emotional responses are produced."[68]

Associative Signification

A macro version of the iconic model may be termed "associative." Under this system an entire song or genre—rather than its symbols, codes, and syntax—can take on a certain meaning based on the context (sometimes lyrical) of its performance.[69] Best uses this model to support his view that *"music has no interior beacon that guarantees permanent meaning. Unlike truth, which is transcultural, absolute, and unchangeable, music can shift in meaning from place to place and time to time."*[70] (Italics original.) He invokes the example of the tune for the hymn "Glorious Things of Thee Are Spoken," which (tune) had a long history of secular service in anthems and concerts, thus indicating that it contains no inherently sacred meaning. Further, he relates that when the tune was attached to the German national anthem, "Deutschland über Alles," it awakened negative feelings among Jews, who were reminded of the Holocaust by it. He also brings up an example of a young man involved in a satanic cult that surprisingly used Bach's music for its liturgies. The man later became a Christian and was terrified whenever he heard the same music played in church.[71] Consequently, Best concludes that "there is no other way to explain this phenomenon other than that music, as music, is completely relative."[72]

There is, of course, another explanation. Throughout his argument Best has maintained that the meaning of the music was determined by its context, but this is only partially correct. The actual extramusical referents of the musical symbols and syntax in the above examples—apart from any lyrics or association—would remain basically the same. Those who are conversant with the codes of western music would probably use terms like "reverent," "melodious," "majestic," "serious," "orderly," and even "joyous" to describe them. The actual referents of the musical codes (reverence, majesty, order, etc.) have not been altered; what has changed is the larger context with which these referents are variously associated. Whether as an anthem, entertainment, a hymn, or even in satanic ritual the qualities described above remain relatively intact, even though their application has changed.[73] What has taken place in the exceptional cases that Best has mustered is that strong reactions have occurred, not to the musical codes per se, but to a negative setting (including lyrics) that the musical piece as a whole has triggered. But this is no support for the neutrality of music.

In the same way, if a light, cheerful song (both in tune and *lyrics*) was playing in the background when someone was informed of the death of a loved one, that happy song, by association with the painful event could for some time be a source of great sorrow for that person.[74] This does not mean, however, that the tune or the lyrics are sorrowful or sad. It has become so by accidental association and circumstance alone, not by any sad properties in the music or even the lyrics.[75]

Most importantly, this example reveals that associative meaning can also take place with *words*—which Best exalts as unambiguous carriers of propositional truth[76]—thus demonstrating that examples of associative signification in no sense prove that "music is completely relative." The associative model only suggests that true signification and communication can, in a fallen universe, be distorted or reversed by unfortunate circumstances or perverse applications, not that the linkage between symbol and referent is entirely arbitrary and unlimited. In fact Davies recognizes how the associative model actually distorts our understanding of how music means:

> If now I am delighted by the slow movement of Beethoven's Symphony No. 3 because I happened to be listening to it when, in the past, I received news of my lottery win, then my delight is not to be counted as a response to the music as such. Put another way, the variety of response labeled by Kivy as "they are playing our song" is to be dismissed, since responses of this type result from private associations that such music calls to mind rather than from attention to features of the music.[77]

Therefore, we should realize that the associative model is not the manner in which music ordinarily signifies, nor is it supposed to be. Extraordinary circumstances and idiosyncratic reactions to music or any symbol should not serve as paradigms of normal musical significa-tion or musical neutrality. Thus, personal responses may be better handled under the rubric of the psychology of music than under semiot-ics. The associative model also suffers from the same problems as the purely iconic one, as will be discussed later.

Primacy of the Bioacoustic System

I will now argue that the bioacoustic model of musical symbolism should be considered the ultimate point of reference and cornerstone of musical semiology. This is not to say that music cannot participate in iconic methods of symbolism or refer to paramusical phenomena other than emotions. It certainly can and should. What I am appealing for is a semiotic that allows for such freedom so long as it does not at the same time undermine, reverse, or confuse the bioacoustic method of mean-ing.

Biblical Model

Evidence from the Bible indicates that the biblical writers held to a bioacoustic model of musical signification. Job 30:31 is especially instructive in that the original language literally conveys the sense of the harp and the flute being transformed into the emotional states of mourning and weeping respectively: "My harp has been turned into mourning, and my flute into the sound of weeping." Here the meaning is certainly not one of a material substance being changed into a non-material entity (emotion). It is rather a poetic and emphatic way of relating that these musical instruments articulated emotional states (in the sphere of sound ordered in time and space) so accurately that they could actually be thought of as becoming those very emotions. Therefore, a freer translation such as "my harp reproduces the sounds/sensations of mourning, and my flute reproduces the sound of weeping" would accurately capture the meaning of that verse.

Here then we have the clearest example of bioacoustic signification in the Bible. In Job 30:31 the text is transparent enough to detect with certainty that the relationship between the symbol and the referent (emotion) is primarily homological or mimetic, and not merely iconic. This is most evident in the second half of the verse, which literally states that "my flute has been turned into the sound of weeping." I have argued earlier that passages like this cannot refer to the unique sound qualities of instruments, since the same instruments participate in the expression of divergent and conflicting emotions like sadness and joy. What is actually referred to by terms such as the "pleasant harp" (Psalm 81:2) are melodic structures played on the instruments, structures that at least in Job 30:31—and most likely other texts—imitate through the agency of sound, space, and time what we feel internally and manifest externally as we experience various emotions. Job 30:31 can mean no less than that.

Moreover, the musical reenacting of emotions was so convincing and accurate to the Israelites that the comparison could actually be reversed so that the genuineness of one's emotions could be measured against the emotional qualities conveyed by certain kinds of music.

This is why both Isaiah and the Lord himself could describe their feelings by comparing them to dirge melodies played on flutes and harps: "Therefore, [said the Lord] my heart moans for Moab like flutes, and my heart moans for the men of Kir Heres like flutes" (Jeremiah 48:36); "Therefore, my heart moans for Moab like a harp, and my deepest emotions for Kir Heres" (Isaiah 16:11).[78] Notice that neither said that the flute and harp were played in a manner that intoned their feelings, but rather, to impress the genuineness of their feelings, they compared them with what society already considered to be a dramatic but faithful expression of those feelings in dirge-music played on the flute and harp.[79] Again the pattern of comparison and imitation fits much better with a bioacoustic system of signification than with an iconic, or exclusively iconic, one. This is because they compare their distress to the sorrowful melodies of dirges (this is doubtless the reference here), which in turn received their intonation from those elements of human lamentation that could be musically reproduced. It is doubtful that they would be so willing to define common feelings by means of instrumental music if there was no or little organic link between their experience and the musical codes of the genre that they chose for comparison.

Although other references to music and emotions in the Bible do not offer the same lucidity with respect to the semiotic system employed, I don't think it is pushing matters to assume that the above examples are characteristic of Israel's musical semiotic, rather than accidental. Certainly, none of the other references undermines this thesis (e.g., Isaiah 24:8), while some like Isaiah 30:29, "You shall have gladness of heart as one who marches to the sound of a flute," add considerable support to the proposal that the bioacoustic semiotic evident in Job 30:31, Isaiah 16:11, and Jeremiah 48:36 was the standard model among the Israelites, and perhaps even among other ancient Near Eastern cultures.

Absurdity

The second reason for insisting on the primacy of the bioacoustic model is because of the impossibility of the opposite and the absurdity resulting from an exclusively or primarily iconic or relativistic understanding of musical signification. If the relationship between musical symbols and the emotions they signify is entirely arbitrary, as it is with language, and if the symbols have no natural or organic affinity with those emotions, then it would actually be conceivable for us to equate a harsh, rapid, loud, dissonant, and heavily accented instrumental piece with sensations of peace, calmness, and rest. The concept is unthinkable since our experience of those sensations in no way coincides with the sonorous characteristics of such a performance; our feelings flatly contradict the tempo, intensity, movement, and volume of the sounds claimed to represent peacefulness, calmness, and restfulness.

Yet this is the logical outcome of a semiotic system that refuses to acknowledge the primacy of the bioacoustic model in encoding emotions. Tagg provides a similar example: "No lullaby will work if yelled jerkily at a brisk rate and no war march will have the desired effect if crooned mellifluously at a snail's pace."[80] John Sloboda, who like Tagg is no champion of the bioacoustic model, nevertheless admits:

> This does not deny the possibility of some primitive responses to music shared by the whole species. For instance, loud fast music is arousing, whilst soft, slow music is soothing. Certain pitch ranges and timbres seem particularly attractive to infants, as do simple repetitive rhythms.[81]

Douglas N. Morgan, despite holding to an iconic model of signification, is forced to temper his position:

> It must be understood that there are important limits [to iconic signification], still imperfectly understood, to the freedom of such interchange [between musical sign and referent], and that the connections between music and meanings are *not wholly arbitrary*. Taps, for example, would be as unlikely to arouse men in the morning as would reveille to make them sleepy in the evening, again because of our biological natures.[82] (Emphasis added.)

Davies takes this principle and applies it cross-culturally:

> I think that there is a common expressive element found in the musics of different cultures. I know of no culture that consistently expresses sadness with jaunty, fast, sprightly music, nor of any that expresses happi-

ness with slow, dragging music. To take one example, Westerners formerly unacquainted with Javanese music are very unlikely to take the gamelan music that accompanies the weeping of puppet characters in *wayang kulit* for happy music, or to mistake battle pieces for funeral music.[83]

Finally, Hospers' insights on the bioacoustic model (his "expression theory") bear consideration:

> If somebody said to us that the last movement of Beethoven's Ninth Symphony, which we take to be expressive of joy or exultation, was mournful, dour, and depressing, we would probably dismiss his claim as absurd and assert with complete confidence that he had not even begun to listen to the music.[84]

He also explains how such claims can be verified,

> If someone were to insist that a fast sprightly waltz was really sad or melancholy, we would refer him to the behavioral features of sad people and show him that when people are in that state they do exhibit the qualities in question (i.e., the qualities of sad music), rather than speed or sprightliness.[85]

Thus the bioacoustic model of musical communication, which secures itself in an analogical and organic relationship to the emotions it represents, provides music with a reliable connection to the emotions that it attempts to signify and prevents music from getting lost in the postmodern wilderness of indeterminacy. Further, it is in the bioacoustic code that we come closest to music as a universal language.[86] I earlier explained that the biological changes that occur when we experience similar emotions are generally the same in everyone. As music accurately encodes those changes through the audible means of melody, rhythm, and harmony, the possibility of cross-cultural musical understanding becomes real. The primitiveness and transcendence of the bioacoustic code, though often encrusted with plentiful layers of iconic symbols, testifies to its superiority and indispensability among other systems of musical symbolism. Even so, no better case can be made for the legitimacy of the bioacoustic scheme, as the primary gauge in all matters of emotional signification, than the intolerable ramifications and irrationalism that its dethronement would bring.

Iconic Signification and Moral Meaning

From the outset I have insisted that whether music is a universal language or not cannot determine whether music is moral or amoral. I have argued that music is generated and enjoyed within culture and receives its meaning within a cultural context.[87] Whether it carries the same meanings outside of that culture is of little significance to the CCM debate in that CCM aims to be *culturally* relevant rather than universal in influence. The problem is that even within the membrane of culture, conventional or learned musical codes, which are not necessarily universal or homologously related to their referents, can still be extremely resilient and meaningful signifiers. In fact they can be so powerful that most listeners consider them to be natural, automatic, and universal, rather than learned.[88] According to McClary and Walser,

> the music of one's own culture often seems completely transparent. Music appears to create its effects directly, without any mediation whatsoever. Listeners are usually not aware of any interpretation on their part, of any cognitive processes that contribute to their understanding of a piece of music.[89]

Moreover, there is sufficient evidence to indicate that within a culture group, people usually understand their musical codes in consistent ways. Drawing on Hevner, Sloboda maintains that "listeners within a musical culture generally agree on the emotional character of a given piece of music, even though they may have never heard it before...."[90] This and many other examples indicate that even if music had meaning on an exclusively cultural level, where musical codes are learned, those codes are not likely to be successfully altered (at least not without a great deal of time and effort) in order to convey contrary meanings.

An example from visible symbols, where the symbol-referent relationship is more easily recognized, may be helpful. A Nazi swastika is not an inherently evil symbol. Apart from its association with Hitler's oppressive totalitarian regime, it could serve as a sign for a variety of wholesome and decent enterprises, for example a logo for an insurance company, a daycare center, or a bakery. Nevertheless, due to its immediate association with Nazi Germany and white supremacy, it would be foolhardy to attempt to rehabilitate the insignia to take on new positive meanings, even if the purpose was to use the symbol to attract modern Nazis in order to eventually convert them to non-Nazis. Such attempts would lead to countless misunderstandings, alienation, and reprisals until the meaning of the swastika, if possible, could be reversed.[91] I say, "if possible," because the swastika is not simply a forgotten artifact of history, but an ever-present reminder of the senseless carnage of the Holocaust. Further, if it was used to attract Neo-Nazis, skinheads, or white supremacists, it could not do so without misleading them (at least initially) since the external referents that these groups would connect with the swastika would be the opposite of those intended by its new promoters.

CCM faces many of the same obstacles in its attempt to contest and reverse predominately negative associations between the sounds of rock music and their counter-Christian referents.[92] This is because rock music is an omnipresent entertainment medium that dominates western culture (even eastern culture) and continues to thrive, develop, and reinforce its codes with far more volume and intensity than its stepchild CCM can ever hope to do. The exercise becomes all the more counterproductive when we realize that one of CCM's main purposes is to spread the gospel to unbelievers through culturally relevant music. It is detrimental because non-Christians would naturally share the meanings of the musical codes as they develop in the larger secular arena, rather than in private Christian circles, renovated lyrics or not. The point cannot be stressed enough: even if musical signs are iconic and nothing else, they cannot be divorced from their referents and reassigned at will—apart from cultural consent—simply by changing the lyrics and the context of their performance.

Ethnomusicology

No matter how successfully one may contend for music as a universal language, whether it be via the bioacoustic model or something

else, valid cases of cross-cultural miscomprehension of musical meanings—sometimes consisting of interpretations entirely at variance with
those of the original culture—gravely jeopardize the position of musical universalism. Edgar mentions one such example where the musical
meaning of Anglican hymns has been misconstrued by evangelized
peoples unfamiliar with western music to the effect that a fast tempo
signified sadness rather than joy.[93] Sloboda relates a similar story:

> I can still recall the surprise I felt when, after hearing a rather jolly
> sounding Greek folk song, my Greek companion indicated that this was
> a desperately sad piece of music. No doubt, an understanding of the
> words was partly responsible for her different view of the music; but I
> realized that my own response was determined by the major key, the
> simple and open harmonies, and the general rhythmic impetus. These
> qualities are, in fact, common to most Greek folk music.[94]

Below I defend the primacy of the bioacoustic model by explaining
how misinterpretations such as these can take place, apart from pure
musical relativism.

Emotions and Interpretation

Social scientists and musicologists recognize that, although human
beings biologically and psychologically experience emotive sensations
in an almost identical manner, emotions may be interpreted or understood differently and have different value in different cultures. Blacking's challenge is significant and discourages a simplistic hermeneutic
concerning the relationship between music and emotions: "It is not
enough to accept verbal statements of common sentiment.... We have
to find out what people mean by such statements, how they are related
to other areas of behavior, and to what extent common values are felt
and internalized, as well as stated."[95] As Nattiez explains, "Feelings of
love appear to be a universal characteristic of human beings;... But this
universality does not mean that the feeling always manifests itself,
translates itself, in an identical way from one era to another, or from
one culture to another."[96] Lidov expands on the previous insights by
remarking that "culture sets the outer patterns of gesture. It also regulates, to a considerable extent, the feelings which are aroused in various

social situations and determines what is desirable or acceptable to express."[97] Davies adds, "In some cultures, for example, death might be an occasion for public celebration rather than for private grief. A person not realizing this might be surprised to find raucous, seemingly joyous music played at funerals."[98]

An example of this may be illustrated by a culture in which fear takes on highly negative connotations, such as failure, inferiority, weakness, even femininity. Consequently, fear may be expressed in music by codes that signify the negative characteristics associated with fear, such as weakness, rather than by reproducing the actual biological and emotional sensations experienced by all human beings when they are afraid. Such a scenario would obviously short-circuit any form of cross-cultural communication in music. This is just one way in which factors such as the interpretation and ideology of emotions can undercut universal meaning in music.

With obvious dependence on Ogden-Richards' triangle for linguistic symbols, the triangle below attempts to demonstrate that in many cases, if not most, the path from pure emotion to musical sign is not direct, but must first travel through a maze of cultural interpretation. Further, the broken line from emotion to musical sign indicates the indirectness of the exchange.

Interpretation of Emotions

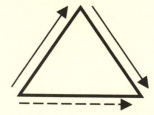

Emotions   Musical Symbol of
                            Interpreted Emotions

Perhaps overlooking this factor in musical signification can explain how Frank Harrison on the one hand can recognize the possibility of a bioacoustic musical code and yet on the other deny its validity:

It is true that certain music-sounds incite the making of more or less obvious parallels with sounds in the non-musical sphere, with gestures, with visual shapes and so on. This is analogous to certain kinds of mimetic or suggestive language usages, such as onomatopoeia. In both music and language such structure-referent connections may well be actual or potential universals, related to human activities that are actually or potentially universal. Their existence as a special and relatively limited group cannot be held to invalidate the general hypothesis that music-structure has no inherent meaning. It is not, indeed, an uncommon experience to find that a structure-referent perception based on mimetic insights current in a particular culture do not apply to those current in another culture.[99]

As I have suggested, the reason that Harrison and others find no musical universals at this very basic level may be because they have not sufficiently considered the various ways in which people interpret and understand emotions within their worldview. Here Meyer is of immense help:

> It must be remembered that the musical characterization of an activity or concept depends upon the attitude of the culture toward the concept as well as upon the psychological mechanisms of association. Ostensibly similar concepts may be characterized differently in different cultures, or even within a single culture, *not because the process of association is inconstant*, but because the concept is viewed in different ways. In our own culture, for example, Death is generally considered to be solemn, fearful, and mysterious; but it also has been regarded as an expected friend or as the sardonic mocker of human pretensions. Obviously, each of these views would give rise to a different musical characterization.[100] (Emphasis added.)

Thus, musical cues may not be an expression of universal feelings, but of the value or ideological significance of those feelings within a certain culture. Here there is a definite mandate for cultural critique to determine whether a society's outlook on God-given emotions reflects a covenantal understanding of those emotions or not. Meaning in music can be easily corrupted at this stage by the intrusion of human depravity as it distorts how God intended emotions to be experienced, understood, and valued. This then is an important reason why misconceptions of the emotional meaning of music take place from one culture to another.

Iconic Symbolism

There is another reason why the emotional properties of music often do not transcend culture. Musical codes for feelings, values, and other extramusical phenomena within cultures are sometimes constructed by reproducing environmental sounds (animals), industrial sounds (machinery), traditional musical sounds that become detached from their original referent, etc.[101] In this model two or more divergent cultures may share the same understanding of an emotion, but because the representation of that emotion in music is not naturally related to the emotion, cross-cultural meaning becomes difficult if not impossible. This is because the connections between the emotion and musical symbol are secondary or tertiary. For instance, it may be that joy is associated with the tone or pattern of a particular environmental sound in a particular culture, like a waterfall, which (waterfall) may have been a source of great joy to that society and have carried positive, almost heroic, connotations. Or a feeling may be associated with the sound of an animal, like the call of a special bird that symbolizes important cultural values. These sounds have no essential connection with the emotions that they represent, making the relation of the emotion or value to the musical symbol secondary or mediated. Consequently, because it is not direct, it is ripe for misunderstanding by those outside the culture who end up attaching other more familiar referents to the musical symbols.

A related factor that disrupts cross-cultural musical understanding is the use of different conventions in encoding the dynamics of music—such as movement, and tension and release—which may be the crucial components in the expression of emotion in music.[102] Davies explains:

> In Western music after the twelfth century, the production of musical movement depends on the use of polyphony and harmony set in a tonal or modal context. A person at home only with monodic music would be in no position to perceive the dynamism [motion] of contrapuntal music or could easily be mistaken about its character.[103]

As with iconic symbolism, the manner in which these dynamic features are perceived and expressed would be affected by a number of cultural and ideological factors.

Non-Emotional Referent

A third form of cross-cultural interference occurs simply because in some cases the musical symbols do *not* primarily represent emotions. Studies reveal that in many cultures musical symbols can stand for specific non-emotive entities.[104] Some elements of music can represent things such as events, objects, values, natural phenomena, and colors. For instance, far eastern cultures associate musical scales with planets of the solar system or hours of the day.[105] Another example is Bach's use of a sharply ascending melody to represent the sky.[106] Here not only would cross-cultural understanding be nearly impossible (although there is a homological relation between the rising melody and the sky), but comprehension may also be difficult for members of the indigenous culture. Nettl rightly questions whether "the audience at any level understood the relationship, whether this kind of elaborate symbolism was lost to them...."[107] In other cases societal hierarchy may be subtly encoded by the dominance and priority of certain elements of the music, as is the case with classical music in Iran.[108] Components of Indian classical music can represent such specific elements as fire, rain, or even "a youth, wearing a red cloth."[109] It is obvious that the variety of non-emotive elements that music can signify is unlimited. The more specific the referent (e.g., a youth, wearing a red cloth) the less perceptible it will be to non-indigenous listeners (or even indigenous ones) without assistance.

Conclusion

So then, the route from the emotion to the musical sign is certainly more complex than first imagined. We have seen that there are important factors that interfere with emotions and their musical symbols, making music difficult to understand for outsiders. Likewise, a culture's concept of time, movement, space, repetition, and variety will also affect the production and understanding of their music.[110] Further, musical misunderstanding may be the result of several rather than just one of these factors. For example, confusion may be attributed to both a culture-specific interpretation of an emotion and the use of iconic symbols to represent that emotion. It may also be the case that the musical cues of a culture are quite transparent, but because the musical expectations of the outsider have been shaped by the (different) musical codes of his own culture, he may be unable to properly understand the non-indigenous music. A legion of other combinations is possible.

Biblically, there should be no objection to the use of musical symbols in signifying non-emotive phenomena, as long as that code does not inadvertently signify something that is bioacoustically undesirable or perverse. Likewise, the use of iconic symbols for emotive and non-emotive entities is perfectly legitimate and unavoidable.[111] Examples from the Bible such as that of a harp mourning, though primarily bioacoustic, also contained iconic signifiers for those emotions. These iconic signifiers contribute to the uniqueness, style, and creativity of the music and should in no wise be discouraged. The problem of course occurs when the iconic sign system dominates to such a degree that it represents a meaning on an iconic level that contradicts the meaning on the bioacoustic one. Deviations in this area can be manifestations of depravity and call for critique or even abandonment of a style or elements thereof.

Finally, the proper use of symbols should be viewed as a divinely-ordained human activity, as is apparent in Adam's naming of the animals and the woman. It is logical to assume, as most do, that he named them based on their unique characteristics or circumstances related to them—as is most evident in the case of the woman:[112]

> So the Lord God formed from the ground every wild animal of the field and bird of the sky and brought them to the man to see what he would name them. And whatever name the man gave to the living creature, that was its name. And the man gave names to all the cattle and the birds of the sky and every wild animal of the field.... And the man said, "This is now the bone of my bones and the flesh of my flesh, and she shall be called woman because she was taken out of man" (Genesis 2:19-23).[113]

Additionally, this kind of naming is akin to God's own naming in creation (Genesis 1:5, 8, 11), making it a derivative activity for mankind. It would be correct then to assume that a similar kind of "naming" takes place in musical signification, even though there are important differences between language and music.[114] Musical signification is based on seeing legitimate relationships and analogies between the musical sign and its extramusical referent, just as in naming, Adam focused on the origin of the woman—as derived from the man—and used the resources of language to express this by adding a feminine ending to a noun for man. Of course, since the fall of man and the entrance of sin, not all attempts at constructing this relationship have been successful or correct, thus hampering or undermining meaning and communication in language and music. As I insisted earlier in regard to aesthetics, musical signification—which involves fallen attributes such as the intellect, will, and emotions—cannot be free from error and corruption. This depravity can also apply to entire systems of signification such as the iconic, which may, if improperly used, subvert the bioacoustic model, which I have stressed must be normative.

Endnotes

[1]Bruno Nettl, *The Study of Ethnomusicology: Twenty-Nine Issues and Concepts* (Urbana, IL: University of Illinois Press, 1983), 2.

[2]Ibid., 36-37; Leonard B. Meyer, "Universalism and Relativism in the Study of Ethnic Music," *Ethnomusicology* 4, no. 1 (January 1960): 49.

[3]Nettl, *Ethnomusicology*, 37.

[4]Cf. Frank Harrison, "Universals in Music: Towards a Methodology of Comparative Research," *The World of Music* 19, no. 1/2 (1977): 34; Susan McClary, *Feminine Endings: Music, Gender, and Sexuality* (Minneapolis: University of Minnesota Press, 1991), 8, 25; William Edgar, *Taking Note of Music* (London: Third Way Books, 1986), 59, 63; Robert Walser, *Running with the Devil: Power, Gender, and Madness in Heavy Metal Music* (Hanover, NH: Wesleyan University Press, 1993), 37; John Sloboda, *The Musical Mind: The Cognitive Psychology of Music* (Oxford: Clarendon Press, 1985), 2.

[5]Meyer, "Universalism and Relativism," 49. Cf. Alan P. Merriam, *The Anthropology of Music* (Evanston, IL: Northwestern University Press, 1964), 261, 263, 268.

[6]McClary, *Feminine Endings*, 8.

[7]Harold M. Best, *Music Through the Eyes of Faith* (San Francisco: Harper, 1993), 54.

[8]Edgar, *Taking Note of Music*, 19; Bruno Nettl, "On the Question of Universals," *The World of Music* 19, no. 1/2 (1977): 4-5, 6, 7; Philip Tagg, "Musicology and the Semiotics of Popular Music," *Semiotica* 66 (1987): 286; David Lidov, "Mind and Body in Music," *Semiotica* 66 (1987): 69, 81-82; Sloboda, *The Musical Mind*, 1.

[9]Nettl, *Ethnomusicology*, 40.

[10]Deryck Cooke, *The Language of Music* (Oxford: Oxford University Press, 1959), 272.

[11]Edgar, *Taking Note of Music*, 64. Cf. Robert H. Mitchell, *I Don't Like That Music* (Carol Stream, IL: Hope Publishing Co., 1993), 8; Donald P. Hustad, "Music Speaks... But What Language?" *Christianity Today*, 6 May 1977, 18.

[12]Edgar, *Taking Note of Music*, 65. See also p. 70.

[13]John Blacking, "Can Musical Universals Be Heard?" *The World of Music* 19, no. 1/2 (1977): 17.

[14]Stephen Davies, *Musical Meaning and Expression* (Ithaca, NY: Cornell University Press, 1994), 244.

[15]Blacking, "Musical Universals," 19. See also pp. 18, 21.

[16]Davies, *Musical Meaning and Expression*, 243.

[17]Ibid., 225.

[18]Cf. Davies, *Musical Meaning and Expression*, 250-51.

[19]Davies, *Musical Meaning and Expression*, 214-15.

[20]Ibid., 215-16.

[21]Ibid., 216.

[22]Cf. Davies, *Musical Meaning and Expression*, 262.

[23]Cf. Davies, *Musical Meaning and Expression*, 289.

[24]Cf. Davies, "Few qualified listeners would describe the overture to Mozart's *Marriage of Figaro* as expressive of sadness; though these listeners might choose to describe the overture with different emotion terms, they would be terms denoting feelings or emotions belonging in the 'happy,' not the 'sad,' category." *Musical Meaning and Expression*, 250-51.

[25]Cf. Millard J. Erickson, *Christian Theology* (Grand Rapids: Baker Book House, 1983), 513-14.

[26]Cf. Erickson, *Christian Theology*, 269, 270.

[27]Nettl, *Ethnomusicology*, 201-05; Tagg, "Musicology," 280, 285; Meyer, "Universalism and Relativism," 51.

[28]Robert Walser, "Bon Jovi's Alloy: Discursive Fusion in Top 40 Pop Music," *OneTwoThreeFour* 7 (Winter 1989): 16; Susan McClary and Robert Walser, "Start Making Sense! Musicology Wrestles with Rock," in *On Record: Rock, Pop, and the Written Word*, ed. Simon Frith and Andrew Goodwin (New York: Pantheon, 1990), 278. See Jim Grieves, "Style as Metaphor for Sym-

bolic Action: Teddy Boys, Authenticity and Identity," *Theory, Culture, & Society* 1, no. 2 (September 1982): 41.

[29]Philip Gordon, "Review of Tipper Gore's *Raising PG Kids in an X-Rated Society* and *Dee Snider's Teenage Survival Guide*," *Popular Music* 8, no. 1 (January 1989): 120; Walser, *Running with the Devil*, 141.

[30]Edgar, *Taking Note of Music*, 71. Cf. Davies, *Musical Meaning and Expression*, 321-22.

[31]Edgar, *Taking Note of Music*, 89.

[32]Ibid., 99.

[33]Ibid., 12; Anne H. Rosenfeld, "Music, the Beautiful Disturber," *Psychology Today*, December 1985, 56.

[34]Walser, *Running with the Devil*, 56.

[35]Jeffrey Jensen Arnett, *Metalheads: Heavy Metal Music and Adolescent Alienation* (Boulder, CO: WestviewPress, 1996), 140.

[36]Ibid., 10.

[37]Robert P. Snow, "Youth, Rock 'n' Roll, and Electronic Media," *Youth & Society* 18, no. 4 (June 1987): 334. Similar conclusions have been drawn from studies of rhythm. James D. Graham, "Rhythms in Rock Music," *Popular Music and Society* 1 (Fall 1971): 37-38.

[38]James Lull, "Listener's Communicative Uses of Popular Music," in *Popular Music and Communication*, ed. James Lull (Beverly Hills, CA: Sage Publications, 1987), 148.

[39]Davies, *Musical Meaning and Expression*, 322.

[40]Nettl, *Ethnomusicology*, 201, 204-05; John Blacking, *How Musical is Man?* (Seattle: University of Washington, 1974), 9; Dane L. Harwood, "Universals in Music: A Perspective from Cognitive Psychology," *Ethnomusicology* 20, no. 3 (September 1976): 530; Tagg, "Musicology," 280; Edgar, *Taking Note of Music*, 53.

[41]McClary, *Feminine Endings*, 21; Walser, *Running with the Devil*, 29.

[42]Tagg, "Musicology," 285.

[43]Jean-Jacques Nattiez, *Music and Discourse: Toward a Semiology of Music*, trans. Carolyn Abbate (Princeton, NJ: Princeton University Press, 1990), 111.

[44]Ibid., 111-13; Edgar, *Taking Note of Music*, 53-54.

[45]Nattiez, *Music and Discourse*, 117; Edgar, *Taking Note of Music*, 54-55. Cf. David B. Pass, *Music and the Church* (Nashville: Broadman Press, 1989), 50.

[46]My selection of the terms "bioacoustic" and "iconic" is drawn from a pool of words that musicologists, linguists, and semoticians have regularly used to represent various types of signification. The lack of consistent terminology brought me to choose those that would be the most self-defining. For example, linguist Ferdinand de Saussure uses the term "symbol" when there is an analogical relationship between the sign and referent, and the term "sign"

when it is arbitrary. David Lidov prefers "index" for the former and "icon" (which I have borrowed) for the latter. The self-explaining term "bioacoustic" is thankfully provided by Philip Tagg for describing the primitive affinity between certain musical elements and bodily functions. Nattiez, *Music and Discourse*, 36; Lidov, "Mind and Body," 73; Tagg, "Musicology," 286-87.

[47]Alf Gabrielsson and Patrik N. Juslin, "Emotional Expression in Music Performance: Between the Performer's Intention and the Listener's Experience," *Psychology of Music* 24, no. 1 (1996): 68.

[48]John Hospers, "Aesthetics, Problems of," in *The Encyclopedia of Philosophy*, ed. Paul Edwards (New York: The Macmillan Company & The Free Press, 1967), 47.

[49]R. Francès, *La perception de la musique* (Paris: Vrin, 1958), 299; quoted in Nattiez, *Music and Discourse*, 118-19.

[50]Gabrielsson and Juslin, "Emotional Expression in Music Performance," 69.

[51]Susanne K. Langer, *Feeling and Form: A Theory of Art* (New York: Charles Scribner's Sons, 1953), 28. It should be made clear that in Langer's version of this model, it is the *concept* of feelings that music symbolizes rather than the feelings themselves. Predating Langer and influencing her was Carroll C. Pratt's *The Meaning of Music: A Study in Psychological Aesthetics*. Davies, *Musical Meaning and Expression*, 125, 133, 134; Charles L. Stevenson, "Symbolism in Nonrepresentational Arts," in *Introductory Readings in Aesthetics*, ed. John Hospers (New York: The Free Press, 1969), 193.

[52]Susanne K. Langer, *Philosophy in a New Key* (Cambridge, MA: Harvard University Press, 1957), 238. Also *Feeling and Form*, 27.

[53]Meyer, "Universalism and Relativism," 51-52.

[54]Ibid., 52.

[55]Lidov, "Mind and Body," 69.

[56]Tagg, "Musicology," 286-87.

[57]Rosenfeld, "Music," 51.

[58]Ibid.

[59]See also Sloboda, *The Musical Mind*, 1; Blacking, "Musical Universals," 17, 18, 19.

[60]Gabrielsson and Juslin, "Emotional Expression in Music Performance," 68, 85-87. Another study, however, concluded that tempo was not a deciding factor in perceiving emotion in music. Stuart B. Kamenetsky, David S. Hill, and Sandra E. Trehub, "Effect of Tempo and Dynamics on the Perception of Emotion in Music," *Psychology of Music* 25, no. 2 (1997): 149-60.

[61]Gabrielsson and Juslin, "Emotional Expression in Music Performance," 69. See also Kamenetsky, Hill, and Trehub, "Effect of Tempo and Dynamics," 150.

[62]Gabrielsson and Juslin, "Emotional Expression in Music Performance," 86.

[63]Ibid., 68. See also p. 87.

[64]Ibid., 87.

[65]Lidov, "Mind and Body," 73. See also E. F. Carritt, "Beauty as Expression," in *Introductory Readings in Aesthetics*, ed. John Hospers (New York: The Free Press, 1969), 131.

[66]Nettl, *Ethnomusicology*, 209. See also p. 244.

[67]Meyer, "Universalism and Relativism," 51. See also Walser, *Running with the Devil*, 29; McClary, *Feminine Endings*, 102.

[68]Edgar, *Taking Note of Music*, 71.

[69]Gabrielsson and Juslin, "Emotional Expression in Music Performance," 68.

[70]Best, *Music*, 54. Likewise Mitchell, *I Don't Like That Music*, 64.

[71]Best, *Music*, 39, 54.

[72]Ibid., 54.

[73]These qualities could even be associated with the devil or rituals devoted to him, but only through severe distortion of the devil's true nature and the attributes that really characterize him.

[74]Cf. Rosenfeld, "Music," 56; David Di Sabatino, "The Power of Music: What to Keep in Mind While Under Its Influence," *Worship Leader*, May/June 1999, 21. This happens more often than realized because of the omnipresence of music in our society. For example, lovers sometimes break up in a setting where a certain song is playing in the background. The song, whether it is happy or sad, can then become a source of pain until it is given new associations or the hurt of the breakup is healed.

[75]Cf. Davies, *Musical Meaning and Expression*, 187, 190.

[76]Best, *Music*, 46-47, 55. More so, since even the title of the song (i.e., words) can trigger such emotions, reactions by association fail to prove the neutrality of music.

[77]Davies, *Musical Meaning and Expression*, 250.

[78]"Moan," seems to me to be the best *single* English equivalent that captures the sense of the Hebrew verb *hāmāh* (cf. RSV). More precisely, the verb in this context describes the kind of emotional turbulence felt in times of deep sorrow and loss, which could be reproduced on musical instruments like the flute and harp. Hence the NASB and NKJV in Jeremiah 48:36 translate *hāmāh* as "wail." See also W. R. Domeris, "*hmh*," in *New International Dictionary of Old Testament Theology and Exegesis*, ed. Willem A. VanGemeren, vol. 1 (Grand Rapids: Zondervan, 1997), 1042-43.

[79]It is interesting that Frith makes a similar observation concerning how rock music encodes a society's view of sexuality and at the same time shapes and contours it. Simon Frith, "Afterthoughts," in *On Record: Rock, Pop, and the Written Word*, ed. Simon Frith and Andrew Goodwin (New York: Pantheon Books, 1990), 420-21.

[80]Tagg, "Musicology," 286-87.

[81]Sloboda, *The Musical Mind*, 1.

[82]Douglas N. Morgan, "Must Art Tell the Truth?" in *Introductory Readings in Aesthetics*, ed. John Hospers (New York: The Free Press, 1969), 234.

[83]Davies, *Musical Meaning and Expression*, 244.

[84]John Hospers, "The Concept of Artistic Expression," in *Introductory Readings in Aesthetics*, ed. John Hospers (New York: The Free Press, 1969), 163.

[85]Hospers, "Aesthetics," 47. Hospers *does* endorse this theory, though with some reservations. "The Concept of Artistic Expression," 165-66.

[86]Tagg, "Musicology," 286.

[87]Cf. McClary, *Feminine Endings*, 21, 102.

[88]Nattiez, *Music and Discourse*, 121-23; Edgar, *Taking Note of Music*, 67, 71.

[89]McClary and Walser, "Start Making Sense," 278; Walser, "Bon Jovi," 16; *Running with the Devil*, 29.

[90]Sloboda, *The Musical Mind*, 2. Cf. Walser, *Running with the Devil*, 32-33; Rosenfeld, "Music," 51; Tagg, "Musicology," 290; Kamenetsky, Hill, and Trehub, "Effect of Tempo and Dynamics," 150.

[91]Laing wisely discerns that when punk rock groups claim to wear swastikas for shock effect, rather than as a statement of racial or ideological allegiance, they ignore the bevy of negative meanings that this sign conveys in the public arena—however non-racist their personal intentions may be. He states: "And in the case of a long-established political *symbol* like the swastika, the accent placed on it in public discourse cannot easily be obliterated by the practice of such a provisional discursive formation as that of punk." *One Chord Wonders: Power and Meaning in Punk Rock* (Philadelphia: Open University Press, 1985), 96-97.

[92]Cf. Jay R. Howard and John M. Streck, *Apostles of Rock: The Splintered World of Contemporary Christian Music* (Lexington, KY: The University Press of Kentucky, 1999), 18.

[93]Edgar, *Taking Note of Music*, 120.

[94]Sloboda, *The Musical Mind*, 2.

[95]Blacking, "Musical Universals," 21.

[96]Nattiez, *Music and Discourse*, 105. See also p. 106.

[97]Lidov, "Mind and Body," 78. Cf. McClary, *Feminine Endings*, 46.

[98]Davies, *Musical Meaning and Expression*, 244n.

[99]Harrison, "Universals in Music," 34.

[100]Meyer, "Universalism and Relativism," 52.

[101]Nettl, *Ethnomusicology*, 179.

[102]Davies, *Musical Meaning and Expression*, 244, 277.

[103]Ibid., 244-45. See also p. 186.

[104]Tagg, "Musicology," 293.

[105]Nattiez, *Music and Discourse*, 123.

[106]Nettl, *Ethnomusicology*, 205.

[107]Ibid.

[108]Ibid., 207.

[109]Ibid., 209-10.

[110]Cf. Nettl, *Ethnomusicology*, 208; Davies, *Musical Meaning and Expression*, 244-46.

[111]Davies, *Musical Meaning and Expression*, 245-46.

[112]I am indebted to William Edgar for this idea. *Taking Note of Music*, 73-74.

[113]In Semitic thinking, naming was a form of exercising dominion over some-one else. In this passage we can also distill Adam's ability to recognize char-acteristic features of animals and represent them in words, an evidence of man's ability and calling to correctly use symbolism and language.

[114]Edgar, *Taking Note of Music*, 74, 58-64; Davies, *Musical Meaning and Expression*, 1-49.

Appendix D

Bill Hybels Faces His Critics

BILL HYBELS, PATRIARCH OF the seeker-sensitive approach to ministry, defends his motives and methods in a 1994 *Christianity Today* interview.[1] To his credit, the interview discloses some of the benevolent activities of Willow Creek Community Church and his sincere desire to win unbelievers. Hybels also may have a point when he questions the practical soul-winning experience of his critics.

On the negative end, however, censures of his methods are often skillfully sidestepped. In responding to charges that he uses marketing techniques, Hybels testifies that his church uses only one percent of its budget for marketing (p. 22). But here he only denies using *formal* marketing opportunities like television ads and billboard promotions, when his critics are referring to the marketing strategy of satisfying the consumer, which is evident in his evangelistic methods.

Further, he deflects allegations of using entertainment techniques by first consenting that preaching is the primary method of communicating the gospel and then stating that "we add texture and feeling and perspective to it through the use of music and media and drama" (p. 23). Like CCM advocates, he resorts to reductionism, breaking down entertainment into some of its unobjectionable components, "texture," "feeling," and "perspective," and offering these as the objective of his stage-oriented methods (p. 23). Not only is this a clever evasion of an inflammatory word like "entertainment," but it also brings up the question of why Hybels could not have added texture, perspective, and feeling through the spoken word if that was really all that he was after. Hybels also claims that no one who has attended his services would label these productions as "mere entertainment." This is first of all quite an ambitious and sweeping prediction in itself. But no one that I am aware of has accused the seeker-sensitive service of just trying to entertain people. It is quite apparent that they are attempting to minister and communicate biblical truths through these methods. The question that needs to be asked, however, is whether entertainment techniques have any place at all in the proclamation of the gospel. As has been painstakingly explained in pervious chapters, Scripture tolerates no such theory.

His remarkable comment that his imitators have gone to an unhealthy extreme is a red herring, I fear. For to what greater extreme can one go than performing a skit about sex, with a scene in which a man (clothed) mounts for intercourse a woman (also clothed) lying on the church floor, as was staged at Willow Creek Community Church (1989/90)?

Finally, Hybels' response to David Wells' suspicion that Hybels and his followers accept culture as neutral again fails to answer the real question at hand (p. 24). It is apparent that Wells is concerned about Hybels' method of evangelism as a spin-off of (unbiblical) cultural values, whereas Hybels entirely avoids the issue by affirming his awareness of the anti-Christian ethos of American society. No mention is made that his pragmatic posture is in harmony with the same values in pop culture. Consequently, I don't think Hybels successfully answers his critics. He responds to the most important questions by parrying them, using reductionism, or downplaying the critic's concern—hardly a persuasive defense.

Endnotes
[1]Michael G. Maudlin and Edward Gilbreath, "Selling Out the House of God?" *Christianity Today*, 18 July 1994, 20-25.

Appendix E

Vain Philosophies: Al Menconi and Secular Rock

ONE OF THE MOST outspoken critics on the lyrical content of most secular rock songs (as well as other styles) is Al Menconi.[1] He perceives even subtle anti-Christian philosophies in a great deal of secular music and strongly advocates replacing it with corresponding Christian alternatives, including all varieties of CCM. But I wonder if Menconi is aware of how many CCM stars live on a steady diet of secular rock; after all, secular rock is where they derive most of their musical material. But beyond just listening dispassionately for instructional purposes, many CCM musicians enjoy secular rock (including the Beatles, Led Zeppelin, Mötely Crüe, and Judas Priest),[2] draw their inspiration from it, and speak glowingly of its performers; for example Michael Sweet, formerly with Stryper, lists as his favorite groups Van Halen, Journey, and the Beatles.[3]

Michael W. Smith once went ballistic after speaking on the phone with Mick Jagger, jumping around the studio and exclaiming, "Mick Jagger is on that phone. I talked to Mick Jagger."[4] Imagine demonstrating that level of adulation for one of history's most accomplished fornicators, an androgyne who wore negligées in concert, recorded "Sympathy for the Devil," and committed many other unspeakable crimes against the Most High. One would think that *Contemporary Christian Music* magazine would be embarrassed to report this. Think again; they treated it as a highlight.

Consider also Steve Mason's (Jars of Clay) fawning admiration of Christ-denying infidels who are leading millions to a godless eternity:

> "I was tripping," says guitarist Steve Mason, recalling the parade of [secular] celebrities he saw. "I was like, 'You're Joan Osborne! You're Seal!'" The 21-year old's eyes and smile widen as he repeats, like a mantra, the name of Seal's leggy backstage companion who clearly made the biggest impression that day: "You're Tyra Banks! You're Tyra Banks!"[5]

For those who are unaware, pop singer Joan Osborne is a dedicated feminist and abortion rights advocate. She has a popular song entitled, "Let's Just Get Naked." Her video "Right Hand Man," glorifies one night stands and features an appearance by the Hindu god Krishna— about which she comments, "Sexuality and spirituality are so closely related to me that to put the two right next to each other in the same song isn't a contradiction."[6] More inexcusable is Mason's childlike excitement over Tyra Banks, a sexy supermodel, actress, and porn queen. When Banks is not posing in the nude, she likes to be photographed in string bikinis or underwear, which she is sometimes in the process of divesting. The disparity between Mason's professed Christian faith and his reaction to Banks did not escape the *Rolling Stone* reporter as he patronizingly remarked, "Luckily for Mason, God forgives him because of grace."[7]

Furthermore, some CCM artists sing secular rock songs, air secular rock music during concerts, and even go on tour with non-Christian groups. Mylon LeFevre, for instance, has played the music of Thirty-Eight Special during intermission; Jars of Clay opened for several Sting concerts in fall of 1996;[8] and Susan Ashton recently toured with country music's premiere lady-killer, Garth Brooks, who to boot is a big fan of KISS, as Menconi himself discloses.[9] Moreover, MxPx once opened for the Sex Pistols and in 1998 toured with Rancid and the overtly anti-Christian punk band Bad Religion, which has a cross-buster as its logo, a black cross voided out with a red diagonal.[10] MxPx themselves admit that "Bad Religion influences thousands of kids to hate God. I went to its show in Seattle. It felt so evil."[11] After acknowledging these things, they, nevertheless, excuse the band and their desire to tour with them with a theology of sin annexed right out of *Reader's Digest* or *Guideposts*: "And it's not that the guys in the band are evil or anything— they're nice guys who just don't know God." Something doesn't add up: they influence "thousands of kids to hate God," are all atheists, openly oppose Christianity, and yet they are not evil? It is not that the members of Bad Religion don't deserve to hear the gospel, but that touring with them would make it impossible for MxPx to denounce or counter their blasphemous message, which is what MxPx should have been doing.

As mentioned earlier, CCM is even represented on MTV with a regular host, Peter King of Dakoda Motor Company.[12]

An example that ought to hit Menconi closer to home is Andraé Crouch, from whom Menconi claims to have drawn tremendous spiritual blessing.[13] But Crouch sang backups on Madonna's *Like a Prayer* album, whose music and life-style Menconi sternly inveighs.[14] Crouch has also performed on *Saturday Night Live*, and has worked closely with "model citizens" like Michael Jackson and bisexual Elton John.[15]

Where is the consistency? Are CCM performers and producers any more immune from counter-Christian lyrics than the rest of us? Should Christians forsake secular rock and embrace CCM, whose artists have cohabitated with secular rock and its empty philosophies since its beginning? Further, what would happen if the CCM industry went on Menconi's "30-Day Christian Music Diet," a month long abstinence from all secular entertainment, to be replaced with Christian music or books, which (diet) he recommends for every believer?[16] I seriously question whether a parasitic movement like CCM could survive if it were cut off so violently from its source.[17]

Endnotes

[1]There is certainly need for concern here. John E. Reid, Jr.'s study demonstrates that most of the Christian teenagers he surveyed (ninety percent) "felt it was okay to listen to [secular] rock music." More so, fifty-eight percent of the males and seventy percent of the females acknowledged that they listened to secular rock all the time. The study revealed that Christian teens who listen to CCM "are still likely to listen to mainstream rock...." "The Use of Christian Rock Music by Youth Group Members," *Popular Music and Society* 17, no. 2 (Summer 1993): 37, 39, 41. See also Jay R. Howard and John M. Streck, *Apostles of Rock: The Splintered World of Contemporary Christian Music* (Lexington, KY: The University Press of Kentucky, 1999), 99.

[2]David W. Cloud, *Contemporary Christian Music Under the Spotlight* (Oak Harbor, WA: Way of Life Literature, 1999), 138-39, 374-75, 386.

[3]On the World Wide Web at http://www.michaelsweet.com.

[4]Michael McCall, "Smitty Gets Gritty," *Contemporary Christian Magazine*, June 1986, 16.

[5]Eric Boehlert, "Holy Rock and Rollers," *Rolling Stone*, 3 October 1996, 24.

[6]On the World Wide Web at http://www.mercuryrecords.com/mercury/artists/osborne_j/j_osborne_bio.html.

[7]Boehlert, "Holy Rock and Rollers," 24.

[8]Ibid.

[9]April Hefner, "Ashton, Becker, Denté: A Trio of Vocal Wealth," *Contemporary Christian Music*, October 1997, 50; Al Menconi and Dave Hart, *Staying in Tune: A Sane Response to Your Child's Music* (Cincinnati, OH: The Standard Publishing Co., 1996), 88.

[10]Mark Joseph, *The Rock and Roll Rebellion: Why People of Faith Abandoned Rock Music—And Why They're Coming Back* (Nashville: Broadman & Holman, 1999), 234-35.

[11]Ibid., 235.

[12]Michael Ciani, "All Aboard," *Contemporary Christian Music*, July 1996, 37.

[13]Menconi and Hart, *Staying in Tune*, 14.

[14]Steve Rabey, "Age to Age," *Contemporary Christian Music*, July 1998, 40; Menconi and Hart, *Staying in Tune*, 97.

[15]Carol Flake, *Redemptorama: Culture, Politics, and the New Evangelicalism* (New York: Penguin Books, 1984), 176; Joseph, *Rock and Roll Rebellion*, 27.

[16]Menconi and Hart, *Staying in Tune*, 201ff.

[17]CCM's dependence and slavish imitation of secular rock is not disputed by any in the industry. Musically, the only thing that separates CCM from its secular counterparts is the lyrics. William D. Romanowski, "Roll Over Beethoven, Tell Martin Luther the News: American Evangelicals and Rock Music," *Journal of American Culture* 15, no. 3 (Fall 1992): 82-83; John E. Reid, Jr. and Joseph R. Dominick, "A Comparative Analysis of Christian and Mainstream Rock Music Videos," *Popular Music and Society* 17, no. 3 (Fall 1993): 95; Howard and Streck, *Apostles of Rock*, 8, 230; Charlie Peacock, *At the Crossroads: An Insider's Look at the Past, Present, and Future of Contemporary Christian Music* (Nashville: Broadman & Holman, 1999), 100; Angelo De Simone, *Christian Rock: Friend or Foe* (New Haven: Selah Production Agency, 1993), 57, 134; Bill Young, "Contemporary Christian Music: Rock the Flock," in *The God Pumpers: Religion in the Electronic Age*, ed. Marshall Fishwick and Ray B. Browne (Bowling Green, OH: Bowling Green State University Popular Press, 1987), 142, 152.

For a much more detailed and exhaustive coverage of this topic see Cloud, *Contemporary Christian Music Under the Spotlight*, 103, 137-42, 219-21, 243-44, 273, 372-73, 374-75, 377, 386, 398.

Bibliography

Abraham, Gerald. *The Concise Oxford History of Music.* Oxford, England: Oxford University Press, 1988.

Ahlstrom, Sydney F. *A Religious History of the American People.* New Haven: Yale University Press, 1972.

Alford, Henry. *Acts-II Corinthians.* 1875; repr. *Alford's Greek Testament: An Exegetical Critical Commentary,* vol. 2. Grand Rapids: Baker Book House, 1980.

Allen, Karen, and Jim Blascovich. "Effects of Music on Cardiovascular Reactivity Among Surgeons." *Journal of the American Medical Association* 272, no. 11 (September 1994): 882-84.

Allen, Roy. "Aesthetic Transformations: The Origins of Dada." In *Dada the Coordinates of Cultural Politics.* Vol. 1 of *Crisis and the Arts: The History of Dada,* edited by Stephen C. Foster, 59-82. New York: G. K. Hall & Co., 1996.

Alter, Robert. *The Art of Biblical Narrative.* New York: Basic Books, 1981.

Altshuler, Bruce. *The Avant-Garde in Exhibition: New Art in the 20th Century.* New York: Harry N. Abrams, 1994.

Anderson, A. A. *2 Samuel.* Word Biblical Commentary, vol. 11. Waco, TX: Word Books, 1989.

Anderson, Warren. "Beyond Rock." *Contemporary Christian Music,* June 1990, 34-35.

———. "Josh McDowell: Bridging the Gap." *Contemporary Christian Music,* June 1990, 36.

Andes, Linda. "Growing up Punk: Meaning and Commitment Careers in a Contemporary Youth Subculture." In *Youth Culture: Identity in a Postmodern World,* edited by Jonathan S. Epstein, 212-31. Malden, MA: Blackwell Publishers, 1998.

Arnett, Jeffrey Jensen. "Adolescents and Heavy Metal Music: From the Mouths of Metalheads." *Youth & Society* 23, no. 1 (September 1991): 76-98.

———. *Metalheads: Heavy Metal Music and Adolescent Alienation.* Boulder, CO: WestviewPress, 1996.

Arnold, Gina. *Kiss This: Punk in the Present Tense.* New York: St. Martin's Griffin, 1997.

Balmer, Randall. "Hymns on MTV." *Christianity Today,* 15 November 1999, 32-39.

Bangs, Lester. "Heavy Metal." In *The Rolling Stone Illustrated History of Rock & Roll: The Definitive History of the Most Important Artists and*

Their Music, edited by Anthony De Curtis and James Henke, 459-63. New York: Random House, 1992.

Bar-Efrat, Shimon. *Narrative Art in the Bible*. Translated by Dorothea Shefer-Vanson. Journal for the Study of the Old Testament Supplement Series, vol. 70. Sheffield: The Almond Press, 1989.

Barnes, Deborah. "Green Cathedrals." *Contemporary Christian Music*, August 1998, 22-23, 25-26, 28.

Barrett, C. K. *A Commentary on the First Epistle to the Corinthians*. Harper's New Testament Commentaries. New York: Harper & Row, 1968.

Bartlett, Robert M. *The Faith of the Pilgrims*. New York: United Church Press, 1978.

Bauer, Walter. *A Greek-English Lexicon of the New Testament and Other Early Christian Literature*. Translated by William F. Arndt and F. Wilbur Gingrich. 2d ed. Chicago: University of Chicago Press, 1979.

Baum, W., E. Cunitz, and E. Reuss, eds. *Ioannis Calvini Opera Quae Supersunt Omnia*. Brunswick: C. A. Schwetschke and Sons, 1863-1900.

Bavinck, Herman. *Our Reasonable Faith: A Survey of Christian Doctrine*. Translated by Henry Zylstra. Grand Rapids: Baker Book House, 1956.

Bayton, Mavis. "Women and the Electric Guitar." In *Sexing the Groove: Popular Music and Gender*, edited by Sheila Whiteley, 37-49. New York: Routledge, 1997.

Beardsley, Monroe C. "The Instrumentalist Theory of Aesthetic Value." In *Introductory Readings in Aesthetics*, edited by John Hospers, 308-19. New York: The Free Press, 1969.

———. "Reasons in Aesthetic Judgments." In *Introductory Readings in Aesthetics*, edited by John Hospers, 245-53. New York: The Free Press, 1969.

Beasley-Murray, G. R. *Baptism in the New Testament*. Grand Rapids: Eerdmans, 1962.

Beaver, R. Pierce, et al. *Eerdmans' Handbook to the World's Religions*. Grand Rapids: Eerdmans, 1982.

Begbie, Jeremy S. *Voicing Creation's Praise: Toward a Theology of the Arts*. Edinburgh: T. & T. Clark, 1991.

Bell, Clive. "Significant Form." In *Introductory Readings in Aesthetics*, edited by John Hospers, 87-99. New York: The Free Press, 1969.

Bell, Verle L. "How the Rock Beat Creates an Addiction." In *How to Conquer the Addiction of Rock Music*, 81-85. Oak Brook, IL, 1993.

Benson, Louis F. *The English Hymn: Its Development and Use in Worship*. Philadelphia: The Presbyterian Board of Publication, 1915.

Berkowitz, Leonard. "The Case for Bottling Up Rage." *Psychology Today*, July 1973, 24-31.

Bessy, Claude. "Less Than Total Recall, by What's His Face." In *Make the Music Go Bang! The Early L.A. Punk Scene*, edited by Don Snowden, 159-74. New York: St. Martin's Griffin, 1997.

Best, Harold M. "There is More to Redemption Than Meets the Ear." *Christianity Today*, 26 July 1974, 12-13, 15-16, 18.

————. "Music: Offerings of Creativity. An Interview with Harold Best" (interview by Cheryl Forbes). *Christianity Today*, 6 May 1977, 12-15.

————. *Music Through the Eyes of Faith*. San Francisco: Harper, 1993.

Bill, J. Brent. *Rock and Roll*. Old Tappan, NJ: Revell, 1983.

Blacking, John. *How Musical is Man?* Seattle: University of Washington, 1974.

————. "Can Musical Universals Be Heard?" *The World of Music* 19, no. 1/2 (1977): 14-22.

Blanchard, John, Peter Anderson, and Derek Cleave. *Pop Goes the Gospel: Rock in the Church*. 1983. Enlarged and revised. Darlington, England: Evangelical Press, 1989.

Blomberg, Craig L. *The Historical Reliability of the Gospels*. Downers Grove, IL: Inter-Varsity Press, 1987.

Bloom, Allan. *The Closing of the American Mind*. New York: Simon and Schuster, 1987.

Blume, Friedrich. *Protestant Church Music*. New York: W. W. Norton & Company, 1974.

Bobgan, Martin, and Deidre Bobgan. *PsychoHeresy: The Psychological Seduction of Christianity*. Santa Barbara, CA: Eastgate, 1987.

Boehlert, Eric. "Holy Rock and Rollers." *Rolling Stone*, 3 October 1996, 23-24.

Bousset, Wilhelm. *Kyrios Christos*. Translated by John E. Steely. New York: Abingdon Press, 1970.

Braun, Roddy. *1 Chronicles*. Word Biblical Commentary, vol. 14. Waco, TX: Word Books, 1986.

Brown, Bruce A. "Justice." *Contemporary Christian Music*, October 1998, 58-60.

Brown, Charles. *The Art of Rock and Roll*. Englewood Cliffs, NJ: Prentice-Hall, 1983.

Brown, Francis, S. R. Driver, and Charles A. Briggs. *The New Brown-Driver-Briggs-Gesenius Hebrew and English Lexicon*. Peabody, MA: Hendrickson, 1979.

Bubel, Kathy. "DC Talks At Last." *Release*, 4 May/June 1994, 16-18.

Carlozo, Lou. "Super Tone Deaf." *Contemporary Christian Music*, February 1999, 18-19, 22.

Carlson, R. A. *David, the Chosen King: A Traditio-Historical Approach to the Second Book of Samuel*. Stockholm: Almqvist & Wiksell, 1964.

Carritt, E. F. "Beauty as Expression." In *Introductory Readings in Aesthetics*, edited by John Hospers, 129-41. New York: The Free Press, 1969.

Carson, Donald A. *The Gagging of God: Christianity Confronts Pluralism.* Grand Rapids: Zondervan, 1996.

Chambers, Iain. "Popular Culture, Popular Knowledge." *OneTwoThreeFour* 2 (Summer 1985): 9-19.

―――. *Urban Rhythms: Pop Music and Popular Culture.* New York: St. Martin's Press, 1985.

Chute, James. "What Hath Pop Wrought in Jesus' Name?" *The Milwaukee Journal*, 17 August 1986, 8E.

Ciani, Michael. "All Aboard." *Contemporary Christian Music*, July 1996, 34-39.

Cline, Cheryl. "*Essays from* Bitch: The Women's Rock Newsletter with Bite." In *The Adoring Audience: Fan Culture and Popular Media*, edited by Lisa A. Lewis, 69-83. London: Routledge, 1992.

Clines, D. J. A. "X, X Ben Y, *Ben* Y: Personal Names in Hebrew Narrative Style." *Vetus Testamentum* 22 (1972): 266-87.

Cloud, David W. *Contemporary Christian Music Under the Spotlight.* Oak Harbor, WA: Way of Life Literature, 1999.

Coates, Norma. "(R)Evolution Now? Rock and the Political Potential of Gender." In *Sexing the Groove: Popular Music and Gender*, edited by Sheila Whiteley, 50-64. New York: Routledge, 1997.

Cohen, Sara. "Men Making a Scene: Rock Music and the Production of Gender." In *Sexing the Groove: Popular Music and Gender*, edited by Sheila Whiteley, 17-36. New York: Routledge, 1997.

Cohn, Nik. *Rock from the Beginning.* New York: Stein and Day Publishers, 1969.

―――. *AwopBopaLooBopaLopBamBoom: Pop from the Beginning.* London: Paladin, 1970.

Collins, Raymond F. *First Corinthians.* Sacra Pagina Series, vol. 7. Daniel J. Harrington, gen. ed. Collegeville, MN: The Liturgical Press, 1999.

Conomos, Dimitri. "Bardaisan." In *The New Grove Dictionary of Music and Musicians*, edited by Stanley Sadie, vol. 2, 150. London: Macmillan Publishers Limited, 1980.

Cooke, Deryck. *The Language of Music.* Oxford: Oxford University Press, 1959.

Cooper, Wendy. *Hair: Sex, Society, Symbolism.* New York: Stein and Day, 1971.

Corbitt, J. Nathan. *The Sound of Harvest: Music's Mission in Church and Culture.* Grand Rapids: Baker Books, 1998.

Corduan, Winfried. *Neighboring Faiths: A Christian Introduction to World Religions.* Downers Grove, IL: InterVarsity Press, 1998.

Cripe, Frances F. "Rock Music as Therapy for Children with Attention Deficit Disorder: An Exploratory Study." *Journal of Music Therapy* 23 (1986): 30-37.

Croteau, Roberta. "House of Amy." *Release*, September/October 1994, 22-27.

Curtis, Edward Lewis, and Albert Alonzo Madsen. *A Critical and Exegetical Commentary on the Book of Chronicles*. The International Critical Commentary. New York: Charles Scribner's Sons, 1910.

Curtis, Olga. "Music That Kills Plants." *Denver Post*, 21 June 1970, 8-11M.

Darsey, Steven. "John Wesley as Hymn and Tune Editor: The Evidence of Charles Wesley's 'Jesu, Lover of My Soul' and Martin Madan's Hotham." *The Hymn* 47 (January 1996): 17-24.

Davies, Horton. *Worship and Theology in England: From Watts and Wesley to Maurice, 1690-1850*. Princeton: Princeton University Press, 1961.

Davies, Stephen. *Musical Meaning and Expression*. Ithaca, NY: Cornell University Press, 1994.

Davis, Brad. "Hot Pink Refrigerators." *Reformed Perspective*, April 1994, 17.

De Simone, Angelo. *Christian Rock: Friend or Foe*. New Haven: Selah Production Agency, 1993.

DeLuca, Dan. "Sex, Thugs, Rock and Roll." *The Philadelphia Inquirer*, 24 October 1999, Arts and Entertainment: 1, 16.

DeMol, Karen A. "Sound Stewardship: How Should Christians Think About Music?" *Pro Rege* 26, no. 3 (March 1998): 1-20.

Desmond, Roger Jon. "Adolescents and Music Lyrics: Implications of a Cognitive Perspective." *Communication Quarterly* 35, no. 3 (Summer 1987): 276-84.

Di Sabatino, David. "The Power of Music: What to Keep in Mind While Under Its Influence." *Worship Leader*, May/June 1999, 20-22.

Diamond, John. *Your Body Doesn't Lie*. New York: Warner Books, 1979.

Dillard, Raymond B. *2 Chronicles*. Word Biblical Commentary, vol. 15. Waco, TX: Word Books, 1987.

Dixon, Amy. "To Mosh or not to Mosh? Christian Rock Concerts Incite Controversy." *Contemporary Christian Music*, February 1996, 22, 24.

Dockery, David S. "*krr*." In *New International Dictionary of Old Testament Theology and Exegesis*, edited by Willem A. VanGemeren, vol. 2, 728. Grand Rapids: Zondervan, 1997.

Dome, Malcolm, and Mick Wall. "World View: Metal Crusade in Global Gear." *Billboard*, 27 April 1985, HM-12.

Domeris, W. R. "*hmh*." In *New International Dictionary of Old Testament Theology and Exegesis*, edited by Willem A. VanGemeren, vol. 1, 1042-43. Grand Rapids: Zondervan, 1997.

Donaldson, Devlin. "Barnabas: Forging Musical Horizons." *Contemporary Christian Music*, October 1998, 69.

Ducasse, Curt J. "The Subjectivity of Aesthetic Value." In *Introductory Readings in Aesthetics*, edited by John Hospers, 282-307. New York: The Free Press, 1969.

Dudley-Smith, Timothy. "Why Wesley Still Dominates Our Hymnbook." *Christian History* 10, no. 31: 9-13.

Duncan, Robert. *The Noise: Notes from a Rock 'n' Roll Era*. New York: Ticknor & Fields, 1984.

Dyer, Richard. "In Defense of Disco." In *On Record: Rock, Pop, and the Written Word*, edited by Simon Frith and Andrew Goodwin, 410-18. New York: Pantheon Books, 1990.

Edelstein, Robert. "Heavyosity." *Rolling Stone*, 15-29 December 1988, 124-25.

Edgar, William. *Taking Note of Music*. London: Third Way Books, 1986.

Ehrenreich, Barbara, Elizabeth Hess, and Gloria Jacobs. "Beatlemania: Girls Just Want to Have Fun." In *The Adoring Audience: Fan Culture and Popular Media*, edited by Lisa A. Lewis, 84-106. London: Routledge, 1992.

Eischer, Mark. "*Images* Kathy Troccoli." *Contemporary Christian Music*, December 1986, 32.

Ellsworth, Donald Paul. *Christian Music in Contemporary Witness: Historical Antecedents and Contemporary Practices*. Grand Rapids: Baker Book House, 1979.

Enroth, Ronald M., Edward E. Ericson, Jr., and C. Breckinridge Peters. *The Jesus People: Old-Time Religion in the Age of Aquarius*. Grand Rapids: Eerdmans, 1972.

Epstein, Jonathan S., David J. Pratto, and James K. Skipper, Jr. "Teenagers, Behavioral Problems, and Preferences for Heavy Metal and Rap Music: A Case Study of a Southern Middle School." *Deviant Behavior* 11 (1990): 381-94.

Erickson, John D. "The Cultural Politics of Dada." In *Dada the Coordinates of Cultural Politics*. Vol. 1 of *Crisis and the Arts: The History of Dada*, edited by Stephen C. Foster, 7-28. New York: G. K. Hall & Co., 1996.

Erickson, Millard J. *Christian Theology*. Grand Rapids: Baker Book House, 1983.

Erlhoff, Michael. "Performances." In *Dada the Coordinates of Cultural Politics*. Vol. 1 of *Crisis and the Arts: The History of Dada*, edited by Stephen C. Foster, 155-70. New York: G. K. Hall & Co., 1996.

Fadiman, Anne. "Heavy Metal Mania." *Life*, December 1984, 102-12.

Farley, Christopher John. "Reborn to Be Wild." *Time*, 22 January 1996, 62-64.

Fee, Gordon D. *The First Epistle to the Corinthians*. The New International Commentary on the New Testament. Grand Rapids: Eerdmans, 1987.

Ferguson, Everett. "Did They Sing Hymns?" *Christian History* 12, no. 37: 14.

————. *Backgrounds of Early Christianity*. 2d ed. Grand Rapids: Eerdmans, 1993.

Ferraiuolo, Perucci. "Whitecross Unveiled." *Contemporary Christian Music*, October 1994, 30, 32.

————. "Church Leaders Troubled by Christian Music." *Contemporary Christian Music*, May 1995, 65.

Fineberg, Jonathan. *Art Since 1940: Strategies of Being*. New York: Harry N. Abrams, 1995.

Fishbane, Michael. "Use, Authority and Interpretation of Mikra at Qumran." In *Mikra: Text, Translation, Reading and Interpretation of the Hebrew Bible in Ancient Judaism and Early Christianity*, edited by Martin Jan Mulder and Harry Sysling, 339-77. Minneapolis: Fortress Press, 1990.

Fisher, Tim. *The Battle for Christian Music*. Greenville, SC: Sacred Music Services, 1992.

Flake, Carol. *Redemptorama: Culture, Politics, and the New Evangelicalism*. New York: Penguin Books, 1984.

Flam, Jack D. "Foreword." In *The Dada Painters and Poets: An Anthology*, edited by Robert Motherwell. 2d ed., xi-xiv. Boston: G. K. Hall & Co., 1981.

Foley, Edward. *Foundations of Christian Music: The Music of Pre-Constantinian Christianity*. American Essays in Liturgy. Edward Foley, gen. ed. Collegeville, MN: The Liturgical Press, 1996.

Fontaine, Craig W., and Norman D. Schwalm. "Effects of Familiarity of Music on Vigilant Performance." *Perceptual and Motor Skills* 49 (1979): 71-74.

Frame, John M. *Contemporary Worship Music: A Biblical Defense*. Phillipsburg, NJ: Reformed & Presbyterian, 1997.

Freeman, Judi, and John C. Welchman. *The Dada & Surrealist Word-Image*. Cambridge, MA: The MIT Press, 1989.

Friebel, Melanie. "Dancin' in the Church: Spreading the Good News Through Sanctified Dance." *Contemporary Christian Music*, November 1994, 51-53.

Friesen, Bruce K., and Warren Helfrich. "Social Justice and Sexism for Adolescents: A Content Analysis of Lyrical Themes and Gender Presentations in Canadian Heavy Metal Music, 1985-1991." In *Youth Culture: Identity in a Postmodern World*, edited by Jonathan S. Epstein, 263-85. Malden, MA: Blackwell Publishers, 1998.

Frith, Simon. *Sound Effects: Youth, Leisure, and the Politics of Rock 'n' Roll*. New York: Pantheon Books, 1978.

————. "Art Versus Technology: The Strange Case of Popular Music." *Media, Culture, and Society* 8 (1986): 263-79.

————. "Towards an Aesthetic of Popular Music." In *Music and Society: The Politics of Composition, Performance, and Reception*, edited by Richard

Leppert and Susan McClary, 133-49. Cambridge: Cambridge University Press, 1987.

———. "Afterthoughts." In *On Record: Rock, Pop, and the Written Word*, edited by Simon Frith and Andrew Goodwin, 419-24. New York: Pantheon Books, 1990.

Frith, Simon, and Angela McRobbie. "Rock and Sexuality." In *On Record: Rock, Pop, and the Written Word*, edited by Simon Frith and Andrew Goodwin, 371-89. New York: Pantheon Books, 1990.

Frost, Maurice, ed. *Historical Companion to Hymns Ancient and Modern.* Rev. ed. London: William Clowes and Sons, 1962.

Gabrielsson, Alf, and Patrik N. Juslin. "Emotional Expression in Music Performance: Between the Performer's Intention and the Listener's Experience." *Psychology of Music* 24, no. 1 (1996): 68-91.

Garcia, Guy. "Heavy Metal Goes Platinum." *Time*, 14 October 1991, 85.

Garlock, Frank, and Kurt Woetzel. *Music in the Balance.* Greenville, SC: Majesty Music, 1992.

Garside, Charles, Jr. "The Origins of Calvin's Theology of Music: 1536-1543." In *Transactions of the American Philosophical Society.* Philadelphia: The American Philosophical Society, August, 1979.

Gaster, Theodor H. *The Dead Sea Scriptures.* Garden City, NY: Doubleday & Co., 1956.

Gill, Chris. "Dialing for Distortion: Sound Advice from 10 Top Producers." *Guitar Player*, October 1992, 84-94.

Gillett, Charlie. *The Sound of the City: The Rise of Rock and Roll.* Rev. ed. New York: Pantheon Books, 1983.

Gilmore, Mikal. "Mick Jagger." *Rolling Stone*, 5 November-10 December 1987, 30-35.

Gleizes, Albert. "The Dada Case." In *The Dada Painters and Poets: An Anthology*, edited by Robert Motherwell. 2d ed., 298-303. Boston: G. K. Hall & Co., 1981.

Godet, Frédéric. *Commentary on the First Epistle of St. Paul to the Corinthians.* Translated by A. Cusin. Edinburgh: T. & T. Clark, 1886.

Godwin, Jeff. *The Devil's Disciples: The Truth About Rock Music.* Chino, CA: Chick Publications, 1985.

———. *Dancing with Demons: The Music's Real Master.* Chino, CA: Chick Publications, 1988.

———. *What's Wrong with Christian Rock?* Chino, CA: Chick Publications, 1990.

Goldberg, Michael. "Amy Grant Wants to Put God on the Charts." *Rolling Stone*, 6 June 1985, 9-10.

Gordon, Philip. "Review of Tipper Gore's *Raising PG Kids in an X-Rated Society* and *Dee Snider's Teenage Survival Guide*." *Popular Music* 8, no. 1 (January 1989): 120-22.

Gowensmith, William Neil, and Larry J. Bloom. "The Effects of Heavy Metal Music on Arousal and Anger." *Journal of Music Therapy* 34, no. 1 (1997): 33-45.

Graebner, William. "The Erotic and Destructive in 1980s Rock: A Theoretical and Historical Analysis." *Tracking: Popular Music Studies* 1, no. 2 (1988): 8-20.

Graham, James D. "Rhythms in Rock Music." *Popular Music and Society* 1 (Fall 1971): 33-43.

Gray, Patrick. "Rock as a Chaos Model Ritual." *Popular Music and Society* 7, no. 2 (1980): 75-83.

Greene, Bob. "Words of Love." *Esquire*, May 1984, 12-13.

Gregory, Andrew H., and Nicholas Varney. "Cross-Cultural Comparisons in the Affective Response to Music." *Psychology of Music* 24, no. 1 (1996): 47-52.

Grieves, Jim. "Style as Metaphor for Symbolic Action: Teddy Boys, Authenticity and Identity." *Theory, Culture, & Society* 1, no. 2 (September 1982): 35-49.

Grossberg, Lawrence. "Rock and Roll in Search of an Audience." In *Popular Music and Communication*, edited by James Lull, 175-97. Beverly Hills, CA: Sage Publications, 1987.

———. "Is There a Fan in the House? The Affective Sensibility of Fandom." In *The Adoring Audience: Fan Culture and Popular Media*, edited by Lisa A. Lewis, 50-65. London: Routledge, 1992.

Gruber, Mayer I. "Ten Dance-Derived Expressions in the Hebrew Bible." *Biblica* 62 (1981): 328-46.

Haïk-Vantoura, Suzanne. *The Music of the Bible Revealed: The Deciphering of Millenary Notation*. Translated by Dennis Weber. Berkeley, CA: Bibal Press, 1991.

Halbersberg, Elianne. *Heavy Metal*. Cresskill, NJ: Sharon Publications, 1985.

Hamilton, Michael S. "The Triumph of the Praise Songs: How Guitars Beat Out the Organ in the Worship Wars." *Christianity Today*, 12 July 1999, 28-32, 34-35.

Hanna, Judith Lynne. *Dance, Sex, and Gender: Signs of Identity, Dominance, Defiance, and Desire*. Chicago: University of Chicago Press, 1988.

———. "Moving Messages: Identity and Desire in Popular Music and Social Dance." In *Popular Music and Communication*, edited by James Lull. 2d ed., 176-95. London: Sage Publications, 1992.

Hanser, Suzanne B. "Controversy in Music Listening/Stress Reduction Research." *The Arts in Psychotherapy* 15 (1988): 211-17.

Harrell, Robert Lomas. "A Comparison of Secular Elements in the Chorales of Martin Luther with Rock Elements in Church Music of the 1960's and 1970's." M.A. Thesis, Bob Jones University, 1975.

Harris, Clarke S., Richard J. Bradley, and Sharon K. Titus. "A Comparison of the Effects of Hard Rock and Easy Listening on the Frequency of Observed Inappropriate Behaviors: Control of Environmental Antecedents in a Large Public Area." *Journal of Music Therapy* 29, no. 1 (Spring 1992): 6-17.

Harris, R. Laird, Gleason L. Archer, Jr., and Bruce K. Waltke. *Theological Wordbook of the Old Testament.* Vol. 2. Chicago: Moody Press, 1980.

Harrison, Frank. "Universals in Music: Towards a Methodology of Comparative Research." *The World of Music* 19, no. 1/2 (1977): 30-36.

Harrison, R. K. *Introduction to the Old Testament.* Grand Rapids: W. B. Eerdmans Publishing Co., 1969.

Hart, David S. "Heavy Metal Thunder." *Contemporary Christian Music,* January 1988, 18-20.

Hart, Lowell. *Satan's Music Exposed.* Huntingdon Valley, PA: Salem Kirban, 1981.

Harwood, Dane L. "Universals in Music: A Perspective from Cognitive Psychology." *Ethnomusicology* 20, no. 3 (September 1976): 521-33.

Hawkins, Stan. "The Pet Shop Boys: Musicology, Masculinity and Banality." In *Sexing the Groove: Popular Music and Gender,* edited by Sheila Whiteley, 118-33. New York: Routledge, 1997.

Hazard, David. "Holy Hype: Marketing the Gospel in the '80s." *Eternity,* December 1985, 32-34, 39-41.

Hebdige, Dick. *Subculture: The Meaning of Style.* London: Routledge, 1979.

Hefner, April. "Ashton, Becker, Denté: A Trio of Vocal Wealth." *Contemporary Christian Music,* October 1997, 48, 50, 52.

Hefner, April, and Lindy Warren. "Grant, Chapman Announce Separation." *Contemporary Christian Music,* February 1999, 10.

Heller, Karen. "The Sacred and the Sensual." *The Philadelphia Inquirer,* 26 May 1999, D1, D10-11.

Hendrickson, Lucas W. "For God and Country." *Contemporary Christian Music,* November 1996, 47.

Herrin, Scott. "Disciple Wrestling Match." *HM Electronic Magazine,* no. 78 (July/August 1999).

Hildebrandt, Franz, and Oliver A. Beckerlegge, eds. *A Collection of Hymns for the Use of the People Called Methodists.* Vol. 7 of *The Works of John Wesley.* Nashville: Abingdon Press, 1983.

Hiwatt, Susan. "[Phallic] Rock." In *Twenty-Minute Fandangos and Forever Changes: A Rock Bazaar,* edited by Jonathan Eisen, 141-47. New York: Random House, 1971.

Holland, Nancy J. "Purple Passion: Images of Female Desire in 'When Doves Cry.'" *Cultural Critique* 10 (Fall 1988): 89-98.

Hospers, John. "Aesthetics, Problems of." In *The Encyclopedia of Philosophy*, edited by Paul Edwards, 35-56. New York: The Macmillan Company & The Free Press, 1967.

————. "The Concept of Artistic Expression." In *Introductory Readings in Aesthetics*, edited by John Hospers, 142-67. New York: The Free Press, 1969.

Howard, Jay R., and John M. Streck. *Apostles of Rock: The Splintered World of Contemporary Christian Music.* Lexington, KY: The University Press of Kentucky, 1999.

Huelsenbeck, Richard. "Dada Lives!" In *The Dada Painters and Poets: An Anthology*, edited by Robert Motherwell. 2d ed., 279-82. Boston: G. K. Hall & Co., 1981.

————. "En Avant Dada: A History of Dadaism." In *The Dada Painters and Poets: An Anthology*, edited by Robert Motherwell. 2d ed., 21-48. Boston: G. K. Hall & Co., 1981.

Hunter, James Davison. "The New Class and the Young Evangelicals." *Review of Religious Research* 22, no. 2 (December 1980): 155-69.

————. *American Evangelicalism: Conservative Religion and the Quandary of Modernity.* New Brunswick: Rutgers University Press, 1983.

————. *Evangelicalism: The Coming Generation.* Chicago: University of Chicago Press, 1987.

Hunter, Kellye. "Playing with Fire: The Risks and Benefits of Selling Super Hot Sauces." *Fiery Foods Magazine Online.*

Hustad, Donald P. "Music Speaks... But What Language?" *Christianity Today*, 6 May 1977, 16-18.

"In the News: Artists, Pastors and Industry Leaders Discuss Issue of 'Fame and Ministry.'" *Contemporary Christian Music*, July 1996, 22, 24.

Iwanaga, Makoto. "The Effects of Repetitive Exposure to Music on Subjective and Physiological Responses." *Journal of Music Therapy* 33, no. 3 (1996): 219-30.

Japhet, Sara. *I and II Chronicles: A Commentary.* The Old Testament Library. Louisville, KY: Westminster/John Knox Press, 1993.

Jenni, Ernst, and Claus Westermann. *Theological Lexicon of the Old Testament.* Translated by Mark E. Biddle. Peabody, MA: Hendrickson, 1997.

Jessop, T. E. "The Objectivity of Aesthetic Value." In *Introductory Readings in Aesthetics*, edited by John Hospers, 271-81. New York: The Free Press, 1969.

Johansson, Calvin M. *Music and Ministry: A Biblical Counterpoint.* Peabody, MA: Hendrickson, 1984.

————. *Discipling Music Ministry: Twenty-First Century Directions.* Peabody, MA: Hendrickson, 1992.

Johnson, Jan. "How Can We Welcome the Next Generation into the Church? Getting the Gospel to the Baby Busters." *Moody*, May 1995, 48-53.

Jonsson, Johannes C. "BOBFEST '99-Stockholm, Sweden." *HM Electronic Magazine*, no. 78 (July/August 1999).

Joseph, Catherine, and A. K. Pal. "Effect of Music on the Behavioral Organization of Albino Rats Using the Operant Conditioning Technique." *Indian Journal of Applied Psychology* 19 (July 1982): 77-84.

Joseph, Mark. *The Rock and Roll Rebellion: Why People of Faith Abandoned Rock Music—And Why They're Coming Back.* Nashville: Broadman & Holman, 1999.

Kaiser, Susan B. *The Social Psychology of Clothing.* New York: Macmillan, 1990.

Kamenetsky, Stuart B., David S. Hill, and Sandra E. Trehub. "Effect of Tempo and Dynamics on the Perception of Emotion in Music." *Psychology of Music* 25, no. 2 (1997): 149-60.

Kaplan, E. Ann. *Rocking Around the Clock: Music Television, Postmodernism, and Consumer Culture.* New York: Methuen, 1987.

Kavanaugh, Patrick. *The Music of Angels: A Listener's Guide to Sacred Music from Chant to Christian Rock.* Chicago: Loyola Press, 1999.

Keil, C. F., and F. Delitzsch. *Biblical Commentary on the Books of Samuel.* Translated by James Martin. Grand Rapids: Eerdmans, 1971.

Kenneson, Philip C. "Selling [Out] the Church in the Marketplace of Desire." *Modern Theology* 9, no. 4 (October 1993): 319-48.

Kilby, Clyde S. *Christianity and Aesthetics.* IVP Series in Contemporary Christian Thought, vol. 3. Chicago: Inter-Varsity Press, 1961.

Kivy, Peter. *Music Alone: Philosophical Reflections on the Purely Musical Experience.* Ithaca, NY: Cornell University Press, 1990.

Klapp, Orrin E. "Style Rebellion and Identity Crisis." In *Human Nature and Collective Behavior: Papers in Honor of Herbert Blumer*, edited by Tamotsu Shibutani, 69-80. New Brunswick, NJ: Transaction Books, 1970.

Kleinig, John W. *The Lord's Song: The Basis, Function and Significance of Choral Music in Chronicles.* Journal for the Study of the Old Testament Supplement Series, vol. 156. Sheffield, England: JSOT Press, 1993.

Koehler, Ludwig, and Walter Baumgartner. *The Hebrew and Aramaic Lexicon of the Old Testament.* Vol. 3. Translated by M. E. J. Richardson. Leiden: E. J. Brill, 1996.

Kopf, L. "Arabische Etymologien und Parallelen zum Bibelwörterbuch." *Vetus Testamentum* 8 (1958): 161-215.

Kuyper, Abraham. *Calvinism: Six Stone Foundation Lectures.* Grand Rapids: Eerdmans, 1943.

Laing, Dave. *One Chord Wonders: Power and Meaning in Punk Rock.* Philadelphia: Open University Press, 1985.

Lamp, Jeff. "Gospel and Rhetoric in 1 Corinthians 1-4: Ruminations Over Implications for Christian Apologetics." Presented at the 47th Annual

Meeting of the Evangelical Theological Society. Philadelphia, PA, November, 1995.

Landegent, David. "Having a Good Time is Not What Counts." *The Banner*, 15 May 1995, 19.

Langer, Susanne K. *Feeling and Form: A Theory of Art*. New York: Charles Scribner's Sons, 1953.

————. *Philosophy in a New Key*. Cambridge, MA: Harvard University Press, 1957.

LaRene, Janet. "Anti Rock and Roll Crusade." In *Twenty-Minute Fandangos and Forever Changes: A Rock Bazaar*, edited by Jonathan Eisen, 89-93. New York: Random House, 1971.

Larson, Bob. *Rock and the Church*. Carol Stream, IL: Creation House, 1971.

————. *The Day the Music Died*. Carol Stream, IL: Creation House, 1972.

Laver, James. *Costume*. New York: Hawthorn Books, 1963.

Lawhead, Steve. *Rock Reconsidered: A Christian Looks at Contemporary Music*. Downers Grove, IL: Inter-Varsity, 1981.

————. *Rock of This Age: Real and Imagined Dangers of Rock Music*. Downers Grove, IL: Inter-Varsity, 1987.

Leaver, Robin A. "The Hymn Explosion." *Christian History* 10, no. 31: 14-17.

LeBlanc, Albert. "All Part of the Act: A Hundred Years of Costume in Anglo-American Popular Music." In *Dress and Popular Culture*, edited by Patricia A. Cunningham and Susan Voso Lab, 61-73. Bowling Green, OH: Bowling Green State University Popular Press, 1991.

Leighton, Anne. "Rush: The Fine Art of Metal." *RIP*, June 1989, 63, 97.

Leupold, Ulrich S., ed. *Luther's Works*. Philadelphia: Fortress Press, 1965.

————. "Learning from Luther? Some Observations on Luther's Hymns." *Journal of Church Music* 8 (July-August 1966): 2-5.

Levin, Robert. "Rock and Regression: The Responsibility of the Artist." In *Twenty-Minute Fandangos and Forever Changes: A Rock Bazaar*, edited by Jonathan Eisen, 265-70. New York: Random House, 1971.

Levine, Harold G., and Steven H. Stumpf. "Statements of Fear Through Cultural Symbols: Punk Rock as a Reflective Subculture." *Youth & Society* 14, no. 4 (June 1983): 417-35.

Lewis, George H. "Popular Music: Symbolic Resource and Transformer of Meaning in Society." *International Review of the Aesthetics and Sociology of Music* 13, no. 2 (December 1982): 183-89.

————. "Patterns of Meaning and Choice: Taste Cultures in Popular Music." In *Popular Music and Communication*, edited by James Lull, 198-211. Beverly Hills, CA: Sage Publications, 1987.

Liddell, Henry George, and Robert Scott, comps. *A Greek-English Lexicon*. 9th ed. Oxford: Clarendon Press, 1996.

Lidov, David. "Mind and Body in Music." *Semiotica* 66 (1987): 69-97.

Liemohn, Edwin. *The Chorale*. Philadelphia: Muhlenberg Press, 1963.

Lipkin, Richard. "Jarring Music Takes Toll on Mice." *Insight*, 4 April 1988, 58.

Litfin, Duane. *St. Paul's Theology of Proclamation: 1 Corinthians 1-4 and Greco-Roman Rhetoric*. Cambridge, England: Cambridge University Press, 1994.

Locher, David A. "The Industrial Identity Crisis: The Failure of a Newly Forming Subculture to Identify Itself." In *Youth Culture: Identity in a Postmodern World*, edited by Jonathan S. Epstein, 100-17. Malden, MA: Blackwell Publishers, 1998.

Long, James. "Mirror Christianity." *Contemporary Christian Music*, May 1995, 71-72.

Longman, Tremper, III. *Literary Approaches to Biblical Interpretation*. Foundations of Contemporary Interpretation, vol. 3. Grand Rapids: Zondervan, 1987.

———. *Fictional Akkadian Autobiography: A Generic and Comparative Study*. Winona Lake, IN: Eisenbrauns, 1991.

———. "rnn." In *New International Dictionary of Old Testament Theology and Exegesis*, edited by Willem A. VanGemeren, vol. 3, 1128-32. Grand Rapids: Zondervan, 1997.

———. "rwꜥ." In *New International Dictionary of Old Testament Theology and Exegesis*, edited by Willem A. VanGemeren, vol. 3, 1081-84. Grand Rapids: Zondervan, 1997.

Lull, James. "Listener's Communicative Uses of Popular Music." In *Popular Music and Communication*, edited by James Lull, 140-74. Beverly Hills, CA: Sage Publications, 1987.

———. "Popular Music and Communication: An Introduction." In *Popular Music and Communication*, edited by James Lull, 10-35. Beverly Hills, CA: Sage Publications, 1987.

Lurie, Allison. *The Language of Clothing*. New York: Random House, 1981.

Luther, Martin. "Against the Heavenly Prophets in the Matter of Images and Sacraments," translated by Bernhard Erling. In *Church and Ministry II*. Vol. 40 of *Luther's Works*, edited by Conrad Bergendoff and Helmut Lehmann. American, 79-223. Philadelphia: Muhlenberg, 1958.

———. "To the Councilmen of All Cities in Germany that They Establish and Maintain Christian Schools," translated by Albert T. W. Steinhaeuser. In *The Christian Society*. Vol. 45 of *Luther's Works*, edited by Walter I. Brandt and Helmut Lehmann. American, 347-78. Philadelphia: Muhlenberg, 1962.

———. "Concerning the Order of Public Worship," translated by Paul Zeller Strodach. In *Liturgy and Hymns*. Vol. 53 of *Luther's Works*, edited by Ulrich S. Leupold and Helmut Lehmann. American, 11-14. Philadelphia: Muhlenberg, 1965.

————. "Preface to Georg Rhau's Symphoniae Iucundae," translated by Ulrich S. Leupold. In *Liturgy and Hymns*. Vol. 53 of *Luther's Works*, edited by Ulrich S. Leupold and Helmut Lehmann. American, 321-24. Philadelphia: Muhlenberg, 1965.

————. "Preface to the Wittenberg Hymnal," translated by Paul Zeller Strodach. In *Liturgy and Hymns*. Vol. 53 of *Luther's Works*, edited by Ulrich S. Leupold and Helmut Lehmann. American, 315-16. Philadelphia: Muhlenberg, 1965.

————. "To George Spalatin," translated by Gottfried G. Krodel. In *Letters II*. Vol. 49 of *Luther's Works*, edited by Gottfried G. Krodel and Helmut Lehmann. American, 68-70. Philadelphia: Muhlenberg, 1972.

————. "To Louis Senfl," translated by Gottfried G. Krodel. In *Letters II*. Vol. 49 of *Luther's Works*, edited by Gottfried G. Krodel and Helmut Lehmann. American, 426-29. Philadelphia: Muhlenberg, 1972.

Lutkin, Peter Christian. *Music in the Church*. 1910 reprint. New York: AMS Press, 1970.

Lynch, Ken. *Gospel Music: Blessing or Blight*. Chester, PA: n.p., 1987.

MacArthur, John F., Jr. *Ashamed of the Gospel: When the Church Becomes Like the World*. Wheaton, IL: Crossway Books, 1993.

Machen, J. Gresham. *The Origin of Paul's Religion*. New York: The Macmillan Co., 1936.

Mack, Burton L. *Rhetoric and the New Testament*. Minneapolis: Fortress Press, 1990.

Manoff, Tom. *Music: A Living Language*. New York: W. W. Norton & Company, 1982.

Marshall, Madeleine Forell. "Irrational Music Sung by a Mob of Extremists?" *Christian History* 10, no. 31: 35.

Martin, Bernice. "The Sacralization of Disorder: Symbolism in Rock Music." *Sociological Analysis* 40, no. 2 (1979): 87-124.

Mason, A. J. "The First Latin Christian Poet." *Journal of Theological Studies* 5 (1904): 413-32.

Maudlin, Michael G., and Edward Gilbreath. "Selling Out the House of God?" *Christianity Today*, 18 July 1994, 20-25.

McCall, Michael. "Michael's Forever Friends." *Contemporary Christian Magazine*, June 1986, 18-19.

————. "Smitty Gets Gritty." *Contemporary Christian Magazine*, June 1986, 16-19.

McCarter, P. Kyle, Jr. *II Samuel: A New Translation with Introduction, Notes and Commentary*. The Anchor Bible. Garden City, NY: Doubleday & Company, 1984.

McClary, Susan. *Feminine Endings: Music, Gender, and Sexuality*. Minneapolis: University of Minnesota Press, 1991.

McClary, Susan, and Robert Walser. "Start Making Sense! Musicology Wrestles with Rock." In *On Record: Rock, Pop, and the Written Word*, edited by Simon Frith and Andrew Goodwin, 277-92. New York: Pantheon, 1990.

McKenna, Kristine. "Burned Bridges & Vials of Blood." In *Make the Music Go Bang! The Early L.A. Punk Scene*, edited by Don Snowden, 39-46. New York: St. Martin's Griffin, 1997.

McKinnon, James. *Music in Early Christian Literature*. Cambridge, England: Cambridge University Press, 1987.

McNeill, John T., ed. *Calvin: Institutes of the Christian Religion*. Vol. 20 of The Library of Christian Classics. Translated by Ford Lewis Battles. Edited by John Baillie, John T. McNeill, and Henry P. Van Dusen. Philadelphia: The Westminster Press, n.d.

McRobbie, Angela. "Dance and Social Fantasy." In *Gender and Generation*, edited by Angela McRobbie and Mica Nava, 130-61. London: Macmillan, 1984.

McVey, Kathleen E., trans. and ed. *Ephrem the Syrian: Hymns*. The Classics of Western Spirituality. New York: Paulist Press, 1989.

Meeks, Wayne A. "The Image of the Androgyne: Some Uses of a Symbol in Earliest Christianity." *History of Religions* 13 (1974): 165-208.

Menconi, Al. "What's Wrong with Christian Music? An Open Letter to Contemporary Christian Musicians." *Contemporary Christian Music*, June 1987, 19-20.

———. "A Serious Look at Christian Heavy Metal: 'Vengeance Is Mine,' Saith the Lord—Or Is It?" *Media Update*, January-February 1989, 12-14.

Menconi, Al, and Dave Hart. *Staying in Tune: A Sane Response to Your Child's Music*. Cincinnati, OH: The Standard Publishing Co., 1996.

Merriam, Alan P. *The Anthropology of Music*. Evanston, IL: Northwestern University Press, 1964.

Meyer, Leonard B. *Emotion and Meaning in Music*. Chicago: University of Chicago Press, 1956.

———. "Universalism and Relativism in the Study of Ethnic Music." *Ethnomusicology* 4, no. 1 (January 1960): 49-54.

Miller, Kevin A. "Silent String." *Christian History* 10, no. 31: 4.

Miller, Leon K., and Michael Schyb. "Facilitation and Interference by Background Music." *Journal of Music Therapy* 26 (1989): 42-54.

Miller, Lisa. "Singing Songs of Love, Not God: It's Getting Harder to Find the Religion in Religious Bands." *The Wall Street Journal*, 23 April 1999, B1, B4.

Miller, Steve. *The Contemporary Christian Music Debate: Worldly Compromise or Agent of Renewal?* Wheaton, IL: Tyndale House, 1993.

Mitchell, Robert H. *I Don't Like That Music*. Carol Stream, IL: Hope Publishing Co., 1993.

Moon, Troy. "Audio Adrenaline Vocalist: Christian Rock Differs Little from Secular Rock Music." *Pensacola News Journal*, 1 March 1998, Life: 6E.

————. "Christian Rock Embraces Diverse Styles and Attitudes." *Pensacola News Journal*, 1 March 1998, Life: 1, 6E.

Morgan, Douglas N. "Must Art Tell the Truth?" In *Introductory Readings in Aesthetics*, edited by John Hospers, 225-41. New York: The Free Press, 1969.

Morris, Canon Leon. *The First Epistle of Paul to the Corinthians: An Introduction and Commentary*. Tyndale New Testament Commentaries, vol. 7. Leicester, England: Inter-Varsity Press, 1987.

Morris, Keith. "Bring on the Guinea Pigs." In *Make the Music Go Bang! The Early L.A. Punk Scene*, edited by Don Snowden, 47-66. New York: St. Martin's Griffin, 1997.

Morrison, Shawn. "Down to the Nitty Gritty." *Contemporary Christian Music*, May 1997, 80-81.

Mounce, Robert H. *The Essential Nature of New Testament Preaching*. Grand Rapids: Eerdmans Publishing Co., 1960.

Munson, Marty, and Rosemary Iconis. "Plugged-In Preemies." *Prevention* 47, no. 7 (July 1995): 42.

Murphy-O'Connor, Jerome. "Sex and Logic in 1 Corinthians 11:2-16." *Catholic Biblical Quarterly* 42 (1980): 482-500.

Murray, John. *Collected Writings of John Murray*. Select Lectures in Systematic Theology, vol. 2. Edinburgh: Banner of Truth Trust, 1977.

"Music Interview—One Bad Pig." *Cornerstone* 15:79, 45-46.

Nappa, Mike. "Destination Known." *Contemporary Christian Music*, February 1997, 34-36.

Nattiez, Jean-Jacques. *Music and Discourse: Toward a Semiology of Music*. Translated by Carolyn Abbate. Princeton, NJ: Princeton University Press, 1990.

Nettl, Bruno. "On the Question of Universals." *The World of Music* 19, no. 1/2 (1977): 2-7.

————. *The Study of Ethnomusicology: Twenty-Nine Issues and Concepts*. Urbana, IL: University of Illinois Press, 1983.

Nettl, Paul. *Luther and Music*. Translated by Frida Best and Ralph Wood. Philadelphia: Muhlenberg Press, 1948.

Newcomb, Brian Quincy. "Flick Shines Bright with *Kellulight*." *Contemporary Christian Music*, October 1998, 16.

————. "On Her Majesty's Secret Service." *Contemporary Christian Music*, March 1999, 36-37.

————. "Pope Visits St. Louis: Christian Artists Headline Catholic Youth Events." *Contemporary Christian Music*, April 1999, 12-13.

Nite, Norm N. *Rock On: The Illustrated Encyclopedia of Rock 'n' Roll—The Video Revolution*. New York: Harper and Row, 1985.

Noebel, David A. *The Marxist Minstrels*. Tulsa: American Christian College Press, 1974.

————. *Christian Rock: A Stratagem of Mephistopheles*. Manitou Springs, CO: Summit Ministries, n.d.

Noll, Mark A. "We Are What We Sing: Our Classic Hymns Reveal Evangelicalism at Its Best." *Christianity Today*, 12 July 1999, 37-41.

Orloff, Katherine. *Rock 'n' Roll Woman*. Los Angeles: Nash Publishing, 1974.

Ortlund, Raymond C. "The Power of the Gospel in the Church Today." *Trinity Journal* 18 (1997): 3-13.

O'Hara, Craig. *The Philosophy of Punk: More Than Noise!!* Edinburgh: AK Press, 1995.

Pareles, Jon. "Metallica Defies Heavy Metal Stereotypes." *Minneapolis Star Tribune*, 13 July 1988, 12 Ew.

Pass, David B. *Music and the Church*. Nashville: Broadman Press, 1989.

Patrick, Millar. *The Story of the Church's Song*. Richmond, VA: John Knox Press, 1962.

Peacock, Charlie. *At the Crossroads: An Insider's Look at the Past, Present, and Future of Contemporary Christian Music*. Nashville: Broadman & Holman, 1999.

Peck, Richard. *Rock: Making Musical Choices*. Greenville, SC: Bob Jones University Press, 1985.

Pepper, Stephen C. "Aesthetic Design." In *Introductory Readings in Aesthetics*, edited by John Hospers, 61-77. New York: The Free Press, 1969.

Persson, Roland S., and Colin Robson. "The Limits of Experimentation: On Researching Music and Musical Settings." *Psychology of Music* 23, no. 1 (1995): 39-47.

Peters, Dan, Steve Peters, and Cher Merrill. *What About Christian Rock?* Minneapolis: Bethany House, 1986.

Phifer, Steve. "God's Favorite Music." *Pentecostal Evangel*, 24 April 1994, 6-7.

Podhoretz, John. "Metallic Rock That's Designed to Shock." *U.S. News & World Report*, 7 September 1987, 50-51.

Poggi, Christine. *Defiance of Painting: Cubism, Futurism, and the Invention of Collage*. New Haven: Yale University Press, 1992.

Porter, J. R. "The Interpretation of 2 Samuel VI and Psalm CXXXII." *Journal of Theological Studies* 5 (1954): 105-07.

Price, Deborah Evans. "'Tis the Season for Sounds of Joy." *Contemporary Christian Music*, December 1994, 22-24.

Prinsky, Lorraine E., and Jill Leslie Rosenbaum. "'Leer-Ics' or Lyrics: Teenage Impression of Rock 'n' Roll." *Youth & Society* 18, no. 4 (June 1987): 384-97.

Quebedeaux, Richard. *The Worldly Evangelicals*. San Francisco: Harper & Row, 1978.

Rabey, Steve. *The Heart of Rock and Roll.* Old Tappan, NJ: Fleming H. Revell, 1986.

————. "Brother to Brother." *Contemporary Christian Music,* July 1996, 44-46.

————. "Age to Age." *Contemporary Christian Music,* July 1998, 18-22, 24, 26, 28, 30, 32, 34, 36, 38, 40, 42, 44.

————. "The Prophets of Praise: The Praise and Worship Music Industry Has Changed the Way the Church Sings." *Christianity Today,* 12 July 1999, 32-33.

————. "What Makes Music 'Christian?'" *Contemporary Christian Music,* May 1999, 55, 58, 60, 62, 64.

Rawlings, David, et al. "Toughmindedness and Preference for Musical Excerpts, Categories and Triads." *Psychology of Music* 23, no. 1 (1995): 63-80.

Reese, Gustave. *Music in the Middle Ages.* New York: W. W. Norton & Co., 1940.

Reid, John E., Jr. "The Use of Christian Rock Music by Youth Group Members." *Popular Music and Society* 17, no. 2 (Summer 1993): 33-45.

Reid, John E., Jr., and Joseph R. Dominick. "A Comparative Analysis of Christian and Mainstream Rock Music Videos." *Popular Music and Society* 17, no. 3 (Fall 1993): 87-97.

Reynolds, Simon. *Blissed Out.* London: Serpent's Tail, 1990.

Reynolds, William J. "Three Hymnals That Shaped Today's Worship." *Christian History* 10, no. 31: 36-37.

Reynolds, William J., and Milburn Price. *A Survey of Christian Hymnody.* Carol Stream, IL: Hope Publishing Co., 1987.

Ribemont-Dessaignes, Georges. "History of Dada." In *The Dada Painters and Poets: An Anthology,* edited by Robert Motherwell. 2d ed., 101-20. Boston: G. K. Hall & Co., 1981.

Rice, William C. *A Concise History of Church Music.* New York: Abingdon Press, 1964.

Ridderbos, Herman. *Paul: An Outline of His Theology.* Translated by John Richard De Witt. Grand Rapids: Eerdmans, 1992.

Riddle, Melissa. "Heartbreak Hotel." *Contemporary Christian Music,* May 1999, 37-38, 40.

————. *"Touched by an Angel: The Album."* *Contemporary Christian Music,* January 1999, 45-46.

Rivadeneira, Caryn D. "The Secrets of His Success." *Marriage Partnership,* Spring 1999, 26, 29, 44-45.

Robertson, Archibald, and Alfred Plumber. *A Critical Exegetical Commentary on The First Epistle of St. Paul to the Corinthians.* International Critical Commentary. Edinburgh: T. & T. Clark, 1929.

Robinson, Gnana. *Let Us Be Like the Nations: A Commentary on the Books of 1 and 2 Samuel.* International Theological Commentary. Grand Rapids: Eerdmans, 1993.

Romanowski, William D. "Roll Over Beethoven, Tell Martin Luther the News: American Evangelicals and Rock Music." *Journal of American Culture* 15, no. 3 (Fall 1992): 79-88.

————. "Move Over Madonna: The Crossover Career of Gospel Artist Amy Grant." *Popular Music and Society* 17, no. 2 (Summer 1993): 47-68.

Rosenfeld, Anne H. "Music, the Beautiful Disturber." *Psychology Today,* December 1985.

Rothwell, Helen F. *Ira D. Sankey a Great Song Leader.* Fort Pierce, FL: Faith Baptist Church Publications, 1995.

Rouse, Ted. *Contemporary Christian Music: Where's the Controversy.* Wauwatosa, WI: New Creation Christian Fellowship, 1995.

Routley, Erik. *The Music of Christian Hymnody: A Study of the Development of the Hymn Since the Reformation, with Special Reference to English Protestantism.* London: Independent Press, 1957.

————. *Church Music and Theology.* London: SCM Press, 1959.

————. *The Musical Wesleys.* London: Herbert Jenkins, 1968.

————. *Christian Hymns Observed.* Princeton: Prestige Publications, 1982.

Rubin, Nathan. *Rock and Roll: Art and Anti-Art.* Dubuque, IA: Kendall/Hunt Publishing Co., 1993.

Rubinstein, Raphael. "Abstraction Out of Bounds." *Art in America,* November 1997, 104-15.

Rubinstein, Ruth P. *Dress Codes: Meanings and Messages in American Culture.* Boulder, CO: Westview Press, 1995.

Ruef, J. S. *Paul's First Letter to Corinth.* The Pelican New Testament Commentaries. Middlesex, England: Penguin Books, 1971.

Rumburg, Gregory. "Yahweh Rocks." *Contemporary Christian Music,* January 1999, 10-11.

Rumburg, Gregory, and Thom Granger. "Hot New Bands." *Contemporary Christian Music,* November 1994, 34-35.

Ryan, Bramwell. "Where Are They Now?" *Faith Today,* September/October 1995, 17-21.

Ryken, Leland, James C. Wilhoit, and Tremper Longman III, eds. "Hair." In *Dictionary of Biblical Imagery,* 359-60. Downers Grove, IL: Inter-Varsity Press, 1998.

Quasten, Johannes. *Music and Worship in Pagan and Christian Antiquity.* Translated by Boniface Ramsey. Washington, D.C.: National Association of Pastoral Musicians, 1983.

Sachs, Curt. *World History of the Dance.* New York: W. W. Norton & Company, 1937.

Sallee, James. *A History of Evangelistic Hymnody.* Grand Rapids: Baker Book House, 1978.

Santiago-Lucerna. "'Frances Farmer Will Have Her Revenge on Seattle:' Pan-Capitalism and Alternative Rock." In *Youth Culture: Identity in a Postmodern World,* edited by Jonathan S. Epstein, 189-94. Malden, MA: Blackwell Publishers, 1998.

Saurman, Mary E. "The Effect of Music on Blood Pressure and Heart Rate." *EM News* 4, no. 3 (August 1995): 1-2.

Savage, Jon. "The Enemy Within: Sex, Rock, and Identity." In *Facing the Music,* edited by Simon Frith, 131-72. New York: Pantheon Books, 1988.

————. *Time Travel: Pop, Media and Sexuality 1976-96.* London: Chatto & Windus, 1996.

Schaeffer, Francis A. *How Should We Then Live? The Rise and Decline of Western Thought and Culture.* Old Tappan, NJ: Fleming H. Revell Co., 1976.

Schafer, William J. *Rock Music: Where It's Been, What It Means, Where It's Going.* Minneapolis: Augsburg Publishing House, 1972.

Schaff, Philip, and Henry Wace, eds. *A Select Library of Nicene and Post-Nicene Fathers of the Christian Church.* New York: Christian Literature Co., 1890.

Schalk, Carl F. *Luther on Music: Paradigms of Praise.* St. Louis: Concordia Publishing House, 1988.

Schreckenberg, Grevasia M., and Harvey H. Bird. "Neural Plasticity of *Mus Musculus* in Response to Disharmonic Sound." *Bulletin of The New Jersey Academy of Science* 32, no. 2 (Fall 1987): 77-86.

Schubert, Emery. "Enjoyment of Negative Emotions in Music: An Associative Network Explanation." *Psychology of Music* 24, no. 1 (1996): 18-28.

Schuller, Robert H. *Self-Esteem: The New Reformation.* Waco, TX: Word Books, 1982.

Schultze, Quentin J., et al. *Dancing in the Dark: Youth, Popular Culture, and the Electronic Media.* Grand Rapids: Eerdmans Publishing Co., 1991.

Schweitzer, Albert. *J. S. Bach.* Translated by Ernest Newmann. Leipzig: Breitkopf & Hrtel, 1911.

Schwitters, Kurt. "Merz." In *The Dada Painters and Poets: An Anthology,* edited by Robert Motherwell. 2d ed., 57-66. Boston: G. K. Hall & Co., 1981.

Seashore, Carl E. *Psychology of Music.* New York: Dover, 1967.

Seel, John. *Evangelical Forfeit: Can We Recover?* Grand Rapids: Baker Books, 1993.

Seerveld, Calvin. "In Search of the Aesthetic." Unpublished Paper. Philadelphia, January 1976.

Seidel, Leonard J. *Face the Music: Contemporary Church Music on Trial.* Springfield, VA: Grace Unlimited Publications, 1988.

Sendrey, Alfred. *Music in Ancient Israel.* New York: Philosophical Library, 1969.

Severn, Bill. *The Long and Short of It: Five Thousand Years of Fun and Fury Over Hair.* New York: David McKay Co., 1971.

Silva, Moisés. *Biblical Words and Their Meaning: An Introduction to Lexical Semantics.* Grand Rapids: Zondervan Publishing Co., 1983.

————. *Has the Church Misread the Bible? The History of Interpretation in Light of Current Issues.* Foundations of Contemporary Interpretation, vol. 1. Grand Rapids: Zondervan Publishing Co., 1987.

————. *God, Language and Scripture: Reading the Bible in the Light of General Linguistics.* Foundations of Contemporary Interpretation, vol. 4. Grand Rapids: Zondervan Publishing Co., 1990.

Simels, Steven. *Gender Chameleons: Androgyny in Rock 'n' Roll.* New York: Timbre Books, 1985.

Slivka, Rose. "The Dynamics of Destruction." *Art in America,* January 1999, 84-89.

Sloboda, John. *The Musical Mind: The Cognitive Psychology of Music.* Oxford: Clarendon Press, 1985.

Smallwood, Dean. "Christian Rockers All Set to Jam in Jesus' Name." *Huntsville Times,* 20 September 1998, G5.

Smith, Kimberly, and Lee Smith. *Oh, Be Careful Little Ears: Contemporary Christian Music...Is That in The Bible?* Mukilteo, WA: Wine Press, 1997.

Smith, Preserved. *Life and Letters of Martin Luther.* London: John Murray, 1911.

Smith, Roberta. "De Maria: Elements." *Art in America,* May/June 1978, 103-05.

Smith, Sandy. "Halos and Hay Bales." *Country America,* June 1994, 39-44.

Snow, Robert P. "Youth, Rock 'n' Roll, and Electronic Media." *Youth & Society* 18, no. 4 (June 1987): 326-43.

Sogin, David W. "Effects of Three Different Musical Styles of Background Music on Coding by College-Age Students." *Perceptual and Motor Skills* 67 (1988): 275-80.

Spence, H. T. *Confronting Contemporary Christian Music: A Plain Account of Its History, Philosophy, and Future.* Dunn, NC: Companion Press, 1997.

Spiegler, Marc. "Scouting for Souls." *American Demographics,* March 1996, 42-49.

Spitz, Lewis W. *The Renaissance and Reformation Movements.* vol. 2, rev. ed. St. Louis, MO: Concordia Publishing House, 1987.

Stevenson, Charles L. "Symbolism in Nonrepresentational Arts." In *Introductory Readings in Aesthetics,* edited by John Hospers, 185-209. New York: The Free Press, 1969.

Stevenson, Robert M. *Patterns of Protestant Church Music.* Durham, NC: Duke University Press, 1953.

Stolnitz, Jerome. "The Aesthetic Attitude." In *Introductory Readings in Aesthetics*, edited by John Hospers, 17-27. New York: The Free Press, 1969.

Stratton, Valerie N., and Annette H. Zalanowski. "The Relationship Between Music, Degree of Liking, and Self-Reported Relaxation." *Journal of Music Therapy* 21 (1984): 184-92.

———. "The Relationship Between Characteristic Moods and Most Commonly Listened to Types of Music." *Journal of Music Therapy* 34, no. 2 (1997): 129-40.

Street, John. *Rebel Rock: The Politics of Popular Music*. Oxford: Basil Blackwell, 1986.

Stuessy, Joe. *Rock and Roll: Its History and Stylistic Development*. Englewood Cliffs, NJ: Prentice Hall, 1990.

Styll, John W. "Editor's Comment: How to Tell the Sheep from the Wolves." *Contemporary Christian Music*, June 1986, 4.

Subotnik, Rose Rosengard. *Developing Variations: Style and Ideology in Western Music*. Minneapolis: University of Minnesota Press, 1991.

Sutton, Val. "Disciple." *HM Electronic Magazine*, no. 78 (July/August 1999).

Swaggart, Jimmy, and Robert Paul Lamb. *Religious Rock 'n' Roll: A Wolf in Sheep's Clothing*. Baton Rouge, LA: Jimmy Swaggart Ministries, 1987.

Swahn, J. O. *The Lore of Spices: Their History, Nature, and Uses Around the World*. New York: Barnes & Noble, 1991.

Tagg, Philip. *Fernando the Flute*. Göteborg, Sweden: Gothenberg University, 1981.

———. "Musicology and the Semiotics of Popular Music." *Semiotica* 66 (1987): 279-98.

———. *Fernando the Flute: Musical Meaning in an Abba Mega-Hit*. Liverpool: Liverpool University, 1991.

Tame, David. *The Secret Power of Music: A Study of the Influence of Music on Man and Society, from the Time of the Ancient Civilizations to the Present*. Wellingbrough, Northamptonshire: Turnstone Press Limited, 1984.

Tavris, Carol. "Anger Defused." *Psychology Today*, November 1982, 25-35.

Taylor, Jenny, and Dave Laing. "Disco-Pleasure-Discourse: On 'Rock and Sexuality.'" *Screen Education* 31 (Summer 1979): 43-48.

Thompson, Cynthia L. "Hairstyles, Head-Coverings, and St. Paul: Portraits from Roman Corinth." *Biblical Archaeologist* 51 (June 1988): 99-115.

Thompson, J. A. *Handbook on Life in Bible Times*. Downers Grove, IL: InterVarsity Press, 1986.

Tomkins, Calvin. *The World of Marcel Duchamp 1887-*. New York: Time, 1966.

Townsend, James. "Radicals in Times of Revolution." *Christian History* 10, no. 31: 8.

Trigg, Joseph W. *Biblical Interpretation*. Wilmington, DE: Michael Glazier, 1988.

Turner, Steve. *Hungry for Heaven: Rock and Roll and the Search for Redemption*. London: Kingsway Publications, 1988.

Urbanski, Dave. "The Preacher's Life." *Contemporary Christian Music*, February 1997, 24-29.

————. "With or Without You." *Contemporary Christian Music*, December 1998, 30-32, 34, 38.

Van Manen, Adrian. *Their Rock is not Our Rock*. N.p., n.d.

Van Pelt, Doug. "Mosh for the Master?" *Contemporary Christian Music*, February 1989, 20-21.

Van Til, Cornelius. *Christian Apologetics*. Phillipsburg, NJ: Presbyterian and Reformed Publishing Co., 1976.

————. *Christian Theistic Ethics*. In Defense of Biblical Christianity, vol. 3. Phillipsburg, NJ: Presbyterian and Reformed Publishing Co., 1980.

Vermes, Geza. *The Dead Sea Scrolls in English*. 4th ed. Sheffield, England: Sheffield Academic Press, 1995.

Vetrocq, Marcia E. "The New York Pre-School." *Art in America*, June 1997, 82-87.

vonEhrenkrook, Jason Q. "A Rhetorical Analysis of the Areopagus and Its Missiological Implications." *Calvary Baptist Theological Journal* 14 (Fall 1998): 1-15.

Vos, Geerhardus. *The Pauline Eschatology*. 1930; reprint. Phillipsburg, NJ: Presbyterian & Reformed, 1994.

Wagner, Ann. *Adversaries of Dance: From the Puritans to the Present*. Chicago: University of Illinois Press, 1997.

Wagner, Norman E. "*Rinnah* in the Psalter." *Vetus Testamentum* 10 (1960): 435-41.

Walser, Robert. "Bon Jovi's Alloy: Discursive Fusion in Top 40 Pop Music." *OneTwoThreeFour* 7 (Winter 1989): 7-19.

————. "Forging Masculinity: Heavy Metal Sounds and Images of Gender." In *Sound and Vision: The Music Video Reader*, edited by Simon Frith, Andrew Goodwin, and Lawrence Grossberg, 153-81. London: Routledge, 1993.

————. *Running with the Devil: Power, Gender, and Madness in Heavy Metal Music*. Hanover, NH: Wesleyan University Press, 1993.

Waltke, Bruce K. "1 Corinthians 11:2-16: An Interpretation." *Bibliotheca Sacra* 135, no. 537 (January-March 1978): 46-57.

Walton, John H. *Ancient Israelite Literature in Its Cultural Context: A Survey of Parallels Between Biblical and Ancient Near Eastern Texts*. Grand Rapids: Zondervan Publishing House, 1989.

Ward, Ed, Geoffrey Stokes, and Ken Tucker, eds. *Rock of Ages: The Rolling Stone History of Rock & Roll*. New York: Rolling Stone Press, 1986.

Ward, W. Reginald, and Richard P. Heitzenrater, eds. *Journal and Diaries III (1743-54).* Vol. 20 of *The Works of John Wesley.* Nashville: Abingdon Press, 1991.

————, eds. *Journal and Diaries V (1765-75).* Vol. 22 of *The Works of John Wesley.* Nashville: Abingdon Press, 1993.

————, eds. *Journal and Diaries VI (1776-86).* Vol. 23 of *The Works of John Wesley.* Nashville: Abingdon Press, 1995.

Warren, Lindy. "Piano Man." *Contemporary Christian Music,* November 1998, 39-40.

Waterman, Mitch. "Emotional Responses to Music: Implicit and Explicit Effects in Listeners and Performers." *Psychology of Music* 24, no. 1 (1996): 53-67.

Webster, Douglas D. *Selling Jesus: What's Wrong with Marketing the Church?* Downers Grove, IL: Inter-Varsity Press, 1992.

Weinstein, Deena. *Heavy Metal: A Cultural Sociology.* New York: Lexington Books, 1991.

Weiss, Piero, and Richard Taruskin, eds. *Music in the Western World: A History in Documents.* New York: Schirmer Books, 1984.

Wenham, Gordon J. *Numbers: An Introduction and Commentary.* The Tyndale Old Testament Commentaries. Leicester, England: Inter-Varsity Press, 1981.

————. *Genesis 1-15.* Word Biblical Commentary, vol. 1. Waco, TX: Word Books, 1987.

Wesley, John. *Explanatory Notes Upon the New Testament.* 1754; repr. Alec. R. Allenson Inc., 1966.

Westermann, Claus. *The Psalms: Structure, Content, and Message.* Translated by Ralph D. Gehrke. Minneapolis: Augsburg Publishing House, 1980.

Whiteley, Sheila. "Little Red Rooster v. the Honky Tonk Woman: Mick Jagger, Sexuality, Style and Image." In *Sexing the Groove: Popular Music and Gender,* edited by Sheila Whiteley, 67-99. New York: Routledge, 1997.

————. "Seduced by the Sign: An Analysis of the Textual Links Between Sound and Image in Pop Videos." In *Sexing the Groove: Popular Music and Gender,* edited by Sheila Whiteley, 259-76. New York: Routledge, 1997.

Wicke, Peter. *Rock Music: Culture, Aesthetics and Sociology.* Translated by Rachel Fogg. Cambridge, England: Cambridge University Press, 1990.

Wienandt, Elwyn A. *Opinions on Church Music: Comments and Reports from Four-and-a Half Centuries.* Waco, TX: Baylor University Press, 1974.

Wiles, Maurice, and Mark Santer, eds. *Documents in Early Christian Thought.* New York: Cambridge University Press, 1993.

Wilhoit, Mel R. "'Sing Me a Sankey': Ira D. Sankey and Congregational Song." *The Hymn* 42 (January 1991): 13-19.

Wilkerson, David. *Set the Trumpet to Thy Mouth.* Springdale, PA: Whitaker, 1985.

Wilson, John. "Handel and the Hymn Tune: I, Handel's Tunes for Charles Wesley's Hymns." *The Hymn* 36 (October 1985): 18-23.

————. "Handel and the Hymn Tune: II, Some Hymn Tune Arrangements." *The Hymn* 37 (January 1986): 25-31.

Wilson, Kenneth T. "Should Women Wear Headcoverings?" *Bibliotheca Sacra* 148, no. 592 (October-December 1991): 442-62.

Wilson-Dickson, Andrew. *The Story of Christian Music: From Gregorian Chant to Black Gospel an Authoritative Illustrated Guide to All the Major Traditions of Music for Worship.* Oxford: Lion, 1992.

Young, Bill. "Contemporary Christian Music: Rock the Flock." In *The God Pumpers: Religion in the Electronic Age,* edited by Marshall Fishwick and Ray B. Browne, 141-58. Bowling Green, OH: Bowling Green State University Popular Press, 1987.

Young, Charles M. "Heavy Metal: In Defense of Dirtbags and Worthless Puds." *Musician,* September 1984, 40-44.

Youngblood, Ronald F. "1, 2 Samuel." In *Deuteronomy-2 Samuel.* Vol. 3 of *The Expositor's Bible Commentary,* 551-1104. Grand Rapids: Zondervan, 1992.

Other Titles at Old Paths Publications

COMMENTARY ON REVELATION, **James Durham**	$49.99
SERMONS ON MELCHIZEDEK & ABRAHAM:	
Justification, Faith & Obedience, **John Calvin**	$33.99
THE HAPPY MOURNER:	
Consolation of God & Sympathy for the Bereaved, **William Jay**	$20.99
PILGRIMS PROGRESS - <u>PART</u> <u>THREE</u>:	
Genuine or Counterfeit?, **"John Bunyan"**	$9.99
THE CHRISTIAN FATHER AT HOME:	
A Manual of Parental Instruction, **W. C. Brownlee**	$14.99
BELIEVER'S POCKET COMPANION:	
Poor Sinners Rich & Miserable Sinners Happy, **William Mason**	$15.99
THE WESTMINSTER STANDARDS - 1648	
(An Original Facsimile), **Westminster Assembly**	$29.99
THE WESTMINSTER STANDARDS - 1648	
(Facsimile) Computer CD-Rom Ed., **Westminster Assembly**	$15.99
COMMENTARY ON THE PSALMS, **George Horne**	$25.99
SERMONS ON GALATIANS, **John Calvin**	$37.99
SERMONS ON THE DEITY OF CHRIST, **John Calvin**	$26.99
SERMONS ON PSALM 119, **John Calvin**	$29.99
SERMONS ON ELECTION & REPROBATION, **John Calvin**	$28.99
PASTORAL THEOLOGY	
The Pastor in the Various Duties of His Office, **Thomas Murphy**	$24.99
EARNESTNESS IN PREACHING:	
Admonition from the Fathers, **Ernest Springer**	$6.99
A TREATISE ON SANCTIFICATION	
Explication of Romans Chapters 6, 7 & 8:1-4, **James Fraser**	$25.99
MICHAEL & THE DRAGON or,	
Christ Tempted & Satan Foiled, **Daniel Dyke**	$22.99
SINCERITY MEETS THE TRUTH, **John Pedersen**	$8.99
REVEALED TO BABES:	
Children in the Worship of God, **Richard Bacon**	$6.99

Include 10% (S & H) with Order (Minimum $3.00)
VISA & MASTERCARD ACCEPTED
(Include Expiration Date)

Old Paths Publications   1 BITTERSWEET PATH
WILLOW STREET, PENNSYLVANIA, USA 17584
Phone toll-free: 1-800-999-4541 or Fax: 717-464-6964
www.oldpathspublications.com   oldpaths@flash.net